Preface

Unreal Engine 4 is a powerful game engine used by many professional and indie game developers. When using a tool such as Unreal Engine for the first time, figuring out where to begin can be a daunting task. This books provides a starting point by introducing you to the interface, workflow, and many of the editors and tools Unreal Engine 4 has to offer. It will help you get a strong foundation you can later build on, and it will spark your interest to explore Unreal Engine and game design further. Each chapter is designed to get you up and running quickly in key areas.

Who Should Read This Book

If you want to learn to make games, applications, or interactive experiences but don't know where to begin, this book and Unreal Engine are for you. This book is for anyone interested in understanding the fundamentals of Unreal Engine. Whether you are new to game development, a hobbyist, or a student learning to become a professional, you will find something useful in these pages.

How This Book Is Organized and What It Covers

Following the *Sam's Teach Yourself* approach, this book is organized into 24 chapters that should take approximately 1 hour each to work through:

▶ **Hour 1, "Introducing Unreal Engine 4":** This hour gets you up and running by showing you how to download and install Unreal Engine 4 and introduces you to the Editor interface.

▶ **Hour 2, "Understanding the Gameplay Framework":** This hour introduces you to the concept of the Gameplay Framework, a key component of every project created in UE4.

▶ **Hour 3, "Coordinates, Transforms, Units, and Organization":** This hour helps you understand how the measurement, control, and organizational systems work in UE4.

▶ **Hour 4, "Working with Static Mesh Actors":** In this hour, you learn how to import 3D models and use the Static Mesh Editor.

▶ **Hour 5, "Applying Lighting and Rendering":** In this hour, you learn how to place lights in a level and how to change their properties.

▶ **Hour 6, "Using Materials":** This hour teaches you how to use textures and materials in UE4.

▶ **Hour 7, "Using Audio System Elements":** In this hour, you learn to import audio files, create Sound Cue assets, and place Ambient Sound Actors into a level.

▶ **Hour 8, "Creating Landscapes and Foliage":** In this hour, you learn to work with UE4's landscape system to create your own landscapes and how to use the foliage system.

▶ **Hour 9, "World Building":** In this hour, you apply what you learned in the previous hours and create a level.

▶ **Hour 10, "Crafting Effects with Particle Systems":** In this hour, you learn the fundamental controls of Cascade, which you can use to craft dynamic particle effects.

▶ **Hour 11, "Using Skeletal Mesh Actors":** In this hour, you learn about the Persona Editor and the different asset types needed to bring characters and creatures to life.

▶ **Hour 12, "Matinee and Cinematics":** In this hour, you learn to use the Matinee Editor and animate cameras and meshes.

▶ **Hour 13, "Learning to Work with Physics ":** In this hour, you learn to make Actors simulate physics to respond to the world around them, and you also learn how to constrain them.

▶ **Hour 14, "Introducing Blueprint Visual Scripting System":** In this hour, you are introduced to basic scripting concepts and learn to use the Level Blueprint Editor.

▶ **Hour 15, "Working with Level Blueprints":** In this hour, you learn about Blueprint event sequences and create a collision event that responds to the player's actions.

▶ **Hour 16, "Working with Blueprint Classes":** In this hour, you learn how to create a Blueprint class, use Timeline, and create a simple Pickup Actor.

▶ **Hour 17, "Using Editable Variables and the Construction Script":** In this hour, you learn to use the Construction Script and editable variables to make modifiable Actors.

▶ **Hour 18, "Making Key Input Events and Spawning Actors":** In this hour, you learn to make a keyboard input event that spawns an Actor during gameplay.

▶ **Hour 19, "Making an Action Encounter":** In this hour, you use an existing Game mode and Blueprint classes to design and create your own first- or third-person action-based obstacle course.

▶ **Hour 20, "Creating an Arcade Shooter: Input System and Pawns":** In this hour, you begin work on a 1990s arcade-style space shooter. You learn about the input system and user-controlled Actors called Pawns.

▶ **Hour 21, "Creating an Arcade Shooter: Obstacles and Pickups":** In this hour, you continue working on the arcade shooter game, creating asteroid obstacles and health pickups, and you learn how to utilize Blueprint class inheritance.

▶ **Hour 22, "Working with UMG":** In this hour, you learn to use the Unreal Motion Graphics UI designer and make a start menu.

▶ **Hour 23, "Making an Executable":** In this hour, you learn the quick path to preparing a project for deployment to other devices.

▶ **Hour 24, "Working with Mobile":** In this hour, you learn optimization guidelines and techniques for working with mobile devices and some simple ways to utilize touch and motion sensors.

We hope you enjoy this book and benefit from it. Good luck on your journey with the UE4 game engine!

Companion Files: To gain access to project files and downloads, go to the book's companion website at www.sty-ue4.com.

About the Authors

Aram Cookson is a professor in the Interactive Design and Game Development (ITGM) department at the Savannah College of Art and Design (SCAD). He has a B.F.A in Sculpture and an M.F.A. in Computer Art. After finishing his M.F.A., he went on to help start the ITGM program and served as the graduate coordinator for 9 years. Over the past 15 years, Aram has developed and taught a range of game art and design courses in classrooms and online, utilizing the Unreal Engine technology.

Ryan DowlingSoka is a technical artist working on the Gears of War franchise at Microsoft Studio's The Coalition, located in Vancouver, British Columbia. He works primarily on content features for the team, crafting systems for destruction, foliage, visual effects, post-processes, and user interfaces in Unreal Engine 4. Previously, he worked at Microsoft, developing experiences for the Microsoft HoloLens in Unity5. Ryan is an expert in a variety of entertainment software creation packages, including Maya, Houdini, Substance Designer, Photoshop, Nuke, and After Effects. Ryan holds a B.F.A. in Visual Effects from Savannah College of Art and Design. With a passion for interactive storytelling, rooted in playing 1990s console role-playing games (*Baldur's Gate II* and *Planescape: Torment*), Ryan focuses on applying interactive technical solutions to solving difficult problems in modern gaming. When not working on video games, Ryan can be found swing dancing his evenings away with his wife.

Clinton Crumpler is currently a senior environment artist at Microsoft Studio's The Coalition, located in Vancouver, British Columbia. Previously an artist at Bethesda's Battlecry Studios, KIXEYE, Army Game Studio, and various other independent studios, Clinton's primary focus areas are environment art, shader development, and art direction. Clinton has released multiple video tutorials in collaboration with Digital Tutors, with a focus on game art development for Unreal Engine. He completed an M.F.A. in Interactive and Game Design and a B.F.A. in Animation at Savannah College of Art and Design (SCAD) in Savannah, Georgia. Prior to attending SCAD, he received a B.F.A. in Graphic Design at Longwood University, located in Farmville, Virginia. More information and his digital works are available at www.clintoncrumpler.com.

Dedication

Tricia, Naia, and Elle: I love you all. —Aram

To Grandpa Bob: Thank you for the constant support through my education and career. Without your contributions to my future, I would not be where I am today, and I am ever grateful. —Ryan

To Amanda: Thanks for driving me across the desert while I wrote. —Clinton

Acknowledgments

To my family: Thank you for being so understanding and patient, and for giving me the time to get this done.

Mom and Dad: Thank you for buying my first computer (TRS-80).

Luis: Thank you for thinking of me. You were an awesome department chair.

To Laura, Sheri, Olivia, and all the reviewers: Thank you for all your efforts.

Epic Games: Thank you for developing, and continuing to develop, such amazing technology and games.

—Aram

A big thank you to Samantha for tolerating and accommodating my weekends being entirely consumed at a keyboard. Your patience and support through this process have been invaluable.

—Ryan

Big thanks go out to my best friend, Brian, for always helping me become a better writer and editing my works and always increasing my confidence through brotherly support.

Thanks to Amanda and her family for supporting me while I wrote this during our move cross-country. Your understanding and help are always appreciated.

—Clinton

We Want to Hear from You!

As the reader of this book, *you* are our most important critic and commentator. We value your opinion and want to know what we're doing right, what we could do better, what areas you'd like to see us publish in, and any other words of wisdom you're willing to pass our way.

We welcome your comments. You can email or write to let us know what you did or didn't like about this book—as well as what we can do to make our books better.

Please note that we cannot help you with technical problems related to the topic of this book.

When you write, please be sure to include this book's title and author as well as your name and email address. We will carefully review your comments and share them with the author and editors who worked on the book.

Email: feedback@samspublishing.com

Mail: Sams Publishing
ATTN: Reader Feedback
         800 East 96th Street
         Indianapolis, IN 46240 USA

Reader Services

Register your copy of *Sams Teach Yourself Unreal Engine 4 Game Development in 24 Hours* at informit.com for convenient access to updates and corrections as they become available. To start the registration process, go to informit.com/register and log in or create an account*. Enter the product ISBN, 9780672337628, and click Submit.

*Be sure to check the box that you would like to hear from us in order to receive exclusive discounts on future editions of this product.

HOUR 1
Introducing Unreal Engine 4

What You'll Learn in This Hour:

▶ Installing the Epic Games Launcher
▶ Installing Unreal Engine
▶ Creating a new project
▶ Using the Unreal Engine Editor interface

Welcome to Unreal Engine! Unreal Engine 4 (UE4) is a game engine and Editor developed by Epic Games to create games and applications ranging from the AAA console market to indie mobile development. Unreal Engine runs on both Windows and Mac operating systems and can publish to Windows, Mac, PlayStation 4, Xbox One, iOS, Android, HTML5, and Linux platforms. In its simplest form, Unreal Engine 4 is a collection of Editors used by different disciplines in any game or application production.

In this hour, you learn to download and install the Unreal Engine, create your first project, and become familiar with the Editor interface. You start with creating a user account and downloading and installing the Epic Games Launcher. From there, you download UE4. Once that is done, you create your first project, learn to navigate the Editor interface, and learn to move around a Level and playtest the default map.

NOTE

Unreal Engine Is Free!

That's right, UE4 is completely free to use! You have access to everything—for free! Why does Epic Games make it free? You never know where the next great game or application is going to come from. How does Epic do it? Not until you release a game and start to make money do you need to pay Epic 5% of royalties. The details, of course, can be found on Epic's website. Epic also has a marketplace where you can purchase and download content for your projects. You don't need to because you can, of course, make everything from scratch, but not reinventing the wheel can certainly speed up production.

Installing Unreal

Installing Unreal Engine is a simple three-part process:

1. Create a new user account.

2. Download and install the Epic Games Launcher.

3. Download Unreal Engine.

Downloading and Installing the Launcher

The Launcher helps you keep track of the different versions of Unreal Engine that you have installed. From it, you can manage your projects, access free sample projects, and get to the marketplace, where you can purchase content to use in your projects; it also keeps you updated with community news and links to online learning resources and documentation.

NOTE
_____

Operating Systems and Hardware Requirements

To effectively use Unreal Engine, you need a Windows PC or Macintosh computer that meets the following criteria:

▶ **OS:** Windows 7 or 8 64-bit or Mac OS X 10.9.2

▶ **Processor:** Quad-core Intel or AMD, 2.5 GHz or faster

▶ **Graphics card:** NVIDIA GeForce 470 GTX or AMD Radeon 6870 series card or higher

▶ **Memory:** 8 GB RAM
_____

Follows these steps to download and install the Epic Games Launcher:

1. Go to the Unreal Engine website (www.unrealengine.com), as shown in Figure 1.1.

2. Click the **Get Unreal** button.

3. When prompted, create a new user account.

4. Choose Windows or Mac download, depending on your operating system, and download the installer file to your download folder (.msi for Windows or .dmg for Mac).

5. Run the installer, choose an install location, and follow any onscreen prompts.

WHAT IS UNREAL ENGINE 4?

FIGURE 1.1
Unreal Engine website.

TIP

Hard Drive Space

Game engines take up a lot of hard drive space. When you download a new version of UE4, it is automatically installed in the same location as the Launcher. Choose an install location for the Launcher
that has at least 20 GB of free space. While the initial install does not require this much space, as
you download sample content or purchase assets from the marketplace, the demand for space will
increase. Fortunately, as you create your own projects, you can save them to any location you want.

Downloading and Installing Unreal Engine

Once the Launcher is installed, you can download and install UE4 through the Launcher. UE4 is
much larger than the Launcher and takes a few minutes to download. Epic is always improving its
software and, as a result, there are many versions of UE4. When you start out, it is best to install
the most recent official version.

CAUTION

Preview Versions

Epic often releases previews of the next version it is working on for bug testing. When you're just
getting to know UE4, it is best to download the most recent version that is not a preview version.
You can always upgrade projects to the newest version once it is made available.

The following steps walk you through the process of downloading and installing UE4 through the Epic Games Launcher:

1. Open the Launcher and click the **Library** link (see Figure 1.2).

2. Go to the Unreal Engine version section and click **Add Version** to add a new version slot.

3. Go to the newly created version slot, click the drop-down arrow, and select the desired version.

4. Click **Install**, and the Launcher downloads and installs Unreal Engine. UE4 is large, so it takes time to download.

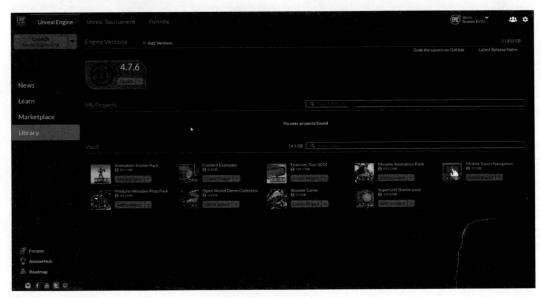

FIGURE 1.2
Launcher Library tab.

Creating Your First Project

Once UE4 has been downloaded, it is time to create your first project. When you launch UE4 for the first time, it opens the Project Browser. The Project Browser has a Projects tab that shows you all the projects you are currently working on and a New Project tab for creating new projects based on existing common game mode templates.

GO TO ▶ HOUR 2, UNDERSTANDING THE GAMEPLAY FRAMEWORK, for more in-depth information about the anatomy of a project.

The Project Browser

When you're starting a new project from the Project Browser, you have to make a few choices. First, you can create either a Blueprint-based project or a C++-based project. This book focuses on Blueprint-based projects only. You also need to choose the target hardware: either Desktop/Console or Mobile/Tablet. And you can choose either Maximum Quality and Scalable 3D or 2D for target graphics. These options change the project's default settings for content development. Finally, you need to decide if you want to start off with default art content. If you choose **With Starter Content**, you have assets to Play around with.

NOTE

Blueprint Versus C++ Projects

Blueprint is the visual scripting environment used to script functionality for a game project. C++-based projects allow users to script functionality in the traditional manner of writing code. A C++-based project requires you to install a compiler, such as Visual Studio 2013. If you have never scripted before or if you have but have never used UE4 before, it is a good idea to become familiar with the Editor and workflow before you move to a C++-based project.

CAUTION

Project Size

When projects are first created, they are not very large, but project file sizes grow rapidly, depending on the amount of content and the quality of content, such as model details and texture sizes. UE4 also generates auto saves and backup files as you work; while these files take up space, they are helpful when anything goes wrong.

TRY IT YOURSELF ▼

Create a Project

You can create projects anywhere you have enough hard drive space. Pick a location that has at least 2 GB of free space and is easy to find. Figure 1.3 shows you the basic settings for your first project, and these are the steps to follow:

1. In the Launcher, click **Launch**.

2. Select the **New Project** tab.

3. Select the **Blueprint** tab.

4. Choose the **First Person** template.

5. Select **Desktop/Console** for target hardware.

6. Pick **Scalable 3D or 2D** for target graphics quality.

7. Select **With Starter Content**.

8. Pick a location that has at least a few gigabytes of free space.

9. Give the project a name.

10. Click **Create Project**.

FIGURE 1.3
Settings used to create your first project.

NOTE

Modifying Project Settings

You can modify project settings, such as target hardware and target graphics, after you have created a project. You can do this in Project Settings, which is found under the Edit tab on the main menu.

Learning the Interface

Now that you have installed UE4 and created your first project, it is time to jump in and get your feet wet. As stated earlier, UE4 is a collection of Editors and tools for different disciplines in game production. For now, focus on learning the key areas of the main interface and learning to moving around a Level. The main interface, referred to as the Level Editor, is primarily used for world and Level building and for asset placement.

The Editors main interface has seven key panels that you need to be familiar with: the menu bar, the Modes panel, the World Outliner panel, the Details panel, the Content Browser panel, the Level Editor toolbar, and the Viewport panel (see Figure 1.4). The following sections show each individual panel and describe them.

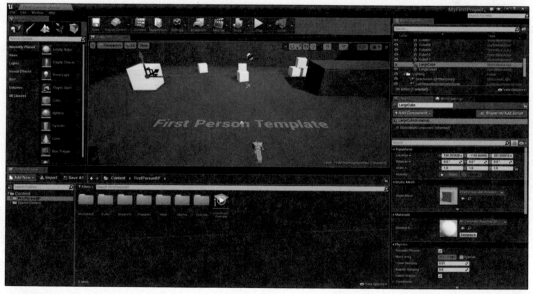

FIGURE 1.4
The UE4 Editor default main interface.

NOTE

Interface Layout

The Editor interface layout is modifiable. You can easily reposition panes and windows to improve workflow. In this book, all interface elements are left in their default locations for consistency, but as you become a more experienced user, you will most likely want to reposition elements to increase productivity.

Menu Bar

The menu bar, as in most other modern applications, consists of File, Edit, Window, and Help menus. File contains operations for loading and saving projects and Levels. Edit has your standard copy and paste operations, as well as Editor preferences and project settings. Window opens Viewports and other panels. If you ever close a window or panel, you can go to the Window menu to open it again. Help contains links to external resources, such as online documentation and tutorials.

Modes Panel

The Modes panel displays the various Editing modes of the Level Editor (see Figure 1.5). It allows for specialized Editing interfaces for working with certain types of Actors and geometry.

TIP

What Is an Actor?

The key to learning any software is learning its interface, workflow, and vocabulary. Unreal has a lot of terms to learn, and you will be exposed to them throughout this book. The term *Actor* refers to any asset that has been placed in a Level. For example, a 3D model in the Content Browser panel is referred to as a *Static Mesh asset*. But once an instance of the Static Mesh asset has been placed in a Level, the instance is referred to as a *Static Mesh Actor*.

The Modes panel consists of different tool modes for the Level Editor that allow you to change the main performance of the Editor. In it, you can select a specialized task such as placing new assets in the world, sculpting landscapes, creating geometry brushes and volumes, generating Foliage, or painting on meshes. Table 1.1 lists the Editor modes and describes their effects.

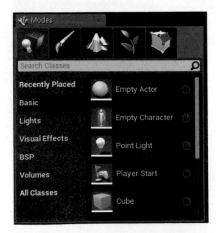

FIGURE 1.5
Modes panel.

TABLE 1.1   Editor Modes

Action	Effect
Place mode	For placing Actors in a scene.
Paint mode	For painting vertex color data on Static Mesh Actors.
Landscape mode	For Editing Landscape Terrain Actors.
Foliage mode	For painting instanced Foliage Actors in a Level.
Geometry Editing mode	For Editing BSP Brush Actors on the vertex edge face Level.

World Outliner Panel

The World Outliner panel displays all the Actors within the current Level in a hierarchical tree view (see Figure 1.6). You can select an Actor simply by clicking its name in the World Outliner panel, and its properties show up in the Details panel. If you double-click a name, the Viewport panel focuses on the asset.

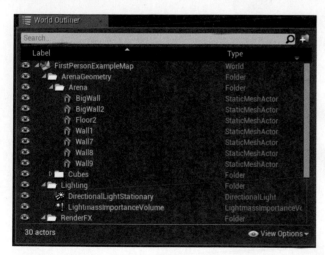

FIGURE 1.6
World Outliner panel.

Details Panel

The Details panel is one of the areas in UE4 that you will use the most. There is a Details panel in just about every one of the subeditors. The Details panel displays all the editable properties for the selected Actors in the Viewport. The properties that appear depend on the type of Actor selected, but there are some common properties found on most Actors (see Figure 1.7). Typical properties include the name of the Actor; transform edit boxes for moving, rotating, and scaling Actors; and rendering display properties.

NOTE

Selecting Actors

To select an Actor, click the Actor in a Viewport or in the World Outliner panel. The Actor is then highlighted, and its base properties appear in the Details panel. It is possible to select multiple Actors at one time:

▶ In a Viewport and World Outliner panel, hold down Ctrl or Shift key while adding or removing multiple Actors from the current selection.

▶ In a Viewport only, press **Ctrl+Alt+click** and drag to create a bounding box selection around multiple Actors.

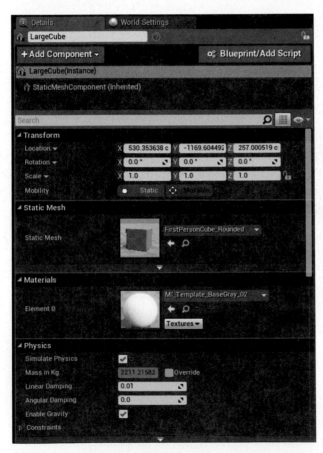

FIGURE 1.7
Main Editor Details panel.

Content Browser Panel

The Content Browser panel is the primary area for managing assets in a project (see Figure 1.8). You use this browser for general tasks related to content, such as creating, viewing, modifying, importing, and organizing. The Content Browser also allows you to manage folders and execute basic operations on assets, like viewing references, moving, copying, and renaming. The Content Browser panel also has a search bar and filter flags for quickly locating assets.

It can help to think of the Content Browser panel as a never-ending toy box of assets. Any time you need something, you can pull an *instance* (that is, a copy) of an asset out of your toy box and place it into a Level. Once an instance has been placed in a Level, it is referred to as an *Actor*. The initial instance of a placed Actor is an exact copy of the original asset found in the Content Browser panel. Once you have placed an Actor, you can modify it individually in the Details panel. On the left side of the Content Browser is the Source panel, which displays the content folder hierarchy. The Source panel can be expanded or collapsed by clicking on the icon in the upper-left corner under the green Add New button. The right side of the Content Browser is referred to as the Asset Management area, which displays the asset in the selected folder in the Source panel.

FIGURE 1.8
Content Browser panel, with the source view on the left and asset management area on the right.

TIP

Folder Organization

Projects can grow in complexity rapidly, so file organization is crucial to maintaining an efficient working environment. A good rule of thumb is to organize asset content by type in separate folders. You can nest folders within each other to allow for maximum organization and flexibility.

Viewport Panel

Viewports are windows into the worlds you create. You use the Viewport panel to move around the current Level. The Viewport panel has many different modes, layouts, and settings, all of which help you create, edit, and manage your Levels (see Figure 1.9).

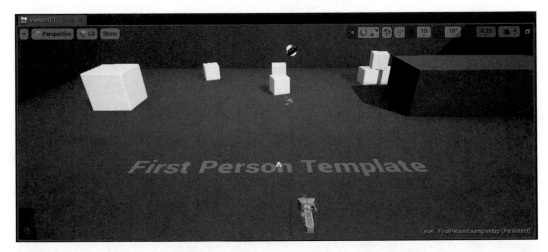

FIGURE 1.9
The Viewport panel.

Viewport Panel Layout

By default, the Viewport panel displays a single-pane Perspective view, but you can easily change it to a two-, three-, or four-pane layout by clicking the Viewport drop-down menu, selecting Layouts, and selecting the desired format (see Figure 1.10). You can change each pane in the Viewport panel to a different view mode.

Viewport Types

There are two basic Viewport types: Perspective and Orthographic (see Figure 1.11). Perspective Viewports display the world in 3D with vanishing points, while Orthographic Viewports show the world in a 2D schematic view. The Perspective view will most likely be your primary working environment, but Orthographic views are great for fine-tuning Actor placement in a scene.

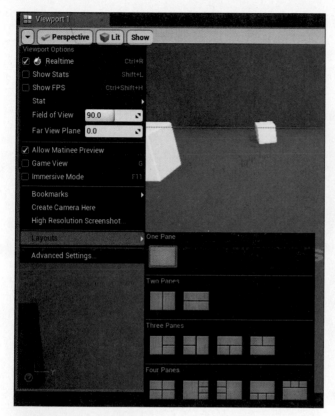

FIGURE 1.10
Viewport panel layout options.

FIGURE 1.11
Viewport view type settings.

View Modes and Visualizers

View modes (see Figure 1.12) change the visual display of the world in a Viewport, regardless of the view type, and they can provide important feedback on the state of a Level. Table 1.2 lists the commonly used view modes.

FIGURE 1.12
View modes.

TABLE 1.2   Common View Modes for Viewports

Mode	Effect
Lit	Shows the final result of a scene with materials and lighting applied.
Unlit	Removes all lighting from the scene, showing base color from assigned materials.
Wireframe	Shows all the polygon edges of Actors in the scene.
Detail Lighting	Displays a neutral material across the entire scene, using the normal maps of the assigned materials.
Lighting Only	Displays neutral material that is affected only by lighting without normal maps data.

NOTE
Visualization

More than 13 different view modes, along with other visualization tools, are available. You can use them to get feedback on a Level and to debug and troubleshoot.

Show Flags

Like view modes, show flags help display relevant information directly within the Level Viewport, such as displaying Actor collision hulls or bounding boxes.

Navigating a Scene in the Perspective Viewport

Now that you have a basic understanding of each of the key areas of the main interface, you need to become familiar with using the Viewport to move around a Level. Tables 1.3 and 1.4 list the most commonly used controls for moving around in a Level in the Viewport.

TABLE 1.3   **Viewport Movement Controls**

Control	Action
Perspective View	
Click+drag	Moves the Viewport camera forward and backward and rotates left and right.
Right-click+drag	Rotates the Viewport camera in place without forward or backward movement.
Click+right-click+drag	Moves the Viewport camera up and down in the world.
Orthographic Views (Top, Front, Side)	
Click+drag	Creates a marquee selection box.
Right-click+drag	Pans the Orthographic view left and right.
Click+right-click+drag	Zooms the Orthographic view in and out.

NOTE

Level Navigation

Unlike in 3D modeling applications, which are set up for focusing and orbiting around a single asset as it's being built, the Unreal Engine Viewport movement controls are designed for set-dressing large game Levels. So moving through large areas quickly is key.

TABLE 1.4 Orbiting, Dolly, and Track Viewport Controls

Control	Action
F	Pressing the F key focuses the Viewport camera on the selected Actor in the Viewport.
Alt+LMB+drag	Tumbles the Viewport around a single pivot or point of interest.
Alt+right-click+drag	Dollies (zooms) the camera toward and away from a single pivot or point of interest.
Alt+middle-click+drag	Tracks the camera left, right, up, and down in the direction of mouse movement.

TIP

Game-Style Navigation

While you're in the Perspective view, if you hold down the right mouse button, you can use W, A, S, and D keys to move through the Level as you would in a typical first-person shooter.

Level Editor Toolbar

The Level Editor toolbar provides quick access to commonly used tools and operations, such as saving the current Level, building pre-calculated lighting for Static Actors, changing Editor display properties, and playtesting the current Level. Figure 1.13 shows the Level Editor toolbar.

FIGURE 1.13
Level Editor toolbar.

Playing a Level

When you create a project, a default Level is already made for you, and it is one of the first things you see in the Editor when you open the project. Playtesting a Level involves using the input system your players will use when interacting with your game. There are a few different modes for playtesting a Level (see Figure 1.14). For now, try out the primary Play in Editor (PIE) modes: Selected Viewport and New Editor Window. You can click the Play icon to Play your Level or click the drop-down arrow to the right of the Play icon and choose one of the Play modes.

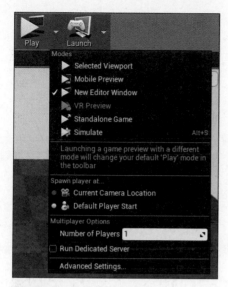

FIGURE 1.14
Play modes.

TIP

Playtesting a Level

The last Play mode you use automatically becomes the default Play mode on the Level Editor toolbar. If you want to use a different Play mode from the default, click the Play drop-down and choose another Play mode.

Summary

In this hour, you downloaded and installed Unreal Engine, familiarized yourself with key areas in the main interface, created your first project, learned how to move around a Level in a Viewport, and learned to playtest a Level. The more familiar you are with these tasks, the better off you will be.

Q&A

Q. What is the purpose of the Epic Games Launcher?

A. The Epic Games Launcher allows you to manage projects and gives you access to the marketplace for purchasing content and keeping UE4 updated.

Q. Where is UE4 installed?

A. UE4 is installed in the same location as the Launcher.

Q. Where should I save my projects?

A. You should save projects on a hard drive that has sufficient free space and is easy to locate.

Workshop

Now that you have finished the hour, see if you can answer the following questions.

Quiz

1. True or false: The Mode panel allows you to switch between different Editing modes.

2. If you want to focus a Viewport on a selected Actor, what key or key combination do you use?

3. True or false: Any asset placed in a Level is referred to as an Actor.

4. You use the _____ for managing and creating new projects.

5. True or false: The main interface layout is completely modifiable.

6. True or false: PIE stands for Play in Editor.

Answers

1. True. The Mode panel allows you to switch between placing Actors, creating Terrain and creating Foliage.

2. The F key will focus the Viewport on to the currently selected Actor.

3. True. Regardless of type, once an asset is placed into a Level it is an instance of the original asset and is referred to as an Actor.

4. Project Browser. You can work on many projects at one time. The Project Browser allows you to switch between projects

5. True. If you click and drag on a panel's tab, you can move to different locations in the interface.

6. True. PIE stands for Play in Editor. You can preview a Level in separate window or in the selected Viewport.

Exercise

On your own, spend time becoming familiar with the UE4 interface. For this exercise, practice creating a new Level and placing Actors in it and then save the Level. These are simple but fundamental skills, and the more comfortable you are with these basics, the more successful you will be as you work further with Unreal Engine.

1. Create a new default Level by selecting File > New Level or pressing **Ctrl+N**.

2. To place a point light Actor in the Level, go to the **Place** tab in the Modes panel.

3. Place a Static Mesh asset in the Level. You can find this asset in the StarterContent folder in the Content Browser.

4. To save your Level, right-click the Content folder in the Content Browser and select **Add New Folder** and name the new folder **Maps**.

5. Save your Level in the newly created Maps folder by selecting File > Save.

HOUR 2
Understanding the Gameplay Framework

What You'll Learn in This Hour:

▶ Downloading and setting up a content example project

▶ Importing assets

▶ Migrating content from one project to another

▶ Introducing the Gameplay Framework

Unreal Engine 4 (UE4) is a deep and rich application that can be used to create anything from 2D indie Games to 3D AAA titles to interactive applications, architectural visualizations and VR experiences. UE4 can create content for various platforms ranging from PC and consoles to mobile as well as web-based HTML. The UE4 Editor takes many of the complicated processes of development and puts them into an easy-to-use developer's application environment. As with any other application, there is a learning curve with UE4. This hour introduces you to some of the terminology, the anatomy of a project, and the basic Gameplay Framework of UE4.

Available Resources

One of the great things Epic has done with the release of version 4 of Unreal Engine and its Editor is to provide quality online documentation and project examples. In the Epic Games Launcher is a Community section that offers news, project spotlights, and links to forums, blogs, and the engine development road map. The Learn section also provides links to online documentation, video tutorials, and sample projects demonstrating various topics. There are categories for projects that highlight features of the engine, for common Gameplay examples, examples of complete Game projects, and sample projects contributed from the Unreal community and Epic partners. Once you are familiar with the interface and the workflow of UE4, one of the best ways to learn is to deconstruct existing projects.

▼ TRY IT YOURSELF

Download the Content Example Project

To see some of the amazing things that can be done with Unreal Engine 4, go to the Learn section of the Epic Games Launcher and explore the Content Examples Project found in the Engine Feature Samples category. Download and set up a project using sample content:

1. In the Epic Games Launcher, navigate to the **Learn** tab.

2. Under Engine Feature Samples, find the Content Examples Project and click it to open it.

3. Next to the word **Download**, make sure the version matches the version of the engine you installed and then click **Download**. The download process starts for this 2+ GB project. Once the Content Examples Project is installed, it shows up in the Vault section in the Library tab in the Launcher.

4. In the Launcher, navigate to the Library tab and look for the Vault section. Then click Create Project under the Content Example header.

5. Give the project a name or leave the default.

6. Pick a location on your hard drive or leave the default.

7. Verify/choose the version to match the version of the engine you downloaded.

8. Click **Create**. After a few seconds, the Launcher creates a new project with the feature content.

9. Open the project in the Editor. Under My Projects, double-click the newly created project.

10. Once the project is loaded into the Editor, select **File > Open Level**.

11. Select any level to open and then double-click it or select it and click **Open**.

12. Once the level is open, preview it by clicking **Play** on the main Editor toolbar.

13. Continue opening and previewing as many levels as you like so you can see and interact with all the features the project has to demonstrate.

Play in Editor (PIE)

Play in Editor (PIE) refers to a collection of options that allows you to playtest a level without having to compile or package content beforehand. The PIE preview options are found on the Level Editor main toolbar, under the Play button (see Figure 2.1). If you click the downward-facing tringle to the right of the Play button on the Level Editor toolbar, you see that there are many options for previewing a level. By default, UE4 uses the Selected Viewport option, which is great when you're testing functionality. At some point, you may need to preview the level in the resolution or aspect ratio of the target platform.

Selecting the New Editor Window option changes the preview play icon and launches a preview of the level in a new window. At the bottom of the preview options is the option Advanced Settings, which you can select to bring up the Editor preferences. Then on the right side of the screen, under Play in New Window, you can set the resolution of the window by using a dropdown list that includes common settings. You can also set the location of the window, which is by default set to 0, 0 to indicate the upper-left corner of your monitor. Enable the Always Center Window to Screen check box if you want the new Editor preview window to be displayed in the center of your monitor.

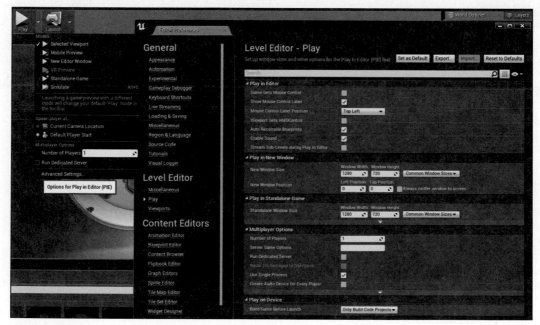

FIGURE 2.1
Play in Editor (PIE) options in the Editor preferences.

Project Folder Structure

When you first create a Blueprint-based project from scratch through the Epic Games Launcher, you need to specify a location and a name for the project. The Editor then copies a collection of default folders and files into the project folder for you. If you look at a project folder after it has been made, you find Config, Content, Intermediate, and Saved folders, as well as an .uproject file:

▶ **Config:** This folder contains default .ini files that store default Editor and project settings and preferences.

▶ **Content:** This folder stores all the assets in the project that are either imported or created directly in the Editor.

▶ **Intermediate:** This folder stores the project's working .ini setting and preference files, along with a CachedAssetRegistry.bin file.

▶ **Saved:** This folder contains Editor autosave and backup files, a Collections folder for assets organized into collections in the content browser, project Config settings for target platforms, Editor log files, and the project thumbnail .png image file that you see in the Launcher.

As you work on a project, more files and folders are added to it.

▼ TRY IT YOURSELF

Create a Blank Project Without Starter Content

To familiarize yourself with a typical project directory structure, in this Try It Yourself you will create a blank project without starter content:

1. In the Launcher, under the Library tab, open the version of the Editor installed from Hour 1, "Introducing Unreal Engine 4," by clicking Launch under the version number.

2. In the Unreal project browser, select the **New Project** tab.

3. Under Blueprints, select the **Blank Project** template.

4. Make sure the **Desktop/Console** setting is selected.

5. Make sure **Graphics Level** is set to a quality level that your hardware supports.

6. Make sure **No Starter Content** is selected.

7. Choose a location for the project.

8. Name the project **MyHour02**. When naming a project, do not use blank spaces in the name.

9. Click **Create Project**. Once the project has been created, it opens automatically.

10. Save it on your hard drive and minimize the project.

If you look through all the folders, you see that some files have already been created, such as config files. Any file with .ini extension is a config file—a text file that stores Editor, engine, and Game preferences. Whenever you make changes to the project or Editor preferences in the Editor, these files are modified and updated.

NOTE

Editor Preferences and Project Settings

You can find Editor Preferences and Project Settings by selecting to Edit on the Level Editor menu bar.

Content Folder

The Content folder is where the Editor stores all the imported and migrated content for a project (see Figure 2.2). In it you typically find two file types: .uasset and .umap. Once you import an external asset, it is saved as a .uasset file in the Content folder for the project. Every time you make a new map and save it, UE4 creates a .umap file and stores it in Content. When you use the Content Browser in the Editor, you see the directory structure of the Content folder.

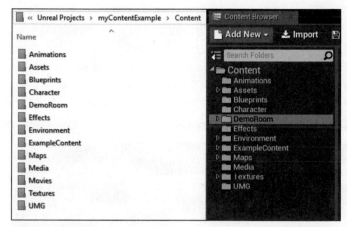

FIGURE 2.2
The project Content folder on the left and the Content Browser Source View on the right.

Importing Content

Unreal Engine 4 supports a variety of file types for importing content. Table 2.1 shows some of the most common files types and which asset types they are associated with.

TABLE 2.1   Common External File Types That Can Be Imported into the Editor

Asset Type	File Extension
3D model, skeletal meshes rigs, animation data	.fbx, .obj
Texture and images	.bmp, .jpeg, .pcx, .png, .psd, .tga, .hdr
Fonts	.otf, .ttf
Audio	.wav
Video and multimedia	.wmv
PhysX	.apb, .apx
Other	.csv

TIP

Identifying File Types

Operating systems tend to hide file extensions by default. When you start working on a project that has a lot of content, it can be hard to keep track of which file is what type. Turning on the option for showing file extensions in your OS can help you quickly identify what type of file you are looking for.

There are a few ways to bring content into a project. For example, you can import content created in an external Editor, such as 3DS Max or Maya for models, Photoshop for textures, and Audacity for sound.

There are two ways to import new content created in an external application. One way is to use the Content Browser as described in the following Try It Yourself. Another way is to go to your operating system's file manager, select the file you want to import, and drag it into the Asset Management Area in the Content Browser (see Figure 2.3).

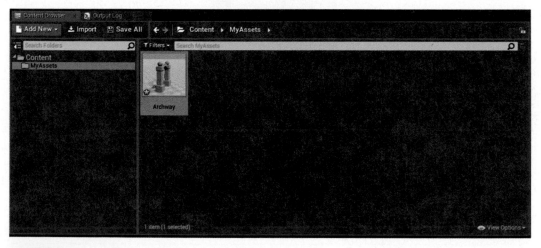

FIGURE 2.3
Content Browser with Source View on the left and Asset Management Area on the right.

▼ TRY IT YOURSELF

Create a Folder in the Content Browser and Import an External Asset

Importing an asset is one of the most common operations you will perform. In this Try it Yourself you will learn a common method for importing an asset into a project.

1. Open the MyHour02 project you created in the previous Try It Yourself.

2. Click on the **Show or Hide Source view** icon below the green **Add New** button to show the Source View in the Content Browser.

3. In the source panel of the Content Browser, right-click the **Content** folder, select **Add New Folder**, and name the new folder **MyAssets**.

4. With the **MyAssets** folder selected in the source panel of the Content Browser, right-click in the **Asset Management Area** and select **Import Asset > Import To**. The Asset dialog box appears.

5. In the Asset dialog box, navigate to the Hour_02 folder from the book's companion website at www.sty-ue4.com select one of the files in the RawAssets folder, and click **Open**. The file is added to the Content folder.

6. Right-click on the **Asset** thumbnail and click **Save** to save the newly imported asset.

TIP

Asset Icons

Asset icons in the Content Browser give you a preview of most assets so you don't have to open them up. If you roll the cursor over an icon, you see relevant information about the asset. For example, a small asterisk in the lower-left corner of an asset's icon tells you that the asset has not been saved. Any time you import an asset for the first time or modify it in some way, the asterisk shows up, letting you know that the changes need to be saved. If you close the Editor without saving an imported or modified asset, you will lose that asset or any changes you have made. Press **Ctrl+S** to save all the assets or right-click an asset and choose **Save**.

Migrating Content from an Existing Project

Another way to add content to a project is to migrate it from an existing project. Every project created has its own Content folder that stores all the assets for the project. Migrating allows you to move assets from one project to another. When you migrate assets, you also move their dependencies while maintaining the folder structure.

TRY IT YOURSELF ▼

Migrate Content

Follow these steps to migrate content from one project to another:

1. Open the Content Examples project you used at the beginning of this hour.

2. In the Source View of the Content Browser, select **Content** (at the top of the directory).

3. In the Asset Management Area to the left of the search bar, click **Filters** and toggle on particle systems. You now see all the Particle Systems in this project in the Asset Management Area.

4. **Ctrl+click** to select a few of the Particle Systems you want to migrate into your project.

5. After you select three or four Particle Systems, right-click one of the highlighted particle systems and select **Asset Actions > Migrate** (see Figure 2.4).

FIGURE 2.4
Content Browser migration.

6. In the Asset Report window, which shows not just the particle systems but also all their dependencies, click **OK**.

7. To find the Content folder of the project you want to copy these assets into, in the Browse for Folder window, navigate to the Content folder of the MyHour02 project and with this folder selected, click **OK**.

NOTE

Content Browser Filters

The more content you have in a project, the harder it can be to find what you are looking for. This is why folder organization and naming conventions are important. At the top of the asset view in the Content Browser are a search box and filter tools. Both of these are relevant to the folder that is selected in the source panel—that is, they show only what is in the folder that is currently selected as well as its subfolders. If you select the Content folder at the top, for example, the search box and filter tools apply to Content and all its subfolders.

Other Asset Types

Many assets are not imported but are created directly in the Editor (for example, Blueprint classes, particle systems, and camera animation data). Over the next 22 hours, you'll learn to add and create some of these asset types.

TIP

Creating a Raw Asset Folder for Your Projects

When working on large projects with large groups, you need some kind of project management software to stay organized. When you first start out, something as simple as adding a folder in your project's root directory to keep track of your raw files can go a long way toward keeping external content organized outside the Editor.

Here is sample directory structure for keeping common external assets organized before importing them into a project:

▶ Raw Assets folder

   ▶ Models subfolder

   ▶ Audio subfolder

   ▶ Textures subfolder

Asset References and the Reference Viewer

You may be tempted to move .uasset files around manually or copy them from one project to another. Although doing that technically works, it is not good practice because of dependencies. You should always make changes to locations and folder structure in the Content Browser so the Editor can update dependencies.

The Reference Viewer shows the dependencies for an asset (see Figure 2.5). For example, if you assign a material to the Static Mesh in the Static Mesh Editor, the Static Mesh needs to know the location of the material in the Content Browser. In turn, the material needs to know the location of the textures that it is dependent on. If you move the material to a new folder in the Content Browser, the Editor automatically updates the Static Mesh asset references. To see the asset references for an asset, right-click it in the Content Browser and select **Reference > Reference Viewer**.

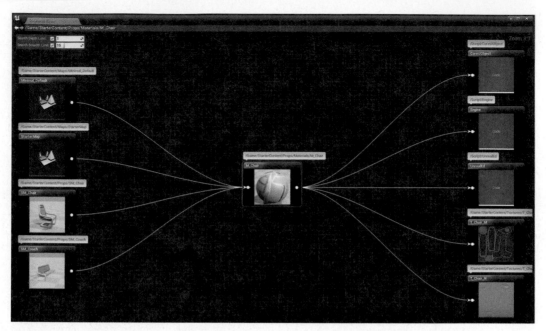

FIGURE 2.5
The Reference Viewer, displaying the dependencies for the M_Chair Material Asset.

Saved Folder

The Saved folder contains four subfolders: AutoSaves, Backup, Config, and Logs. The Editor uses the AutoSaves and Backup folders to create backup files and temporary working files for anything you have opened or modified. You can use these files to save the day if the Editor ever crashes on you. But they also increase the size of your project greatly as you work, so you may want to periodically flush these folders to keep the project size down. The Config folder contains .ini files that are used to store project settings.

Gameplay Framework

The Gameplay Framework is a collection of C++ or Blueprint classes that manages the rules of the Game, player input and avatars, cameras, and player HUDs in every project.

NOTE

More Than Games

Don't let the terminology fool you. While UE4 has been developed to make Games and much of the terminology is Game related, this engine can be used to make many different applications. For example, a 3D artist could make a model viewer to display 3D models in the portfolio website.

GameMode Class

In the Gameplay Framework, the GameMode class is used to set the rules of the Game and store all the other classes that are needed to define the Game's core functionality. For example, the GameMode class is a good place to script respawn systems for a first-person shooter or a timer for a race Game. The following is a list of the classes in the Gameplay Framework that are assigned to the GameMode class:

- DefaultPawn class

- HUD class

- PlayerController class

- Spectator class

- ReplaySpectator class

- PlayerState class

- GameState class

After a Game mode and its dependencies have been created, you can assign the Game mode to the project or to each individual level in a project. Most projects have two or three Game modes, but of course only one can be assigned as the default mode. You do this in the project settings, under **Maps & Modes > Default Modes**. Once a Game mode has been set as the default mode, it is the mode used by every level in the Game unless the Level has been set to override the default Game mode in the GameMode Override property on the World Settings tab of the Editor.

Controller Classes

A controller class controls a pawn in a Game. The PlayerController class takes the input from the player and uses it to direct the player's pawn. There are two basic types of controller classes: PlayerController and AIController. The PlayerController class manages inputs from the player and directs a pawn in the Game by possessing it. Player inputs can be anything from mouse and keyboard or Game pads to touch screens or an Xbox Kinect. The PlayerController class is also where you can turn on visibility of the mouse cursor and set how the Game will respond to mouse-click events. Every human player in a Game has an instance of the PlayerController class assigned to him or her. For example, every time a player joins a multiplayer Game, an instance of the PlayerController class is created within the GameMode class and assigned to that player for the rest of the Game session. PlayerController classes do not have physical representations in the Game world.

Pawn and Character Classes

In Unreal Engine, the term *Pawn* refers to the player's avatar. Pawn classes take the input from the PlayerController class and use it to direct the physical representation of the player in the Game. This can be as basic as just representing the player's location in the level or as complex as an animated Skeletal Mesh with a collision hull moving around the Game world. There are several classes that can be assigned to the DefaultPawn class property in a Game mode, such as the Pawn, Character, and Vehicle classes. A Pawn class is a generic class for creating a variety of Pawn types, while Character and Vehicle classes are set up for dealing with specific but common Pawns found in most Games. Since pawns take direction from a controller class, Pawns can be controlled by the PlayerController class or the AIController class.

HUD Class

The HUD class is used to draw 2D interface content to the player's screen and create in-Game heads-up display (HUD). A Game's entire HUD system can be scripted in the HUD class. Epic has also provided an interface Editor called Unreal Motion Graphics (UMG), which is a collection of tools and classes for building complex interfaces and HUDs. (See Hour 22, "Working with UMG.")

The project templates that Epic has provided already have Game modes set up for common Game types. Typically, you choose a Game mode template every time you created a new project.

▼ TRY IT YOURSELF

Add a Game Mode to a Project

At the beginning of this hour, you created a blank project that you can now use to practice adding the Game modes as a features pack. Follow these steps to add a Game mode to the blank MyHour02 project:

1. Open the MyHour02 project you created in the previous Try It Yourself.

2. In the Content Browser, click the green **Add New** button above the source panel.

3. In the pop-up window at the top, select **Add Feature or Content Pack**. This opens the Add Content to the Project window (see Figure 2.6).

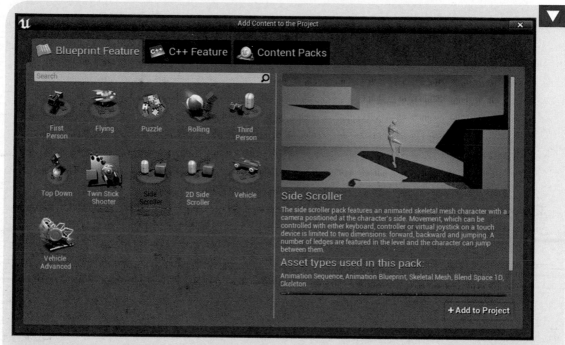

FIGURE 2.6
Add Content to the Project window.

4. On the Blueprint Features tab, select **Side Scroller** and click the green +**Add to Project** button to add it to your project.

5. On the Content Packs tab, select the starter content and click the green +**Add to Project** button to add it to your project.

6. Close the Add Content to the Project window.

In the Content Browser you will now see a few new folders that have been added to your project. Navigate to the SideScrollerBP/Maps folder and double-click on the SideScrollerExampleMap Level to open it. Preview the Level by clicking on the **Play** button on the Level Editor toolbar. As you can see you now have the beginnings of a side scroller Game. However, if you open any of the other levels that were added with the Starter Content they use a different Game mode. Navigate to the StarterContent/Maps folder and open the Minimal_Default level and preview it. You can see that the Side Scroller Game mode does not work. You need to set the Default Game Mode of the project.

▼ TRY IT YOURSELF

Set the Default Game Mode to a Project

Follow these steps to set the Default Game Mode of your project:

1. Open the MyHour02 project you created in the previous Try It Yourself.

2. In the Content Browser, click the green **Add New** button above the source panel.

3. On the Level Editor menu bar select **Edit > Project Settings**.

4. Under Project on the left-hand side of the Project Settings window, select **Maps & Modes** (see Figure 2.7).

FIGURE 2.7
Project Settings.

5. On the right-hand side, select **SideScrollerGameMode** from the **Default GameMode** drop-down list.

6. Close the Project Settings window and preview the Minimal_Default level again.

You can also assign Game modes to individual levels by going to the GameMode Override property on the World Settings tab of the Editor and selecting any of the Game modes that have been added to the project.

Summary

In this hour, you learned to import assets, migrate content from one project to another, and add various features to an existing project. You were also introduced to concepts related to Game modes and learned to set the default Game mode for a project.

Q&A

Q. Do I need to assign a Game mode to every level I create?

A. No. You need to assign a mode only if the level needs a different Game mode than the rest of the project. When a Game mode is set up in the Project Settings, all levels in the Game use that Game mode.

Q. When I migrated content, the Editor asked if I wanted to overwrite the existing content.

A. When you migrate content, some assets have the same dependencies as others, and if they are migrated at different times, the Editor warns you that some of the original assets will be overwritten, which breaks the dependency of the asset that is migrated first. You have to fix the dependencies manually after you migrate assets.

Q. What is an .ini file?

A. An .ini file is simple text file that stores preferences and settings for both the Editor and a project. While .ini files can be opened and edited in a simple text Editor, there is not much need to do this because they are managed through the UE4 Editor.

Workshop

Now that you have finished the hour, see if you can answer the following questions.

Quiz

1. True or false: The best way to move content from one project to another is to copy the .uasset file.

2. True or false: You don't need to save an asset in the Content Browser after it has been imported or modified.

3. True or false: The Reference Viewer allows you to see an asset's dependencies on other assets.

Answers

1. False: The proper way to move content from one project to another is to migrate it.

2. False: When you first import an asset or modify an existing asset, you need to save it.

3. True: The Reference Viewer enables you to visualize an asset's dependencies.

Exercise

Create a blank project and import external assets. Add two Game Mode templates and Mobile Starter Content; assign one of the Games as the default Game mode, and assign the other to a level.

1. Create a new Blank project.

2. From the Content Browser add **Third Person** Game Mode.

3. From the Content Browser add **Flying** Game Mode.

4. From the Content Browser add **Mobile Starter Content**.

5. In the Content Browser, create a new folder called **MyContent** and import external content from the book's Hour_02 folder.

6. Assign the **Third Person** Game Mode as the project's default Game mode.

7. Create a new level and set GameMode Override to **FlyingGameMode** in the Levels property on the World Settings tab of the Editor.

HOUR 3
Coordinates, Transforms, Units, and Organization

What You'll Learn in This Hour:

▶ Cartesian coordinates and how they relate to UE4 transformations

▶ Scaling, moving, and rotating

▶ The grid system and measurements for Actors

▶ Scene organization and structure

▶ Actor grouping, layers, and attaching

In this hour, you learn about using coordinates and transforms, and you develop an understanding of how to use the grid to create content in a 3D space. This hour looks at what types of transformations are used to control particular Actors in the Editor. Then it looks at how to control these transforms and what tools can maximize their use. Next, you examine the grid system and the measurements that make multi-software package information translate correctly into UE4. Finally, you examine some organizational systems used in UE4 to keep projects tidy and readable.

Understanding Cartesian Coordinates

Understanding any type of 3D content creation requires understanding the use of three-dimensional coordinates—that is, Cartesian coordinates. *Cartesian coordinates* are a system of calculations from which you can derive information or points within a given field or space. If you have taken a geometry or calculus class in school, then you have probably already used Cartesian coordinates. When placing a point on a 2D plane, as shown in Figure 3.1, you must pick two numbers, one for the X axis and one for the Y axis. Then you can simply find the place where the points meet, and you have found the intended coordinate or position within that space. This process is exactly the same in 3D spaces, except that now there are three axes that define where the points meet. Instead of using just two numbers, a 3D plane uses X, Y, and Z coordinates. Each letter corresponds to an axis, where Z is up and down, Y is left to right, and X is front to back. All 3D graphics are generated by plotting out one single point Relative to specific values. By using a string of these intersection points, you can make connections between the points to create a shape or volume. You can also use the points for manipulation and movement to plot out placement and Scale of an object in 3D space.

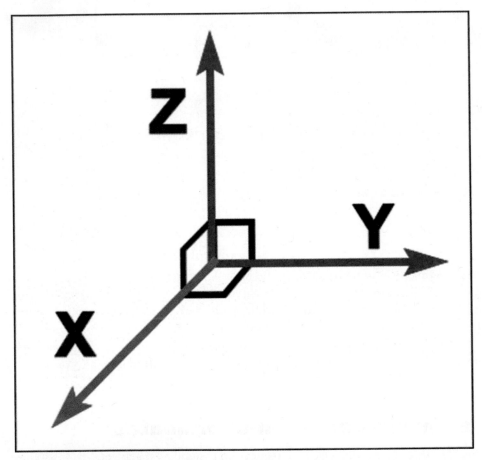

FIGURE 3.1
Each direction in a 3D coordinate system has an associated letter X, Y, or Z.

Working with Transforms

The following sections look at how to achieve movement, scaling, and Rotation with the transformation tools in the UE4 Editor.

Transformation Tools

A transformation tool manipulates or translates within the 3D space in UE4. There are three transformation types (see Figure 3.2):

▶ Move

▶ Scale

▶ Rotate

FIGURE 3.2
The transformation widget representing each transformation type. Beginn
transformations for move, Scale, and rotate and their corresponding widget

One of the most important features of the World Outliner is that it enables you to find Actors within the scene. All Actors in the scene are listed and searchable through the search bar at the top of this panel. You can use this search bar to search the whole scene or look for specific types of Actors within the scene. You can also exclude words from your search by adding the - character before a keyword search. For instance, say that you are making a map with two areas, and you have labeled the ground Actors as **area1_ground** or **area2_ground**. If you want to find an Actor with the word **ground**, but you want to search all the ground Actors without the word **area1**, you could simply type **ground, -area1** in the search bar. The result would be all the Actors containing the word **ground** but without the word **area1**.

Folders

The World Outliner is organized in much the same way as your computer's file browser. There are individual files and groupings of files in folders, and those folders can be organized and nested inside one another. This system is used in many digital organizational systems to maintain consistency, allowing for easy use and efficacy. You can easily make and organize folders in this type of system. At the top right of the World Outliner panel is a small icon that is a plus symbol on a folder. You can click this icon to add a new folder to your World Outliner and name it.

▼ TRY IT YOURSELF

Create a New Folder and Move Actors

This Try It Yourself gives you practice creating folders and moving Actors around within them. With the Unreal Editor open, follow these steps:

1. Navigate to the World Outliner panel.

2. Select the **Create a New Folder** option in the top-right corner.

3. Name the new folder.

4. Navigate to the Viewport and click an Actor in the level to select it. Notice that the actor you selected in the scene is now highlighted in the World Outliner.

5. Back in the World Outliner panel, click and drag the Actor name from the World Outliner into the new folder.

New Folders

...ly have an Actor selected in the World Outliner and make a new folder, that Actor is ... placed in the new folder.

As shown in Figure 3.6, each folder in the World Outliner has an eye symbol located next to it. By clicking this symbol you can toggle the visibility of Actors in the scene on and off. This is useful when you want to hide certain Actors or groups of Actors located in folders quickly while working with a scene. For instance, you might want to hide all of your lighting while you are moving Actors around to avoid selecting and moving the wrong Actors.

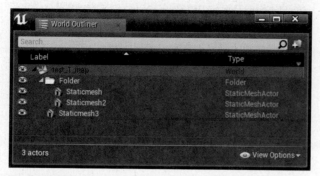

FIGURE 3.6
The World Outliner with folders. Notice that Folder contains Staticmesh and Staticmesh2, but Staticmesh3 remains outside Folder.

Grouping

Grouping is another easy way to quickly organize aspects of a project within a scene. Grouping is similar to using folders, in that it turns a selection of Actors into an individually placed Actor on the World Outliner. You can group Actors in a scene by clicking one Actor and holding down the **Ctrl** key as you click other Actors you want to add to the grouping. Then you can right-click any of the selected Actors and select **Group** from the Context Menu. You can also use the short-cut key **Ctrl+G** to group the selected Actors together.

By grouping together a set of Actors, you can move, Scale, and rotate them all at one time. When you apply movement, scaling, or Rotation to a group of Actors, keep in mind that the transformations apply to the center of all the Actors in the group; it's important to keep this in mind if you decide to group Actors that are far apart within a scene.

NOTE

Grouping Actors

An Actor can belong to only one group at a time. This means you cannot group an Actor into more than one group.

A few options allow you to change how a group is set up. Each group can be unlocked and locked. By default, all groups created are locked, which means all the parts of it transform as one unit. To manipulate each part inside a group, right-click the group to open the Context Menu and select **Groups > Unlock**. While the group is unlocked, you can manipulate the Actors in the group individually. When you are done making changes, you can lock the group again by simply right-clicking any of the Actors in the group and selecting **Lock Group**. This resets the constraints of the Actors to act as one Actor group again.

Layers

Another method for keeping your project organized is the layer system. In UE4, the layer system is similar to the systems in 3D programs such as Maya or Max. To access the Layers panel, simply select **Window > Layers** from the main menu. In this panel, you can control what parts of the scene are grouped into layers and can be toggled on and off. When you right-click in the Layers panel, all available options, such as New Layer, for creating a new layer, are available (see Figure 3.7).

You can add Actors in a scene to layers in a couple ways. One way is to click names of Actors in the World Outliner and left-click and drag them to the appropriate layer in the Layers panel. Another method is to select all the Actors you want to add to a layer, right-click that layer in the Layers panel, and select **Actors to Layer** from the Context Menu provided. You can also remove previously added Actors from layers: Right-click an Actor and select **Remove Selected Actors from Layer** from the Context Menu.

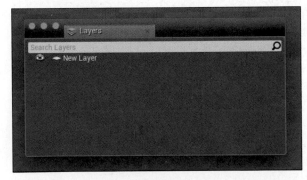

FIGURE 3.7
The Layers panel.

To select all Actors in a layer, right-click the layer and choose **Select Actors** from the Context Menu. This is a powerful way to keep similar Actors in a scene paired together and easily selectable all at once. For instance, by using layers, you can put all the lights for a scene in one layer, all the Static Meshes in one layer, and all the post-processing effects and particles in one layer. You can control layers in the World Outliner much the way you control Actors there. You can toggle a layer on and off by using the eye symbol located beside the name of the layer.

NOTE

The Difference Between Groups and Layers

There are a few differences between groups and layers, but the biggest one is the ability to put a single Actor in multiple layers. While an Actor can be in only one group at a time, that Actor can be in multiple layers at once. This difference maximizes flexibility for Actor pairing and selection.

Attaching

Attaching Actors to one another allows you to create a parent-child relationship between them. Once two Actors have been attached (see Figure 3.8), one will be the parent and the other the child. The child Actor's transforms become Relative to its parent. This means that when you move, Scale, or rotate the parent, the child will follow. However, changing the transforms of the child Actor does not affect its parent. A parent can have any number of child Actors attached to it, but a child can have only one parent. To attach one Actor to another, select the Actor you want to be the child in the World Outliner by clicking on its name and dragging it onto the name of the Actor you want to be the parent. To break an attachment, in the World Outliner click and drag the child back onto the parent's name.

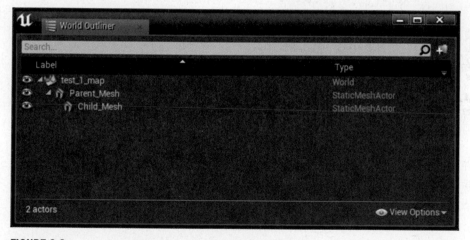

FIGURE 3.8
World Outliner showing attached Static Mesh Actors.

Because the Location, Rotation, and Scale transforms for Actors are each set to type Relative by default, the child mimics the changes made to the parent transforms. You can change the transform type for Location, Rotation, and Scale independently of each other from Relative to World. For example, there may be times when you want a child to follow its parent's position but not its Rotation or Scale. To do this, Location needs to be set to type Relative, but Rotation and Scale need to be set to type World. To change the transform type of Location, Rotation, Scale for the child, select the Actor and in the Details panel under Transform, click the triangle next to Location, Rotation, or Scale and choose the transform type (see Figure 3.9).

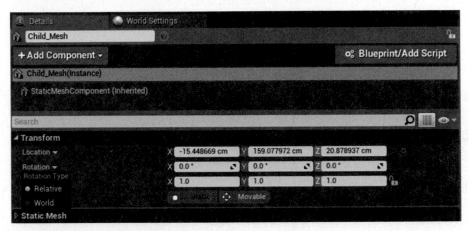

FIGURE 3.9
Details Panel showing Rotation Type property.

Summary

In this hour, you learned about using the transform tools to manipulate and alter the state of the Actors within a scene. You also looked at the ways you can control these transforms for maximum flexibility. You now understand how to alter the default settings to suit your needs and project. This hour you examined the grid system and using snaps in UE4 to increase efficiency and maintain precise movements and measurements while manipulating Actors within a scene. Finally, you took a look at keeping up with your Actors during development by organizing them into layers and groups. Using these tools, you can now feel confident in your use of coordinates, transforms, units, and organization in UE4.

Q&A

Q. Can I use the old Unreal system of measurement that uses 2, 4, 8, 16, 32, 64, and so on that was in the UDK?

A. Yes, you can use this system this by going to the main menu and selecting **Edit > Editor Preferences > Grid Snapping** and turn on **Use Power of Two Snap Size**.

Q. How do I move an Actor back to using the grid after I have moved it off?

A. Right-click an Actor that has been moved off the grid and select **Transform > Snap/Align > Snap Origin to Grid** from the Context Menu.

Q. How can I find an Actor in a scene after I find it in the World Outliner?

A. Select the Actor in the World Outliner and, in the Main Scene panel, simply press the **F** key to focus on that Actor.

Q. What happens when a group has only one Actor in it?

A. It automatically turns back into a single Actor rather than a group.

Workshop

Now that you have finished the hour, see if you can answer the following questions.

Quiz

1. What are the three types of transformation tools?
2. What is 1 uu equal to in real-world measurements?
3. If you toggle off the grid view, will the Actor still move along the grid measurements?
4. Can you add a new light to a preexisting layer?
5. Can an Actor that is already in a group be selected and removed from the group?

Answers

1. Move, Rotate, and Scale are the three types of transformation tools.
2. 1 uu equals 1 cm.
3. Yes, even with the grid toggled off, the Actor will still move as if it were snapping to the grid.
4. Yes, you can add a new light to a layer by selecting the Actor first and right-clicking and selecting **Add to Layer**.
5. Yes, first right-click the group and select **Unlock** and then select the undesired Actor within the group. Delete the Actor and then relock the group.

Exercise

For this exercise, you open the Editor and make a few changes to how you control the scalar parameters of an Actor. Then you group that Actor and put it into different layers to control its visibility. Understanding the controls for doing all this gives you versatility to control all the transformations of your Actors within the Editor. Also, it's important to understand how to organize Actors for maximum control of project organization and structure through groups and layers.

1. Bring any Actor into the level.

2. Scale up the object on the X axis by 15.

3. Rotate the Actor 25 degrees to the right.

4. Move the Actor 12 uu on the Y axis.

5. Move the Actor 140 uu on the Z axis.

6. Bring a second Actor into the level.

7. Group the two Actors.

8. Unlock the group, select the second Actor, and delete it.

9. Move the remaining Actor into a new layer.

10. Name the layer **Newtestlayer**.

HOUR 4
Working with Static Mesh Actors

What You'll Learn in This Hour:

▶ Becoming familiar with the Static Mesh Editor
▶ Importing 3D model files
▶ Assigning materials and collision hulls to Static Mesh assets
▶ Placing Static Mesh Actors
▶ Changing mesh and materials references on Static Mesh Actors
▶ Setting collision responses on Static Mesh Actors

Static Meshes are some of the most common art assets and Actor types you will work with in UE4. Static Meshes are 3D models imported from applications such as 3DS Max or Maya. They are primarily used for set dressing and world building. Just about every Level you make will need statics meshes. In this hour you familiarize yourself with importing 3D models, using the Static Mesh Editor, editing collision hulls, learning the key elements of working with Static Mesh assets and Actors, and assigning materials to Static Mesh assets and Actors.

NOTE

Hour 4 Setup

Create a new project with the Third Person Template and Starter Content.

Static Mesh Assets

Static Mesh assets store the pivot point (local axis), vertices, edges, and polygons that define the visual look of a model, as well as Levels of detail (LODs). Static Mesh assets also store collision hulls, sockets, and the UV layouts used for materials, textures, and lightmaps. The more comfortable you are working with and understanding the attributes of Static Mesh assets and Actors, the easier other concepts will be in later hours.

NOTE

LODs

LOD are simply versions of a mesh at different polygonal resolutions. The farther a mesh is from the camera, the less polygonal detail is needed to display the model. This is an efficiency technique for keeping rendering frame rates high during gameplay.

Static Mesh Editor

The Static Mesh Editor allows you to edit, modify, and set base properties for Static Mesh assets stored in the Content Browser. The Static Mesh Editor consists of a menu bar, a toolbar for turning on and off display elements, a Viewport window that allows you to view a mesh, a Details panel for editing and modifying a mesh's properties, a Socket Manager panel for adding and editing sockets, and a Convex Decomposition Hull panel for creating unique collision hulls (see Figure 4.1).

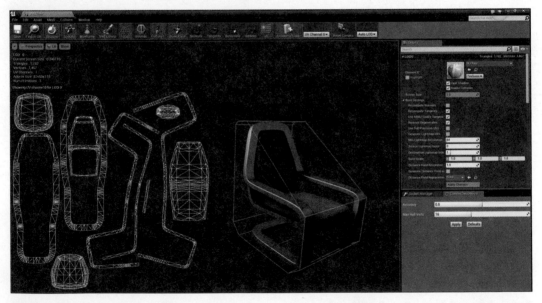

FIGURE 4.1
Static Mesh Editor interface.

Opening the Static Mesh Editor Window

To view a Static Mesh in the Static Mesh Editor, double-click the Static Mesh asset in the Content Browser, and the Static Mesh Editor opens in a new window. Each Static Mesh asset you double-click opens its own Static Mesh Editor window.

Use the Static Mesh Editor to View a Static Mesh Asset

Open the Static Mesh Editor for an existing Static Mesh asset using the following steps:

1. In the Launcher, open the project you created in Hour 1, "Introducing Unreal Engine 4."

2. In the Content Browser, navigate to the StarterContent folder. If you did not add starter content to your project back in Hour 1, click the green Add New button and select **Add New Feature or Content Pack**. In the pop-up window, select the **Content Pack** tab, highlight the starter content, and then click **Add to Project**.

3. In the StarterContent folder, navigate to the **Props** folder (see Figure 4.2).

FIGURE 4.2
Finding a Static Mesh asset in the Content Browser. Left pane: Source View. Right pane: Asset Management Area.

4. In the Asset Management Area (right pane in the Content Browser) double-click any of the Static Mesh assets to open it in the Static Mesh Editor.

5. Practice moving around the Static Mesh Editor Viewport and toggling on and off the display options on the toolbar.

NOTE

Using the Static Mesh Editor Viewport

The Static Mesh Editor Viewport window works the same way as the main Editor Viewport. Press **F** to focus the view on the mesh and **Alt+click+drag** to orbit around the mesh.

Importing Static Meshes

Two file types are commonly used for importing 3D models into the Editor: .obj and .fbx. When you import either file type, you open up an FBX Import Options window, which offers a lot of options. If you do not have a lot of experience working with 3D models, the options to focus on for now are Auto Generate Collision, Import Materials, and Import Textures. All three of these options are selected by default. Auto-generating collision hulls and lightmap UVs on import can speed things up, but you can also edit and modify collision hulls and lightmap UVs in the Static Mesh Editor.

▼ TRY IT YOURSELF

Import a Static Mesh Asset

Now that you know how to open the Static Mesh Editor for an asset, follow these steps to import a new Static Mesh into a project:

1. Open the project you created in Hour 1.

2. Go to the Content Browser and pick a folder or create a new one for storing the Static Mesh asset.

3. Right-click in the asset management view of the Content folder and select **Import To, or** click on **import** on the navigation bar at the top of the Content Browser.

4. In the Open File dialog that appears, locate the .obj or .fbx file for the Archway asset from the Hour_04 Models folder (available on the book's companion website at www.sty-ue4.com) and double-click the file, or select the file and click **Open.** (You can bypass this step by simply dragging the file into the asset view of the Content Browser straight on your OS File menu.) After the file has been selected and opened, the FBX Import Options menu is displayed.

5. In the FBX Import Options window that appears (see Figure 4.3), make sure **Auto Generate Collision** is selected.

FIGURE 4.3
The FBX Import Options window.

6. Click **Import**.

7. Once the mesh has been successfully imported, it is good practice to save it. In the Content Browser, right-click on the asset thumbnail and click **Save** from the list.

TIP

Pivot Points

When you import a mesh asset, the Static Mesh's pivot point is determined by the model's position relative to the world coordinate in the 3D application it was exported from—not the model's local axis. In the FBX Import Options window, under Transform, you can change the mesh's relative position to the pivot point by editing the position, rotation, and scale values.

Viewing UV Layouts

Before a material can be properly displayed on the surface of a model, it needs a UV map layout, also known as a UV channel. If a model has been created properly in a 3D modeling application, it should already have at least one UV channel set up. Static Meshes can have multiple UV channels. Typically there is at least one UV channel for a material (UV Channel 0) and one for the lightmap data (UV Channel 1). To view the UV channels for a Static Mesh, click the **UV** button on the toolbar to toggle it on and off. The current UV channel is displayed in the Viewport window. You can change which UV channel is displayed by selecting a channel from the drop-down on the toolbar (see Figure 4.4).

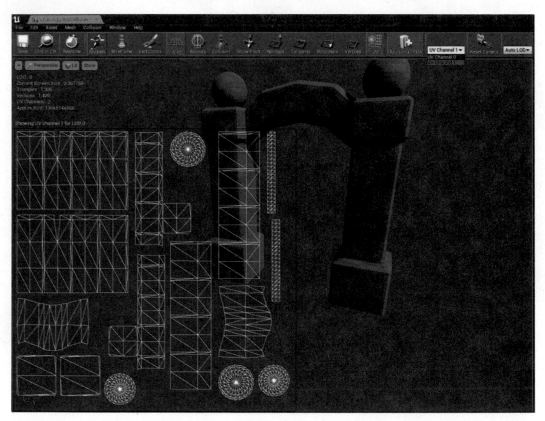

FIGURE 4.4
The mesh UV channel displayed in the Static Mesh Editor Viewport.

NOTE

Lightmap UV Channel

The lightmap UV channel is used for storing light and shadow information on the surface of a mesh. The Editor auto-generates a UV channel for lightmaps during import, but you can also create one after import by using the Static Mesh Editors Details panel options. The default lightmap UV channel is 1, which is the second UV channel because the UV channel index starts at 0. Although you can technically use any UV channel you want for lightmaps, when starting out it is best to use the default settings.

Assigning a Material to a Static Mesh Asset

Because a Static Mesh asset is a base asset, it is a good idea to prep the asset for continual use. One way to do this is to assign a default material so that every time the asset is placed in a Level as a Static Mesh Actor, it already has a material that you can replace, if desired.

TRY IT YOURSELF ▼

Assigning a Material to a Static Mesh

To assign a material to a Static Mesh asset, follow these steps:

1. Open one of the Static Meshes in the Static Mesh Editor.

2. Select the **Details** panel and find the LODO bar.

3. Under element 0, click the drop-down arrow to the right of the **Material** thumbnail and select a material from the list. You can also drag a material from the Content Browser to the thumbnail to change the material assignment.

4. Click **Save** on the Static Mesh Editor toolbar to save the changes to the Static Mesh asset.

Collision Hulls

A *collision hull* is a simple primitive shape that surrounds a mesh and is used to identify collision events. A *collision event* occurs when two Actor collision hulls hit, touch, or overlap with each other. When you import a 3D model, the Editor auto-generates a simple collision hull.

Viewing Collision Hulls

You can view a collision hull in the Static Mesh Editor by clicking the **Collision** icon on the Static Mesh Editor toolbar (see Figure 4.5).

FIGURE 4.5
Static Mesh Editor toolbar showing Collision toggled on.

You can then interact with the collision hull by clicking any of its wireframe edges. You can move, scale, and rotate the hull simply by pressing the **Spacebar** to cycle through Transform gizmos (see Figure 4.6). You can remove a selected collision hull by pressing the **Delete** key.

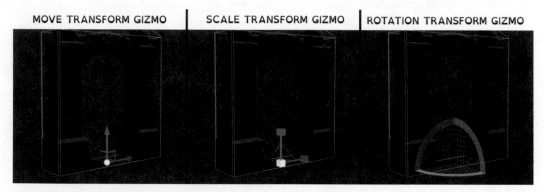

FIGURE 4.6
Move, Scale, and Rotate Transform Gizmos. The X axis is red, the Y axis is green, and the Z axis is blue.

Editing Collision Hulls

Auto-generating collision hulls during import can save you time, but depending on the shape of the mesh asset, auto-generation may not always be the best solution. In Figure 4.7, you can see the auto-generated collision that surrounds the entire Archway mesh. This collision hull will block Actors from passing through the mesh, but it will also stop Actors from walking under the Archway. In this case, the collision hull needs to be modified.

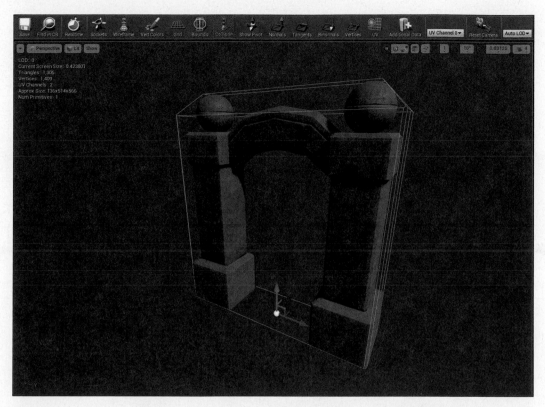

FIGURE 4.7
An auto-generated collision hull.

NOTE

Simplified Collision

You can add multiple collision hulls to one Static Mesh. To add one, click **Collision** on the menu bar and select **Add** *collision you want to add*. Do this as many times as you like. If you need to remove a collision hull, just select it in the Viewport and press **Delete**. If you want to remove all of the collision hulls from the Viewport, select **Collision > Remove Collision**.

▼ TRY IT YOURSELF

Work with Collision Hulls

This is a good time to practice editing collision hulls. Try editing the Archway asset found in the Hour_04 folder (available on the book's companion website at www.sty-ue4.com):

1. Open the Archway mesh in the Static Mesh Editor. (You can use the previously imported asset or duplicate the previously imported asset in the Content Browser, or you can just import a new one altogether.)

2. Select **Collision > Remove Collision**.

3. Select **Collision > Add Box Simplified Collision** (see Figure 4.8).

4. Select the collision hull in the Viewport and press the **Spacebar** to cycle through Move, Scale, and Rotate as needed to place the Box Simplified collision hull over the Archway top.

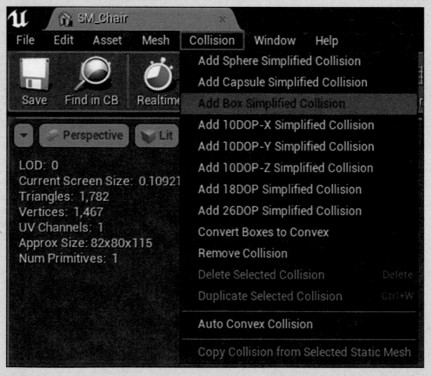

FIGURE 4.8
Selecting **Collision > Add Box Simplified Collision** from the Static Mesh Editor menu bar.

5. Repeat steps 3 and 4 two more times for each of the Archway pillars.

6. Click **Save** on the toolbar to save the changes to the Static Mesh asset in the Content Browser. When finished, your collision should look similar to Figure 4.9.

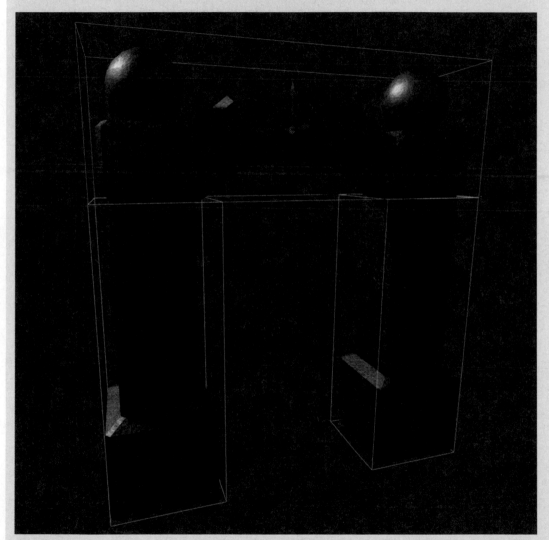

FIGURE 4.9
Manually placed collision Hulls.

Convex Decomposition

Collision hulls are simplified convex primitive shapes for efficiency, but the Static Mesh Editor also has a panel called Convex Decomposition that allows you to auto-generate collision hulls for more complicated models. Altering the complexity of a Static Mesh and the convex decomposition settings will give you varying results (see Figure 4.10). To open the Convex Decomposition panel, select **Collision > Auto Convex Collision**.

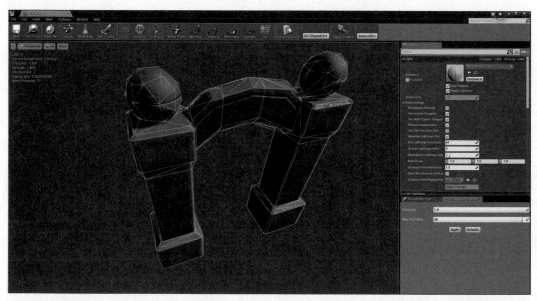

FIGURE 4.10
Collision hulls can be generated with the Convex Decomposition panel.

Per-Poly Collision

You can also set Static Mesh assets to per-poly collision, which is the most accurate collision you can have. It is also the most computational intensive, so you should use it only for specific situations when you need precision. Go to the Static Mesh Settings section of the Details panel and set Collision Complexity to **Use Complex Collision as Simple** (see Figure 4.11). This will tell the Editor to use Complex Collision (per-poly) instead of Simple Primitive Convex Primitive.

FIGURE 4.11
Static Mesh settings for per-poly collision.

CAUTION

Per-Poly Collision Detection

If every Static Mesh Actor onscreen were processing per-poly collision detection during a game, this would take up a lot of processing power and could quickly reduce frame rates at runtime.

Static Mesh Actors

The remainder of this hour focuses on working with Static Mesh Actors. Static Mesh Actors are placed instances of a Static Mesh asset in a Level. Each placed Static Mesh Actor has its own properties that can be modified independently of the referenced Static Mesh asset. Changing a Static Mesh asset's properties can affect all of the Static Mesh Actors that reference it. For example, if you remove the collision hulls completely from a mesh asset, all the Actors that use this Static Mesh will not be able to generate collision responses. However, changing a Static Mesh Actor's properties and settings has no effect on the original Static Mesh asset.

Placing Static Mesh Actors into a Level

Now that you have gone through the process of importing and editing collision hulls for Static Mesh assets, it's a good time to practice placing Static Mesh Actors into a Level. To place a Static Mesh into your Level, locate one in the Content Browser. (You can use the mesh you imported earlier or you can import a new mesh and place it into the Level.) To place the mesh in the current Level, simply **click+drag** the asset from the Content Browser to the current Level in the Level Editor Viewport.

Once you drag a Static Mesh into a Level, you create a Static Mesh Actor that references the original mesh asset. If you select a placed Static Mesh Actor in a Level, it gets a silhouette outline around it, and you see the Transform gizmo appear at the Actor's pivot point. You can see in the Level Editor Details panel that it now has Transform properties that store its position, rotation, and scale in the world (see Figure 4.12).

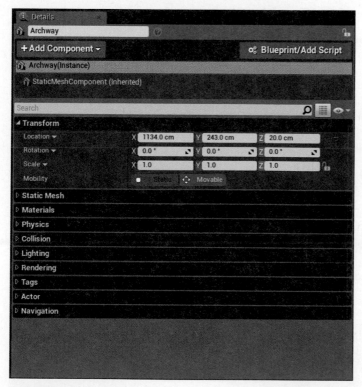

FIGURE 4.12
Static Mesh Actor Transform settings in the main Editor Details panel.

TIP

Duplicating Static Mesh Actors

If you want to quickly duplicate an already-placed Static Mesh Actor, hold down the **Alt** key and move or rotate the Actor by using the Transform gizmo in the Level Viewport.

Mobility Settings

In the Transform section of the Details panel, you can see that a Static Mesh Actor has two possible mobility states: Static and Movable. Changing the mobility state of an Actor ultimately affects how the engine calculates light and shadow information for the Actor. Static tells the engine that lighting needs to be precalculated, and Movable tells the engine to calculate lighting during runtime. If you want to animate a Static Mesh Actor or have it simulate physics, you need to set Mobility to **Movable**. To change the mobility stat of a Static Mesh Actor, simply click on **Static** or **Movable** under the Transform properties.

NOTE

Static Mesh: To Move or Not to Move, That Is the Question

The term *Static Mesh* can be a bit deceiving. In this case, *static* refers to the base state. By default, a Static Mesh is also static in that it will not move during game play. If a mesh is not going to move, you can build (precalculate) lighting data so the target runtime platform does not have to worry about calculating lighting every frame but can simply load and display the precalculated lighting data on the surface of the placed Actor.

Changing the Mesh Reference for a Static Mesh Actor

As you can see in Figure 4.13, a Static Mesh Actor references the initial Static Mesh asset used when the Actor was placed in the Level. You can easily change the mesh reference by dragging a new mesh asset from the Content Browser to the Static Mesh reference thumbnail in the Level Details panel of the selected Static Mesh Actor or by clicking on the drop-down arrow next to the currently assigned mesh and selecting a new mesh. When you have changed the mesh, you see it update in the Level Viewport. Because the Static Mesh Actor stores its own world Transform data, the newly assigned mesh takes on those properties.

FIGURE 4.13
Static Mesh Actor mesh reference.

Replacing the Material on a Static Mesh Actor

A Static Mesh Actor also has a material reference that is initially assigned based on the original material assigned to the mesh asset in the Static Mesh Editor. You can modify the material for each Actor. Figure 4.14 shows the current material assignment in the main Editor Details panel for the selected Static Mesh Actor. You can drag a new material from the Content Browser to the thumbnail image of the current material in the Details panel, or you can click on the drop-down arrow next to the currently assigned material and select from the list, or you can simply click and drag the new material from the Content Browser to any of the Static Mesh Actors in the Level.

FIGURE 4.14
Static Mesh Actor material reference.

Editing Collision Responses on a Static Mesh Actor

You have already learned how to edit collision hulls on Static Mesh assets in the Static Mesh Editor. Now you are ready to modify collision responses on Static Mesh Actors placed in a Level. With a Static Mesh Actor selected in the Level, you can find the collision setting for the Actor in the main Editor Details panel. For now you can focus just on the collision presets, collision responses, and object types. To view Actor collision hulls in the Level Editor Viewport, press **Alt+C** to toggle collision hull visibility. Figure 4.15 shows the Level Viewport with collision hull display turned on.

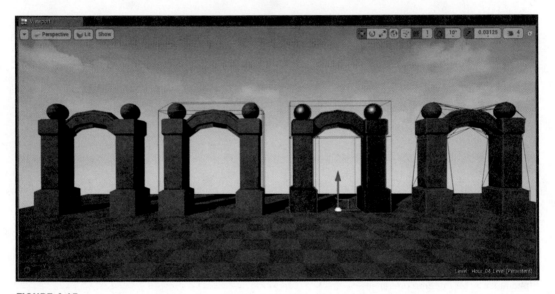

FIGURE 4.15
The Level Editor Viewport, showing four Static Mesh Actors, each referencing a different Static Mesh asset with different collision hulls and the Level Viewport collision hull show flag toggled on.

Collision Presets

By clicking the triangle to the left of Collision Preset in the main Editor Details panel, you can expand the window to show more options. With a preset already assigned, you see that the collision response options are grayed out and can't be modified. The presets define common settings for collision responses for Actors with different object types. To unlock the options, you must choose **Custom Preset**. Figure 4.16 shows the collision settings.

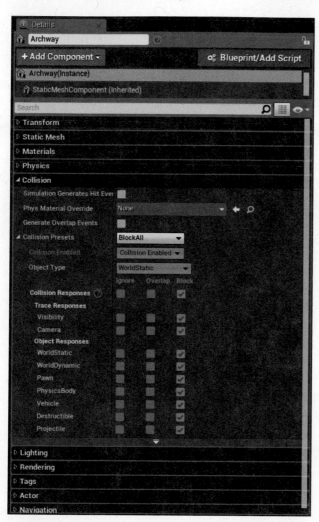

FIGURE 4.16
Static Mesh Actor collision setting in the main Editor Details panel.

TIP

Custom Collision Presets

You can create your own collision presets by selecting **Edit > Project Settings** on the Level Editor Main menu. But when you're first starting out, it is easiest to just choose the custom preset and modify the collision response for each Actor directly on the selected Static Mesh Actor.

Collision Enabled

The Collision Enabled setting on the Details panel lets you turn collisions on and off for the selected Actor. When this is selected, even if the referenced Static Mesh asset for this Actor has a collision hull, this Actor will not process collision interactions and events.

Object Type

The Object Type setting on the Details panel allows you to set what kind of object type this Actor is, so when other Actors collide with it, they will know how to respond. For example, if a Static Mesh Actor is set to Static under Transform, then its object type should be set to **WorldStatic**, but if it is set to Movable under Transform, the object type should be set to **WorldDynamic**.

NOTE

Object Types

Every Actor that can collide has an assigned object type. There are seven object types: WorldStatic, WorldDynamic, Pawn, PhysicsBody, Vehicle, Destructible, and Projectile.

Collision Response Flags

The Collision Responses section of the Details panel allows you to set how this Static Mesh Actor will respond to other Actors with defined object types.

There are three interaction states for collision interactions:

- ▶ **Ignore:** Ignore any collision responses of these object types.
- ▶ **Overlap:** Check to see if the mesh's collision hull is intersecting with another Actor.
- ▶ **Block:** Stop another Actor from passing through the mesh's collision hull.

NOTE

No Collision Hull on the Asset, No Collision Response on the Actor

If a Static Mesh asset does not have an assigned collision hull in the Static Mesh Editor, then any Static Mesh Actors that reference the Static Mesh asset will not be able to process any collision events regardless of the collision response type assigned to the Actors.

Summary

In this hour, you were introduced to Static Meshes and some of the different tools associated with them. You now have some experience with importing 3D models, working with the Static Mesh Editor, creating collision hulls, placing Static Mesh Actors in a Level, and modifying basic collision properties. There is, of course, more to learn about Static Meshes, but you now have a base knowledge to build from.

Q&A

Q. I know you can import a Static Mesh into the UE4, but can you export a Static Mesh as well?

A. Yes, right-click the mesh asset in the Content Browser and select **Common > Asset Action**. In the dialog that appears, click **Export**.

Q. Can I modify the pivot point of a Static Mesh asset?

A. No—at least not directly in the Static Mesh Editor. You can, however, make adjustments to the original mesh asset in an external 3D modeling application and then reimport the mesh. If you don't have the original mesh, you can export the mesh as an .fbx file from the project.

Q. What is the Socket Manager panel, and what is it used for?

A. The Socket Manager panel allows you to create points on a mesh that are used for establishing parent/child hierarchical relationships—that is, for attaching one Actor to another. These relationships are helpful when you're animating or moving an Actor with Blueprint.

Workshop

Now that you have finished the hour, see if you can answer the following questions.

Quiz

1. True or false: It is always best to set a mesh to per-poly collision.

2. What key do you press along with **Alt** to display collision hulls in the Level Editor Viewport window?

3. True or false: By default, lightmap UV layout is stored in UV Channel 1.

4. True or false: If a Static Mesh asset does not have a collision hull assigned, a Static Mesh Actor that references this mesh will still have a collision response.

5. True or false: If you assign a new material to a Static Mesh Actor, it replaces the material assigned to the Static Mesh asset.

Answers

1. False: For efficiency, it is always best to use simple shapes for collision.

2. Alt + C will toggle on the display of collision hulls in the Level Viewport window.

3. True: By default, UE4 uses UV channel 1 for lightmaps.

4. False: If a Static Mesh asset does not have an assigned collision hull, then any Static Mesh Actors that reference the Static Mesh asset will not be able to process any collision events.

5. False: Assigning a new material to a Static Mesh Actor only affects that Actor.

Exercise

Find .fbx and .obj model files on the Internet or use the ones provided in the Hour_04 folder (available on the book's companion website at www.sty-ue4.com) and import them. Edit their collision hulls and place them in a Level.

1. Create a **Maps** folder in the Content Browser.

2. Create a new default map and save it to the newly created Maps folder.

3. Create a Mesh folder in the Content Browser.

4. Import an .obj model file.

5. Import an .fbx model file.

6. Assign a new material to each of the Static Mesh assets.

7. Change their collision hull properties by using the presets and auto decomposition.

8. Place Static Mesh Actors in the Level several times.

9. For each mesh, change the Move, Scale, and Rotate Transforms.

10. Assign unique materials to each of the Static Mesh Actors.

11. Save the Level to the Maps folder.

HOUR 5
Applying Lighting and Rendering

What You'll Learn in This Hour:

▶ Learning lighting terminology
▶ Using different types of lights
▶ How to apply light properties
▶ Building lighting
▶ Using Mobility settings

In this hour, you learn to work with Light Actors. First, you look at the types of lights available. Then you look at how to place Light Actors in a level, modify their settings, and control how they affect other Actors in the world.

Although lights are some of the simplest Actors to place in a level and edit, understanding how they work and interact with other Actors and how to apply rendering settings are difficult skills to master.

NOTE

Hour 5 Setup

Create a new project with the Third Person Template and Starter Content.

Learning Light Terminology

Some basic key concepts help in understanding the options when dealing with Light Actor properties:

▶ *Direct* lighting refers to light that falls on the surface of an Actor, without any interference from other Actors. The light travels directly from the light source to the surface of mesh. So the Static Mesh Actor receives the full color spectrum of the light.

▶ *Indirect or bounced* lighting refers to light that has been reflected off the surface of another Actor in the scene. Because light waves are absorbed or reflected based on the surface properties and colors of a mesh, the reflected light takes on some of the color information and also passes it on to the next surface in its path. Indirect lighting affects the overall scene light intensity.

▶ *Static* lighting refers to lighting for objects and lights that do not move. For things that don't move, lighting and shadows have to be calculated only once (during build), which results in better performance and high quality.

▶ *Dynamic* lighting refers to lights and objects that may move at runtime. Because this type of lighting is calculated every frame, it is often slower and lower quality than static lighting.

▶ *Shadows* are created when the engine takes a snapshot of the silhouette of a mesh from the light's point of view and then projects that image onto the surface of other Actors on the inverse side of the lit Mesh Actor. Both Static Mesh Actors and Light Actors have shadow properties that can be selected.

Understanding Light Types

There are four basic Light Actors in Unreal Engine: Point Light, Spot Light, Directional Light, and Sky Light (see Figure 5.1). They all have some similar property settings. However, each Light Actor type also has settings that are unique.

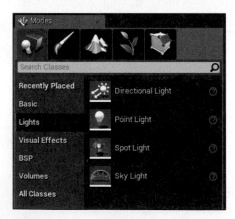

FIGURE 5.1
Light Actors can be found in the Lights section of the Modes panel.

Adding Point Lights

Point Lights work much like a real-world light bulb, emitting light equally in all directions from a single point in space. This is the most common light type, particularly for indoor scenes.

Add a Point Light to a Scene

Follow these steps to create an empty level without lighting and add various types of lighting:

1. Create a new empty level. It should be black.

2. In the Modes panel, select **Basic** and drag a cube into the level.

3. In the Details panel, set Location to **0,0,0** and set Scale to **20,20,1** to create a floor surface.

4. In the Modes panel, select **Lights** and drag a Point Light into the level.

5. In the Details panel, set Location to **400,0,200**.

6. In the Modes panel, select **Basic** and drag a cube into the level. Notice the shadow that is cast on the floor from the Point Light.

7. In the Details panel, set Location to **500,100,90**.

8. Play with adjusting various parameters on the light and the cube to see what effects they have.

9. Save and name the **Level LightStudy**.

Figure 5.2 shows the result of this Try It Yourself.

FIGURE 5.2
Point Lighting.

Adding Spot Lights

In UE4, a Spot Light emits light from a single point in a cone shape toward a specific direction, just like a Spot Light in the real world. The Spot Light direction is set by changing the Spot Light Actor's Rotate transform. You can adjust the attenuation to set the distance the light travels from where the Spot Light is paced. The Inner Cone and Outer Cone angle properties affect how quickly light changes from full intensity at the center of the cone to no light at the edges. The closer these values are to one another, the harder the edge of the light will be.

▼ TRY IT YOURSELF

Add a Spot Light

Follow these steps to add some Spot Lights to the level you created in the previous Try It Yourself:

1. Open the LightStudy level you created in the previous Try It Yourself.

2. Delete the Point Light from the scene.

3. In the Modes panel, select **Lights** and drag a Spot Light into the level.

4. In the Details panel, set Location to **600,60,300**.

5. Play with adjusting the color and adding more lights.

Figure 5.3 shows the result of this Try It Yourself.

FIGURE 5.3
Red and blue Spot Light overlapping each other and creating purple lighting.

Adding Sky Lights

A Sky Light captures the distant parts of a level—everything further than SkyDistanceThreshold—and applies light to it. That means the sky's appearance and its lighting and reflections will match, even if the sky is coming from atmosphere, or layered clouds on top of a skybox, or distant mountains. Using a Sky Light is a good way to brighten up an entire level and affect shadow colors.

NOTE

Fog Actors

Because of how a Sky Light functions, you may need to add an atmospheric fog or exponential fog Actor to a scene to see results of the Sky Light in the scene.

TRY IT YOURSELF ▼

Add a Sky Light

Follow these steps to add a sky and Sky Light to the scene you've been working on:

1. Open the level you created in the previous Try It Yourself. Delete the other lights from the level if you want.

2. In the Modes panel, select **All Classes** and drag a Sky Sphere (**BP_Sky_Sphere**) into the level. This is the sky.

3. In the Modes panel, select **Lights** and drag a Sky Light into the level. Notice that the scene has taken on the color of the sky.

4. Play with the properties on the Sky Sphere and Sky Light to see various effects.

Figure 5.4 shows the result of this Try It Yourself.

FIGURE 5.4
Sky lighting.

Adding Directional Lights

A Directional Light simulates light that is being emitted from a source that is infinitely far away. All shadows cast by this light will be parallel, making a Directional Light the ideal choice for simulating sunlight. When using a Directional Light in your level, it does not matter where you place it, only the direction it is facing.

Add a Directional Light

Follow these steps to add Directional Lighting to your scene:

1. Open the level you created in the previous Try It Yourself.

2. In the Modes panel, select **Lights** and drag a Directional Light into the level.

3. Use the **Rotate** tool to change the direction of the Directional Light and observe the effect.

4. To make a sky, select **Sky Sphere** in the World Outliner panel.

5. In the Details panel, set Directional Light Actor to **Directional Light**. Now the sky controls the Directional Light.

6. Play with the properties on the Sky Sphere and Directional Light to see various effects.

Figure 5.5 shows the result of this Try It Yourself.

FIGURE 5.5
Directional Lighting with Sky lighting.

Using Light Properties

The Properties tab of each light in a scene shows a number of properties, including the ones listed in Table 5.1.

TABLE 5.1 Light Properties

Property	Description
Intensity	Determines the brightness of the light, in lumens, for Point Lights and Spot Lights, where 1700 lumens corresponds to a 100W bulb.
Light Color	Determines the color the light shines. Color is additive, so if you shine a red light on a blue object, it ends up purple.
Attenuation Radius	Determines the maximum distance the light will reach. Illumination fades from maximum at the source of the light to zero at the edge of the radius.
Cast Shadows	Determines whether objects affected by the light cast shadows. Calculating dynamic shadows can be processor intensive.
Inside Cone Angle	Sets the angle in degrees of a Spot Light's bright area.
Outside Cone Angle	Sets the angle in degrees of a Spot Light's falloff area. If this is close to the inside angle, your Spot Light area will be sharp.
Temperature	Allows you to set the color of a light based on Kelvin color temperature scale. This is great if you are trying to match real-world light colors. You need to toggle on the Use Temperature property in order to set this.

There are many more properties, giving you total control over the lighting in a game, but these should be enough to get you started.

CAUTION

Performance

Poorly chosen lighting settings can have a big effect on performance. For example, using too many dynamic lights can cause serious performance issues. In addition, light attenuation radius can have a serious impact on performance, so use larger radius values sparingly.

Building Lighting

UE4's tool for building lighting is called *Lightmass*. Lightmass has many settings that are beyond the scope of this book. However, you can control some of these settings by selecting **Window > World Settings** and looking at all settings under Lightmass.

While UE4 can render all lights and mesh in a level with dynamic lighting, doing so affects both performance and quality. If UE4 knows that a light will not move, it can precalculate the lighting and shadows for that light and all static Actors in the world that it touches. While storing precalculated lighting is less processor intensive during gameplay, it does require memory usage.

You use the build light tools in UE4 to precalculate lighting and shadow information in a level for Static Mesh and Light Actors and BSPs. (See Chapter 9 for information about BSPs.) This information is stored as images embedded in the level, which you can find by selecting **Window > World Settings > Lightmass > Lightmaps**.

Once you have built lighting, the editor displays the precalculated lighting data for any static lights. When you add a new light to a level or move lights and meshes, lights are rendered as dynamic and updated in real time until the lighting is rebuilt.

To build lighting, click the down arrow on the **Build** button on the toolbar (see Figure 5.6). In the submenu that appears, select **Lighting Quality > Preview** to get quick results. When you're ready with your final level, select **Lighting Quality > High**. High quality takes longer to generate but gives more accurate results.

FIGURE 5.6
Build button.

Swarm Agent

Notice that when you build lighting, an application called Swarm Agent automatically launches in the background. Swarm Agent manages communication between the editor and Lightmass. When you build lighting, Swarm Agent keeps track of and displays the build progress. As the complexity of a level increases, so does the amount of time it takes to calculate and build lighting. Swarm Agent can also be set up to communicate with remote machines on a network and utilize their processing power to reduce the amount of computing time. For small projects and levels, this is usually not a concern, but it is nice to know network rendering is there when needed.

NOTE

Rebuilding Lighting

Every time you move a light that is set to cast static shadows or a Static Mesh Actor that is set to static, the editor reminds you to build lighting. The more lights and objects you have, the longer it takes to rebuild the lighting. When working with light, it is best to follow an iterative process and build lighting only when significant changes have been made. You can preview and playtest the level without rebuilding the lighting, but the lighting won't be correct until you rebuild lighting.

▼ TRY IT YOURSELF

Build Static Lighting for a Scene

Follow these steps to add static lighting for the scene you've been working with:

1. Create a new Default Level.

2. Navigate to the Shape_Cube Static Mesh asset found in the StarterContent/Shapes folder in the Content Browser, and place it into the level so it is sitting on the floor.

3. From the main toolbar, click the down arrow next to Build to expand the options.

4. Select **Lighting Quality > Preview**.

5. Click the **Build** icon to build lighting. Once the Lighting build is finished, the shadow of Static Mesh Actor will update and display the newly built lighting and shadow.

6. Now change the quality of the precalculated shadow. Select the Floor Static Mesh Actor that was added when you created the Default level. In the Level Details panel under Lighting, turn on **Overridden Light Map Res** and set its value to **1024**.

7. Click the **Build** icon to build lighting again. You will see the shadow quality change. Figure 5.7 shows the result of changing the Lightmap resolution.

FIGURE 5.7
Static lighting with the default Lightmap resolution on the left and 1024 Lightmap resolution on the right.

NOTE

Adjusting Lightmap Resolution

You can override the Lightmap resolution quality on a per-Actor basis in your level as needed, or you can change the Default Lightmap resolution on Static Mesh asset in the Static Mesh Editor. Increasing the resolution will have an effect on lighting build times.

Mobility

Every light has a Mobility option for which you can choose Static, Movable, or Stationary. These settings help UE4 decide what to light dynamically and what to precalculate and save (bake) in a Lightmap:

▶ *Static* lights are lights that cannot be changed or moved in any way at runtime. The lighting information is built prior to gameplay and stored in a special texture called a *light map*. Static light gives high performance but does not work with movable objects within the light's radius. The primary reason to use the Static setting is for performance, such as on mobile devices.

▶ *Movable* lights cast completely dynamic light and shadows, and they can change position, rotation, color, brightness, falloff, radius, and just about every other property they have. None of the light they cast gets baked into the light maps, and they cannot have any indirect lighting. These lights are usually expensive to render and are not as high quality as static or stationary lights. You might use a movable light on a character that moves, such as a player holding a flashlight.

▶ *Stationary* lights are like static lights in that they cannot move; however, their brightness and color can be changed at runtime. This can be useful, for example, on lights that can be turned on and off that are not movable. The Stationary setting gives medium performance and high quality.

Table 5.2 helps you determine which of these Mobility settings to use for Static Mesh Actors.

TABLE 5.2 Static and Movable Settings for Lights and Meshes

	Light Settings		
Static Mesh Settings	**Static**	**Stationary**	**Movable**
Static	Baked lighting	Baked lighting	Baked lighting
Movable	Dynamic shadows	Dynamic shadows	Dynamic shadows

To change the Mobility setting of any Light Actor in your level, select the light and in the Level Details panel under Transform, select the Mobility setting you need. The Directional Light that is found in the default scene already has a Mobility setting of Stationary. So, if you change the Mobility of the Shape_Cube Static Mesh Actor that you placed in the previous Try it Yourself to Movable, you will change how the editor casts shadows for the Actor.

▼ TRY IT YOURSELF

Casting Dynamic Shadows

Follow these steps to change the Mobility settings of a Static Mesh Actor and to make it cast dynamic shadows:

1. Continue with the level you created in the previous Try it Yourself.

2. In the level, select the Shape_Cube Static Mesh Actor; and in the Level Details panel under Transform, set its Mobility to Movable by clicking on Moveable.

Summary

This hour starts off by highlighting some basic lighting terminology. You learned about the different types of light in UE4 and their purposes, and you learned how to place lights and configure their settings. You also learned about building lighting and how Mobility settings impact static and dynamic lighting. Lighting is one of the most complicated and powerful aspects of UE4, and it can be overwhelming. There is plenty of time to learn the details. For now you are now equipped with everything you need to get started lighting scenes.

Q&A

Q. How many lights can I add to a scene?

A. This question is not easy to answer. If you're talking about small, static lights that do not overlap lots of objects, you can add hundreds or thousands. On the other hand, using just a few large radius dynamic lights covering the entire scene could be too many. The best way is to experiment and see what works.

Q. Why don't the shadows or lighting in my scene look correct?

A. If your lights are static, you may need to build the lighting again by clicking the **Build** button on the toolbar.

Q. How do game makers make some scenes look so realistic?

A. Look at all the sample scenes included with UE4 and examine how the lights are set up. You might be able to figure out some of the tricks used to get various effects. As in magic, smoke and mirrors are used in game development all the time.

Q. Why are the Lightmaps generated during the build lighting process and embedded in the level?

A. The placement of lights and Actors in a level is unique to each level, so the lighting information generated is relevant only to that level.

Workshop

Now that you have finished the hour, see if you can answer the following questions.

Quiz

1. To illuminate an entire scene with one light, which type should you use?

2. When would you use a static or stationary light?

3. When would you use a stationary or movable light?

4. What is Lightmass?

Answers

1. To illuminate an entire scene with one light, use a Sky Light or Directional Light.

2. Use a static or stationary light when your light and everything it casts upon cannot move.

3. Use a stationary or movable light when your light or the Actor the light casts upon needs to be moved.

4. Lightmass is UE4's static lighting engine, which you use when building lighting.

Exercise

In this exercise, build a simple scene by placing BSP, Static Meshes, and all the different light types.

1. Create a new empty level.

2. In the Modes panel, select **BSP** and drag out a box into the Viewport.

3. With the box selected in the Details panel, under Brush Settings set both the X and Y properties to **1000** and the Z property to **20**. UE4 creates a large platform.

4. In the Modes panel, select **Basic** and drag out a player start in the center of the platform just above the surface.

5. In the Modes panel, select **Basic** and drag out two cube Static Meshes. Place them on the platform just above the surface.

6. Select one of the cube Static Mesh Actors and, in the Details panel, under Physics, turn on **Simulate Physics**.

7. Add Directional Light with Rotate set to **0,200,45** and Light Color set to **255,205,105**.

8. Add a Point Light to the scene so it is just above the platform. Set its Intensity to **15000**, Light Color to **255,0,255**, and the Attenuation Radius to **250**.

9. Add a Spot Light to the scene and place it about 300 units above the platform in an empty location. Set its Intensity to **30000**, Light Color to **210,255,15**, Inner Cone Angle to **22**, and Outer Cone Angle to **24**.

10. In the Modes panel, select **Visual Effects** and drag out atmospheric fog into the scene.

11. Add a Sky Light. Set its Intensity to **10** and Light Color to **215,60,15**.

12. Click the **Build** button on the toolbar to build the lighting.

13. Preview the level by walking around the level and pushing the Physics cube around to see how it interacts with the placed lights.

14. Make adjustments to all the Light Actors as desired. Remember to build the light again before you preview the level.

HOUR 6
Using Materials

What You'll Learn in This Hour:

- ▶ Understanding materials and how they are used
- ▶ Using physically based rendering
- ▶ Using the Material Editor
- ▶ Using texture types and sizes and importing textures
- ▶ Understanding the material node and constants
- ▶ Using instances and parameters

In this hour, you learn what materials are and how to use them in UE4. You first get a basic understanding of how to use physically based rendering. Next, you learn about each type of material input and how it renders in real time. Then you get familiar with ideal texture sizes, resolutions, and settings, as well as how to use them in a material setup. You also learn how to create a new material using the Material Editor, and using that material, you learn about instances and node parameters. Finally, you create your own material setup.

NOTE

Hour 6 Setup

Create a new Blank project with Starter Content.

Understanding Materials

A *material*, or *shader*, is a combination of textures, vectors, and other mathematical calculations that work in tandem to create surface descriptions and properties for assets in UE4 (see Figure 6.1). Materials may seem complex at first, but a material is really one of the most visually simple parts of UE4. You can use materials to describe the surface properties of an asset for the player and establish visual context and style. Materials primarily inform UE4 how light reacts to each surface. Assets within UE4 have specific materials applied to them. By default, different objects have standard default UE4 materials applied to them. When you are viewing a rock, a tree, or a concrete wall in a game, each of these assets has a particular material applied that gives it a unique appearance.

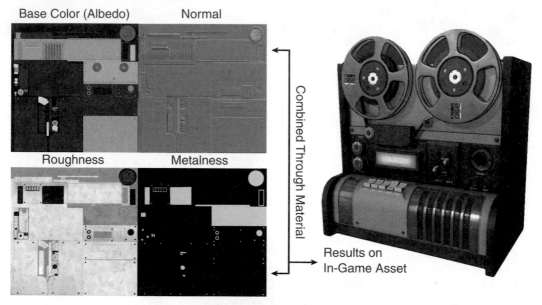

FIGURE 6.1
The aspects and textures combined in a material make the final result that appear in a game.

Physically Based Rendering (PBR)

UE4's material rendering system uses physically based rendering (PBR) for real-time rendering. PBR is a relatively new concept in the world of authoring textures and materials for games. Previously, PBR was part of a process that placed lighting detail directly into textures to give shape and surface volume to assets. A problem became apparent with that method when assets moved into different types of lighting scenarios, and there were viewable discrepancies between shadow and light information and the light direction and shadows within the scene. Such discrepancies tended to cause a visual break in continuity and believability of the game world.

Now, thanks to advances in processing power and UE4 technology, you use material parameters to allow assets to form their own lighting and shadow information. This prevents assets from being "baked," or permanently placed, within the textures. In addition, you can have assets lit in any time of day under any lighting scenario without having to re-author the textures. All this boils down to simpler, more consistent creation of textures for game assets.

NOTE

The PBR Material System

PBR has been adapted to mainstream game development in the past few years, but the film and television industries have been using it for some time with 3D animation and renderings. PBR helps different materials react in different lighting scenarios more realistically. It also allows for reuse of textures and assets during production and a more realistic lighting in each scene.

Material Input Types

To create great materials and textures, you use the Material Editor. The following sections show you the most commonly used Material Editor inputs.

Base Color (Albedo)

Base color, also sometimes referred to as *albedo* or *diffuse*, is the core color description of a surface in a material minus all shadow and lighting detail. Essentially the base color input uses an albedo texture, which is the pure color value of the material you are creating. It should be void of shadow and lighting information and show only the color that you wish to represent in the material. It can use a texture input or even a simple vector value, which is simply a number representing a flat color.

Metalness

The metalness material input is used to describe whether a material is metallic. This input is one of the easiest parts of the Material Editor to understand, and it is also one of the most important inputs to get right for a material to render correctly. The way UE4 uses metalness is very user-friendly and allows for quick control and understanding of which materials are metallic. Each pixel on this texture map is typically black or white, with very few grays. Black represents materials that are not metallic, such as stone, brick, or wood, while white represents the aspects of the material that are metallic, such as iron, silver, or copper. Often, if a material is not metallic, a simple vector of 0 can be used to simplify this input. You can also reduce this input to a grayscale texture or just one channel of a texture because of its simplicity.

NOTE

Metalness Versus Specular-Based PBR

There are two major types of PBR-based systems for authoring textures in games. While UE4 uses a metalness-based system, some other game engines use a specular-based system. Both systems can produce almost identical results. The main difference is in the way the game maker authors textures so the engine can best understand it.

Roughness

Roughness (also called *gloss* or *micro surface detail*) is the most artistically flexible aspect of the PBR system. You use this texture to represent the roughness and the history of the surface of the material being created. The roughness depicts the miniature details and describes the sheen or amount of light projected from a surface. For instance, if you are authoring a new steel metal material, the metalness and albedo of the material would be fairly simple; you would need to make little change in color or noise variation, but you would use roughness to describe all the small surface detail such as minor scratches, dirt, or grime. Very rarely would you have a single-color roughness, as it is rare that any surface in real life has not had some sort of wear or change to its surface. You can reduce roughness to grayscale textures as no color information is used to describe roughness.

Normal

You use the normal input for normal map textures or three-vector values (X, Y, and Z coordinates, as discussed in Hour 3, "Coordinates, Transforms, Units, and Organization"). Normal inputs describe the direction in which light should react with a surface. Normal maps fake high-definition surface detail and shape in an asset by tricking the light into displaying these details based on a texture map per pixel being lit. The normal input is similar to a bump map in other 3D packages and rendering, but with a few minor changes in the authoring.

Understanding normal inputs can be tough at first, but it is easiest to comprehend if you break down a normal input into the color channels involved in the process. Each channel of a texture map (red, green, and blue) is composited to represent a different surface direction angle per color. Red represents the X-axis, or the left-to-right direction of light hitting the surface. Green represents the Y-axis, or the top-to-bottom direction. Blue represents the Z-axis, or the front-to-back direction (see Figure 6.2).

NOTE

Green Channel

The green channel sometimes changes or flips, depending on what type of 3D software you use. Maya uses a normal format, while Max and UE4 flip the green channel for rendering normal maps. To flip the green channel in UE4, select and open the texture in the Content Browser and select the **Flip Green Channel** option.

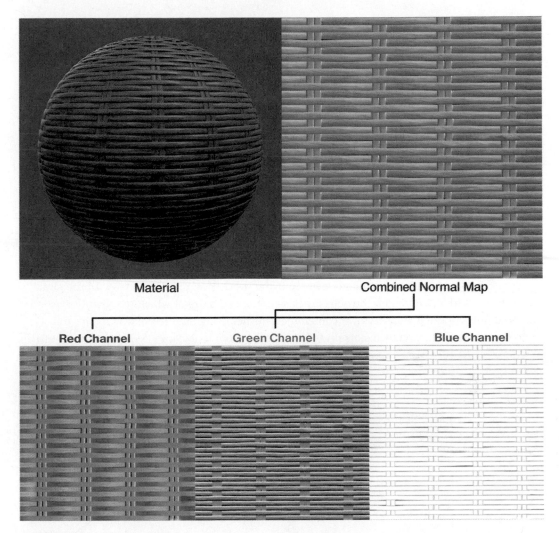

FIGURE 6.2
The channels of a normal map each have directional lighting information that UE4 uses to determine the volume and shape of the surface.

Imagine a flat polygon being lit by a light. When the light hits it, the polygon reacts simply by showing that it is being lit as a flat surface because the light rays hit the polygon and react in one direction. Now think about creating a brick surface. In order to accomplish this, if you have no model that has thousands of polygons, you can create a normal map to emulate the smaller surface details that the bricks would display. This normal map, when hooked up through the Material Editor, notifies UE4 that when a light hits this specific material on a surface, it should react as specified per pixel represented in that map. When you then shine the same light at the surface, it reacts accordingly and gives the illusion of form and detail that is not really there.

Creating Textures

Textures are the foundation for coloring and giving a visual language to materials and assets within UE4. The following sections explore how to create and use them.

Texture Sizes

Texture sizes are an important part of the authoring process. Creating a texture that does not use a specific proportion constraint may lead to the texture not rendering properly, being skewed or distorted, or not being able to be imported at all. Games today use a general set pattern of texture size resolution.

Powers of 2

Understanding how textures are rendered in UE4 is key to knowing the texture size you should specify. In order for UE4 to process textures sizes in real time, all textures are rendered in terms of the distance from the player camera view. So if you are seeing an asset up close in the game world, the texture resolution on the object is close to the exact size at which the texture was authored and imported. As the player camera gets further away, smaller texture details are unnecessary to understand the colors and shapes being represented, and therefore UE4 begins to reduce the texture size by continuously halving it as the player gets farther from the asset. This process is called *mipping* or *mip mapping* (see Figure 6.3).

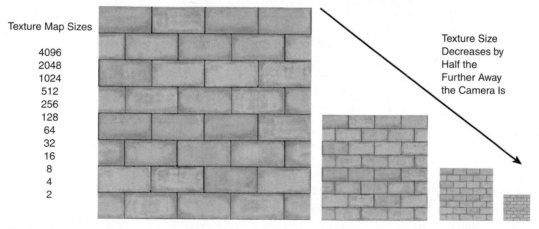

FIGURE 6.3
The size of the texture is directly related to how the texture resizes within UE4 dynamically to save memory.

Now that you have an understanding of how UE4 uses and renders textures, you're ready for a discussion of aspect ratio, or proportion. Texture sizes begin at around 256 pixels (px) and increase in scale by doubling over and over (512, 1024, 2048, and sometimes the rare 4096 pixels). These multiples are important because they enable the texture to be halved or multiplied by 2 for easy use in UE4. Texture sizes can go down if necessary, as well, to 128, 64, 28, 16, 8, 4, and even 2 pixels. A texture can be any of these sizes in height or width, but it must both be using one of these pixel size for its height and width measurements. For instance, most textures are authored within a box or square shape ratio (e.g., 512×512 pixels or 1024×1024 pixels), but this does not mean the same pixel size must be used for each dimension. A texture created at 512 pixels height and 1024 pixels width is perfectly fine because UE4 halves each aspect individually while rendering it; that is, UE4 reduces it to 256×512 pixels and again to 128×256 pixels.

Texture File Types

To create materials from the textures you have created, you need to import the textures into the Content Browser. Certain file types and settings are needed to correctly import and integrate those textures into the Material Editor. The following file types currently work in UE4:

- ▶ .tga
- ▶ .psd
- ▶ .tiff
- ▶ .bmp
- ▶ .float
- ▶ .pcx
- ▶ .png
- ▶ .jpg
- ▶ .dds
- ▶ .hdr

Importing Textures

Now that you understand how to author textures and what formats are acceptable, you can import some textures into the Content Browser.

▼ TRY IT YOURSELF

Import Textures into the Content Browser

To import a your own texture into the editor, open UE4 and follow these steps:

1. Open the Content Browser by clicking the **Content Browser** button on the toolbar or by pressing **Ctrl+Shift+F**.

2. Select the location to import the texture from your computer's folders.

3. Right-click in an empty area on the right side of the Content Browser and select **Import Asset/Import to** *location on your computer where project is stored*.

4. Select **Windows Folder** and navigate to the texture you want to import.

5. **Click Open.**

NOTE

Drag and Drop

To import any content—including textures, models, video files, and other assets—into UE4, you can also simply click from a local file on your computer, drag, and drop it into the Content Browser. For instance, if you have a file saved on your desktop, you can simply click and drag it into the Content Browser.

Making a Material

The following Try It Yourself walks you through creating a new material in the Content Browser.

▼ TRY IT YOURSELF

Create a Material in the Content Browser

To create a material in the Content Browser, open UE4 and follow these steps:

1. Open the Content Browser.

2. Select the location to create the material from the Content folders.

3. Right-click in an empty area on the right side of the Content Browser and select **Create Basic Asset/Material**.

4. Rename the new material from its default name.

After you have made a material, you can freely control all aspects of each input for that material. You can double-click any material in the Content Editor to open it in the Material Editor (see Figure 6.4). In the Material Editor, you can make changes to any of the inputs. Notice that the Material Editor has multiple options available as well as a real-time material preview.

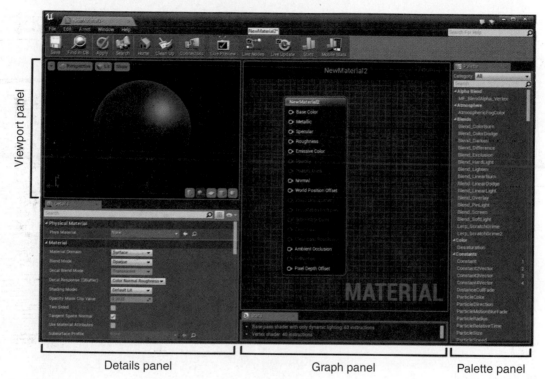

FIGURE 6.4
The Material Editor.

There are primarily four panels to use in the Material Editor, along with the main toolbar:

▶ **Viewport panel:** The top-left corner of the Material Editor is the viewport panel, which gives a real-time preview of the material. It shows the final result of the material being compiled. You can change the object on which the material is displayed by using the shape options below it, and you can change its visual or perspective attributes by using the options above it.

▶ **Details panel:** Directly below the Viewport panel is the Details panel. This is where you can change overall material properties and rendering techniques that the material uses in gameplay space, such as opacity options, subsurface options, and shading models. This panel is useful for advanced material editing.

▶ **Graph panel:** The middle panel is the Graph panel, which is where all the visual editing happens for the material. It allows you to drag in or place textures to route into inputs or use special nodes to create different effects in the material. This is where you link the textures you bring into UE4 to a material to achieve your final result.

▶ **Palette panel:** This is the panel located farthest to the right. It houses all the special nodes and math functions for creating specific effects within a material.

The panels of the Material Editor each play a part in constructing the final material and optimizing the result.

Inputs and Outputs

You can think of the Graph panel as a panel that has an electric current traveling from left to right. When the current reaches the final node, the material node, the Graph panel creates the combination of all the material effects shown in the game. The material node is the default for any new material and contains all the final material attributes (see Figure 6.5).

Each node used in the Graph panel, whether for a texture or a specific node, has outputs and sometimes inputs and connects to the final material node. The output of a node is located on its right side. If there is an input, it is located to the left. You can connect nodes together to create different effects that influence the final result for the material. To connect one node to another, simply click the output connection of one node and drag the visible connection to the input of another node.

NOTE

Extra Nodes

When you're using the Material Editor, it is okay to show floating nodes that you are using to experiment, but they should not appear in the final result. The material takes into account only the nodes that are hooked into the material node. It ignores all other nodes.

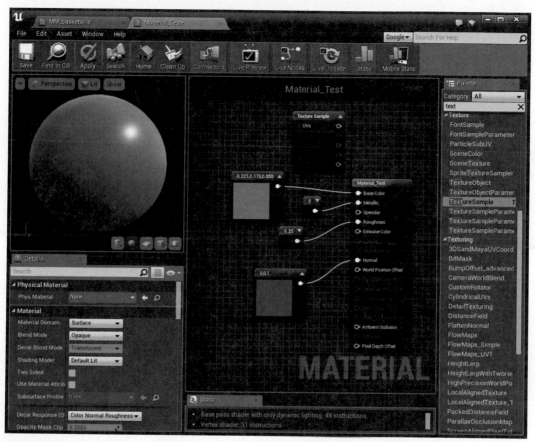

FIGURE 6.5
Nodes connecting through outputs and inputs to the final material node.

Value Nodes

Now that you understand the parts of the Material Editor, you can create a simple material by using constant values. Constant values are numbers that can create values or colors depending on the number of values used. You can get these value nodes from the Palette panel and use them within a material as inputs.

Two commonly used value nodes are the Constant node and the Constant3Vector node. The Constant node represents a single number or value. The Constant3Vector node represents a vector or a set of three numbers, each representing a corresponding RGB value. For instance, if Constant3Vector is set to 1,4,6, it means the setting is 1 for red, 4 for green, and 6 for blue.

Most of the commonly used nodes in the Material Editor have a corresponding shortcut key so you can place them quickly. To place a simple Constant node, for example, press the **1** key and right-click in the Graph panel area. To create a Constant3Vector, press the **3** key and right-click in the Graph panel area. You can also click these nodes in the Palette panel and drag them into the Graph panel to use them. After you have placed one of these value nodes in the Graph panel, you can click the node and use the Details panel to the left to change the value, name, and other aspects of the node. Next you'll practice creating a material using vector values.

▼ TRY IT YOURSELF

Create a Material with Vector Values

To create a material with vector values, open the Material Editor on the new material you just created and follow these steps:

1. Create a Constant value node by pressing the **1** key and right-clicking the mouse in the Graph panel.

2. Click the output of the new Constant node and drag to connect it to the roughness input of the material.

3. Click the Constant value node to see the information for the node in the Details panel.

4. In the Details panel, change the value of Constant to **1** instead of the default 0. (Notice the change in the roughness in the Viewport panel.)

5. Create a Constant3Vector by holding down the **3** key and right-clicking in a blank space in the Graph panel.

6. Click the **Constant3Vector** value node to see the information for the node in the Details panel.

7. In the Details panel, change the value of the R value to **1**. (If the color values are not already exposed in the Details panel, click the small arrow to the left of the Constant option in the Details panel. The R, G, and B options appear, and you can individually change them to control the red, green, and blue values.)

8. Click and drag the output of the Constant3Vector to the base color of the material node. (Notice that the color changes to pure red, as shown in Figure 6.6).

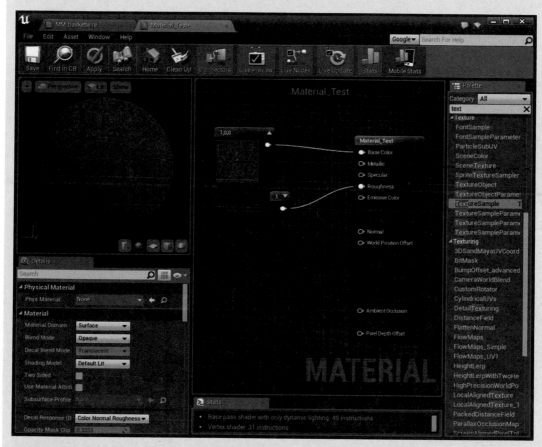

FIGURE 6.6
Notice the change that occurs when the material node receives new inputs.

Instances

Instances are key to reusing materials multiple times and preventing you from having to create the materials over and over again. By changing some of the nodes in a material, you can make specific nodes in the material dynamically changeable. For instance, if your main material is colored with a Constant3Vector node to be green, by changing the node to a parameter, you can easily alter the color in another instance of that material instead of making a whole new material from scratch.

To work with instances, the main material must accommodate the ability to dynamically transform specific nodes into parameter-based nodes. In the Material Editor of the primary material, you right-click any of the constants or vectors nodes and select **Convert to Parameter** from the context menu (see Figure 6.7). After you convert the material to a parameter, you can rename it in the Details panel, and then any value or information you give to the main material in the Details panel will be the default settings for that node until you alter any settings in the material instance. To create a material instance from a material, simply right-click the material in the Content Editor and select **Create Material Instance**. This material instance uses the parameters from the parent material that we originally created.

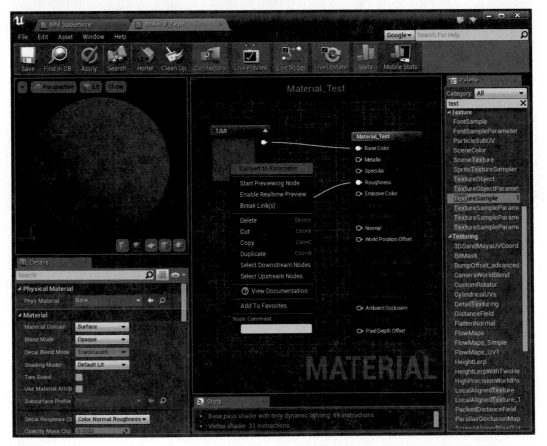

FIGURE 6.7
When a constant is changed to a parameter, it can be renamed and labeled. Then it is available to change dynamically within the material instance.

Now when you double-click the material instance you just created from the main material, you can see the parameter settings in the Parameter Groups section of the Details panel. Clicking the checkmark next to the parameter you want to alter activates that parameter within the instance so that you can alter any of the details of that parameter.

TRY IT YOURSELF ▼

Create a Material Instance

With the Content Editor open, follow these steps to create a material instance:

1. Open the main material you created previously in the Material Editor.

2. Right-click the Constant3Vector that you made previously and select **Convert to Parameter**.

3. In the Details panel, rename the Constant3Vector to **Color Param**.

4. Save changes and close the Material Editor.

5. In the Content Editor, right-click the main material and select **Create Material Instance**.

6. Rename the new material instance you have just created to Mat_inst and then double-click it in the Content Browser to open it.

7. Navigate to the Parameter Groups section of the Details panel and click the **Color Param** box. The parameter is now active.

8. Change color values as follows: Set R to **0**, G to **1**, and B to **0**. (Notice that the color changes to green, as shown in Figure 6.8.)

FIGURE 6.8
Inside the material parameter, you can select the color and change it to any other color without altering the original material.

Summary

You now understand why materials are such a vital part of the production pipeline and how they are created and used in UE4. Understanding PBR can take some practice, but using this new system yields more realistic and overall believable game worlds, assets, and characters. Using material instances and parameters helps you increase production speed and overall memory conservation. In reducing the number of materials a project uses through smarter instancing and parameters, you can save time and energy, create larger game spaces, and easily use assets that have similar material setups. A good material and shader artist finds ways to make innovative and reusable materials that are easy to understand and flexible for multiple instances.

Q&A

Q. Do I have to use the PBR system in UE4? I am used to the old system, and there is still a specular input node in the Material Editor.

A. Yes, you do need to use PBR. Almost all functions and setups are built to accommodate PBR. The specular input node has some influence on the final result, but it is not as powerful as it was in older versions of Unreal Engine.

Q. Can I create and import a texture that is larger than 4096 pixels?

A. Yes, this is possible, but doing it is highly discouraged. Rendering a texture larger than 4096 in real time is difficult for not only UE4 but most computers, and you may find that trying to render such a large texture causes problems with frame rate.

Q. Why are some of the material inputs grayed out and not usable?

A. Material setups use specific inputs to generate the final results. The Details panel of the material node controls what inputs are visible in connection to the type of material. For example, if you are making a glass material, you may need an opacity input, but if you are making a brick wall, an opacity input is not necessary.

Q. Can I have more than one output routing into an input of a node?

A. No, only one output is accepted into one input per node. Sometimes nodes have multiple input nodes for math functions and other special nodes, but there are multiple input slots for these types of nodes.

Q. Can I change what material a material instance is connected to?

A. Yes, this is possible. In the Details panel of the material instance, you can relink a different base material to the material instance. Keep in mind that the material instance then updates and changes relative to the parameters within that new material and may lose some of the previous information that may have been set per parameter.

Q. Can I delete a main material and keep a material instance of it?

A. No, the material instance needs to use the information from a base material. However, you can switch which material it references. You just need to make sure it has a material to get its information from.

Q. If I change the main material, will the instance change?

A. That is the glory of material instances! The instance tries to stay up to date with the changes you make across all instances from one material. If you activate a parameter within an instance, the instance attempts to keep the value but updates the other parameters that are not active or adds new parameters added later during production.

Q. What are all these other nodes in the Palette panel? Can I also use those to create materials?

A. Those nodes are a collection of mathematical equations, figures, and other special nodes to help you achieve special results within the material beyond the basic constant values and texture inputs—and you are free to use them. Experiment and type multiple ones to see what nodes give you the effects you want.

Workshop

Now that you have finished the hour, see if you can answer the following questions.

Quiz

1. What does PBR stand for?

2. Is a texture size of 512×256 pixels a good size to use in UE4?

3. What material input decides the hue of the material?

4. What panel shows a preview of a material in the Material Editor?

5. Why is material instancing important?

Answers

1. PBR stands for physically based rendering.

2. Yes, this is a valid size in UE4. While not the same both vertically and horizontally, the texture size 512×256 still follows the rules and can be sized down in UE4 appropriately.

3. The base color input determines the hue of a material.

4. The Viewport panel shows a preview of a material in the Material Editor.

5. Material instancing allows you to quickly iterate and make changes to parameter values without requiring you to create a whole new material.

Exercise

In this exercise, you create a basic material; create values for its roughness, base color, and metalness; and create a material instance to control variations of the material. Creating materials and instances is an important part of controlling how a scene looks and feels and how light reacts to each aspect of an asset. Understanding how each input directly impacts the visuals of a game is an important aspect for any world builder to fully understand. Finally, understanding instancing and parameters will give you maximum flexibility and reusability with the materials in a project.

1. Create a new material in the Content Editor.

2. Name the material.

3. Open the material and create constant values for both roughness and metalness.

4. Create a Constant3Vector for the base color.

5. Convert all the Constant nodes and the Constant3Vector node into parameters.

6. Rename all the new parameters and give them default values.

7. Create a material instance from the main material.

8. Activate and change the settings of the parameters within the instance.

HOUR 7
Using Audio System Elements

What You'll Learn in This Hour:

▶ Understanding audio basics
▶ Using Sound Actors
▶ Creating Sound Cues
▶ Controlling Sound with audio volumes

In this hour, you learn about audio in Unreal Engine. You start by learning about the basic components of audio in UE4 and then how to place sounds in a scene with Sound Actors. You also learn about the powerful capabilities of Sound Cues and working with the Sound Cue Editor.

NOTE

Hour 7 Setup

Create a new project with the First Person Template and Starter Content.

Introducing Audio Basics

Whatever game you're creating, it's likely that Sound will play a big part in the experience. From ambient Sounds in a scene to spoken dialog between characters and even background music, the audio in a game can make or break the user's experience. Most of the time, players don't realize it, but Sound is a large part of overall gameplay.

Audio Components

The audio system in UE4 is powerful, and it has a large number of components and terminology. At first, it may seem overwhelming, but you'll understand it all in time. If at any point you feel like you're getting deeper into Sound than you want to right now, feel free to skip ahead to later lessons and then come back to this one when you're ready for more complex features.

Here are a few of the fundamental components this lesson covers:

▶ A *Sound Wave asset* represents an imported audio file and settings related to the playback and storage of that file.

▶ An *Ambient Sound Actor* is used to represent an audio source in a scene.

▶ *Sound Cue assets* and the *Sound Cue Editor* enable you to combine Sounds and modifiers to alter the final output.

▶ The *Sound Attenuation* asset defines how a Sound is heard based on the player's distance from the Sound's origin.

Importing Audio Files

UE4 supports importing uncompressed.wav files. If your source audio files aren't in .wav format, you can easily convert them by using the freely available Audacity Sound editor, among others. Epic also provides a great deal of audio content in its sample projects and marketplace to help get you started.

NOTE
_____

Audacity

Audacity can be downloaded at http://www.audacityteam.org.
_____

The easiest way to import audio is simply to drag a .wav file from your operating system's file manager into the **Content Browser** or by clicking **Import** in the Content Browser and finding and choosing the file to import. Once it is imported, you can double-click the audio asset to see its Properties in the Generic Asset Editor's Details Panel. The next Try it Yourself walks you through importing a .wav file.

Import Audio Files

In the Content Browser, create a new folder called **MyAudio**. Then follow these steps to import .wav files:

1. Navigate to the Hour_07 folder (available on the book's companion website at www.sty-ue4.com) and locate the file **storm.wav.**

2. Click and drag storm.wav into the **MyAudio** folder in the Content Browser. A new asset is created.

3. Repeat steps 1 and 2 for the thunder.wav file, also in the Hour_07 folder for this lesson. Figure 7.1 shows the assets you've just imported—storm and thunder—along with a Steam01 asset.

FIGURE 7.1
Sound Wave assets in the Content Browser.

When you have a Sound file imported into the Content Browser, you can edit the Sound Wave asset properties in the Generic Asset Editor by double-clicking the asset. You can set a number of properties, including the compression amount, whether the Sound asset loops by default, and the pitch, and you can even add subtitle information. There isn't anything you need to modify right now, though. Figure 7.2 shows the Generic Asset Editor's Details panel.

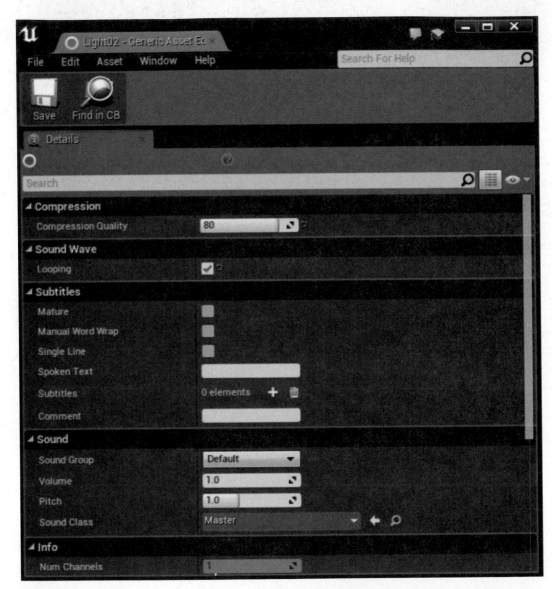

FIGURE 7.2
Sound Wave properties.

Using Sound Actors

Sound Wave assets are of no use without a source to play them! Ambient Sound Actors are the components that allow you to play Sounds in a level. The simplest way to create them is to drag a Sound Wave asset into a scene. You can create many Ambient Sound Actors in a scene and give them various properties. Table 7.1 shows the properties available in the Details panel when an Ambient Sound Actor is selected.

TABLE 7.1   Ambient Sound Actor Properties

Property	Description
Sound	Points to a Sound Wave asset or Sound Cue asset.
Is UI Sound	Determines whether the Sound asset plays when the game is paused.
Volume Multiplier	Sets the overall volume of the Sound.
Pitch Multiplier	Sets the overall pitch of the Sound.
Instance Parameters	Allows addition of per-instance parameters for the Sound.
Sound Class Override	Optionally assigns a group for the Sound asset.

TRY IT YOURSELF ▼

Place an Ambient Sound Actor

Continuing from the previous Try It Yourself, it's time to add an audio source:

1. Open the Content Browser and navigate to one of the Sound Wave assets you imported in the previous Try It Yourself.

2. Click and drag the asset into the scene.

3. You should see your new Actor in the World Outliner panel and the properties exposed in the Details panel.

4. Click **Play**. You should hear the Sound but be unable to discern where it's coming from.

Setting Attenuation

For Sound to appear to have a position in 3D space, you need to specify the Attenuation. *Attenuation* is the falloff of the Sound as you move further away from it in 3D space. Table 7.2 shows the Attenuation properties.

In the next Try It Yourself, you use the Override Attenuation setting to control the distance the Sound can travel from a placed Actor.

TABLE 7.2   Attenuation Properties

Property	Description
Attenuate	Enables the use of Attenuation via volume.
Spatialize	Enables the source to be positioned in 3D space.
Distance Algorithm	Specifies the type of volume versus distance algorithm to use for the Attenuation model.
Attenuation Shape	Specifies the shape of the Attenuation volume, which is usually a sphere.
Radius	Specifies the overall size of the volume. Outside this radius, no Sound will be heard.
Falloff Distance	Specifies the distance over which falloff occurs.
Non-Spatialized Radius	Specifies the distance at which spatialization begins.

▼ TRY IT YOURSELF

Override Attenuation

Continuing from the previous Try It Yourself, it's time to set Attenuation:

1. In the World Outliner panel, select your Ambient Sound Actor from the list.

2. In the Details panel, under the Attenuation category, toggle on **Override Attenuation**. A yellow wireframe sphere appears around the Actor in the level. This represents the distance the sound can travel.

3. Click the little triangle to the left of **Override Attenuation** at the bottom of the category to expand the setting.

4. Set Radius to **200** and Falloff Distance to **50**.

5. Preview the level. If you are standing outside the Attenuation sphere, you cannot hear the sound.

You can adjust the Attenuation for each placed Ambient Sound Actor. You can also create Sound Attenuation assets that can be reused and applied to Sound Wave assets or Ambient Sound Actors.

TIP

Sharing Attenuation Settings

As a project grows, it is a good idea to create a Sound Attenuation asset and share it among many Sound Actors. This makes it easier to adjust settings for a large number of audio sources.

Using Modulation Properties

Modulation effects add motion and depth to Sound. The modulation settings allow you to control the minimum and maximum modulation for both pitch and volume as well as set a high-frequency gain multiplier. Table 7.3 lists and describes the modulation properties.

TABLE 7.3   Modulation Properties

Property	Description
Pitch Modulation Min	Specifies the lower bound to use when randomly determining a pitch multiplier.
Pitch Modulation Max	Specifies the upper bound to use when randomly determining a pitch multiplier.
Volume Modulation Min	Specifies the lower bound to use when randomly determining a volume multiplier.
Volume Modulation Max	Specifies the upper bound to use when randomly determining a volume multiplier.
High Frequency Gain Multiplier	Specifies a multiplier to apply to the high-frequency gain for Sounds generated by the component.

Creating Sound Cues

So far, you've learned how to apply a Sound Wave asset to an Ambient Sound Actor, but for every location where you used a wave, you could have also used a cue. Cues give you an enormous amount of control over your audio. What if you want to alter Sounds randomly, such as footsteps or the wind rustling the trees? Or what if you want to apply modulations and other effects? This is where the Sound Cue steps in. The Sound Cue Editor has the following panels and buttons (see Figure 7.3).

▶ **Graph panel:** This panel displays the flow of the audio from left to right. The output node, which has an image of a speaker on it, represents the final output.

▶ **Palette panel:** This panel lists various Sound nodes that you can drag into the Graph panel and chain together to create complex Sounds.

▶ **Play Cue:** This toolbar button plays an entire Sound Cue, which is equivalent to playing the output node.

▶ **Play Node:** This toolbar button plays just the audio coming from a selected node (which includes those before it).

FIGURE 7.3
Sound Cue Editor.

To open the Sound Cue Editor, you first need to create a Sound Cue asset. In the next Try It Yourself, you create a new Sound Cue object and then add a Wave Player node.

▼ TRY IT YOURSELF

Make a Sound Cue

Continuing from the previous Try It Yourself, here you add a Wave Player node to a Sound Cue.

1. In the Content Browser, click the **Add New** button or right-click in an empty space Asset Management Area in the Content Browser to bring up the New Asset dialog. Under Create Advanced Asset, select **Sound Cue** from the Sound list.

2. Name the new Sound Cue **thunder**, and then double-click it to bring up the Sound Cue Editor.

3. To add the thunder asset, drag a Wave Player Node from the Palette panel into the Graph Viewport panel.

4. In the Details panel for the Wave Player node, select your Sound asset. Drag its output pin to the input pin of the speaker. Your view should look as shown in Figure 7.4.

5. Preview playback of the Sound Cue with the Play Cue button on the toolbar of the Sound Cue Editor.

6. Drag your Sound Cue from the Content Browser into the scene and preview the level.

FIGURE 7.4
Sound Cue Editor playing a sound.

While a Sound Cue is playing, to aid in debugging, the wires of currently active nodes turn red. This makes it easy to follow the Sound Cue's construction in real time.

Mix Sound in a Sound Cue

Continuing from the previous Try It Yourself, build a Sound Cue with a mixer node to create the atmospheric effect of a thunderstorm:

1. Open the Sound Cue you created in the Previous Try it Yourself, and add a second Wave Player node, and assign the Storm.wav file you imported earlier in the hour.

2. Make sure each Wave Player node is set to **Looping**.

3. Drag a mixer node into the Sound Cue Editor from the Palette panel.

4. Drag from the output pin of each wave player to an input pin on the mixer.

5. Drag from the mixer output pin to the output node (the speaker) pin.

6. Test and save your Sound Cue. When you're finished, your Sound Cue should look similar to the one in Figure 7.5.

7. Preview the level.

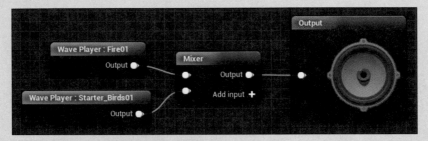

FIGURE 7.5
This Sound Cue mixes two sounds.

Advanced Sound Cues

You can accomplish incredibly complex behavior with Sound Cues that go far beyond what this hour covers. A great next step is to read Epic's documentation and examples, which include detailed information on every type of node available. Figure 7.6 shows an example of one advanced Sound Cue.

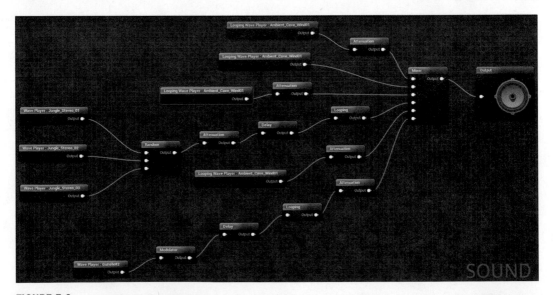

FIGURE 7.6
This Sound Cue mixes together Sound waves with a variety of properties, including Attenuation, randomization, looping, and delays.

Controlling Sounds with Audio Volumes

Audio volumes are not Sound assets, but they can be used to control and apply various Sounds in a scene. You can also use them in zones to control where Sounds can be heard from. For example, an audio volume in a small tunnel may have a reverb effect to simulate the bouncy echo acoustics you'd expect to hear in such a tunnel.

Reverb effects allow you to control elements such as reverb, echo, air absorption, and other parameters. You can easily adjust and apply them to any audio volume placed in a level.

TRY IT YOURSELF ▼

Work with Audio Volumes

In this Try It Yourself, you create an audio volume with some reverb effects to simulate being in an enclosed space. Start from any previous scene from this lesson that doesn't have any enclosed spaces and follow these steps:

1. In the Level Editor, add an audio volume to the level, select **Modes > Volumes > Audio Volume**, and drag the audio volume into your Level. The yellow wire outline indicates the bounds of the volume.

2. With the Audio Volume Actor selected in the level, click **Reverb Effect** in the Level Details panel to add a new Reverb Effect.

3. In the menu that appears, select **Create Reverb Effect** and name your new effect **MyEffect**. This adds a new Reverb Effect asset to the Content Browser.

4. In the Content Browser, double-click on the **MyEffect Reverb Effect** asset you created to open the Generic Asset Editor.

5. In the Details panel of the Generic Asset Editor for your Reverb Effect, hover your mouse over each parameter in the Reverb Parameters list in the Details panel to get a brief description of it. To create an obvious echo/distortion effect, set Density to a very low number and Reflection Gain to a high number. Feel free to experiment with other values, as shown in Figure 7.7. When you're finished, click the **Save** button in the toolbar.

6. In the Level Editor preview, click **Play** and take note of any sounds playing as well as the sound your thunder makes. Now enter the volume and listen again. You should now have a good idea of what you can do with audio volumes.

FIGURE 7.7
Reverb parameters.

Summary

In this hour, you learned about using audio in UE4. You started by learning about the basics of audio and the components required to make it work. From there, you explored the Ambient Sound Actor. You learned how to test audio and use Attenuation. You learned about the Sound Cue Editor and built your first Sound Cue. You finished the hour by learning about Sound volumes.

Q&A

Q. Does UE4 support 2D audio?

A. Absolutely. 2D audio is (usually) Sound without Attenuation, which is covered in this lesson. For Blueprint, there is specifically a PlaySound2D node that is perfect for 2D and user interface audio.

Q. Can I use a different shape other than a sphere when using Attenuation?

A. Yes. In the Override Attenuation settings for the Ambient Sound Actor, look for the Attenuation Shape Property and choose from one of the options there.

Q. I am not happy with the way the Sound in my game attenuates. What can I do to change this?

A. Under the Override Attenuation setting for the Ambient Sound Actor is a property called Distance Algorithm that you can set to change the way Sound fades out while attenuating.

Workshop

Now that you have finished the hour, see if you can answer the following questions.

Quiz

1. True or false: You can only make Sound loop with a Sound Cue asset.

2. True or false: To import a Sound, it must be an uncompressed .wav file.

3. True or false: If you wanted to add a Reverb Effect, you can use an Audio Volume.

4. True or false: You can use Sound Cues to mix Sound.

5. True or false: If you are using an Ambient Sound Actor to play background music in a level, you would want it to have Attenuation.

Answers

1. False. You can set any Sound Wave asset to looping in the Generic Asset Editor. In the Content Browser, double-click on the Sound Wave asset to open the Generic Asset Editor.

2. True. .wav files are a common audio file type.

3. True. You can place as many Audio Volume Actors as you need in a level and apply a different Reverb Effect to each one.

4. True. Sound Cue assets and the Sound Cue Editor give you the ability mix and modify Sound Wave assets.

5. False. Typically background music should Sound the same to the player throughout the level. So you do not want to apply Attenuation.

Exercise

In one of the Try it Yourself exercises this hour, you created a Sound Cue asset that mixed two Sound waves. However, the looping thunder you put in it doesn't Sound realistic. How might you improve this? For this exercise, improve the quality of the effect by using a delay and looping node.

1. Open the Sound Cue you created in the "Mix Sound in a Sound Cue" Try It Yourself.

2. Drag a Delay node from the Palette panel to the Graph Viewport panel. Link the wave player: thunder output pin to the Delay node. In the Sound Cue Editor Detail panel, set the Delay Min to 1 and the Delay Max to 5.

3. Drag a Looping node from the Palette panel to the Graph Viewport panel. Link the delay output pin to the Looping node.

4. Link the Looping node output pin to the already-placed mixer node. When you're finished, your Sound Cue should look similar to the one in Figure 7.8.

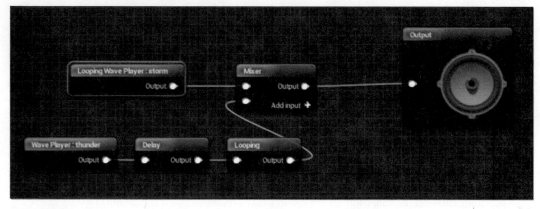

FIGURE 7.8
This Sound Cue has a random delay between loops of the thunder Sound.

5. Preview the level.

HOUR 8
Creating Landscapes and Foliage

This hour looks at landscape creation and use. After creating a custom landscape material, you
use the landscape tools to paint and layer the results into a newly formed landscape. Then you
focus on creating Foliage assets and placing them within the game space using UE4's Foliage tools.

What You'll Learn in This Hour:

▶ Working with landscape tools and settings
▶ Using height maps
▶ How to use landscape materials
▶ How to use Foliage tools and settings

NOTE

Hour 8 Setup

Create a new project with the Third Person Template and Starter Content.

Working with Landscapes

While working on any new project, you may find that Static Meshes cannot cover the space you
need to allow the player to explore, especially if you're creating free-roaming exterior spaces. In
such situations, landscapes are the tools to use. Landscape tools are powerful and allow for vast
swaths of world creation that can be edited per segment, which means you can quickly edit for
game space expansion and tailor the game for efficient rendering.

Landscape Tools

Many tools are available for creating and editing landscapes and their parameters in UE4. You
access the default landscape controls on the left side of the screen in the Modes panel. You click the
Landscape button—the middle button, which contains a mountain icon (see Figure 8.1)—to bring
up the Landscape panel. You can also press **Shift+3** to quickly bring up the Landscape panel.

FIGURE 8.1
You access the Landscape panel by clicking the **Landscape** button on the Modes panel or pressing **Shift+3**.

Three major tabs are available on the Landscape panel:

▶ **Manage:** This tab controls the construction and management aspects of the landscape.

▶ **Sculpt:** This tab changes the volume and form of landscape geometry.

▶ **Paint:** This tab controls the material type applied to the landscape's surface.

The Sculpt and Paint tabs are grayed out and unusable until you create your first base landscape on which to use these options.

Manage Tab

The first section of the Landscape panel is the Manage section. Here you can create and manage existing landscapes. There are two ways to start a new landscape: You can create a new landscape based on set parameters, or you can create a landscape based on an imported height map. This lesson discusses how to create a landscape from scratch.

Height Maps

A *height map* is a texture that provides height variation information based on a grayscale. White surfaces on the texture indicate landscape height increases, while black pixels indicate landscape height decreases. A height map is similar to a bump map in other 3D programs. These textures can be authored in many other sculpting or photo manipulation programs and then imported and used in UE4, or they can come directly from UE4.

A height map can be useful when you are re-creating a specific real-world location and want to use the exact landscape volumes to emulate the area within your game space. Also, you can use a height map as a mask to notify UE4 what areas have specific types of Foliage or landscape material types. In order to use a height map as a mask, you must export it from the editor and resave it as an appropriate file type in an external application, such as Photoshop. Then you can reimport it as a texture and use it as a mask.

While this lesson does not walk you through how to use an external height map to learn about landscape creation, as you create a landscape within UE4, you are authoring an internal height map within UE4 by using the Sculpt tab tools. You can even export the height map from the landscape you sculpt in UE4 to edit in other programs using a texture format. The texture formats are a commonly used texture type that preserves height map variation and details, with little loss of data.

Creating Landscapes

When creating a new landscape, you have a few options to begin your setup. The first is to determine which material is being used on the landscape. We discuss materials in the "Landscape Materials" section a little later on, but for now, note that this is one of the initial places that the material and the layers of that material that can be attached to a new landscape.

Following the material and material layers settings are the transform settings for the new landscape (see Figure 8.2). Here you can specify where the new landscape is placed in world space, as well as its size and rotation.

The next section of the landscape controls is for landscape LODing (level of detailing) techniques, which you can change to enable the landscape to render quickly and efficiently. These controls, labeled Section Size and Sections per Component, relate to how much information is displayed to the player at once. A larger Section Size setting means there is less to render within the component or section, which is easier on the CPU. The higher the Sections per Component setting, the better UE4 is able to divide and decide at what quality to render each section. There is a delicate balance between ensuring a high frame rate and a desirable quality of landscape resolution. Experimentation is key here as there is no easy answer about the optimal numbers for a project.

Next, you can change the settings for the density and size of each landscape tile used to make up the larger landscape whole. UE4 states that, by default, each subdivided landscape section or plane has a density of 1 vertex per meter. In the vertical, or Z, scale, which is by default set to 100, the height range is 256 meters up or down. These are important measurements to know when manipulating and controlling the density and size of these panels for a new landscape. If you know these measurements, you can control the number of vertices on the entire landscape by using the resolution settings and the number of overall landscape segments along with components settings. By combining these settings, you can balance the resolution or density of vertices per landscape section.

NOTE

Section Size

To ensure a good frame rate, Section Size should be the most monitored setting in the Landscape panel. Increasing the Section Size setting too much will cause major drops in frame rate and editor usability because of the intense processing power required.

The final two options for creating a new landscape are the Fill World and Create buttons at the bottom of the Landscape panel. The Create button simply confirms the settings that are currently in place and uses them to create a new landscape. The Fill World button creates a landscape that is the size of the entire game space that is currently available.

FIGURE 8.2
The Manage menu in the Landscape panel for creating a new landscape.

▼ TRY IT YOURSELF

Create a New Landscape

To create a new landscape, open the Landscape panel and follow these steps:

1. Set Section Size to **31×31 quads**.

2. Set Sections per Component to **2×2 sections**.

3. Set Number of Components to **10×10**.

4. Click the **Create** button to create the new landscape.

Landscape Management

Now that you have created a new landscape, new options are available to control and manage the new landscape. On the Manage tab, you can now see that the default tool is the Selection button. You use it to select landscape sections for editing. When you click the Selection button, a drop-down menu shows other options for controlling aspects of the newly created landscape. Some of the options on this menu are for deleting or adding components; you use these options to subtract sections of landscape from the existing landscape or add new sections to it. Another option, Change Component Size, allows you to edit the component values of the originally created landscape if you need more resolution or if the landscape differs from what you originally created. In addition, you can use the Move Levels option under the Manage tool in the Landscape Panel to move sections to particular levels. This is a more advanced development option for stream-specific areas or levels used to reduce rendering power to display areas that are not persistently needed in player view. Finally, you have options for creating additional landscapes, as well as options for controlling splines linked to the landscape currently selected.

NOTE

Splines

Splines are a series of connected points that run on top of the landscape. Splines are helpful for creating malleable roads, sidewalks, and other structures more naturally along the surface of the landscape.

Sculpting Shapes and Volumes

Now that you have created a new landscape, you can begin sculpting shapes and volumes into the landscape. The Sculpt tab has three major drop-down menus: Tool, Brush, and Falloff (see Figure 8.3).

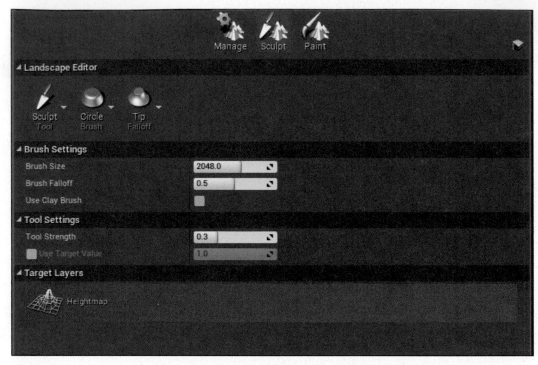

FIGURE 8.3
The Sculpt tab of the Landscape panel.

Tool Menu

The Tool menu contains tools for controlling the surface and volume definition of the landscape.
Each tool has specific settings relative to the type of tool:

▶ **Sculpt:** This tool sculpts up or down into the landscape mesh.

▶ **Smooth:** This tool brushes smoothness or lessens the variation difference between areas
being influenced by the Sculpt tool.

▶ **Flatten:** This tool flattens the landscape to the height specified when you first click the
landscape with the Flatten tool activated. It moves the landscape terrain up or down,
depending on the height value selected.

▶ **Ramp:** This tool connects two areas by ramping the landscape between the two with a
constant change in grade between points.

▶ **Hydro Erosion and Erosion:** This tool simulates general wear of the ground that happens
in a world scenario to emulate this effect on the game space landscape.

- **Noise:** This tool applies a general noise to the landscape and uses the settings to determine the amount and intensity.

- **Retopologize:** This tool reduces the spacing and difference in variation between surface components to reduce stretching.

- **Visibility:** This tool hides or unhides selections of surfaces on the landscape mesh.

- **Selection:** This tool masks selections of the landscape mesh.

- **Copy/Paste:** This tool selects a section of the landscape to paste similar height settings into another section of the landscape.

Brush Menu

The Brush menu allows you to choose the overall shape of the tool being used on the landscape. There are four types of brushes:

- **Circle:** This is the most basic and default brush. It is a circular shaped brush.

- **Alpha:** This brush uses a specific texture as a mask influenced by a grayscale similar to a height map.

- **Pattern:** This brush uses a repeating pattern across the whole of the landscape, which acts as a mask for sculpting.

- **Component:** This brush affects whole component pieces of the area being sculpted.

Falloff Menu

The Falloff menu allows you to control the strength of the brush's influence on the landscape being sculpted. There are four types of falloff:

- **Smooth:** This is the most commonly used type of falloff. It is a soft blend between the strong and weak parts of the brush.

- **Linear:** This is a direct constant falloff.

- **Spherical:** This is a weaker influenced falloff toward the center and increases to a stronger influence toward the edge end of the brush.

- **Tip:** This is a strong influence at the center with a quick falloff to a weaker falloff that slowly dissipates toward the edges.

Painting

You use the Paint tab of the Landscape panel to paint material layers onto the landscape mesh. This tab provides many of the same setups and tools as the Sculpt tab. As in the Sculpt tab, the three main tools in the Paint tab are Tool, Brush, and Falloff. Each of these sections uses the same rules and applications as for the Sculpt tab, but instead applies the rules to the painting of materials.

Landscape Materials

Landscape material setups differ slightly from normal material setups. Creating the material for a landscape follows the same process as making a new material, except that the blending between layers is defined using a special node in the Material Editor called a LandscapeLayerBlend node (see Figure 8.4). With this node, different textures can be used and divided into specific layers called out in the landscape setup menus. To use this node, simply add it from the Palette panel on the right of the Material Editor. Then you can click the node and click the + symbol on the node to add layers. You can add and use more than one layer.

Once placed in a material, textures that would normally be combined or blended into a regular material are instead routed into the layers of the LandscapeLayerBlend node and then placed into the related input of the final material, such as base color or normal. You need to be careful to name these layers properly so UE4 correctly defines the layers in the landscape.

▼ TRY IT YOURSELF

Create a New Landscape Material

To create a new landscape material and set up your own custom textures, follow these steps:

1. Create a new material in the Content Browser and name it **Landscape_Material_Test01**.

2. Enable the use of this material for landscapes by going to the Details panel for the material and turning on **Used with Landscape** under the usage options.

3. Create a LandscapeLayerBlend node from the Palette panel for the new material.

4. Import the desired textures for the landscape materials you want. (For this exercise, we'll use example names of textures Dirt_01 and Grass_01 for clarity.) Then drag into the new material the desired textures from the Content Browser or create a texture sample. The Grass_01 and Dirt_01 base color textures as well as the accompanying textures (normal, roughness, etc.) should now be in the material as texture samples.

5. In the LandscapeLayerBlend node, set up the number of layers to use in the landscape material. To do this, select the LandscapeLayerBlend node and go the Details panel. Click the + button beside the Layers option. Create two additional layers because you want two material blends in the landscape.

6. For the newly created layers in the Details panel of the LandscapeLayerBlend node, use the **Layer Name** option to name the layers **Dirt** and **Grass**. Connect the base color texture of Grass_01 to the Grass layer and the base color of Dirt_01 to the Dirt layer.

7. Connect the LandscapeLayerBlend node to the base color input for the material. For each texture type (normal, base color, roughness, etc.), duplicate the LandscapeLayerBlend node you just created and connect the LandscapeLayerBlend node to the material in its corresponding location.

8. By default, no textures display in the material preview, so to test the layers, go to the LandscapeLayerBlend node and change Preview Weight to any number greater than 0 and less than 1.

Landscape materials are layered differently than are normal materials, and they use a different form of blending. The blending types are available in the details of the LandscapeLayerBlend node for each layer. There are three types of landscape layers blending:

▶ **LB_WeightBlend:** This is the default type of blend for any type of landscape layer. It blends on an additive value of 0 to 1. The more of the layer that is painted on the landscape, the more predominately visible the layer becomes.

▶ **LB_HeightBlend:** This type blends based on the associated height map assigned with the height layer input of the LandscapeLayerBlend node.

▶ **LB_AlphaBlend:** This type is similar to the blending for normal materials in a vertex, which use a mask to divide the transition of textures between layers. Using a specific map, the layers are divided and transition based on the grayscale of the alpha map.

By connecting the textures to their layers and then to their appropriate final material, you can use the material as a layer landscape material. The material can then be applied to the landscape through the Details panel of the desired landscape. Once a texture is connected to a layer, the Palette panel displays the appropriate layers that can now be selected and painted to the landscape.

NOTE

Landscape Material Nodes

There are other landscape nodes in the Material Editor to help control aspects of the landscape's use of layers and textures. Experiment and explore these other nodes to see how they can apply to the landscape for a project.

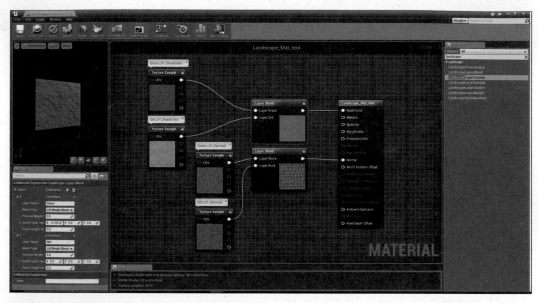

FIGURE 8.4
The LandscapeLayerBlend node in the Material Editor allows you to control multiple landscape layers. Here, you can see a layer blend set up between two types of materials to use to paint the landscape.

▼ TRY IT YOURSELF

Set Up the Landscape with a New Material

Once you have created a landscape and the material for it, you can apply the material to the landscape by following these steps:

1. Select the landscape and navigate to the Details panel.

2. Add your material to the section titled Landscape in the Landscape Material area. The material you previously created is applied to the landscape.

3. In order to paint from the layers you created in your material, you have to create landscape layers, so click the **Landscape** button in the Modes panel (see Figure 8.5).

4. Select the Paint tab in the Landscape panel.

5. Look in the Target Layers options for your layers that were created in your material that is now linked to the landscape. Click the + symbol to the left of each of the layers in the Detail window to create a new Landscape Layer for each of the layers within the material. Now each of those layers should be selectable and enabled to use for painting on the landscape.

6. Select a target layer to paint with and **click+drag** onto the landscape to begin painting. Select another target layer to change to painting that layer.

7. To alter the brush size, brush falloff, or other painting options, change the settings above the Target Layers section in the Brush settings or Tool settings.

FIGURE 8.5
The Landscape panel houses the Manage, Sculpt, and Paint tabs.

Using Foliage

Foliage is a collection of assets placed on top of and in direct relation to the landscape mesh or other assets in a scene. Foliage assets are usually trees, rocks, grass, shrubs, and other assets that are connected to the assets below. The Foliage tab is extremely useful for placing a large number of assets into a scene quickly, while using certain parameters and restrictions on where they can be placed. It would take a long time to hand-place grass plains and trees into a large open area, but by using the Foliage tab, you can quickly place these assets by using a brush tool. Foliage Actors can be any type of Static Mesh that is available through the Content Browser. Simply dragging and dropping a mesh to the Foliage tab (the fourth one from the left, which contains a leaves icon) enables it to be used as a Foliage Brush asset (see Figure 8.6).

Five tabs are available on the left side of the Foliage tab:

▶ **Paint:** The most commonly used tab for Foliage, Paint controls painting options of the Static Meshes and what kinds of surfaces are affected.

▶ **Reapply:** This tab applies current settings to all of the currently placed Foliage Static Meshes. It is useful if changes have been made to the settings of a Foliage Static Mesh after it has been placed within the scene.

▶ **Select:** This tab allows you to select certain groups of selections in the entire world space of Foliage Static Meshes.

▶ **Lasso:** This tab allows you to select certain groups of selections of Foliage Static Meshes.

▶ **Fill:** This tab allows you to fill complete selections in the scene with the desired Foliage Static Mesh.

Settings in the Paint tab control the side of the brush or the area being affected. There are also density options that control how densely the assets are placed while you're using the tool. Finally, the boxes in the Paint tab allow you to control what parts of the scene the brush affects. For instance, if you turn off the landscape selection, only BSPs and Static Meshes are affected and take Static Meshes applied from the brush in the scene.

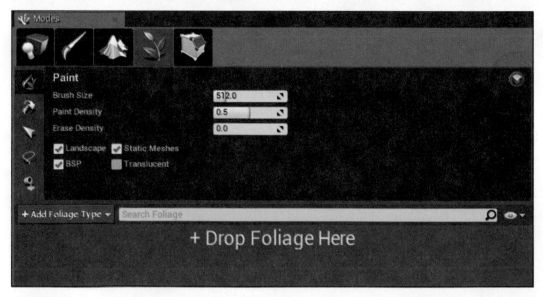

FIGURE 8.6
The Foliage tab.

Placing Foliage

To place Foliage within a scene, you must have Static Meshes added to the Foliage tab (see Figure 8.7). Then you can select and paint all the Static Meshes in groups or individually by toggling them on and off. To toggle on a Static Mesh, simply click the icon of the asset and select the check box in the top-left corner; to toggle it off, deselect the check box. All toggled-on assets paint at once when you're using the Foliage Brush within the scene. You can save each of the Static Meshes in this list for later by clicking the save symbol in the top-right corner of each Static Mesh in the list. Now each asset in this list has its own parameters for how it is spread and used in the brush. Each setting defaults to a value or setting, but if you click a Static Mesh from the list, you can toggle the options displayed below by using the check box beside each one. These options impact density, angle, direction, scale, and many other factors that change how a Static Mesh is placed within a scene.

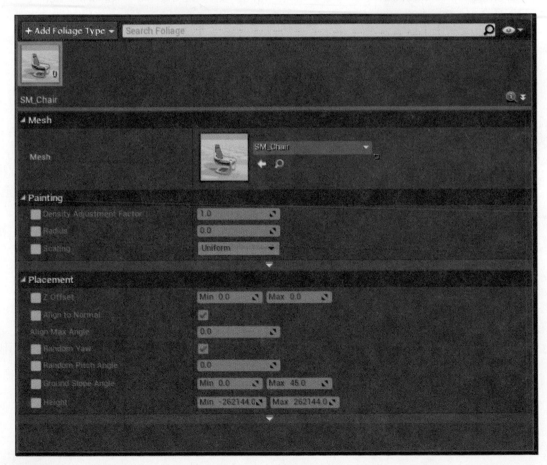

FIGURE 8.7
Foliage Static Mesh settings.

To paint with selected Foliage, simply left-click anywhere in the scene. When you do this, you begin to place assets based on the settings of the brush per Foliage Static Mesh. To delete paint, hold down the **Shift** key and left-click, and drag to paint back onto the area that was previously painted. To remove a Static Mesh entirely from the Foliage tool, simply right-click the desired asset from the Foliage tab types and select **Delete**. All instances of the mesh are then removed from the scene.

▼ TRY IT YOURSELF

Place Foliage

To place Foliage, with the Foliage tab open, do the following:

1. Drag a Static Mesh actor from the Content Browser and drop it in the **Drop Foliage Here** area of the Foliage panel.

2. Change the density of the Foliage Static Mesh to **50**.

3. Change the radius to **2**.

4. Click and paint on the previously created landscape.

5. **Shift+click** the painted area to delete the painted Foliage Static Meshes.

Summary

This hour you examined the landscape tools available in UE4. You learned how to manipulate the shape and surface of landscapes. You also developed an understanding of how to create landscape material layers and paint those layers on landscapes. Then you took a look at the Foliage tools and how to use Static Meshes to paint Foliage into a scene. Understanding these tools will expand your ability to make larger expanses of playable game space and help you quickly populate those landscapes with trees, bushes, and other types of Foliage.

Q&A

Q. Why would I use a landscape instead of a series of Static Meshes?

A. For larger game spaces, landscapes render more efficiently and allow for maximum developer control over aspects of the landscape visuals all at once. Static Meshes must be controlled individually and do not have the culling and rendering development that landscapes do.

Q. Can I select Foliage Static Meshes after I paint them into a scene?

A. Yes. While you're in the Foliage tab, you can select the painted Static Meshes independently and transform them.

Q. Can I have base color, normal, roughness, and metallic material for the landscape, just as with a standard material?

A. Yes. When you're creating the layer setup node for each input, make sure the name of each layer is identical to each of its partners. For instance, the name of the dirt layer in normal, roughness, and base color needs to be the same in each of the landscape layering nodes in order for them to correctly function together.

Workshop

Now that you have finished the hour, see if you can answer the following questions.

Quiz

1. Can you use an animated mesh in the Foliage tab?

2. Once you create a landscape, can you change any of its settings?

3. What is the name of the node used in the material to layer landscape materials?

Answers

1. No, only Static Meshes are allowed. Those Static Meshes can have vertex deformation through their material to simulate motion, but you cannot directly use Skeletal Meshes with specific animations.

2. Yes, you can change the settings of the landscape in the Change Component Size section of the Landscape panel.

3. You use the LandscapeLayerBlend node to layer landscape materials.

Exercise

For this exercise, you create a new landscape with new settings and add variation to the surface. Then you create a landscape layered material and link it to the landscape for use through the Paint tab. Finally, you add a Static Mesh to the Foliage and use it to paint the landscape surface. This exercise helps you understand how to create a new landscape from scratch and paint layered materials and meshes on its surface.

1. Create a new landscape.

2. Use the Sculpt tab to sculpt into the surface.

3. Use the Ramp tool to blend between two areas of the sculpted surface.

4. Use the Smooth tool to blend a sculpted area of the landscape.

5. Create a new layered landscape material.

6. Add the layered landscape material to the landscape.

7. Paint different layers onto the landscape.

8. Add multiple Static Meshes to the Foliage tool.

9. Paint with each Static Mesh from the Foliage tab.

10. Paint with all Static Meshes from the Foliage tab at the same time.

HOUR 9
World Building

What You'll Learn in This Hour:

▶ Adding a level to a project

▶ How to set dress a level

▶ Combining placed Actors into a Blueprint class

The goal of this hour is to solidify your familiarity with the Editor's main interface and learn about the anatomy of a typical level. You will practice your world building and set dressing skills and practice what you've learned in previous hours. World building is the process of placing Actors and art assets within a level. In world building, the lines between level designer and environment artist become blurred. (In some production environments, world building may be the responsibility of the level designer.) In this hour, you make a new project and work with existing assets, create a new level, place assets of varying types, and familiarize yourself with good world building practices.

NOTE

Hour 9 Setup

Create a new project with the Third Person Template and Starter Content.

TRY IT YOURSELF ▼

Set Up a Project

For this hour, you need a new project based on the Third Person project template. Follow these steps to set it up:

1. Open the Launcher and load the main Editor.

2. Select **New Project** to create a new project.

3. On the Blueprint tab, choose the **Third Person** game template.

4. Choose **Desktop/Console**.

5. Choose **Maximum**.

6. Select **With Starter Content**.

7. Click **Create Project**.

NOTE

Content Packs

For this hour, you can use the Starter Content. If you prefer, you can find free content in the Launcher under the Learn section or you can download the free Infinity Blade content packs from the Marketplace. To get these content packs, in the Launcher, under Marketplace, type **Infinity** and then look for Infinity Blade. If you want to use content from an existing project, you need to migrate it into your project. If you download the Infinity Blade content, it will be added to your vault, under the Library tab in the Launcher, and from there you can add it to your project.

Building Worlds

World building needs vary depending on the type of game you're developing, but the fundamental process applies to most productions. For now, you can work with existing assets and don't need to worry about gameplay or modeling, and texturing new content. This way, you can solidify your familiarity with the Editor interface and focus on your world building skills.

Good world building—including the use of scale, color, lighting, sound, and asset placement—establishes a mood and evokes a desired emotional response in players. Set dressing should not only look good but it should help guide players through the level and establish immersion.

Environmental Narrative

If you are working on a game, there is a good chance there already is an established narrative that determines the locations that your levels need to depict. When you are set dressing, it can help to form your own visual narratives for each space you make. Before you begin to build a level, look at all the visual assets you have to work with and create a simple narrative that explains what happened to the space you are creating before the player got there. This will help you make decisions about asset placement and lighting later.

Create a Default Level

Every project starts with a default map that allows you to quickly test the game mode and the players' controls. You have already created a project, and now you need to create a level within it:

1. In the Content Browser, create a new folder and name it **Maps**.

2. On the main menu, select **File > New Level** (or press **Ctrl+N**).

3. In the dialog that appears, choose **Default Level**.

4. Save your newly created level into the Maps folder.

Anatomy of a Level

In the level you have just created, look at the World Outliner panel, and you can see that the default map already has some placed Actors. Take a moment to select and look at the names, Actor types, and properties in the Details panel for each of the already-placed Actors. There is a Floor Static Mesh Actor that establishes a ground plane. A Player Start Actor defines the location where the Pawn will spawn when playing the level. There are two lights: a Sky Light that captures a cube map that contributes to the overall lighting of the scene and a Directional Light that establishes the direction of the sun. There is an Atmospheric Fog Actor that approximates the scattering of light through a planetary atmosphere. Finally, there is a Blueprint class called Sky_Sphere that uses Blueprint to control a dynamic material on a Static Mesh to control the look of the sky in the level. If you switch the viewport to top view and zoom all the way out, you can see that the sky dome is scaled up to be bigger than the grid.

NOTE

Directional Lights

The location of a Directional Light does not matter; only orientation matters. The light from a Directional Light starts from outside the world and travels in the direction the Directional Light is facing. Because the light is infinitely far away, this light is used to mimic the sun and does not have a direct falloff.

World Building Process

Now that you have a project set up, let's talk about process. While set dressing, it is good practice to work in stages, using the following iterative process:

1. **Scale and scope.** You need to establish scale and set the level's footprint, which you typically do with simple, primitive objects.

2. **Shelling and blocking.** This is the process of handling the architectural and structural needs of the level by placing large architectural and structures forms, such as buildings and walls or other structural elements. You can do this with primitive shapes until the final assets have been created.

3. **Prop and asset placement.** This stage involves placing props and decorative assets, such as benches, shrubs, and garbage cans, that are relevant to the project.

4. **Lighting and audio pass.** At this stage, you place lights and Ambient Audio Actors.

5. **Playtest and refine.** This aspect deals with traversing the level from the player's point of view and identifying, tweaking, and fixing any issues.

Repeat steps 3–5 until you're satisfied. The following sections walk through all the parts of this process.

Establishing Scale

When building a level, establishing an appropriate and effective scale for the environment is one of the most import aspects of setting the level's mood. To do this, you need to know the size of the player character. In UE4, remember that 1 Unreal unit (uu) is equal to 1 centimeter (cm) in the real world by default, so if the average character in your game is 6 feet tall, it will be 182.88 cm (1.82 meters) or 182.88 uu tall. Even if you don't have the final character built, placing a temporary visual representation of the character goes a long way toward establishing scale.

▼ TRY IT YOURSELF

Place a Reference for Scale

Using a character asset or even a simple primitive shape that represents the size of an average character can help you set the scale of a level. Follow these steps to place a Skeletal Mesh provided with the Third Person game template:

1. Open the default level you created in the preceding Try It Yourself.

2. In the Content Browser navigate to the **ThirdPersonBP > Character > Mesh** and locate the **SK_Mannequin** asset.

3. Drag the **SK_Mannequin** Skeletal Mesh asset into your level and place it on the Floor Actor.

4. Save and preview the level. Figure 9.1 shows the Sk_Mannequin placed scale reference.

FIGURE 9.1
Character scale reference.

Establishing Scope

Now that you have a default map created and saved, it is time to establish the scope of the level. Bigger is not always better, but many beginning artists and designers make the mistake of overscoping their projects and immediately trying to building massive MMO-sized levels. This will most likely create a lot of frustration and increase the time it takes to solve any problems that crop up. A good rule of thumb to follow when just starting is to choose quality over quantity. As you become more comfortable with UE4 and the Editor, you can increase the complexity of your projects.

This hour shows you how to start with the default Floor Static Mesh and add some minor additions. Go to the Modes panel and select the **Place** tab. Select **BSP** from the list on the left-hand side. You now see list of BSP Actors you can place in your level. Click+drag a box BSP Actor into the viewport of your level. With the Placed Box Actor selected, under Brush Settings, set the Y brush shape to **440** units and the Z brush shape to **50** units. Now position the BSP box at the center of one end of the Floor Static Mesh so the bottom edge of the box lines up with the top edge to the floor. This will be the footprint of the level (see Figure 9.2). It's not exactly epic, but it's a good starting point.

FIGURE 9.2
A box BSP placed to establish the level footprint.

Working with BSP Actors

BSP Actors are procedurally generated geometric primitives native to UE4. BSP stands for *binary space partitioning*, and these Actors are 3D geometry but are treated differently from meshes imported from 3D applications. BSPs are great for quickly blocking out a level. Another term you might hear when talking about BSPs is constructive solid geometry (CSG), which means they are contiguous shapes. You can perform simple Boolean modeling tasks with multiple BSPs by changing them from additive to subtractive states. You texture them in the Editor by using simple planar projections, and you can texture each polygon on a BSP primitive separately by dragging a material from the Content Browser onto the desired surface.

You can perform other simple modeling task on BSP Actors by switching to the Geometry Editing tab in the Modes panel. However, if you need something more complex, you should use a modeling application and import a Static Mesh. When working with BSPs, it is best to set their size directly under Brush Settings in the Details panel and to avoid scaling them.

Shelling and Blocking

When you have the footprint established, you can begin blocking out the level's structural assets. In the Content Browser, in the Starter Content folder named Architecture, you can find Static Meshes to work with. Select the **wall_door_400×300** Static Mesh asset, drag it into your level, and place it on the side of the BSP box that faces the floor. Continue to do this with the other side and roof to make a simple box, as shown in Figure 9.3.

FIGURE 9.3
Level shelling and blocking with BSP Actors.

Once you have built a small room, drag out another box BSP Actor and start making walls around the floor mesh. When you're finished, your final blockout should look something like Figure 9.4.

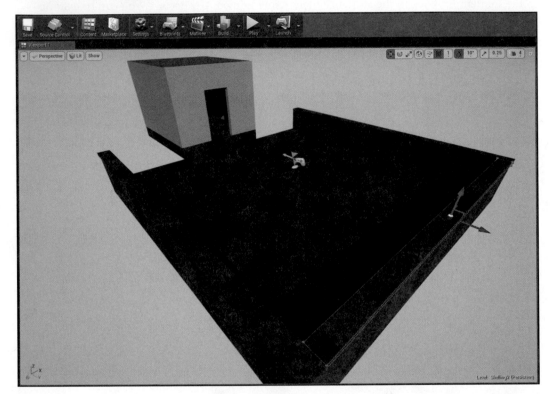

FIGURE 9.4
Level shelling progress.

TIP

Snaps and Working Quad View

Placing assets correctly and getting them lined up can be tedious. Enabling transform snapping when moving, scaling, or rotating Actors can help. (You learned about this in Hour 3, "Coordinates, Transforms, Units, and Organization.") It also helps to change the viewport layout to four panes, so that you can work with top, side, and front views as you line things up. To change the viewport layout, click on the small **Maximize/Restore** icon on the far right of the snap settings (see Figure 9.5).

FIGURE 9.5
Transform and grid snapping and viewport toggle.

The following list identifies the four useful snap setting panes shown in Figure 9.5:

1. Snapping to the grid when dragging

2. Snapping objects to rotation grid

3. Snapping objects to scale grid

4. Maximize/restore viewport

Placing Props and Assets

After you have blocked out and shelled a level, you can place props and assets in it. In the Content Browser, in the Starter Content folder called Props, you can find assets that you can use to set dress your level. Because you are working in a virtual space, you don't have to worry about structural accuracy, but you also don't want your player to see behind the curtain—so you need to strike a balance. Drag out a few instances the SM_Rock Static Mesh from the Props folder place them around the outside of the room and underneath the floor to make it look like the room is built into the side of a mountain. Now is good time to start assigning materials to some of the surfaces. Add whatever meshes you have to work with to decorate the space (see Figure 9.5). Periodically build lighting as you go. You may notice that the more content you add, the longer it takes to build lighting.

Visual Complexity and Framing

Visual complexity is the concept of finding a balance between visual details and asset usage. Randomly placing a large number of assets throughout a level might add details but will most likely create a poorly crafted and cluttered experience. When placing assets, consider the function of the space based on narrative and set the assets to identify key locations for frameable moments (see Figure 9.6). *Framing* is the idea of creating mini compositions in a game world. These areas of detail can grab players' attention and help guide them through the space. Try to create interesting spatial relationships where the player has to move between open and confined spaces to add interest and help define areas of detail.

FIGURE 9.6
Prop and asset placement with assigned materials.

Working with Modular Assets

You will notice that many of the Static Mesh assets provided in the Starter Content are made for modular modeling. Well-modeled modular assets are modeled and based around consistent units, with properly placed local pivots so they easily snap together. This helps reduce the time it takes to set dress, but it also increases the chance of excessive repetition and uniformity. Good set dressing is speedy because of modular assets, but it requires you to disguise the reuse of similar assets to create a convincing space.

TIP

Grids and Snaps

The downside to working with modular assets and grid snapping is that you risk making your level too uniform or gridded. So you have to make a special pass on a level in which you make small transform changes where applicable to ensure that things look as natural as possible.

Combining Actors into a Single Blueprint Class

When set dressing, it is a good idea to combine assets, which you can do in a few ways. As discussed in Hour 3, great ways to keep things organized are to group and attach Actors, move placed Actors into a folder in the World Outliner panel, and assign Actors to layers. Although these methods are quick and have benefits, they are unique to the level you are working on. Combining Actors into a single Blueprint class gives you the benefit of both grouping and attaching. When you do this, you get the added benefit of making the Actors reusable across multiple levels, and you can eventually script functionality.

TIP
___

Combining Assets

When set dressing, you may not always find the asset you need or have a modeler standing by to create new content. If you get creative, often you can build a new asset with the content you already have simply by combining assets into a Blueprint class. After you create these assets and place them in a level, you can move, scale, and rotate them like any other Actors.
___

TRY IT YOURSELF ▼

Create a Simple Blueprint Class

Blueprint Classes are covered in more depth in later lessons, but here you learn a simple method for combining multiple Actors into a single reusable Blueprint, a torch:

1. Create a new folder in the Content Browser and name it **MyBlueprints**.

2. Find a cylinder Static Mesh asset in the Starter Content in the Content Browser.

3. Place the cylinder mesh into your level and scale it to a desired size.

4. Assign a material to the placed cylinder by dragging a material from the Content Browser onto the Static Mesh Actor.

5. Find the Fire01_Cure Sound Cue asset in the Starter Content, drag it into the level, and place it on top of the cylinder.

6. Add a Point Light Actor from the Place tab in the Modes panel. Position the light so it is just above the cylinder. Set the color, intensity, and attenuation radius to your desired settings.

7. Find the P_Fire particle system in the Starter Content, add it to the level, and position it just above the cylinder.

8. Select all the placed Actors from steps 2–7 in the level. Then click the **Blueprint** icon on the main toolbar and choose **Convert Selected Components to Blueprint Class**.

9. In the dialog that appears (see Figure 9.7), select a path, give the Blueprint Class the name **P_Fire_Blueprint**, and click **Create Blueprint**.

FIGURE 9.7
Combining placed Actors in to a single reusable Blueprint asset.

10. In the Level Editor main interface, select **File > Save All**.

11. In the Content Browser, locate the newly created Blueprint asset and drag it into your level as many times as needed.

Creating World Beyond

World beyond refers to areas that fall beyond the player's reach. The world beyond creates the illusion that the level is in a much bigger world than it is (see Figure 9.8). Common examples of world beyond are mountain ranges and cityscapes off in the distance. The world beyond concept can also be applied to more immediate spaces, such as rooms a player can see into but not enter, or a fenced courtyard between buildings.

As you build a level, think of different ways you might be able to implement this concept. The following sections provide some suggestions to get you started.

FIGURE 9.8
Common implementation of world beyond.

As you can see in Figure 9.8, a big rock hovering in the air has been placed to establish the world beyond. It might be better if players can't see that the rock hovers. Adding an Exponential Height Fog Actor to the level helps obscure the player's view, as shown in Figure 9.9.

FIGURE 9.9
Image of set dressed level with exponential height fog.

Lighting and Audio Pass

Moving on to the fourth stage of the set dressing process, it's time to start placing lights and Ambient Sound Actors.

Lighting

Lighting is one of the most important aspects of set dressing. It ties the space and all the placed assets into a consistent visual experience, and it establishes the mood and, ultimately, the player's emotional response to the environment. Beginners often focus on adjusting the intensity of lights and forget to tweak the color of the lights in a level. This is one of the most important things to do to set the mood of a level, and varying the color of lights will also help lead the player from space to space.

When working with lights, it can help to switch view modes between Lit, Detailed Lighting, and Lighting Only. This way, you can see each of the placed assets in the level with a gray surface, which allows you to assess the color and intensity of all the lights placed in the world and how they all work together (see Figure 9.10). Add Point and Spot Light Actors to a level as needed. Then adjust the Intensity, Light Color, and Attenuation settings. Don't forget about the already-placed Directional and Sky Light Actors.

GO TO ▶ **HOUR 5, APPLYING LIGHTING AND RENDERING**, to review working with lights.

TIP

View Modes

You can easily change the viewport view mode. Select a mode by using the following keyboard shortcuts:

- ▶ **Wireframe:** Alt+2
- ▶ **Unlit:** Alt+3
- ▶ **Lit:** Alt+4
- ▶ **Detailed Lighting:** Alt+4
- ▶ **Lighting Only:** Alt+5
- ▶ **Lighting Complexity:** Alt+6

FIGURE 9.10
Setting the viewport view mode to Lighting Only helps you visualize the lighting in the level without materials.

TIP

Adding Lights Without Representation

Because Light Actors are easily placed, beginners often light areas in a level but forget to place a visual source. Whether it's a lantern, a lamp, or a torch, be sure to have an Actor that explains where the light is radiating from in order to give logic to lighting the space.

Shadow Colors

Changing the color and intensity of lights in a scene can help establish a mood, but keep in mind that shadows are always black. While you can't directly change the color of shadows in a scene, it is possible to tint their color by placing a Sky Light. Select the Sky Light Actor in the level and in the Details panel, under the Light category, adjust the Light Color and Intensity properties as desired.

Lightmass Importance Volume

If you have been building lighting throughout this process, you may have noticed that the amount of time it takes to build lighting has increased as the amount of content in a level has increased. When you build lighting, Lightmass calculates the number of times light bounces around the level (three bounces by default). If a light hits a surface, bounces off, and continues to travel without ever hitting another surface, UE4 continues to process the light until it leaves the level. To minimize this processing, you can set Lightmass Importance Volume to define the area beyond which the light is no longer processed. When you do this, you can greatly reduce the amount of time it takes to build lighting.

The Lightmass Importance Volume is located in the Volume category in the Modes panel. Once you have added it to a level, you can adjust the size and shape of the volume in the Details panel, under Brush Settings. When placing the volume, you should have it surround the important areas of the level.

Audio

Simple ambient sounds can breathe life into a static level. Audio has a huge impact on player perception. Sounds such as rushing wind, birds chirping, thunder in the distance, and the hum of a generator are good environmental sounds to help inject life into a static world. Ambient sounds typically are looping.

To add an Ambient Sound Actor to a level, find a Sound Wave asset in the Content Browser, drag into the level, and adjust properties. Under Attenuation, uncheck the **Override Attenuation** setting and then adjust the radius and fall distance.

GO TO ▶ HOUR 7, USING AUDIO SYSTEM ELEMENTS, to review working with sound Actors.

Playtesting and Refining

After you have completed the rest of the world building process, such as shelling the level, placing Static Mesh Actors, and setting lighting and audio, you need to check over all your work by playtesting and refining. Hopefully, you have already been periodically playtesting your level as you have been working. If you haven't, now is a good time to click the **Play** button on the Level Editor toolbar and walk around the level.

Try to look at your level from the player's point of view and identify any issues. Look for places that indicate poor attention to detail. This can show up in many ways, such as a surface not being assigned a material or objects floating above the ground or sinking into the floor. Look at asset placement: Are props always placed on the perimeters of rooms, with nothing in the interior spaces? Also ensure that architectural spaces are not perfectly symmetrical and that there are not so many different materials in a level that the player's eye can never rest.

After you make the necessary refinements to the level, you can add a few other Actors that will make a big difference in the final look of the level. You can find these visual effects Actors on the Modes panel, under Visual Effects: Sphere Reflection Capture, Fog, and Post Processing Volume

Actors. When you place these Actors in a level and adjust them properly, these Actors make the final game look professional.

Reflection Capture Actors

Sphere and Box Reflection Capture Actors capture images of the level from their location and project reflections onto other Actors in the vicinity—if the nearby Actors have materials with reflective properties. While these Actors do not create accurate reflections, using them is very effective and efficient because the scene capture is calculated before runtime. You can place them as needed throughout a level.

Fog Actors

Game makers used to use fog to hide the fact that a level was small and had few assets or for occluding far-off assets to improve rendering efficiency. Today, fog is more of an aesthetic choice. Be careful: Fog can easily flatten a scene because it washes out contrast in the lighting.

There are two Fog Actor types that you can place in a scene:

▶ **Atmospheric Fog:** Atmospheric Fog is typically used with exterior levels and approximates atmospheric light scattering. It works directly with a directional light placed in the level.

▶ **Exponential Height Fog:** The Exponential Height Fog Actor controls fog density in the level based on height: Lower areas in a level have higher density than do higher areas.

Post Processing Volume Actors

Post processing allows you to apply camera effects to a scene. You can adjust properties like Depth of Field, Motion Blur, and Scene Color on rendered frames. You can use Post Processing Volume Actors to apply these effects to areas in a scene that are defined by a primitive shape. Once a Post Processing Volume Actor is placed in a level and selected, you can adjust the size and shape of the Actor under Brush Settings in the Details panel. When a camera enters a Post Processing Volume Actor, the effects are applied. Figure 9.11 shows the level before and after the Post Processing Volume Actor has been placed with Color Grading, Scene Color, and Depth Of Field properties adjusted.

While you can place multiple Post Processing Volume Actors in a scene, you can also place a single one and have it affect the entire level by turning on Unbound in the Post Process Volume category under Brush Settings in the Details panel. Here you can also find all the other properties you can control.

FIGURE 9.11
Image of a set-dressed level, before (top) and after post-processing (bottom).

Summary

In this hour, you learned to add a new level to a project and were introduced to a number of new skills involved in set dressing a level. You were also introduced to some basic concepts related to creating worlds and had a chance to apply the skills you acquired in previous lessons. In this hour you saw that a good set dresser should think like an interior designer and a landscape architect, while creating areas of interest and intrigue based on discrete environmental narratives.

Q&A

Q. When I place Static Mesh Actors in a level and they intersect one another, why do some of the overlapping polygons flicker?

A. When placing Static Mesh Actors, it is okay to have them intersect; however if any of the polygons are coplanar (that is, share the same space), the rendering engine doesn't know which polygon to display. This results in a flickering effect as UE4 tries to determine the sorting order. To fix this issue, simply offset one of the assets.

Q. When I preview a level, why am I able to walk though some of the Static Mesh Actors?

A. Most likely, the Static Mesh asset is missing a collision hull. To fix this, find the Static Mesh in the Content Browser, open it up in the Static Mesh Editor, and generate a new collision hull. Refer to Hour 4, "Working with Static Mesh Actors."

Q. When I try to adjust the sky colors on the Sky_Sphere Actor, my choices do not have an effect. Why?

A. By default, the Sky_Sphere colors are determined by the Directional Light. You can either change the rotation of the direction light or, with the Sky_Sphere Actor selected, go to the Details panel and uncheck **Colors Determined By Sun Position**. Then you can modify the override settings on the Sky_Sphere Actor.

Q. Why do I see the word *preview* on some of my placed Static Meshes? And why am I being alerted that lighting needs to be rebuilt?

A. If you have Static Mesh and Light Actors with mobility set to Static, you have to build lighting to create lighting and shadow data for those Actors. If your level is not too large and lighting builds don't take too long, there is no harm in building lighting at regular intervals.

Q. Why do I keep seeing the message "there is no Lightmass importance volume"?

A. You need to add a Lightmass Importance Volume setting to the scene and set its size so that it just fits all the other assets inside its volume.

Q. Do I have to use BSPs to block out my level?

A. Not at all. It is okay to use Static Mesh assets only.

Q. My character can jump over the wall and outside the level. How do I stop that?

A. Depending on the scale of an asset, the player may have the ability to jump higher than the asset. This is really a preplanning issue; it's a good idea to know a pawn's abilities before you set dress an entire space. However, you can place Blocking Volume Actors to define invisible areas the player cannot pass through. Blocking volumes are found on the Modes panel under Volumes.

Workshop

Now that you have finished the hour, see if you can answer the following questions.

Quiz

1. If building lighting for a level is taking a long time, what option can you set to help shorten build times by culling and light rays that travel outside the defined area?

2. If you are using materials with reflective properties but reflections are not showing up, what type of Actors can you add?

3. If the Pawn can jump over walls and fall outside the level, what Actor can you place to create invisible collision hulls?

4. True or false: Grouping and linking Actors in the World Outliner panel are the only ways to combine Actors.

5. True or false: The world beyond concept only refers to far-off distance that the player cannot reach.

Answers

1. If building lighting for a level is taking a long time, you can add a Lightmass Importance Volume setting to help shorten build times.

2. If you are using materials with reflective properties but reflections are not showing up, you should place Sphere and/or Box Reflection Capture Actors in your level.

3. If the Pawn can jump over walls and fall outside the level, you can place Blocking Volume Actors in your level.

4. False; already-placed Actors can be combined in to a Blueprint Class that can reused throughout all the levels in your project.

5. False; while far-off distances are the most common implementation of world beyond it also refers to any nearby areas the players can see but can get to.

Exercise

For this exercise, create and set dress a second level but this time start with the Empty Level template. The Empty Level template does not have any of the preplaced Actors found in the Default template. It is good practice when starting out to familiarize yourself with all the Actors needed to set up a basic level. Set dress a small environment using existing assets and materials. There should be a consistent visual theme to the space and a focal object that brings everything together. You should demonstrate your understanding and ability to implement common set-dressing concepts, such as visual complexity and dealing with world beyond.

1. In the project you created for this hour, from the main menu select **File > New Level** (or press **Ctrl+N**).

2. In the dialog that appears, choose **Blank Level**.

3. Save your newly created level into the Maps folder.

4. Add a BSP box and under Brush Settings in the Details panel, set the brush shape to **2000** for X, **2000** for Y, and **50** for Z.

5. Add a Player Start Actor.

6. Add a Directional Light.

7. Add a Sky Light.

8. Add an Atmospheric Fog Actor.

9. Add the Sky_Sphere Blueprint Actor.

10. Migrate Static Meshes, Materials, Particle Systems, and Audio assets from another project or add content packs from the marketplace.

11. Set dress the level.

12. Add an Exponential Height Fog Actor.

13. Add a Lightmass Importance Volume Actor.

14. Add Sphere Reflection Capture Actors.

15. Add a Post Processing Volume Actor.

HOUR 10
Crafting Effects with Particle Systems

What You'll Learn in This Hour:

▶ Understanding particles and data types
▶ Working with the Cascade Editor
▶ Using emitters and modules
▶ Using the Curve Editor
▶ Setting up materials for particles
▶ Triggering Particle Systems

Particle Systems are the building blocks of visual effects in games. You can use particles for explosions, muzzle flashes, leaves falling in the wind, waterfalls, magical energy, lightning, rain, dust, fire, and much more. In UE4, particles have many different flavors that you can manipulate to create a variety of effects through the particle Editor Cascade. This real-time particle editor and UE4's modular approach to controlling particle behavior allows you to design even the most complex effects quickly and easily. In this hour, you learn about the different types of particles in UE4, how to use Cascade to create and control how particles behave, how to use SubUV textures, and how to utilize particle effects with Level Blueprints.

NOTE

Hour 10 Project

For this hour, you need to open the Hour_10 folder, which is available on the book's companion website at www.sty-ue4.com. This folder contains applicable and useful texture sets and premade Particle Systems that you can explore to further understand the concepts in this hour.

Understanding Particles and Data Types

In video games, a *particle* is a point in space that follows a set of rules that determine its location and various visual attributes. There is usually some form of mesh attached to these points that causes the particles to appear to the player. There are many different types of particles, each with a different type of mesh or construction attached to its points.

UE4 includes the following types of Particle Emitters, each of which has different benefits for different situations:

▶ **Sprites:** By far the most common type of emitter, a Sprite is a single camera-facing quad mesh with a texture to define the visuals. Sprites are most often used for smoke and fire, but they can be used to create many other effects. Effects usually are made with the default camera-facing Sprite Emitters.

▶ **Mesh data:** With this type of emitter, a particle attaches to a single polygonal mesh. This allows for great looking effects such as rockslides or flying debris from explosions.

▶ **Anim-trail data:** Used exclusively with Skeletal Meshes and animations, Anim-Trail Data Emitters create trails using the sockets from Skeletal Meshes. These work well for creating streaks behind swords or other melee weapons.

▶ **Beam data:** This type of emitter draws a camera-facing set of quads that stretch between the recently created particles. This type is often used for lasers, lightning, or similar effects.

▶ **GPU Sprites:** Visually similar to the default Sprites, GPU Sprites have the distinction of being simulated entirely on the graphics processor. This allows you to simulate and render orders of magnitude more particles than their CPU counterparts. Some features available to the default Sprites are not available to GPU Sprites, however, making GPU Sprites most useful when you need to simulate large quantities of distinct individual effects, such as sparks, fireworks, snow, or rain.

▶ **Ribbon data:** This type of emitter draws quads between each pair of recently placed particles, interpolating bends with smooth curves. This type is often used with moving emitters to create engine or projectile trails.

This hour focuses on the three most common Particle Emitters: Sprites, GPU Sprites, and mesh data.

Working with Cascade

Unreal Engine 4 has a powerful particle editor called Cascade. The Cascade interface and the number of options in it can be a bit daunting at first, but the versatility and modular approach to particle behavior makes Cascade an incredibly useful tool.

A *Particle System* is a collection of one or more Particle Emitters (potentially of different types) that make up an effect. Each Particle Emitter spawns an arbitrary number of particles and controls their behavior and appearance. It controls these behaviors through modules that you can add to or remove from any Particle Emitter.

Modules can control effects such as a particle's size, color, velocity, and rotation, and they can also handle collisions.

You open Cascade by double-clicking any particle template in the Content Brower. The Cascade Editor has six major parts, as shown in Figure 10.1 and described in the following list:

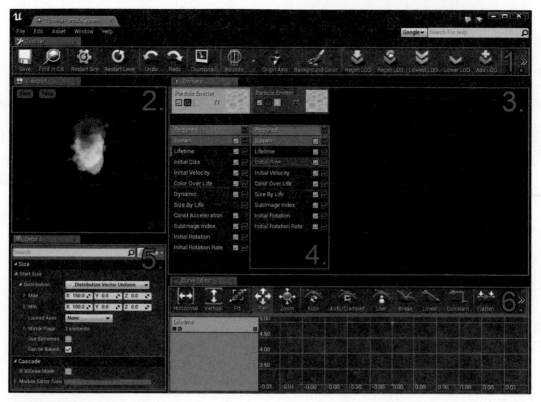

FIGURE 10.1
The six important sections of Cascade.

The six parts are 1) Toolbar; 2) Viewport Panel; 3) Emitters Panel; 4) Modules Panel; 5) Details Panel; 6) Curves Editor. The six sections are described in the following list:

▶ **Toolbar:** As in most other editors in UE4, the toolbar is where you save changes and handle asset-level actions. Important commonly used buttons are Restart Sim and Restart Level, which cause UE4 to refresh a Particle System from scratch.

▶ **Viewport Panel:** This panel provides a full-fledged preview Viewport of your Particle System and allows you to use normal movement controls.

▶ **Emitters Panel:** This panel contains all the emitters held by the selected template. Each emitter is a piece of the effect, controlling distinct particles and represented by a column. You can add a new emitter by right-clicking in the empty space.

▶ **Modules Panel:** This panel holds the behaviors that control the emitter selected in the Emitters panel. Each module is displayed as a row, with a type name and a check box to enable or disable the module. You can add a new modules by right-clicking in this column and using the context menu to choose a specific module.

▶ **Details Panel:** This panel shows the available properties of the selected module. When no module or emitter is selected, it shows the particle template's global properties.

▶ **Curves Editor:** This panel visualizes property values as curves, allowing for complex effects that usually occur over the lifetime of a particle. It is commonly used to fade particles in or out, change their sizes over time, and manipulate their velocities. You can visualize modules' curves in the Curves Editor by clicking the graph icon on the individual module.

Using Emitters and Modules

To understand how to use Cascade to create particle effects, you need to first understand how modules can manipulate particles inside an emitter. The range of modifications and the variety of behaviors that a module can describe is massive.

An *emitter* describes a collection of particles, and how it describes those particles is entirely decided by the modules that make up the emitter. Modules can influence an emitter's movement, its behavior, its color and appearance, what type of data it is drawing, complex events in the particle's lifetime, and much more.

Modules show up as individual rows in an emitter's column in the Emitters panel. You can add modules to an emitter by right-clicking the emitter in the Emitters panel. You can modify the different properties and parameters of a module through the Details panel.

Required Modules

Each emitter comes with three required modules. The first doesn't look like a module at all but is where emitter-specific information like the emitter's name and quality information reside. This module rests at the top of an emitter column and shows the emitter's name, and a thumbnail render of the emitter's effect. It is on this module that you can disable the entire emitter by using the check box underneath the emitter's name.

Under the top-level module is a black bar, which represents a slot that the emitter's type data can be slotted into. This module always exists, but you may choose to leave it empty. Choosing to not slot in a distinct type data will cause the emitter to spawn CPU Sprite particles.

The next required module is actually named the Required module, which holds the parameters a Particle Emitter absolutely requires to function. Information about the applied material, the emitter's lifetime, and whether the emitter loops can be found here. It is a good idea to look at all the parameters held in the Required module and get a feel for everything in here. In the future, you will come back to this module frequently.

Finally, the last required module is the Spawn module, which is responsible for the number of new particles that are created and their frequency or rate of emission. Without this module, no particles would ever be created.

Module Properties

Each module has a set of properties that control how that module affects the particles it contains. The Distribution field controls how each particle determines what value to use for a given property. The available distributions are grouped into a few different types:

NOTE

Vector and Float Distributions

Each of these distributions has versions for singular scalar float values and three float vector values. The type of distribution (whether float or vector) is determined by the property itself and cannot be changed by the user.

For more about distributions and how they work in Cascade, check out the excellent documentation at https://docs.unrealengine.com/latest/INT/Engine/Basics/Distributions.

▶ **Distribution Float/Vector Constant:** Some properties, such as the emitter's Duration property, can have only one value. No matter at what point in the simulation, a constant distribution always comes back the same. Other properties (such as the Lifetime module's Lifetime property) are not required to be constant but can be interpreted as such.

▶ **Distribution Float/Vector Constant Curve:** When properties need to change over the lifetime of the Particle System or the emitter, those properties can be interpreted as curves. At the same point in every particle's lifetime, the property will evaluate the curve the same way. This is often used to change the color or opacity of particles over their lifetimes in a predictable way. Curves are best edited through the Curve Editor, although can be manually adjusted in the Details panel.

▶ **Distribution Float/Vector Uniform:** Properties that are not forced to be constant may be interpreted with a variety of different distribution methods. The simplest distribution method available is the uniform distribution, which takes in minimum and maximum values that can be returned and returns a uniformly random value between the two (see Figure 10.2). These distributions are most often used with modules that affect the initial state of a particle. One example is the Initial Size module, which can have a uniform distribution used to give each particle a random scale.

▶ **Distribution Float/Vector Uniform Curve:** A uniform curve distribution is the most advanced distribution setting for a property, and it offers the benefit of a time-based result—like constant curves do—but with the controlled randomness provided by the uniform distribution. These distributions are best used when an effect needs to be both random and modulated with time. As with the constant curves, it is best to use the Curve Editor to make modifications to uniform curve distributions.

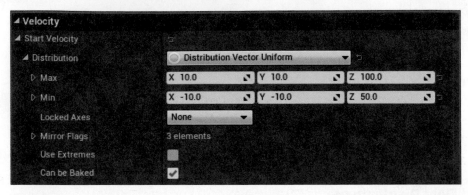

FIGURE 10.2
An example of using the Distribution Vector Uniform setting, which describes the randomized initial velocity of each particle. In this case, the X and Y velocities range from values of –10.0 to 10.0, while the upward Z velocity ranges from 50.0 to 100.0.

NOTE

Initial Versus Over Life

The names of some modules include either *Initial* or *Over Life* (e.g., Initial Color, Color over Life). These names accurately describe the behaviors of a module, and they have measurable differences in terms of how they are evaluated.

When a module name includes *Initial*, curve and uniform curve distributions are evaluated over the emitter's duration, not over the individual particles' lifetimes. For example, if Initial Color is defined as a curve from red to green, as the entire emitter stays active, new particles begin getting more green, while particles spawned earlier remain their initial red color.

Conversely, when a module has *Over Life* in the name, curve and uniform curve distributions are evaluated for the lifetime of each particle. For example, if Color Over Life is defined as a curve from red to green, each new particle begins as red and transitions to green individually.

Using the Curve Editor

Many modules are best utilized with curve distributions. Editing curves manually through the Details panel is possible, but it is somewhat unintuitive. Luckily, Cascade comes with a fully featured Curve Editor that makes manipulating and creating curves simple.

You can see curves in the Curve Editor by clicking the graph icon on individual modules in the Emitters panel. Figure 10.3 shows some of the most important features of the Curve Editor: 1) Toolbar; 2) Channel visualizers; 3) Property visualizer; 4) Key. These features are described in the following list:

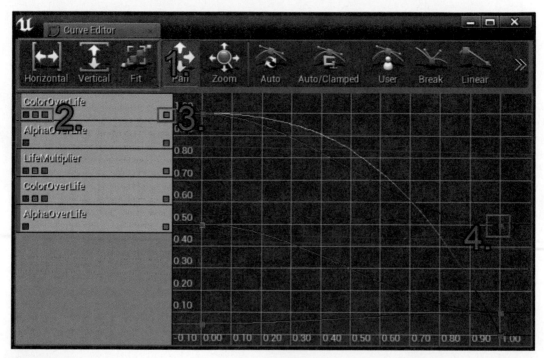

FIGURE 10.3
The Curve Editor showing several curves, with points of interest highlighted.

▶ **Toolbar:** The toolbar has buttons for many tools that are necessary for handling and manipulating curves. The first three buttons highlighted in Figure 10.3 are the framing tools, which are used to quickly set the Curve Viewport to match the minimum and maximum values of all visible curves.

▶ **Channel visualizers:** Each curve distribution is either a singular float curve or a set of curves that make up a vector distribution. In the case of a vector distribution, these three red, green, and blue boxes can be used to visualize individual channels of the vector. When you click any of these boxes, the matching curve in the Editor is either enabled or disabled.

▶ **Property visualizer:** This box enables or disables the visualization of all channels of the associated property. You can use it to disable the display of all curves in a property with one click.

▶ **Key:** As with many other curve or animation editors, this Curve Editor works with placed keys. You can manipulate keys directly through keyboard shortcuts or by right-clicking and setting values manually.

The process of adding keys and navigating around the Viewport can take some getting used to. The controls listed in Table 10.1 are invaluable for effectively using the Curve Editor to define effects.

TABLE 10.1 Curve Editor Controls

Control	Description
Click+drag on the background	Pan view around.
Mouse scroll	Zoom in and out.
Click a key	Select the key.
Ctrl+click a key	Toggle selection of a key.
Ctrl+click a curve	Add a new key at the clicked location.
Ctrl+click+drag	Move the current selection.
Ctrl+Alt+click+drag	Box select.
Ctrl+Alt+Shift+click+drag	Box select and add to current selection.

Using Common Modules

Many modules are available to you. There are, however, some modules that are almost always used and whose versatility and distinct properties are worth mentioning. They are described in the following sections.

Required Module

The Required module, as mentioned previously, handles most of the bare minimum information required by an emitter. Some of this module's most important properties, described in this section, should not be overlooked.

The Emitter category includes the following important properties:

▸ **Material:** This property determines which material is used by each particle in the emitter. (You learn about particle-friendly materials later in the hour.)

▸ **Use Local Space:** This Boolean property determines whether the Particle System should be completely relative to its Actor's position, rotation, and scale or whether it should simulate in world space. This flag is false by default, meaning that as the emitter moves around in the world, the particles stay behind. This also means that particles ignore the rotation of the containing Actor. A good time to turn this flag on is when you need an effect to stay stuck to a character completely—for example, for muzzle flashes or simple engine flares.

▸ **Kill on Deactivated and Kill on Completed:** These two properties are primarily for efficiency, and you can use them to have UE4 automatically clean up your Particle Systems. Kill on Deactivated destroys the emitter whenever it is deactivated, while Kill on Completed destroys the emitter as soon as the Emitter Duration setting's time runs out.

The Duration category includes the following properties of note related to the duration and looping of the emitter:

▶ **Emitter Duration:** This property is a single float value that determines how long a single loop of the Particle System is. This is a value in seconds, so if Emitter Duration is set to 5.0, the emitter will complete one loop in 5 seconds. It is important to note that particles can technically have longer life spans than the Emitter Duration setting.

▶ **Emitter Loops:** This property is an integer value that determines how many times the emitter loops. When this value is 0, the emitter loops endlessly.

Finally, the SubUV category controls the sizing and controls of the different properties that go into using SubUV textures. A series of properties in this module determine how SubUV textures are managed. SubUV textures are commonly used to display simple animations on particles to create complex multilayered effects. You learn about how to use SubUV textures later in this hour.

Spawn Module

The Spawn module is always used to determine how many new particles are created and how often it happens. It can be roughly separated into two categories: per-second spawns and burst spawns. The first category determines how many particles per second are created, and the second category indicates that the emitter should force spawn a set number of particles at a particular time.

The Spawn category includes the following properties:

▶ **Rate:** This property is a float distribution that determines the number of particles to emit per second.

▶ **Rate Scale:** This property is a secondary scalar applied to the Rate property to modulate the number of particles. The result of Rate multiplied by Rate Scale determines the number of particles to emit in a given frame.

The Burst category is slightly more involved than Spawn because it allows you to determine specific times to force emit a particular number of particles. This category includes the following properties:

▶ **Burst List:** This property contains a list of counts and times to spawn a set number of particles. You can add new burst items by clicking the + icon on the burst list array. A burst item has three properties: Count, Count Low, and Time. Count and Count Low determine the minimum and maximum numbers of particles to emit in a given frame, determined by Time. When Count Low is negative, the emitter simply emits the number of particles defined by Count; otherwise, it picks a random number between the two properties.

It is important to note that Time is a value between 0.0 and 1.0, where 1.0 denotes the maximum duration of the emitter.

▶ **Burst Scale:** This property is a distribution that scales the values determined by the Burst List property.

Lifetime Module

In the vast majority of Particle Systems, the Lifetime module should be considered a requirement. This module determines how long particles remain in existence. The module has only one property, and that property can be any of the distribution types. You can use the Lifetime module to give particles a random lifetime.

Something to keep in mind is that many modules work off the lifetime of individual particles, so changing the Lifetime module can drastically change the speed at which other modules modify particle behaviors.

Initial Size and Size By Life Modules

One of the things you most commonly need to control in any Particle System is the size and scale of the particles being displayed. The Initial Size and Size by Life modules are regularly used together in many effects for just this purpose. To find these modules, right-click the emitter and select **Add Module > Size**. Here are some more details about these two modules:

▶ **Initial Size:** The Initial Size module sets the particles' size at the time that they are spawned. It is most often used with the `Distribution Uniform Vector` setting to create some variation of randomness between different particles.

▶ **Size By Life:** This module handles the important task of modulating an individual particle's size over the course of its lifetime. You can use this setting with the Initial Size module to grow or shrink particles as time moves on. One common use is a curve distribution where the size starts near or at 0.0 and then grows quickly to a value near 1.0. This causes the visual effect similar to rapid expansion, a common feature in effects such as explosions.

Initial Color, Scale Color/Life, and Color Over Life Modules

The modules dedicated to handling a particle's color—Initial Color, Scale Color/Life, and Color Over Life—are very similar to the modules dedicated to scale. In addition to the RGB color properties of each particle, these modules can control the alpha (transparency) of each particle. By modifying the alpha, you can easily hide the creation and deletion of each particle, which is especially useful for soft effects like smoke or fire.

Pushing color values above 1.0, in many cases, causes the post-process bloom effect to take effect, which can be used to create glowing bright effects like sparks or flames.

These modules require that the material applied to the Particle Emitter be set up with a particle color node input. Here are some more details about these three modules:

- **Initial Color:** The Initial Color module, like the Initial Size module, sets the color of each particle when it spawns. This module is often used to randomize the starting colors of each particle.

- **Scale Color/Life:** This module takes the existing color of a particle and modulates the result over the lifetime of the particle. Curve distributions can be used to great effect with this module. You can use the Scale Color/Life module with the Initial Color module to create slightly different random particles that change color or alpha over time since the resultant color values are a combination of both modules.

- **Color Over Life:** This module is different from the By Life modules we have previously covered in that this module sets the value of the particle's color directly. This means it stomps over the values set by Initial Color or Scale Color/Life modules. Color Over Life modules are usually used in isolation to fill the role of the other two modules.

Initial Velocity, Inherit Parent Velocity, and Const Acceleration Modules

Cascade maintains several modules that are dedicated to handling particle motion: Initial Velocity, Inherit Parent Velocity, and Const Acceleration Modules. Many particle effects require only the simplest of these—the modules dedicated to applying velocity or acceleration in a constant direction. Here are some details on these three modules:

- **Initial Velocity:** This module determines the starting velocity for any particle. The module works well with uniform distributions to create a small amount of randomness in any direction or magnitude.

- **Inherit Parent Velocity:** This module does exactly what its name implies. If the emitter is moving at any speed when the particle is spawned, the module applies the speed and direction of the parent emitter (or Actor) to the particles. This works best for particle effects that are meant to appear physically based, especially when attached to Actors that move throughout the world.

- **Const Acceleration:** This module applies a consistent amount of acceleration to all particles in an emitter evenly. This is the module best used to approximate gravity. Most particle effects that have distinct physical elements (like sparks, dirt, rocks, or water) should use Const Acceleration with a negative value in the Z component to simulate the effect of gravity.

Initial Location and Sphere Modules

Under the Location category are many modules related to the spawn location of each particle. When none of these modules are used, Cascade simply spawns particles at the emitter's origin. These location modules can often be stacked to create interesting and diverse effects, but often these two simple modules are more than sufficient:

▶ **Initial Location:** By far the most commonly used location module, the Initial Location module uses a vector distribution to pick the starting location of each particle. When used with the `Distribution Uniform Vector` setting, this module can fill a box-like volume with new particles to spawn. This module is great for creating atmospheric area-filling effects.

▶ **Sphere:** Similarly to the Initial Location module, the Sphere module handles spawn locations. Differently, however, the Sphere module distributes particles throughout a sphere volume. The sphere's radius can be set through a distribution, although often a constant distribution is sufficient. In addition to Initial Location, the Sphere module can also be used to apply a velocity scale to each particle. This is useful because the velocities this module applies are aligned to the surface of the sphere. The resultant effect works well for sparks or particulates intended to come from a point source (explosions come to mind).

Initial Rotation and Rotation Rate Modules

One of the limitations of Particle Systems is that it is difficult to make individual particles look very different from their neighbors. Using random sizes and random colors can help create the illusion of diversity, but another important feature is to randomly rotate each particle. The rotation-based modules can help you create interesting motion and diversity in your effects. Here are some details on these two modules:

▶ **Initial Rotation:** This is a simple module that merely sets the starting rotation of each particle. By using a `Distribution Float Uniform` setting, the Initial Rotation module can create much-needed diversity in nearly all effects. The scale for rotation is 0.0 to 1.0, where 1.0 is one full rotation of the particle.

▶ **Rotation Rate:** Sometimes an initial rotation is not quite enough to make an effect shine. In such cases, the Rotation Rate module really comes through. You can use this module to give all particles a unique amount of angular velocity. As with the Initial Rotation module, the scale for the Rotation Rate module is 0.0 to 1.0, where a value of 1.0 means the particle completes a full rotation in a single second.

The Rotation Rate and Initial Rotation modules work together and can be stacked.

Setting Up Materials for Particles

Understanding the interaction between Particle Emitters and the materials applied to the particles is crucial to devising interesting and textured effects. There are a number of modules, including those related to color modulation, that cannot work unless you first set up the materials to interpret those modules.

Emitter modules set properties and parameters on particles, and those properties are then interpreted by the attached materials—but only if the proper nodes are used in the material graph.

Particle Color

Being able to modulate a particle's color is incredibly important and almost always needed. Therefore, setting up a material to interpret this property is extremely common when you're making visual effects.

In its most basic form, a particle material often takes the RGB and A values from an input texture and multiplies them with the respective values of a particle color input node. Figure 10.4 shows a simple unlit translucent material with this setup.

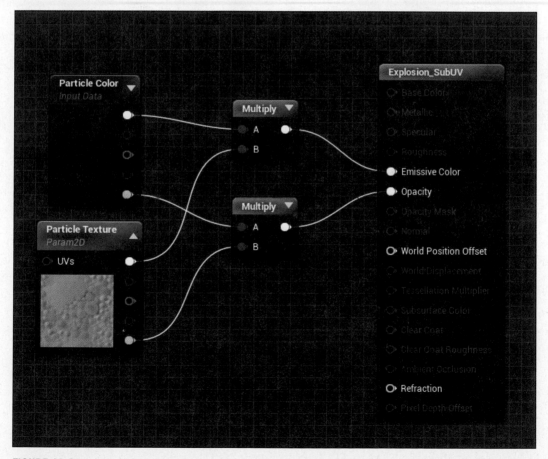

FIGURE 10.4
A simple translucent unlit material set up with the ability to take the color set by an emitter's various color modules.

SubUV Textures

One of the most convenient and versatile ways to make dynamic effects is to use the SubUV options provided by UE4 to create SubUV texture effects.

SubUV texture effects are used for visual effects where distinct frames of an animation are prerendered into a single texture sheet. The different frames are laid out in a grid pattern, and then at runtime, UE4 picks and interpolates between the different frames, giving the illusion of animation.

Figure 10.5 shows the order in which an example of a SubUV texture and the order in which the frames are shown.

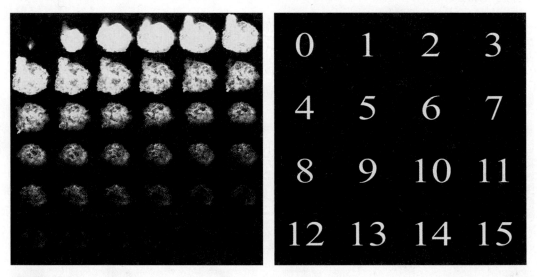

FIGURE 10.5
Two examples of SubUV textures. The left image shows an example of a prerendered 6 × 6 explosion effect made in a third-party package. The right image shows the order the animation goes through, with frame numbers for a 4 × 4 SubUV texture.

Using a SubUV texture requires three distinct steps. The first step is to tell the emitter's Required module the number of columns and rows in the SubUV texture. The second step is to create a SubImage index in the Particle Emitter and set up a curve, picking which frames to show at which time. The final step is to place a `ParticleSubUV` or a `TextureParameterSubUV` node in the material graph of the applied material.

NOTE
_____

SubImage Index

A SubImage index defines a curve where the horizontal axis fits from 0 to 1, where 1 is the lifetime of the particle. The vertical axis is an integer, with the exact frame number to be displayed, starting with 0. So if a texture sheet is 4 × 4, it has 16 frames, and the value to use at the end of the SubUV texture should be 15.

Create a SubUV Texture Effect

Using SubUV textures is one of the best ways to create deep and complex effects with lots of secondary animation. Follow these steps to create a new simple Particle Emitter effect and material setup, using an explosion SubUV texture:

1. In the Content Browser, in the folder for the Hour_10 project (available on the book's companion website), create a new particle template and name it **SimpleExplosion**.

2. Open the Cascade Editor for the **SimpleExplosion** template by double-clicking it.

3. Delete the default **Initial Velocity** module.

4. Open the **Required** module's details and scroll down to the **SubUV category**. Under SubUV, set **Interpolation Mode** to **Linear** and set both **Sub Images Horizontal** and **Sub Images Vertical** to 6.

5. Right-click the Particle Emitter, select **SubUV > SubImage Index.**

6. Set the distribution to **Distribution Float Curve Constant.**

7. Under the distribution field, expand **Point #1** and set **Out Val** to 36.

8. In the Content Browser, create a new material and name it **SimpleExplosion_Material.**

9. Open **SimpleExplosion_Material**'s material graph.

10. In the material's global settings, set **Blend Mode** to **Translucent** and set **Shading Model** to **Unlit.**

11. Add a new **Particle Color** node to the material graph.

12. Create a **TextureSampleParameterSubUV** node and then set **Parameter Name** to **Particle SubUV.**

13. Replace the **Particle SubUV** node's texture with /Game/Textures/T_Explosion_SubUV.

14. Create two **Multiply** nodes.

15. Connect both the **Particle Color** and **Particle SubUV** white RGB pins to the first **Multiply** node.

16. Hook the first **Multiply** node's output into the **Emissive Color** input.

17. Connect the **Particle Color** node's alpha output and the **Particle SubUV** node's red output to the second **Multiply** node.

18. Hook the second **Multiply** node's output to the **Opacity** node's input.

19. In the Cascade Editor for the **SimpleExplosion** template, select the **Required** module and set the **Material** property to **SimpleExplosion_Material**.

20. Lower the **Spawn Rate** setting to **0.0** and create a **burst spawn** item with a value of **1.0**.

21. In the **Required** module, set **Duration** to **1.0**.

22. In the **Lifetime** module, set the **Lifetime** property's distribution to **Distribution Float Constant** and set Constant Value to **1.0**.

23. Place an instance of the **SimpleExplosion** particle system into the level.

Triggering Particle Systems

Some particle effects always need to be active. Other times, more control is needed to fine-tune the activation timing of particle effects.

Auto Activate

For ambient effects, such as some fires or wind effects, often there is no need to ever have the effects be disabled. In cases such as these, the Auto Activate setting on an emitter Actor can be used to simplify the placement and activation of the effects.

To make a Particle System activate as soon as it is placed, after placing a Particle Emitter, select the Actor and look for the Activation category. If the Auto Activate property on an emitter Actor is checked, the emitter automatically activates itself when the game begins.

Activating Particle Systems Through Level Blueprints

In some situations, game designers and developers need more complete control over when and how particle effects simulate. Level Blueprints and Blueprint classes can be used to great effect to control the activation behaviors of different emitters.

In Level Blueprints, you can directly access a reference to an emitter Actor and use it to control the activation state of a Particle System.

Dragging off a reference to a Particle System gives you access to two extremely useful nodes: Activate and Deactivate (see Figure 10.6).

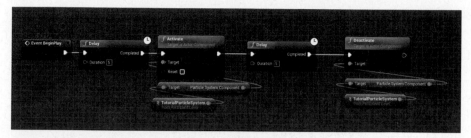

FIGURE 10.6
A simple level event graph that waits 5 seconds before activating a Particle System and then waits another 5 seconds before deactivating that same system.

Summary

This hour, you learned about UE4's modular approach to crafting and controlling particle effects. You learned about the tightly coupled relationship between Particle Systems and the materials attached to them. You saw the powerful SubUV texture technique and learned how to trigger effects from Level Blueprints. Creating Particle Systems is a deep topic and can take time to master, but the fundamentals covered in this hour form the backbone of nearly every effect imaginable.

Q&A

Q. I've made what should be a one-shot effect, but it keeps restarting. How do I fix this?

A. In the Required module of an emitter, the number of loops of a particle is set on the Emitter Loops property. If the value is equal to 0, the emitter repeats endlessly. Try setting its value to 1 to play the effect only once.

Q. I've hooked up my Particle System in Level Blueprints to activate after a trigger, but it keeps playing at the start of the level. How do I stop it from playing until I'm ready?

A. Remember to uncheck the **Auto Activate** property on the emitter Actor in the level. The Auto Activate property is on by default, and as long as it is on, the emitter always starts playing when the game starts.

Q. I'm trying to use a SubUV texture, but the shown texture looks wrong. My effect is being clipped weirdly. What is wrong?

A. The most common reason for clipped or weird textures is inaccurate SubUV settings. In the Required node, try changing the SubUV Horizontal and SubUV Vertical properties to better match your source texture.

Q. **The Color setting modules do not seem to be affecting my particles. What might be happening?**

A. Take a moment to check the material you are using to make sure the particle color input node is being used properly. The RGB properties need to end up in the channels that you want the color to affect. Similarly, the ALPHA output needs to end up in either the Opacity channel or the Opacity Mask channel. If the Opacity and Opacity Mask channels are grayed out, the problem may lie in the material settings. Make sure Blend Mode is set to **Translucent or Masked**.

Workshop

Now that you have finished the hour, see if you can answer the following questions.

Quiz

1. True or false: Each Particle System can have only one Particle Emitter.

2. True or false: An emitter cannot have multiples of the same module active at the same time.

3. True or false: Curve values can be modified either in the Details panel or the Curve Editor.

4. True or false: GPU and CPU particles are identical except for the quantity that can be simulated efficiently.

Answers

1. False. Particle Systems can have any number of emitters.

2. False. Some modules can be stacked. In that case, the modules apply their attributes in top-down order, concatenating their effects together. Some modules stomp over the values previously changed above.

3. True. The Curve Editor provides a more intuitive way to modify curve distributions, but using the Details panel is a perfectly valid way to modify curve attributes.

4. False. GPU particles can be simulated in much higher quantities, but some modules cannot be used with them. When a module that is incompatible with a data type is added, a red X appears, and an error message describes the issue.

Exercise

Practice making new Particle Systems and play around with the different modules available to you for controlling Particle Emitters. Look at the /Game/Particles/P_Explosion Particle System and modify it to become a blue energy explosion.

1. In the Hour_10 project, open the /Game/Particles/P_Explosion Particle System.

2. In the Shockwave emitter, select the **Color Over Life** module. Change the point 0 and 1 colors to a pale electric blue.

3. Change the fireball's **Required** module's material to the provided **/Game/Material/ M_explosion_subUV_blue**.

4. Modify the fireball's **Color Over Life** curve to the same electric blue color chosen in step 2.

5. Repeat steps 2–4 for the remaining modules.

HOUR 11
Using Skeletal Mesh Actors

What You'll Learn in This Hour:

▶ Understanding what a Skeletal Mesh is and how it differs from a Static Mesh
▶ Importing a Skeletal Mesh from a 3D package
▶ Using the Persona Editor
▶ Playing animations on a new Skeletal Mesh Actor

Often, you need to handle more complex animations than simply moving the transform components of Static Meshes. One of the ways to create objects with different parts that move independently is to use a Skeletal Mesh. With Skeletal Meshes, you can breathe life into characters through animation. These animations are often made in third-party packages and imported into UE4. Most of the time when you play a game with a controlled character, that character is a Skeletal Mesh. This hour, you learn the power of Skeletal Meshes, how to import a character from a third-party package, and how to place and animate a Skeletal Mesh.

NOTE

Hour 11 Project Setup

For this hour, you need to open the Hour_11 project found in the Hour_11 folder (available on the book's companion website at www.sty-ue4.com), which contains Unreal animation content examples. If you would rather, though, you may use the marketplace to add the content examples manually.

Defining Skeletal Meshes

If Static Meshes make the game world, Skeletal Meshes make the game world feel alive. The primary difference between Static and Skeletal Meshes is evident in the names: In a Static Mesh, each vertex is bound to a single location, the object's pivot. In a Skeletal Mesh, vertices are manipulated by a skeleton-like hierarchy of independent locations. This hierarchy can make unique parts of a single mesh translate and animate independently of its neighbors. This fundamental ability allows the animation of complex characters, monsters, animals, vehicles, machines, and much more.

Figure 11.1 shows a Skeletal Mesh in UE4; in it, a skinned mesh is on top of the skeleton hierarchy in a resting pose. The white bones (or joints) are where animation will be played back, and the nearby skinned vertices of the mesh will deform to follow them.

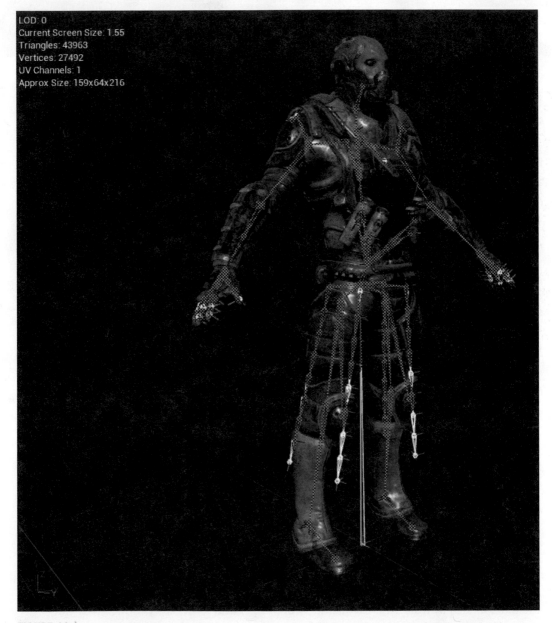

LOD: 0
Current Screen Size: 1.55
Triangles: 43963
Vertices: 27492
UV Channels: 1
Approx Size: 159x64x216

FIGURE 11.1
A Skeletal Mesh from the UE4 Matinee example project. This mesh has a series of bones that make up the skeleton (designated in the screenshot by the white lines). The nearby vertices have been *skinned*, or attached to the bones in a third-party program so they will follow the skeleton around as it animates.

The phrase *skinning* or *skinned mesh* refers to the process of binding vertices to the underlying skeleton. An artist creates a skinned mesh in a third-party content creation tool by telling each vertex which bone it should be bound to. A variety of packages and tools can be used for this process. Many such software packages have visualization modes to show the distribution of skin weights. Figure 11.2 shows an example of this.

FIGURE 11.2
A visualization of the vertex weighting of a character's lower left arm in Blender. In this visualization red indicates that the vertex will completely follow the selected bone, yellow or green indicates that multiple bones contribute to the vertex's position, and blue indicates that the vertex is unaffected by the selected bone.

Once the vertices are skinned to the skeleton, animators can rotate, translate, and scale the character's bones to create dynamic animations. Figure 11.3 shows an animated character.

FIGURE 11.3
A simple punching pose of the Owen character provided in the Unreal Engine 4 content examples.
The Hour 11 project includes this animation and character.

In Unreal Engine 4, animating a Skeletal Mesh takes at least three separate components.
Understanding what these components are and what they are responsible for individually is
imperative to working with Skeletal Meshes:

▶ **Skeletal Mesh:** The primary component, a Skeletal Mesh is the skinned vertices that go
   with a set of internal bones. This is the component that defines the appearance of the
   mesh, including how materials are assigned.

▶ **Skeleton:** Each Skeletal Mesh is attached to a separate asset called a skeleton. A skeleton
   can be shared between many Skeletal Meshes, but a single Skeletal Mesh can have only
   one skeleton. Disparate Skeletal Meshes (potentially with unique hierarchies) can be
   animated by UE4 using the same assets. This level of indirection allows different characters
   to share the same animations.

There are some rules about how Skeletal Meshes can share skeletons. Different hierarchies can be used, as long as the base bone hierarchy is the same. Removing a bone earlier in the hierarchy breaks the connection between the child bone and the skeleton. In addition, naming conventions between the skeleton and the Skeletal Mesh must match. All bones that are controlled by the skeleton must have exactly the same names in the skeleton and the Skeletal Mesh.

▶ **Animation sequence:** An animation sequence is a record of how a skeleton moves, including the keyframe location, rotation, and scale of each animated bone in the skeleton. An animation sequence can be assigned to only one skeleton, so if two Skeletal Meshes want to share the same animation asset, they must also share the same skeleton.

In addition to these three necessary components of animating a mesh, there are two other components of the skeleton system. These components are not absolute requirements, but they allow for extended behavior, especially when you're making characters:

▶ **Physics assets:** When you create characters, or Skeletal Meshes, that need to interact with the physics system, a fourth file, called a physics asset, is created, which defines the simplified collision geometry attached to the skeleton. This asset allows characters to ragdoll after death or to receive damage from ray sources.

▶ **Animation Blueprints:** Characters and meshes with complex animation requirements often make use of animation Blueprints. These specialized Blueprints are responsible for the logic necessary to choose which animation sequences to use at which times. Animation Blueprints are often responsible for handling animated locomotion, as well as blending between different animations based on user input.

Figure 11.4 shows the reference hierarchy of Skeletal Meshes, skeletons, and animations. This visualization shows the interface-like nature of the skeleton.

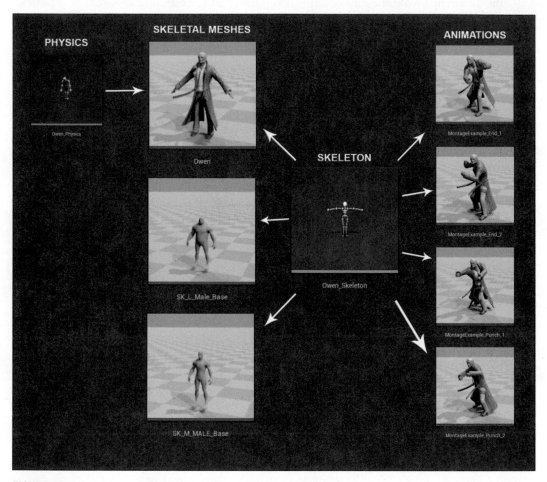

FIGURE 11.4
This is the reference hierarchy of Skeletal Meshes, skeletons, animation sequences, and physics assets. Each arrow points from the reference to the referencer. For example, skeleton assets do not know which animations use it, but each animation sequence knows which skeleton it is applied to.

Importing Skeletal Meshes

Unreal Engine 4 is a game engine, and for the most part, it isn't a content creation tool. As with Static Meshes or textures, to create a Skeletal Mesh you need to use a third-party program. UE4 interfaces with third-party programs through the use of the Autodesk Filmbox format (.fbx). An .fbx file contains the mesh, skeleton, and animation data necessary for UE4 to utilize animated characters.

NOTE

3D Software Packages

Creating your own characters can be an involved process and requires software other than UE4. Several different packages are commonly used, all of which are sufficient for the job. Autodesk's Maya, Autodesk's 3DS Max, and SideFX's Houdini are three professional paid software options, all of which have independent developer pricing. In addition to those packages, the free open source tool Blender can also do everything necessary to create and animate characters.

How to do skinning and animation are both beyond the scope of this book, but this hour does discuss importing Skeletal Meshes and animations into UE4, and there are a few things to keep in mind when importing. Before you import a Skeletal Mesh, it first needs to be exported from the content creation package in which it was made. Although each software package handles this step a bit differently, a few best practices apply to exporting from any package:

▶ Triangulating the mesh prior to export is always preferred.

▶ When exporting, it is best to select the root of the mesh skeleton and use an option such as Export Selected Only.

▶ Smoothing groups should be enabled.

▶ Preserver edge orientation should be enabled.

▶ Tangent and binomials (also known as tangent space) should be disabled.

CAUTION

Editor Unit Scale

Most content packages treat 1 unit to mean 1 meter. Unreal Engine is different, treating 1 unit as 1 centimeter. Therefore, when you're working with content creation packages, it is important to either account for this difference on export or potentially change the Editor in the content creation program to match UE4's unit scale. If changing this option in a content creation package is not possible, you can set the Import Uniform Scale option to 0.01 under Transform Options in UE4's FBX import dialog to fix this discrepancy.

The included Blender file Hour_11/RAW/BlenderFiles/_UE4_StartupFile.blend sets Blender's scale environment to match the scale of UE4. If you use this file, or if you set your package to treat 1 unit as 1 centimeter, will prevent you from having to constantly change import and export scales.

NOTE

Sample Files

The Hour_11/RAW folder (available on the book's companion website) includes a few test assets you can use to practice importing. Some associated Blender scene files are also available in this folder.

Importing a Skeletal Mesh and creating a skeleton for the first time is as simple as dragging and dropping an .fbx file into the Content Browser or importing it by clicking the **Import** button. When you do this, you get the dialog shown in Figure 11.5. This dialog allows you to create a new skeleton if one doesn't yet exist for the imported mesh.

FIGURE 11.5
The FBX Import Options dialog that appears when a Skeletal Mesh is detected in UE4.

It is important to note some of the properties in the FBX Import Options dialog:

▶ **Import as Skeletal:** When this option is checked, the mesh is treated as a Skeletal Mesh. If it is unchecked, the imported mesh is just a Static Mesh.

▶ **Import Mesh:** Unchecking this option causes UE4 to ignore the mesh completely.

▶ **Skeleton:** This asset reference option allows you to use an existing skeleton. If you leave this option blank, however, a new skeleton is created. When importing a Skeletal Mesh for the first time, it is a good idea to leave this empty and to use it only for subsequent meshes.

▶ **Import Animations:** This option allows you to import animations. You can import an animation at the same time you first import a Skeletal Mesh and create a skeleton, but it is usually good practice to first import a mesh with no animations attached and the character in a default bind pose. To only import animations and not the Skeletal Meshes, keep Import Animations checked and uncheck Import Mesh.

▶ **Transform:** Occasionally, different software packages use a scene setup that UE4 cannot account for. You can use the options in the Transform section to correct these differences. In general, it is best to leave these at their default values and modify the software package to better match UE4.

▶ **Import Materials:** Most of the time when you first import a Skeletal Mesh, it is a good idea to import materials. With the Import Materials option checked, new default materials are created next to the Skeletal Mesh, with the same names used in your creation package. Because most creation packages do not use the same material system as UE4, you usually end up replacing these materials later.

▶ **Convert Scene:** The .fbx coordinate system is substantially different from UE4's. In most cases, the Convert Scene check box should remain checked unless you've intentionally changed your .fbx to match UE4. Selecting this check box causes UE4 to convert the Y+ up axis of most content packages to the Z+ up axis of Unreal Engine.

After you click **Import** on the FBX Import Options dialog, the requested files are created, including a new skeleton. Figure 11.6 shows the files UE4 creates with the settings shown in Figure 11.5 when you import Hour_11/RAW/HeroTPP.fbx.

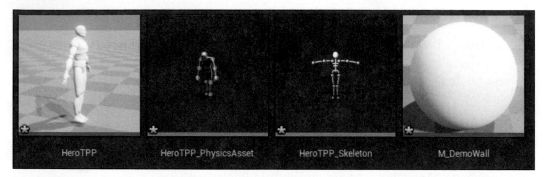

FIGURE 11.6
The files created by the FBX Import Options dialog using the settings defined in Figure 11.5.

TIP

Bones Are Missing from the Bind Pose

Depending on the 3D package you are using to create your content, the .fbx file may or may not include information about the bind pose. If it doesn't, you may get a set of warnings on import starting with:

```
"The following bones are missing from the bind pose:"
```

If the Skeletal Mesh in your 3D Package is in the correct bind pose at frame 0, you should import the Skeletal Mesh again with the **Use T0 as Ref Pose** option enabled. You can find this option by clicking the advanced options downward-pointing arrow at the bottom of the Mesh section of the FBX Import Options dialog.

Before moving on to how to use and modify these assets, use the next Try It Yourself section to practice importing Skeletal Meshes.

▼ TRY IT YOURSELF

Import the Hero

The first step with using an asset is always getting the asset into Unreal Engine 4. Use the provided HeroTPP.fbx file and follow these steps to try importing a new Skeletal Mesh:

1. In Hour 11 Project's Content Browser, navigate to the **TryItYourself** folder, and then open the _1 folder (available on the book's companion website).

2. Click the **Import** button in the top-left corner of the Content Browser.

3. Using the Import dialog, navigate to **/Hour_11/RAW/HeroTPP.fbx** and click **Open**.

4. In the FBX Import Options dialog that appears, make sure **Import as Skeletal** and **Import Mesh** and **Use T0 as Ref Pose** are all checked. (Remember that you find the **Use T0 as Ref Pose** option by clicking the downward-pointing arrow at the bottom of the Mesh section.)

5. Make sure the Skeleton property is set to **None** to ensure that a new skeleton is created.

6. Uncheck the **Import Animations** check box.

7. Ensure that **Convert Scene** at the bottom of the dialog box is checked.

8. Click **Import**.

9. When the import finishes, compare your results to those in Content/TryItYourself/_1_Result.

Just importing animations is similar to importing Skeletal Meshes, but the process is slightly different. When importing an animation for an existing skeleton, it is important that you set the **Skeleton** property in the FBX Import Options dialog to a compatible skeleton. (The bone hierarchy information must be the same as the hierarchy used to create the animation.)

Also, when you import an animation from a 3D package, it is important to make sure the **Import Animation** option is checked, and it's usually best to uncheck the **Import Mesh** option. This way you avoid importing and duplicating your meshes every time you import a new animation.

Learning Persona

Unreal Engine 4 contains a special Editor, the Persona Editor, for working with Skeletal Meshes, skeletons, animation sequences, and animation Blueprints. The Persona Editor is a one-stop shop for everything to do with animating characters.

Persona is a combined Editor with separate editing modes for the different asset types that make up an animated character. This Editor style allows you to make use of the tightly integrated nature of animation assets.

Double-clicking the type of asset you want to edit automatically opens the Persona Editor to the correct editing mode for that asset.

Skeleton Mode

Figure 11.7 shows the Persona Editor's Skeleton mode. The components of the Editor are
1) Reference Pose button; 2) Skeleton Mode button; 3) Skeleton tree; 4) Persona Viewport.
The different components are numbered on the figure and described in the following list:

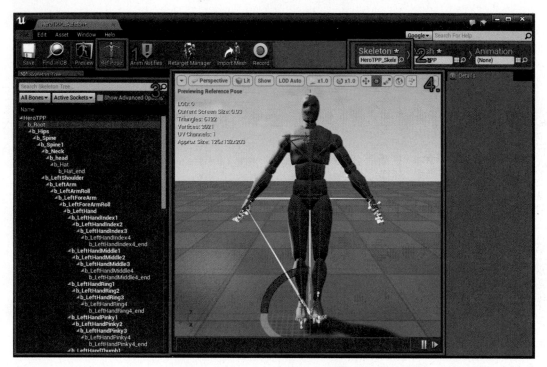

FIGURE 11.7
Persona's Skeleton mode, with points of interest highlighted.

▶ **Reference Pose button:** This commonly used button stops any playing animations and
  returns the character to its reference pose.

▶ **Skeleton Mode button:** This button puts Persona into the Skeleton mode, and it also
  contains an asset reference that allows you to find the edited skeleton in the Content Browser.

▶ **Skeleton tree:** This area displays the hierarchical outline of bones in the skeleton.
  When you select a bone in this hierarchy, you can then manipulate it in the Viewport.
  In addition, right-clicking any bone here allows you to add a socket, which allows for
  additional meshes to be added dynamically.

▶ **Persona Viewport:** The Persona Viewport is a miniature scene view that shows the selected
  skeleton and Skeletal Mesh. In this Viewport, you can reposition, rotate, or scale bones,
  and you can preview animations. You can see additional information about the mesh in
  the top-left corner of this Viewport.

Mesh Mode

Figure 11.8 shows the Persona Editor's Mesh mode. The components of the Editor are 1) Mesh Mode button; 2) LOD settings category; 3) Physics category; 4) LOD Visualizer; 5) Viewport statistics; 6) Morph Target Previews tab. The different components are described in the following list:

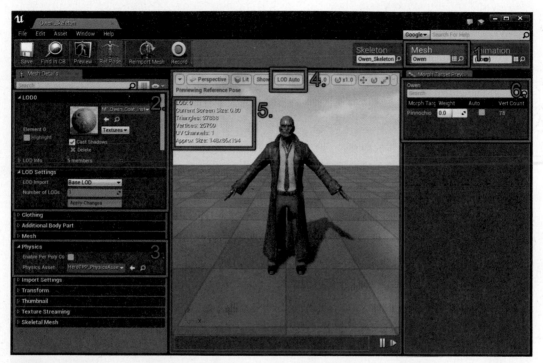

FIGURE 11.8
Persona's Mesh editing mode with points of interest highlighted.

▶ **Mesh Mode button:** This button puts Persona into Mesh mode, and also contains an asset reference that allows a different mesh to be selected and edited through a drop-down menu.

▶ **LOD Settings category:** In this part of the Details panel (which closely resembles the Details panel of a Static Mesh asset), the top categories are reserved for LOD and material information. In this section you can tell UE4 to generate extra LODs, and you can set materials on those LODs.

▶ **Physics category:** In the Details panel, the Physics category is where you can apply a Skeletal Mesh's physics asset. There is also an **Enable per Poly Collision** option. By default, this option is turned off, and in most cases it should be. Per-poly collision cannot be used for physics simulations like ragdolls, but it can be used for ray-cast queries. In most cases you should leave this check box disabled and instead use a Physics asset.

▶ **LOD Visualizer:** This option can override the displayed LOD, allowing you to visualize the different LODs on your mesh. The setting LOD Auto allows the Viewport to automatically LOD the character based on view settings. LODs need to be created for this to work.

▶ **Viewport statistics:** In the top left of the Viewport, you see commonly used statistics about the displayed mesh. These stats include the poly-count, the requested LOD, and the approximate size of the Skeletal Mesh.

▶ **Morph Target Previews tab:** Although this hour doesn't cover morph targets, it is worth noting that this tab is where you can preview morph targets. In the animation content examples provided by Unreal, for example, you can find the Pinnochio morph target example on the Owen Skeletal Mesh. Modifying the weight of the Pinnochio morph target extends Owen's nose out exceptionally far.

Animation Mode

Figure 11.9 shows the Persona Editor's Animation mode. The components of the Editor are 1) Create Asset button; 2) Animation Mode button; 3) Details panel; 4) Anim Asset details; 5) Anim Sequence Editor; 6) Timeline; 7) Asset Browser. The different components are described in the following list:

FIGURE 11.9
Persona's Animation editing mode with points of interest highlighted.

▶ **Create Asset button:** This button provides a convenient way to create new montages, animation sequences, and other animation type assets.

▶ **Animation Mode button:** This button puts Persona into Animation mode, and it also contains an asset reference that allows a different mesh to be selected and edited through a drop-down menu.

▶ **Details panel:** You use this panel to edit socket and anim notify properties.

▶ **Anim Asset details:** This section shows the available properties for editing on the animation asset selected in the Asset Browser. You can use this section to modify asset-specific settings.

▶ **Anim Sequence Editor:** Many animation assets have some properties that are Timeline based. In this section you can modify Additive Animation Curves, Notifications, and Tracks in a Timeline keyframe fashion.

▶ **Timeline:** You can modify the current playback time and animation controls here. By clicking and dragging the red box in the Timeline, you can move the play head to scrub through the selected animation.

▶ **Asset Browser:** This quick browser is for animation assets. Double-clicking an asset in this browser sets it as the edited preview asset. If you mouse over an asset, a quick real-time preview of the animation appears in a pop-up.

In Animation mode, you can make simple animations entirely in the Persona Editor. This process is not as streamlined as in most 3D content creation packages, but it is entirely doable, and for simple animations, this can be very useful. This process takes advantage of the Additive Animation Tracks setting on an animation sequence, and to use it, you set animation keyframes for different bones you want to animate on a skeleton.

To set a key on an existing animation sequence, you select a bone in the skeleton and then click the + **Key** button in the toolbar (see Figure 11.10). Next, you rotate or position the bone (pressing the E key to bring up the rotation handle or **W** to bring up the translation handle) to the new desired location and then press the **Apply** button on the toolbar to save those results. You then move the play head to a new point in the Timeline and repeat the process.

FIGURE 11.10
The highlighted + Key and Apply buttons on the toolbar allow you to create animations of your own directly in the Persona Editor.

After you apply an additive animation to a bone by using this process, you can manually modify the keys through the Curves Editor in the Anim Sequence Editor section below the Viewport. You can add new keys by right-clicking in the Track Viewport. Figure 11.11 shows the different context menus for an edited bone.

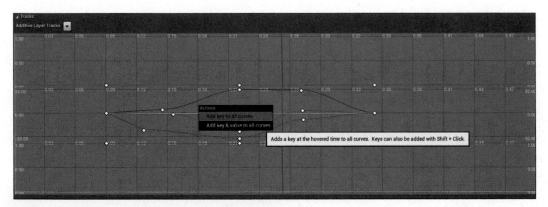

FIGURE 11.11
Right-clicking in a bone's additive curve track allows you to add new keys. You can also manually move keys in this Editor. In addition, the down arrow in the top-left corner allows you to remove or disable individual tracks.

▼ TRY IT YOURSELF

Shake the Hero's Head

Sometimes using the Additive Animation Tracks option is enough to create a simple animation. Follow these steps to create a new animation sequence that shakes the Owen character's head:

1. In the Hour 11 project's Content Browser, navigate to the **TryItYourself/_1** folder. (If you didn't do the first Try It Yourself this hour, navigate to the **Hour_11/TryItYourself/_1_Result** folder instead.)

2. Double-click the **HeroTPP** Skeletal Mesh asset to open the Persona Editor for this Skeletal Mesh.

3. Click the **Animation Mode** tab at the top right of the Persona Editor.

4. Click the **Create Asset** button in the Persona toolbar.

5. Select **Create Animation > From Reference Pose**.

6. To set the length of the animation, right-click the Timeline at the bottom of Persona and select **Append at the End**.

7. In the field that appears, type in **119** to set the animation to 120 frames.

8. Click on the Viewport and press the **E** key to switch to the rotation editing mode. (Alternatively, you can click the **Rotate** tool in the top right of the Viewport.)

9. In the skeleton tree's search box, type **Head** and then select the **b_head** bone.

10. If it isn't already there, drag the **Timeline** slider to frame 0.

11. Click the + **Key** button on the toolbar twice to create a zeroed-out key on frame 0.

12. Drag the **Timeline** slider to the last frame in the sequence (frame 120).

13. Click the + **Key** button on the toolbar twice again to create a zeroed-out key frame on the last frame. This will allow the animation to loop nicely.

14. Move the **Timeline** slider to the first one-third of the animation, around frame 40.

15. Click the + **Key** button and rotate the character's head to the left about 50°.

16. Click the + **Key** button again to confirm your changes.

17. Move the **Timeline** slider to the second one-third of the animation, around frame 60.

18. Click the + **Key** button and rotate the character's head to the right 50°. This should mirror the key frame set on frame 40.

19. Confirm the keyframe by clicking the + **Key** button again.

20. Click the **Apply** button on the toolbar to confirm that you are done making changes.

21. Click the **Play** arrow on the Timeline to preview your animation.

22. Compare your result to the animation sequence available in TryItYourself/_2_Result.

Graph Mode

Figure 11.12 shows the Persona Editor's Graph mode, which is by far the most complicated editing mode in Persona. Graph mode works in conjunction with animation Blueprint assets to handle the logic for blending different animation states and behaviors.

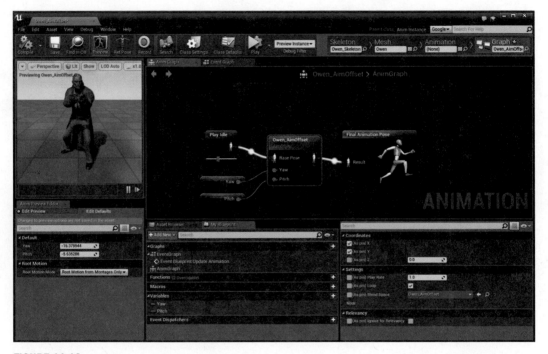

FIGURE 11.12
You use Graph mode to handle the logic behind complex blending of different animations and behaviors.

Unlike the other modes, Graph mode's tab appears only when you're opening an animation Blueprint.

Graph mode is critical when you're working with complex character animations, especially those that are driven by the user. Animation Blueprints control animation on Skeletal Meshes through driving blend space assets or aim offset assets, directly blending two anim sequences, and even directly controlling the bones of a skeleton.

TIP

The powerful set of tools available in Graph mode can be overwhelming at first, and explaining them all is beyond the scope of this book. If you are interested in learning more about animation Blueprints and Persona's Graph mode, take a look into the included animation demo. Open `Hour_11/ExampleContent/AnimationDemo/AnimBlueprint` directory in the `Hour_11` project (available on the book's companion website) to see several different examples of animation Blueprints handling different use cases.

In addition, the excellent video series *3rd Person Game with Blueprints (v4.8)* produced by Epic Games goes into more detail about what animation Blueprints are. This series is available on the Unreal Engine wiki, at http://wiki.unrealengine.com.

Using Skeletal Mesh Actors

One of the primary ways to use animated Skeletal Meshes is simply to place them in a scene as Actors. Luckily, this is as simple as placing any other Actor in a scene. Dragging a Skeletal Mesh from the Content Browser to the Viewport is an efficient way to place a Skeletal Mesh as an Actor.

A Skeletal Mesh Actor does have some unique properties that are worth keeping in mind (see Figure 11.13).

FIGURE 11.13
A placed Skeletal Mesh Actor has settings for playing animations immediately or through an animation Blueprint. The different Details panels for Animation mode are shown here.

In the Animation category of properties for a Static Mesh Actor, controls are available to set animations playing, set whether the animations loop, and at what point they start, as well as the speed at which they play back:

▶ **Animation Mode:** This option allows you to specify whether to use an animation Blueprint or a single animation asset. Setting this option to **Use Animation Asset** makes the following options available.

▶ **Anim to Play:** This option allows you to specify a reference from the Content Browser to a single animation asset.

▶ **Looping:** When checked, the Looping Boolean means the animation will play continuously by looping back to the start of the animation when it finishes.

▶ **Playing:** When checked, the Playing Boolean means the animation will play when the game begins instead of waiting to be set manually through Blueprints or some other method. Turn this off if you want to control when the animation starts playing.

▶ **Initial Position:** You can specify a value (in seconds) that determines the starting time of the animation. Scrubbing this value is a good way to visualize the poses an animation goes through.

▶ **PlayRate:** This value is a multiplier of how fast the animation plays back. Setting it to 0.5 causes the animation to play half as fast as default; on the other hand, a value of 2.0 causes the animation to play twice as fast.

▼ TRY IT YOURSELF

Place the Hero

Animations aren't useful if they aren't ever played. Follow these steps to place HeroTPP into a new scene and set him up to play the head shaking animation you created in the last Try It Yourself:

1. Create a new default level in the Hour 11 project.

2. In the Hour 11 project's Content Browser, navigate to the **TryItYourself/_1** folder. (If you didn't do the first Try It Yourself this hour, navigate to the **Hour_11/TryItYourself/_1_Result** folder instead.)

3. Select the **HeroTPP** Skeletal Mesh, drag it into the world, and place it near the origin.

4. Select the new Skeletal Mesh Actor and in the Details panel for the Actor, switch Animation Mode to **Use Animation Asset**.

5. In the Content Browser, navigate to the **Hour_11/TryItYourself/_2** folder. (If you didn't do the second Try It Yourself this hour, navigate to the **Hour_11/TryItYourself/_2_Result** folder instead.) In this folder, select the **HeroTPP_Skeleton_Sequence** animation sequence.

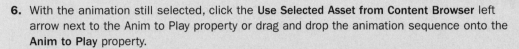

6. With the animation still selected, click the **Use Selected Asset from Content Browser** left arrow next to the Anim to Play property or drag and drop the animation sequence onto the **Anim to Play** property.

7. Ensure that **Looping** and **Playing** are both checked.

8. Click **Simulate** or **Play in Editor** to start the game and see your character animate.

9. Compare your result to the level available inHour_11/TryItYourself/_3_Result.

Summary

Skeletal meshes have an important place in a game maker's toolbox. With these incredibly versatile tools, you can bring to life diverse and interesting 3D characters. In this hour you learned the power and strength of Skeletal Meshes and how to import a brand-new Skeletal Mesh into the Editor. You learned about the many options you need to set to bring your Skeletal Mesh to life and how they work together. You also learned how to use the very powerful Persona Editor to make changes to a Skeletal Mesh and even create simple animations—entirely inside Unreal Engine 4. Finally, you learned how to place and play Skeletal Mesh Actors in a scene.

Q&A

Q. I don't know any 3D packages that can make Skeletal Meshes. Can I use UE4 instead?

A. Unfortunately, at this writing, UE4 does not contain any skinning or modelling tools. All is not lost, however, because there are many packages on the Unreal marketplace that provide prebuilt Skeletal Meshes and animation packs for your projects. In addition to paid options, the company Mixamo provides 15 excellent animated characters for free through the marketplace.

Q. When I import animations, the mesh looks heavily deformed and weirdly positioned—not at all like how the animation plays in the source package. What is happening?

A. Usually, if you experience heavily disparate deformations from the animation source, there is a scale discrepancy. Try setting Import Uniform Scale to **0.01** or **100** as a test. If either of these two options fixes the problem, take some time to check what unit scale your source package uses and whether you can switch it to match UE4 (1 unit = 1 cm).

Q. I don't want my animations to play at startup. Instead, I want them to play later. How do I make this happen?

A. On a Skeletal Mesh Actor, uncheck the **Playing** option. You can use level Blueprints to set the animation playing again by using either **Play** or **Play Animation** from a reference to your Skeletal Mesh Actor. (For more on level Blueprints, check out Hour 15, "Working with Level Blueprints.")

Workshop

Now that you have finished the hour, see if you can answer the following questions.

Quiz

1. True or false: Animation sequences and assets can play on any number of skeletons.

2. True or false: Each Skeletal Mesh requires a unique skeleton asset.

3. True or false: UE4 treats 1 unit as 1 cm.

4. True or false: Animations cannot be made in UE4 and must be made in an external package.

Answers

1. False. Each animation sequence is bound to the skeleton it is imported with. Although you can retarget an animation sequences to a new skeleton, doing so creates a unique asset.

2. False. Multiple different Skeletal Meshes can share the same skeleton, and this is why the same animations can be played on different Skeletal Meshes. With this in mind, all Skeletal Meshes that attempt to share the same skeleton must have the same base bone hierarchy and bone naming conventions. Any disruptions to the bones in the chain require a new skeleton asset to be used.

3. True. This is important when you're transferring any assets from one software package to another.

4. False. Although making animations is substantially easier in a dedicated program, you can make simple Skeletal Mesh animations in the Persona Editor by using the Additive Animation Tracks option.

Exercise

With the provided content examples, practice placing a variety of animations into a scene.

1. In the Hour_11 project (available on the book's companion website), create a new Level.

2. In the Content Browser, open the **ExampleContent/AnimationDemo/Animations** folder.

3. Pick a few Skeletal Mesh animations, such as **Jumping Jacks** or **Run Right**, from this folder and drag them into the scene.

4. Ensure that the animations are set to play and loop and then press **Simulate**.

HOUR 12
Matinee and Cinematics

What You'll Learn in This Hour:

▶ Working with Matinee Actors
▶ Using the Matinee Editor
▶ Working with Camera Actors
▶ Moving and rotating Actors over time

This hour introduces the Matinee Editor in UE4, which allows you to create in-game cut scenes, title sequences, and ambient environment animations. The Matinee Editor is the tool used mostly by cinematic artists, animators, and level designers. Over the next hour, you will learn about Matinee Actors, the Matinee Editor, and how to animate a short sequence.

NOTE

Hour 12 Project Setup

For this hour, you can create a new project with the First Person template and Starter Content, or you can use the book project and work in the Hour_12 folder (available on the book's companion website at www.sty-ue4.com).

Matinee Actors

Matinee in UE4 is a complete tool set and pipeline for creating in-game cinematics. Matinee can be used to animate various properties of many Actor types. You can use it to create videos, and you can export and import keyframe data through the use of the .fbx file format. You can have as many Matinee Actors in a single level as you need, and you can control Matinee Actors and pass events to Blueprint. This hour focuses on setting up and animating cameras.

Before you can begin to use the Matinee Editor, you first need a Matinee Actor in your level. The Matinee Actor does two main things: First, it allows you to set preferences on how the Matinee should behave in the level, and second, it points to a Matinee Data asset that stores the group, tracks, and keyframes for the Matinee sequence. You can add a Matinee Actor to a level in two ways: As with any other Actor, you can drag a Matinee Actor from the Modes panel or you can click the **Cinematics** icon on the Level Editor toolbar and select **Add Matinee**. Once you have placed a Matinee Actor in a level, you should give it a descriptive name in the Level Details panel (see Figure 12.1).

NOTE

Adding a Matinee Actor

If you add a Matinee Actor using the Cinematics icon on the Level Editor toolbar, the Matinee Editor opens automatically. To see the Matinee Actor's properties, you need to close the Editor and select the Matinee Actor in the Level Viewport.

Matinee Actor Properties

If you select a Matinee Actor and look at its properties in the Details panel, you can find the play rate of the Matinee under Play (see Figure 12.1). This value is normalized, so a value of 1 is 100% of the play rate, and 0.5 is 50%, or half speed. You also see a Play on Level Load option, which you can select to start the Matinee playing as soon as the level is loaded in memory. In addition, the Looping option allows you to set the Matinee to play continuously. The next section that is important to look at is Cinematic. Here you can find the ability to temporarily toggle on and off player movement and rotation inputs, and you can hide the player and HUD while the Matinee is playing. These options are typically meant for Matinees that use Director groups and Camera Actors.

NOTE

Playback Speed and Frame per Second

While Matinee uses a normalized value to determine the playback speed, the actual number of frames per second (FPS) is set inside the Matinee Editor through Snap Settings.

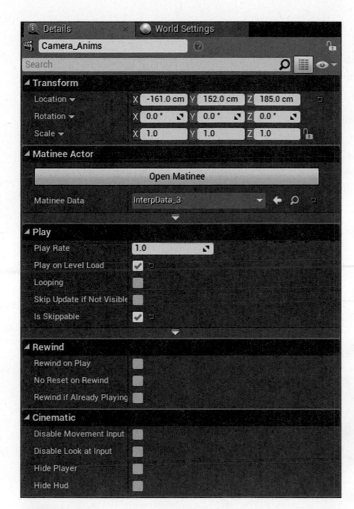

FIGURE 12.1
Matinee Actor properties.

Matinee Editor

Matinee Editor is the interface for editing animation sequences (see Figure 12.2). To open the Matinee Editor, select a Matinee Actor and, in the Details panel, click **Open Matinee**. The key areas of the Matinee Editor are indicated in Figure 12.2 and described in the following list:

▶ 1) **Menu bar:** You use the menu bar to perform operations such as importing and exporting Matinee data as an .fbx file or stretching a keyframe.

▶ 2) **Toolbar:** The toolbar has common operations such as playback and Snap Settings.

▶ 3) **Curve Editor:** The Curve Editor allows you to refine interpolation data through the use of splines.

▶ 4) **Tracks panel:** The Tracks panel allows you to manage groups and tracks and also set keyframes.

▶ 5) **Details panel:** The Details panel displays the properties of a selected track or group.

▶ 6) **Time Bar:** The Time Bar indicates times during the sequence.

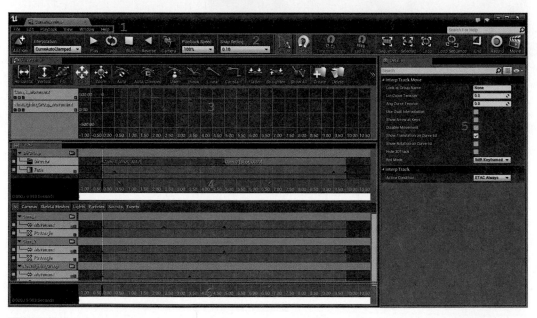

FIGURE 12.2
Matinee Editor.

NOTE

When Working in the Matinee Editor

Much of the work you do in Matinee requires you to have the Matinee Editor and Level Viewport visible at the same time. Although dual monitors are not required, having two monitors—and a mouse with a scroll wheel—make big difference when you're working with Matinee.

NOTE

Useful Controls and Shortcuts When Working with Matinee

Here are some useful shortcuts for use in Matinee:

▶ Rolling the middle mouse wheel up or down zooms in and out of the Timeline.

▶ Clicking the sequence icon on the Matinee tool fits the Timeline to the Viewport.

▶ Pressing the Enter key adds a keyframe to the selected track at the current time.

Tracks Panel

The Tracks panel is the area where you will spend the majority of your time when working with Matinee. The Track panel uses Groups and Tracks to keep things organized. At the top you see operations for displaying groups based on assigned Actor types. On the left side you have the group and track list, and at the bottom of the Tracks panel are the frame and time count, the play head, and the sequence length.

Setting Sequence Length

At the bottom of the Tracks panel, you can find the Timeline info, the play head, and the current time, as determined by the position of the play head. The total length of time of the sequence is indicated by the red triangle markers and the active work area by the green triangle markers, as shown in Figure 12.3. To set the length of time for the sequence, you need to position the red triangle markers. Click the red marker on the right side and drag it to the right to add more time or drag it to the left to reduce the length of time. If you are already at the end of the Tracks panel, remember that you can roll the middle mouse wheel to zoom out and display more time.

NOTE

Dead Space

When first starting out, many people make the mistake of thinking that a sequence ends with the last keyframe. This is not the case. Matinee plays all the way up to the red triangle marker. If you have finished setting keys, and there is dead space between the last key and the right red marker, you can drag the marker back to the last keyframe.

Play Head

The play head, or time marker, as shown in Figure 12.3, shows where you are in time while editing a sequence and allows you to place keyframes in a track at specific times. Clicking any empty space at the bottom of the Timeline moves the play head to that location. You can click+drag to scrub (that is, manually play) the sequence. The following areas are identified in Figure 12.3 with numbers: 1) Group; 2) Tracks; 3) Play Head/Scrub Bar; 4) Key; 5) Red Markers; 6) Green Markers.

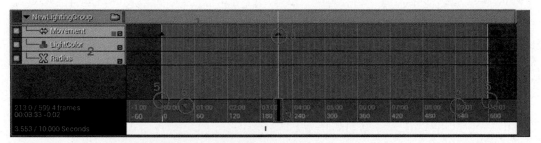

FIGURE 12.3
Red and green markers, play head, time, and frame count.

Groups

In Matinee, *groups* store the Actor or Actors that you want to control and the tracks that you are using to affect the assigned Actors (see Figure 12.4). There are five group presets: Empty group, Camera group, Particle group, Skeletal group, and Lighting group. With the exception of the Empty group, all the groups have preassigned tracks for working with specific Actor types identified by their names. The Empty group works with any Actor type, but you have to manually assign your own tracks based on the Actor you are animating and its properties.

To add a group, you first need to place the Actor you would like to control into a level. Then, with the Actor selected, you can add a group to the Matinee. Matinee automatically assigns the Actor to the group. To add a new group, right-click an empty area of the groups and tracks list on left side of the Tracks panel. In the dialog that appears, select the group that matches the placed Actor. If there is not a group listed for your Actor types, select Empty group and give it a name. After you do this, you are ready to assign new tracks and set keyframes.

TIP
_____

Assigning a New Actor to an Existing Group

If you need to change the Actor assigned to a group, select the new Actor in the Level Viewport and right-click the group name in the Tracks panel. In the dialog that appears, select **Actors > Replace Group Actors with Selected Actors.** When you add a Static Mesh Actor to a group, Matinee automatically changes its mobility settings to movable.
_____

Tracks

Tracks are used to set and store keyframe data over time for specified properties, and they are assigned to groups (see Figure 12.4). For example, the movement track stores the position and rotation data of an Actor. There are more than 16 predefined tracks. For some properties of an Actor that you might want to animate there may be a track that does not show up in the track list. The data type of the property determines what type of track you need. For example, the scale of a Static Mesh Actor can be animated, but there is no scale track in the list of tracks. Some properties are defined by their data type. Scale, for instance, stores the scale of an Actor as a vector (X, Y, Z). So if you want to modify the scale of an Actor, you need to add a vector property track to the group that has a Static Mesh asset assigned to it. Matinee shows you a list of the properties of the data type that can be affected. As another example, if you want to modify the intensity of a Point Light Actor, which is stored as a float, you need a float property track. Adding the float property track to a group that has a Point Light Actor assigned to it brings up a list of all the properties of the Point Light Actor that use a float value.

FIGURE 12.4
Groups and tracks.

GO TO ▶ CHAPTER 14, INTRODUCING BLUEPRINT VISUAL SCRIPTING SYSTEM, to learn more about variable data types.

NOTE
Keyframes

A key stores property settings data over time. The type of data depends on the Actor and the track you are using. Just about any Actor's properties and can animated over time. As Matinee plays, it interpolates between the stored values in each keyframe.

Folders

Folders are used to organize groups in Matinee. For example, you might have four or five groups, each set up to control a camera. In the Tracks panel, you can create a folder to store just the camera groups. Using folders helps you stay organized as the complexity of a Matinee sequence grows.

TIP
Order of Operations When Setting Keyframes

While adding a keyframe is a straightforward process, order of operations makes a big difference. The mantra to remember when you are first starting out is this: Move in time, move in space, add a key.

▶ **Move in time:** Move in time means to move the play head in the Tracks panel to the desired spot where you want to add a key.

▶ **Move in space:** Move in space means to move or rotate the Actor in the Level Viewport assigned to the group that contains the movement track you are adding the key to.

▶ **Add a key:** Add a key means to set a key at the current time on the relevant track to store the change in value.

Animate Static Mesh Actors and Set Keyframes in Matinee

Follow these steps to set keyframes and create a basic looping animation in Matinee:

1. Drag out a Static Mesh cube either from the Content Browser or from the Place tab in the Modes panel.

2. Drag out a Matinee Actor from the Place tab in the Modes panel and place it next to the cube in the level.

3. Select the Matinee Actor in the level and change its name in the Level Details panel to **move cube**. Then click **Open Matinee**.

4. In the Matinee Editor, right-click in the dark gray area on the left side of the track window and select **Create New Empty Group**.

5. Give the group the name **Cube_A**.

6. To assign a Static Mesh Actor to the group, in the Level Viewport, select the cube you placed in step 1, right-click the **Cube_A** group in the Matinee Editor, and select **Actors** > **Add Selected Actors**.

7. Turn on frame snapping by clicking the magnet icon on the Matinee toolbar and make sure Snap Setting is set to **0.5**.

8. To set the length of the Matinee to 3 seconds, at the bottom of the Tracks panel, drag the red triangle on the right side to 3 seconds.

9. Right-click the newly created group and add a new movement track from the list tracks.

10. To add a key, make sure the play head is at 0 seconds and that the Movement track is selected. Then click the **Add Key** icon on the Matinee toolbar or press **Enter**.

11. Move the play head to the end of the Matinee time (3 seconds, in this case) and add a second key by clicking the **Add Key** icon or pressing **Enter**. You now have two keys, one at the beginning and one at the end, that are storing the same position and rotation transform data at different times.

12. Move the play head to the middle of the Timeline, 1.5 seconds, and with the Matinee Editor window still open, select the placed cube in the Level Viewport and move it up on the Z axis about 500 units.

13. Select the movement track again and add a third key by clicking the **Add Key** icon or pressing **Enter**. A yellow spline appears in the Level Viewport, showing the path of the cube over the length of the sequence, which in this case is a straight line.

14. Scrub the play head back and forth, and you see the cube animate up and down. Click **Play** or **Looping** on the Matinee toolbar to preview the animation (see Figure 12.5).

15. To set the properties on the Matinee Actor, close the Matinee Editor and select the Matinee Actor in the Level Viewport. Then, in the Details panel of the main Editor, toggle on **Play on Level Load and Looping**.

16. Preview the level.

FIGURE 12.5
Groups and Tracks with red keyframes.

Curve Editor

The Curve Editor in Matinee gives you the ability to micromanage interpolation data represented as a spline. A *spline*, in this case, is a visual representation of the interpolated data over time. Just about every type of a track's keyframe data can be displayed and modified in the Curve Editor. The Curve Editor has its own toolbar for working with curves. To display a track's keyframe data in the Curve Editor, you need to toggle on the **Show on Curve Editor** box, which is the tiny box farthest to the right of the name of the track (see Figure 12.6). By default, when this box is dark gray, it is off; and when it's yellow, it is on. The following areas are identified in Figure 12.6 with numbers: 1) Lock View toggle; 2) Toggle Track on or off; 3) Show on Curve Editor toggle; 4) Show Spline path in Level Viewport.

FIGURE 12.6
Toggle on the Show on Curve Editor box.

Once you have toggled on **Show on Curve Editor** to display a track in the Curve Editor, the group and track name show up on the left side of the Curve Editor. You can have many tracks displaying curve data in the Curve Editor at one time if needed. You also most likely need to center the view. Press the **A** key to fit and display all active curves. Depending on the type of data a track is storing, you may have one or multiple curves associated with the track. For instance, a fade track used in a Director group uses only a float value, whereas a movement track has six curves: three for position (X, Y, and Z) and three for rotation (pitch, yaw, and roll). You can turn the visibility of each individual curve on or off in the Matinee Details panel with the track selected (see Figure 12.7). The following toggles are identified in Figure 12.7 with numbers: 1) Toggle visibility of X transition on Curve; 2) Toggle visibility of Y transition on Curve; 3) Toggle visibility of Z transition on Curve.

FIGURE 12.7
Display curve toggles in the Curve Editor.

NOTE

Movement Track

The movement track only displays curves for position by default. To show rotation data, you need to select the movement track, and in the Matinee Details panel, turn on **Show Rotation on Curve Editor**. You also might have noticed that position and rotation are stored in the same key. If you need to separate them, you can right-click the movement track and select **Split Translation and Rotation**, but once you make changes, you cannot go back without deleting the movement track and starting over.

Interpolation Modes

Interpolation (interp) modes, which are assigned to individual keys, determine how the spline transitions from one keyframe to the next. There are five types of interpolation modes, but for now we focus on three:

- ▶ **Curve (red):** This type of mode is used to control ease-in and ease-out effects. This is the mode to use when you want to edit a curve in the Curve Editor.

- ▶ **Linear (Green):** This type of mode stratifies the change in values between keyframes evenly over time.

- ▶ **Constant (Black):** This type of mode holds the last keyframes value for all the in-between frames until the next keyframe.

To change the interpolation of a key, right-click a keyframe in the Tracks panel and select **Interp Mode** and then the desired mode.

▼ TRY IT YOURSELF

Use the Curve Editor to Refine Animation Interpolations

Follow these steps to use the Curve Editor to control the rotation of an animated mesh:

1. Open the Matinee Editor for the Matinee Actor (MoveCube) from the previous Try It Yourself exercise.

2. In the Tracks panel, add another group and name it **Cube_B**.

3. Place another cube next to the first cube and assign it to the Cube_B group.

4. Add a movement track to the Cube_B group.

5. Add a key to frame 0 on the newly created movement track for group Cube_B.

6. In the Tracks panel move the play head to the end of the Matinee (3 seconds, in this case).

7. In the Viewport, rotate the new cube approximately 300 degrees on the Z axis.

8. Set a key. Now if you scrub the play head or press **Looping** on the Matinee toolbar, you see that the cube rotates the shortest distance. You could add more keyframes, but that would get messy, take more time, and be harder to edit later.

9. Display the Cube_B group's movement track on the Curve Editor and click the gray box on the right side of the movement track. At the moment, the Curve Editor is displaying only positional data.

10. With the movement track selected, in the Details panel toggle off **Show Translation on Curve Ed** and toggle on **Show Rotation on Curve Ed**.

11. In the Curve Editor toolbar, click the **Fit** icon to center and fit the curve data for the Cube_B movement track. Because only the Z axis has a change in rotation, you can turn off the display of the X and Y axes. In the Curve Editor window, under the Cube_B movement, click the red and green boxes so they are grayed out. Red is the X axis, green is the Y axis, and blue is the Z axis.

12. In the Curve Editor, right-click the first keyframe and set its value to **0**.

13. Right-click the second key and set its value to **359**.

14. Preview the level, and you see the cube now rotates 360 degrees and is looping, but because the default interpolation curve settings are set to **CurveAutoClamp**, there is ease in and ease out, which causes the cube to slow down and speed up. To change this, find the movement track for the Cube_B group in the Tracks panel, hold down **Ctrl**, and click the first and last keys so they are both selected.

15. Right-click one of the selected keys and choose **Interp Mode Linear** to straighten the curve so the rotation data will be evenly interpolated over the length of the animation.

16. Preview the level, and you should see that the cube rotates smoothly and continuously around the Z axis.

Working with Other Tracks

Thus far this hour you have been working with the Movement track, one of the most common tracks in the Matinee Editor. However, there are many more tracks you can work with, such as the Event track used to call events in Blueprint with a Matinee Controller node or an Animation track used to play animation sequences on a Skeletal Mesh Actor. For now, you will use a Sound track to play a sound through Matinee.

Sound Track

A Sound track in Matinee allows you to play a Sound Wave asset or a Sound Cue asset at a specific time in the Matinee sequences. The sound asset does not need to be an Actor in the level with its own group. You can just add a Sound track to an existing group.

When you set a keyframe on a Sound track, you need to have a Sound Wave or Sound Cue asset selected in the Content Browser. This sets a key and adds the sound asset to the track. The Selected Sound asset's name is displayed on the track along with a visual representation of its length. After you have a sound asset keyed, you can change the volume and pitch of the sound by right-clicking the key and selecting **Set Sound Volume or Sound Pitch**.

NOTE

Sound Asset Lengths

Sound assets already have set lengths determined by the original imported Sound Wave. If you need a shorter or longer sound, you can edit the asset in a sound editing program such as Audacity, or use a different sound asset.

▼ TRY IT YOURSELF

Add a Sound Track to an Existing Group

Follow these steps to play a sound in Matinee at a specific time during the sequence.

1. Open the Matinee Editor for the Matinee Actor (MoveCube) from the previous Try It Yourself exercises.

2. In the group and track list on the right side of the Tracks panel, right-click group Cube_A and select **Add a New Sound Track**.

3. In the Content Browser or Starter Content, click the **Explosion01** Sound Wave asset.

4. Move the play head to frame 0.

5. With the Sound track selected, add a key. Once the key is placed, you see a visual representation and the name of the Sound Wave in the Sound track.

6. Preview the Matinee by clicking **Play** on the Matinee toolbar.

Working with Cameras in Matinee

The real power in Matinee lies in working with cameras to create in-game cut scenes. For this last part of the hour, you look at working with Camera Actors and Camera groups in Matinee and using the Director group to switch between cameras.

Camera Groups and Actors

The Camera group places a Camera Actor automatically. The Camera group already has a FOVAngle and movement track for animating a Camera Actor. There are, however, many more properties of a camera that can be animated with a Camera Actor assigned to the Camera group. For example, if you add a float property track to a Camera group you get a huge list of properties that can be keyframes.

NOTE

Camera Actors

The Camera group places a Camera Actor automatically, but if you already have a Camera Actor, you can just use any empty group and assign movement and/or an FOVAngle track, as needed. If you add a track and decide you don't need it, you can simply select the track and press **Delete** to remove it.

TRY IT YOURSELF ▼

Add and Animate Two Cameras

Follow these steps to create a new 10-second Matinee sequence and animate two cameras.

1. Add a new Matinee Actor and name it **Camera_anims**.

2. In the Tracks panel, add a new Camera group and name it **Cam_1**. Matinee automatically adds a Camera Actor to the level and adds a field of view (FOVAngle) track and a movement track to the Camera group. It even creates the first keyframe on frame 0 for you. (You don't have to animate the FOVAngle if you don't want. You can leave it, or you can select the track and press **Delete** to remove it. If you change your mind later, you can simply add a new FOVAngle track back to the group.)

3. In the Tracks panel, set the Matinee time by dragging the red triangle on the right side to 5 seconds.

4. Turn on the Lock view camera icon to the right of the Cam_1 group to change the view in the Viewport so it looks through the camera assigned to this group. Then, if you move around the level with the Matinee Editor still open, you will be moving this camera around. Don't worry—the camera position will not be recorded until you set a key. If you scrub the play head, the camera resets to its last keyframe.

5. While looking through the camera, move the play head to 2.5 seconds, and then move the camera by navigating in the Viewport.

6. To set a key for the camera, ensure that the camera is placed where you want it, select the **Cam_1 movement** track in the Matinee Editor, and set a keyframe.

7. Move the play head to 5 seconds and move the camera to a new position. Set the last keyframe.

8. To add a second camera, move to a new location in the Level Viewport, add another Camera group, and name the group **Cam_2**. Because the first camera is set up to animate over the first 5 seconds, you need to animate the second camera for the last 5 seconds. Remember that the first keyframe is automatically created when you add the Camera group. Move the play head to 5 seconds without moving the new camera and add a keyframe.

9. To create a simple camera pan, make sure the camera view icon is not selected and move the play head to the last 10 seconds. (Making sure the camera view icon is not selected allows you to move and rotate the camera without looking through it.)

10. Move the second camera on one of its axes for about 200 units and set a key.

11. Scrub the play head or click **Looping,** and you see the cameras animate. The first camera moves for the first 5 seconds, and the second camera moves for the last 5 seconds.

Director Group

The Director group is a unique group that allows you to work like a film editor. When added, the Director group shows up at the top of the Tracks panel. You can have only one Director group per Matinee. A Director group with a Director track that has a Camera group assigned to it takes over the player's view while the Matinee sequence plays. The Director group gives you the ability to switch between cameras through the use of a director track and add cinematic effect such as fade-ins and fade-outs and slow motion.

Director Group Tracks

Some tracks are unique to the Director group, such as fade and slomo tracks. Director group tracks affect an entire sequence, regardless of the camera that is being used. Setting a keyframe on a track in a Director group works the same as for any other track: Move the play head to the desired frame, select the track, and add a key. Keyframes for most of the director tracks can be displayed and edited in the Curve Editor for further refinement.

Here is a list the Director group tracks and what they are used for:

- ▶ **Director:** This track switches the current view between Camera groups throughout the sequence.

- ▶ **Fade:** This track allows you to set fade-ins/fade-outs over the sequence on the active camera, as determined by the director track. A keyframe value of 0 is visible and the keyframe value 1 is black.

- ▶ **Slomo:** This track uses keys to temporarily change the playback speed of the sequence.

- ▶ **Audio master:** This track controls the volume and pitch of all the audio tracks in the sequence.

- ▶ **Color scale:** This track changes the color tinting of the rendered frame while the Matinee sequence is playing. RGB values must be set in the Curve Editor.

To add a track to the Director group, right-click the Director group in your Matinee and add the desired track from the list, as shown in Figure 12.8.

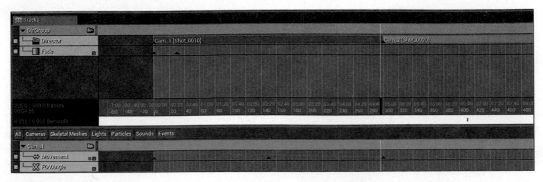

FIGURE 12.8
Director Group with a Director track and a Fade track.

NOTE

Camera Groups

If you are going to loop a Matinee, do not use a Director track in the Director group. Because the Director track tells the Matinee to take over the player's view, the player will be stuck watching the Matinee forever.

TRY IT YOURSELF ▼

Use the Director Group to Cut between Cameras

Use a Director group to change which camera the player sees through:

1. Right-click on a blank location on the left side of the Tracks panel and select **Add New Director Group**. Matinee splits the Tracks panel into two sections, with the Director group at the top. The Director group already has a director track, which is unique to a Director group.

2. Move the play head to frame 0, and with the Director track selected, add a keyframe. In the dialog that appears, choose **Cam_1** and click **OK**.

3. Move the play head to 5 seconds and add another keyframe to the Director track, only this time pick **Cam_2** and click **OK**. Now when the Matinee is played, it switches the view between the two Camera groups.

4. Toggle on the camera icon for the Director group so you are looking through the Director group's view, and scrub the animation or click **Looping** on the Matinee toolbar. You should be able to see from both cameras' points of view as the Matinee plays.

5. To prep the Matinee Actor so it plays when the level loads, close the Matinee Editor, select the Matinee Actor, and in the Details panel turn on **Play on Level Load**.

6. Preview the Level.

Working with Matinee Data Assets

By default, every time you place a new Matinee Actor, you create a Matinee asset that is embedded in the Matinee Actor. Most of the time this is all you need. If, however, your project needs to reuse the same cinematics and animation repeatedly, you can benefit by creating a Matinee Data asset. A Matinee Data asset stores group, track, folder, and keyframe data and is accessible through the Content Browser, which means you can also use it with Matinee Actors in other levels as well.

Here are the steps to take to create your own Matinee Data asset:

1. Create a folder called **MatineeData** for your project in the Content Browser.

2. Right-click in the folder select **Create Advanced Asset** > **Miscellaneous,** and click on **Matinee Data.**

3. Give the new Matinee Data asset a name and save it.

4. Place a Matinee Actor in the level. In the Details panel for the Matinee Actor, click the Matinee Data Properties drop-down and select the Matinee Data asset you created in steps 2 and 3.

You can now assign this data asset to as many Matinee Actors as needed. If you edit this data, it updates across all the Matinee Actors that reference the Matinee Data asset.

Summary

This hour you learned about working with the Matinee Editor to animate Static meshes and Camera Actors. The Matinee workflow is primarily for creating passive cut scenes and controlling looped ambient environment animated sequences. If you want to create animated assets that the player can interact with, you should use Blueprints and the Timeline, as discussed in Hour 16, "Working with Blueprint Classes."

Q&A

Q. The player still has control of the pawn while a cinematic is playing. How can I turn this off?

A. In the Details panel for the placed Matinee Actor, go to the Cinematic section. Here you can turn off player movement and hide the player pawn or HUD while the Matinee is playing.

Q. Is it possible to select multiple keyframes at one time?

A. Yes, in the Tracks panel or the Curve Editor, you can **Ctrl+Alt+click+drag** to create a drag selection or you can **Ctrl+click** to add to the current selection.

Q. How do I change the position of an individual keyframe?

A. Select the key, hold down **Ctrl,** and drag the key to a new location in the Timeline.

Q. How do I delete a group, a track, or a keyframe?

A. Simply select any of these and press the **Delete** key.

Q. I created a great animation, but it plays too fast. Can I change the spacing of the keyframes in order to change the timing of the animation?

A. Yes. You can manually select and move each keyframe, which could take forever, depending on the number of keyframes. A better way is to drag a selection to select the keys you want to change and then select **Edit > Stretch Selected Keyframes**. In the dialog that appears, you can set new timing for the selected keyframes.

Q. I am trying to animate a door opening and closing, but the pivot point of the mesh is in the wrong location. How do I change the pivot point of a Static Mesh Actor that I am trying to animate?

A. The best way is to edit the mesh in a 3D application and reimport it. But as a workaround, you can also attach the door mesh to a parent Actor and then animate the parent Actor. The parent Actor effectively becomes the pivot point. You can set the parent Actor's render properties in the Level Details so it is hidden in game and only the door mesh will be seen.

Workshop

Now that you have finished the hour, see if you can answer the following questions.

Quiz

1. True or false: It is possible to change the Actor that is being controlled by a group in a Matinee.

2. True or false: Cameras have to be animated in a separate Matinee from other Actors.

3. True or false: The scale of a Static Mesh cannot be animated.

4. True or false: A Matinee Data asset can be used across multiple levels.

Answers

1. True. You can assign and reassign Actors to existing groups in Matinee.

2. False. Cameras and other assets can be animated in a single Matinee Actor.

3. False. The scale of Static Mesh can be animated with a Vector Property track.

4. True. Matinee Data assets are stored in the Content Browser and can be used across multiple Matinee Actors in different levels.

Exercise

Create a 15-second cinematic of an epic door opening. The cinematic should use several cameras and fade in on the first camera and fade out on the last camera.

1. Create a new default map.

2. Add a Matinee Actor to the level.

3. In the Level Details panel under Play, set the Matinee Actor's **Play on Level Load** property to On. Do not turn on looping.

4. In the Level Details panel under Cinematic, set the Matinee Actor **Disable Movement Input, Disable Look at Inputs, Hide Player,** and **Hide Hud** properties to On.

5. Block out the level with only the Actors that you will need to animate, such as the door and the door frame.

6. Open the Matinee Editor and add the necessary groups and movement track to animate the pieces of the door as it opens.

7. Use sound tracks in each group as necessary.

8. Add three Camera groups and animate each camera.

9. Add a Director group with a Director track to switch between the cameras.

10. Add a fade track to the Director group and set keys for a fade-in on the first camera and a fade-out on the last camera.

HOUR 13
Learning to Work with Physics

What You'll Learn in This Hour:

▶ Making a Static Mesh Actor simulate physics
▶ Creating and assigning Physical Materials
▶ Using Physics Constraint Actors
▶ Using Physics Thruster and Radial Force Actors

This hour introduces physics in UE4. You start off learning how to set up a simple rigid physics body from a Static Mesh Actor. Then you look at working with Physical Materials and Constraint Actors. You finish up the hour creating and using Force Actors. Physics simulation is a large topic, so establishing a framework and a basic understanding of working with physics to build on is the goal of this hour.

NOTE

Hour 13 Project Setup

For this Hour, you use the Hour_13 project from the book's companion website at www.sty-ue4.com. The provided project has a Game Mode that uses a First person character with a physics gun that can be used to interact with Actors simulating physics.

Using Physics in UE4

A *physics body* is an Actor that responds to external forces and collisions. Physics in UE4 is handled by the NVIDIAs PhysX physics Engine. The PhysX Engine uses the CPU or GPU, depending on the system, to process rigid bodies, soft bodies, cloth, destructibles, and particles. The UE4 Editor has interface tools for setting up and modifying physics properties. This hour focuses on working with rigid bodies. A *rigid body* is a solid, non-deformable objects, such as a 2×4 piece of wood or a beach ball.

Common Physics Terms

When you start working with physics, it is a good idea to familiarize yourself with some of the terms:

▶ *Physics body* is a generic term used to describe any object that is set to simulate physics.

▶ A *rigid body* is solid non-deformable objects.

▶ A *soft body* is a deformable object that conforms to the world around it when it collides with something.

▶ *Cloth* is a type of soft body.

▶ *Destructible* is a term that applies to a rigid body that fractures and crumbles when enough force has been applied.

▶ *Linear* refers to directional force that changes the position of an Actor in a level.

▶ *Angular* refers to rotational forces that change the orientation of an Actor.

▶ *Mass* refers to the amount of a matter in a given body, regardless of the amount of gravity applied.

▶ *Density* is the amount of mass by volume in a given physics body.

▶ *Damping* refers to how quickly a physics body comes to a rest after a force has been applied. It is the dissipation of energy over time.

▶ *Friction* is the amount of resistance applied to a sliding or rolling body.

▶ *Restitution* refers to the amount of bounce a physics body has and how quickly the body comes to rest.

▶ *Force* is applied to a mass for a duration.

▶ *Impulse* is an instantaneous hit.

Assigning the Physics Game Mode to a Level

To test out physics simulation, you need a Pawn with a physics gun so you can interact with physics bodies. Open the provided project for this hour, Hour_13 project. This project contains a Game Mode set up with a physics gun for you to use, along with some sample maps. Create a new level and open the World Settings panel for the level by clicking the **Settings** icon on the main Editor toolbar above the Viewport window and selecting **Project Settings** (see Figure 13.1).

FIGURE 13.1
Opening the project settings.

Under Game Mode in the World Settings panel, set GameMode Override to
SimplePhysicsGameMode, as shown in Figure 13.2. Playtest the level, and you should see a
simple red crosshair.

FIGURE 13.2
Setting GameMode Override.

Project and World Physics Settings

Now that the Game Mode has been set for the level, you can focus on locating the default
project settings for physics. You need to do this in several areas. First, you set a default setting for
the entire project. To do this, select **Settings > Project Settings** (refer to Figure 13.1). The Project
Settings tab that appears allows you to set many attributes related to physics for a project, but

you only need to look at two for now. As shown in Figure 13.3, you can set Default Gravity, which is roughly the rate of acceleration per second squared on a body as it falls due to the force of gravity. The default value is –980 cm on the Z-axis. You can also set Default Terminal Velocity, which is the top speed a physics body will be allowed to move. The default value is 4000. These settings apply to all levels in the project, unless you override them in a level's World Settings panel or on individual Actors.

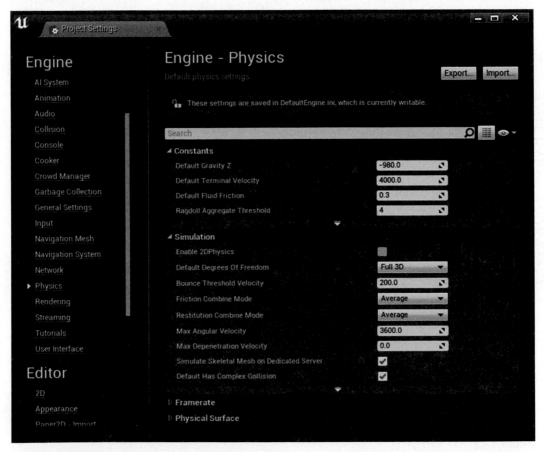

FIGURE 13.3
Project Settings panel.

Next, you can set default physics attributes on an individual level. With a level open, select the World Settings tab and look for the Physics section, which shows the default settings for the level (see Figure 13.4). Here you can override the project's default gravity settings just for the current level. You might do this, for example, if you are working on a physics-based game and certain levels need different gravity settings from the rest of the project.

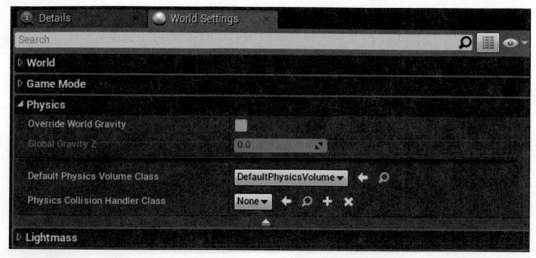

FIGURE 13.4
Overriding a project's default gravity settings for a level in World Settings.

Simulating Physics

A basic physics body in UE4 is nothing more than a Static Mesh that has been set to simulate physics. To make a Static Mesh Actor simulate physics, simply place one in your level. Then on the Details panel, go to the Physics section, where you can toggle on and off Simulate Physics, as shown in Figure 13.5. Toggling it on automatically changes the mobility of the placed Static Mesh Actor to movable and changes the Collision preset to Physics Actor. If you preview the level, the Static Mesh Actor now simulates physics, though it might not be moving if it's already on the ground and force has not yet been applied. Placing the Actor 500 units above the ground plane allows the default gravity settings to affect the object. Also on the Level Details panel, you can see that the Actor has a default mass based on its size in kilograms (kg). If you scale the Actor up or down, you can see the mass of the Actor change relative to its size. As you can see, you can override this setting and put in any value you like.

Two other properties to look at right now are Enable Gravity and Start Awake. If you turn off Enable Gravity, you override the project or level default gravity settings for the Actor, effectively making it respond like an asteroid in space. Toggling off Start Awake tells the Actor not to start simulating physics until it is influenced by an external force other than gravity.

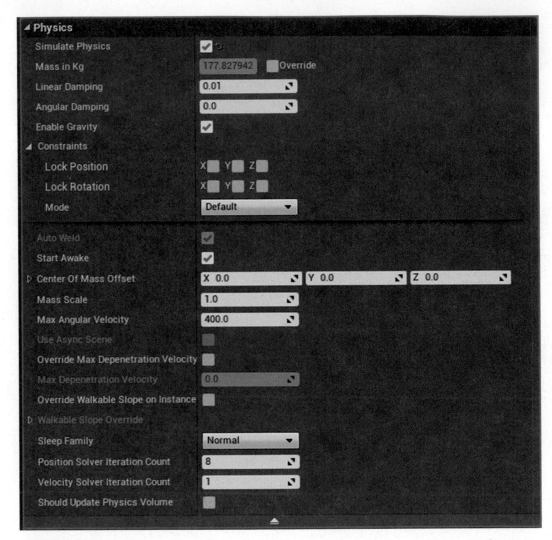

FIGURE 13.5
Physics properties for a Static Mesh Actor.

TIP

No Collision Hull

If a Static Mesh Actor does not allow you to set Simulate Physics, it is most likely because the Static Mesh asset that has been assigned to the Actor does not have a collision hull. In that case, locate the Static Mesh asset in the Content Browser, open it in the Static Mesh Editor, and assign a collision hull. Remember to save it.

Now that you have placed a Static Mesh Actor set to simulate physics, you can preview your level and interact with it using the simple physics gun. Move close to the physics body and point the HUD crosshairs on it. Click to grab the object and pick it up; right-click to release the object. If you right-click an object when you are not holding anything, you poke it.

Table 13.1 lists the key physics properties you can set for a Static Mesh Actor.

TABLE 13.1   Physics Properties for a Static Mesh Actor

Property	Description
Simulate Physics	Toggles physics simulation on and off for the Actor.
Mass in KG	Mass of the body, in kilograms, based on the Actor's size in the world. This property can be set manually by turning on Override.
Linear Damping	Drag force added to reduce linear movement.
Angular Damping	Drag force added to reduce angular movement.
Enable Gravity	Whether the object should have the force of gravity applied.
Constraints	Controls which axises the Actor can move and rotate on when simulating physics.
Modes	Presets for constraint assignments.
Start Awake	Whether the object should start awake or initially be sleeping.
Center of Mass Offset	Specifies the offset for the center of the mass of this object from the calculated location.
Mass Scale	Per-instance scaling of mass.
Max Angular Velocity	Limits the amount of angular velocity that can applied.
Use Async Scene	If this is selected, the body is put into the asynchronous physics scene. If it is not selected, the body is put into the synchronous physics scene. If the body is static, it is placed into both scenes, whether Use Async Scene is selected or not.
Sleep Family	The set of values used in considering when to put this body to sleep.
Position Solver Iteration Count	The physics body's solver iteration count for position. Increasing this setting is more CPU-intensive but yields better stabilization.
Velocity Solver Iteration Count	The physics body's solver iteration count for velocity. Increasing this setting is more CPU-intensive but yields better stabilization.

TIP

Details Panel

Just about every subeditor in UE4 has a Details panel, and every Details panel has a search bar. If you can't find a particular property, type its name in the search bar of the ac-tive Details panel, and it will show up.

Using Physical Materials

Physical Materials enable you to modify the behavior of a physics body. The term *Physical Materials* can be a bit misleading because these are not actually rendering materials at all, but rather materials in the substance sense. They can be applied to individual Static Mesh Actors in your level, or they can be assigned to regular materials that, when assigned to a Static Mesh Actor simulating physics, will also affect the Actor's physics simulations behavior.

Creating a Physical Material Asset

Physical Material assets can be created in the Content Browser. They allow you to set properties such as Friction, Density, and Restitution on a physics body (see Figure 13.6).

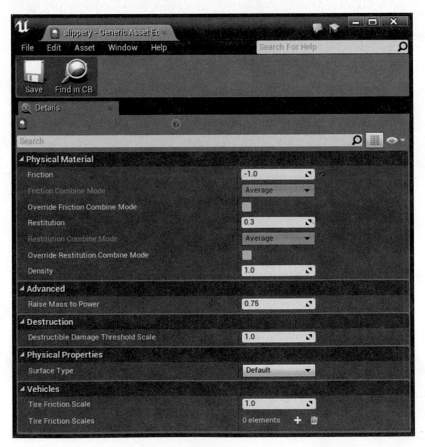

FIGURE 13.6
Physical Material properties.

To create new Physical Material in the Editor, go to the Content Browser and create a new folder. In the asset management area, right-click and select **Physics > Physical Material** (see Figure 13.7). Give the newly created asset a name and then double-click it to open its properties. After you modify any values, remember to save the changes by right-clicking the modified asset in the Content Browser and selecting **Save**.

FIGURE 13.7
Creating a Physical Material asset.

Assigning a Physical Material to a Static Mesh Actor

To assign a Physical Material to a Static Mesh Actor, select the Actor in the level and go to the Collision section in the Levels Details panel. You will see the Phys Material Override property (see Figure 13.8). Drag the Physical Material asset from the Content Browser next to this property to set it.

FIGURE 13.8
Assigning a Physical Material to a Static Mesh asset in the Collision section of the Details panel.

Assigning a Physical Material to a Material

The advantage of assigning a Physical Material to a regular material is that every time you assign the material to a Static Mesh Actor, it will have the visual surface properties of the regular material, and it will also use the Physical Material properties if the Actor ever has its state changed to simulate physics at runtime.

To assign a Physical Material to a regular material, simply open the desired material in the Material Editor, select the final material node, and look for the Phys Material Override property in the Material Editor's Details panel. Drag the Physical Material asset onto the property, save, and close the Material Editor.

The Following Try it Yourself walks you through creating Physical Material assets and assigning them to Static Mesh Actors and a Regular material.

TRY IT YOURSELF ▼

Assigning Physical Materials to Static Mesh Actors

This is a good time to practice creating and assigning Physical Materials to Static Mesh Actors, so follow these steps:

1. Drag out three Static Mesh Actors—one cube and two spheres—from the Place tab in the Modes panel. Set them all to simulate physics.

2. Create a folder in the Content Browser to store your Physical Materials.

3. Create three Physical Materials.

4. Name the first Physical Material **Slippery** and set its Friction property to **-1**. Assign this to the placed Cube Static Mesh Actor's Phy Material Override property.

5. Name the second Physical Material **Bouncy** and set its Restitution property to **1.6**. Assign this to one of the placed Sphere Static Mesh Actor's Phy Material Override property.

6. Name the third Physical Material **Heavy** and set its Density property to **10**.

7. Create a new regular material and in the Material Editor and Name it **Heavy_Mat**. Assign it a color and link the constant vector 3 material expression to the Base Color.

8. In the Material Editor, select the **Primary** material node and in the Material Editor's Details panel, assign the **Heavy** Physical Material Asset created in step 6 to the Phys Material property, as shown in Figure 13.9.

9. Save and close the material.

10. Drag the Heavy_Mat material onto the last placed Static Mesh Actor in the level.

11. Preview the level and interact with each of the physics bodies.

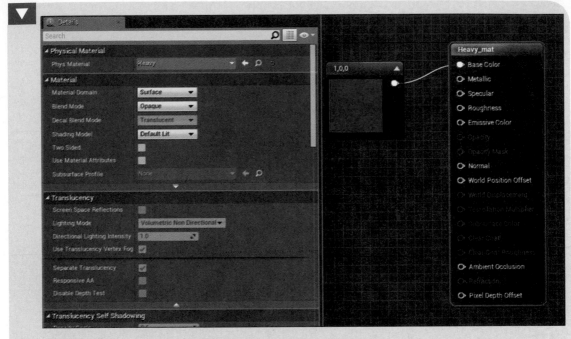

FIGURE 13.9
Assigning a Physical Material to a material.

Working with Constraints

Constraints allow you to control the movement of a physics body by locking movement and rotation on a specific axis. You set properties for a constraint in the Constraint section of the Level Details panel for the Static Mesh Actor. Here you find properties that allow you to lock the physics body to specific positional and rotational axes (see Figure 13.10). There is even a mode property with presets, which is great when working with an individual physics body that has specific needs. For example, you can lock the X and Y movement so the physics body can move only along the Z-axis; or you can lock the rotation only, so the physics body can move but not rotate.

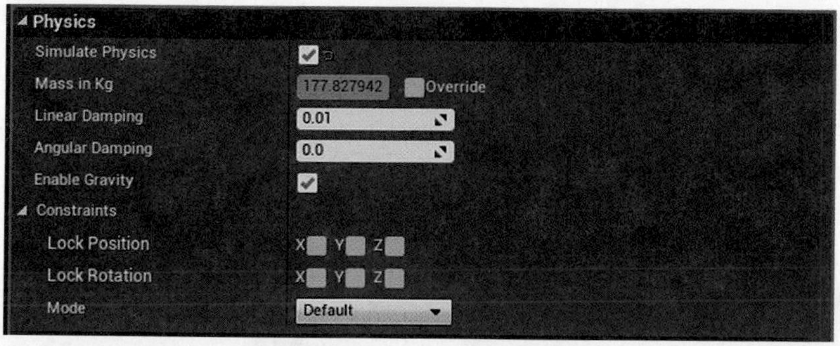

FIGURE 13.10
Actor Constraints.

Attaching Physics Actors

In previous hours, you learned about parent/child relationships and attaching Actors together. Unfortunately, because physics objects dynamically respond to the world around them in real time, through collision and external forces, attaching them together has no effect. A physics body can be a parent to another movable Actor, but attaching a physics body as a child to a parent Actor has no effect at runtime, and the attaching relationship is ignored.

NOTE

Attaching Physics Bodies

The Editor allows you to attach a Physics Actor. If a Static Mesh has been set to simulate physics and the child Actor is movable, the child will follow the position and rotation of the parent Physics Actor.

Physics Constraint Actors

Due to the limitations of attaching physics bodies, Epic has provided a Physics Constraint Actor that allows you to link Physics Actors to any other Actor, as shown in Figure 13.11. You use a Constraint Actor to create a joint, or a hinge, between two physics bodies. A Constraint Actor differs from standard attaching method, in that the movement of both the parent (Constraint Actor 1) and the child (Constraint Actor 2) have effects on each other's movement and rotation. Since the Physics Constraint Actor works like a joint, there are presets for the type of joint to use. Choosing the preset automatically adjusts the linear and angular settings between **Free**, meaning no constraint at all, **Lock**, meaning no movement at all, and Limited, which allows you set a range of movement.

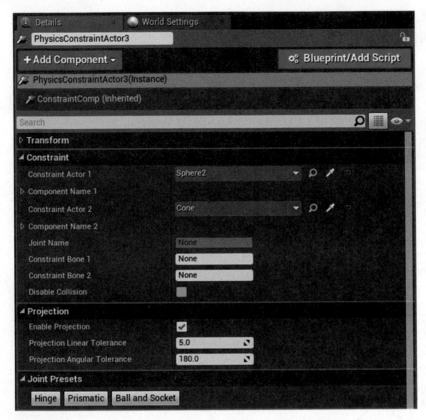

FIGURE 13.11
Physics Constraint Actor properties.

▼ TRY IT YOURSELF

Create a Swinging Lamp Using a Constraint Chain

Follow these steps to set up your own constraint chain by creating a hanging lamp:

1. Place a Static Mesh Cube Actor in your level, 400 units above the floor. Leave it static; that is, do not select Simulate Physics.

2. Place a Static Mesh Sphere directly under the cube. Set its X, Y, and Z scaled to **0.4** and select **Simulate Physics**.

3. Place a second Static Mesh Sphere directly under the first sphere. Set its X, Y, and Z scaled to **0.4** and select **Simulate Physics**.

4. Place a Static Mesh Cone Actor just underneath the bottom sphere and select **Simulate Physics**.

5. Drag out a Spot Light Actor so it is directly under the cone. Set its color to red and increase its intensity to 40,000.

6. Attach the spotlight to the Cone Actor in the World Outliner panel.

7. Drag out a Physics Constraint Actor and place it in between the cube and the top sphere.

8. On the Details panel for the Constraint Actor, look for the Constraint tab. For Constraint Actor 1, click the eye dropper icon to the right and then click the cube in the Viewport. This assigns the Cube Static Mesh Actor to the Constraint Actor 1 property. If you have done it correctly, you should see the cube surrounded by a red wireframe box.

9. Repeat step 8 for the Constraint Actor 2 property, but this time choose the top sphere. If you have done it correctly, you should see the sphere surrounded by a blue wireframe box.

10. Repeat steps 7 through 9 twice, and each time place the new Constraint Actor between the next two Static Mesh Actors and assign the mesh just above the newly placed Physics Constraint to Constraint Actor 1 and the bottom mesh to Constraint Actor 2. You should have a total of three Physics Constraint Actors when you are done. See Figure 13.12 for proper placement and arrangement of the Actors.

11. Preview the level and use the physics gun to interact with the constraint chain to make the light swing.

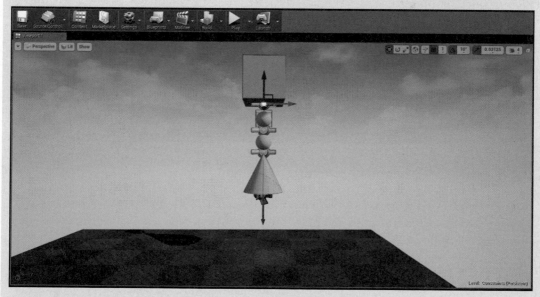

FIGURE 13.12
Lamp constraint chain.

Instead of using presets, you can micromanage linear or angular movement limits on a joint. If you select **Limited** on any of the axes under Angular Limits on the Details panel, more properties show up that allow you to set the stiffness and damping, as well as limit the swing and twist angles of the joint, as shown in Figure 13.13. You can even set linear and angular breakable thresholds that break the joint constraints when enough linear or angular force is applied.

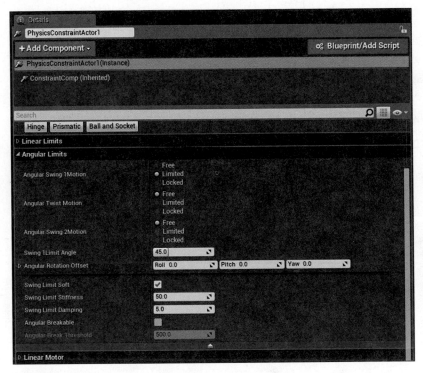

FIGURE 13.13
Physics constraint Actor Angular Limits properties.

Now that you have a constraint chain set up, play around with these properties and see what happens. Make small adjustments and playtest often until you get a good sense of what all the properties are doing and how they work.

NOTE

Simulating Metal Chains and Ropes

You might be tempted to use the method described here to make an actual chain, and while that may technically be possible, it is not the best way to go about it. If you want to simulate a chain, or even a rope, that is best done in the Physics Asset Tool (PhAT) Editor, using a Skeletal Mesh Actor that relies on bone and joint hierarchies.

Using Force Actors

You can do a lot with physics bodies through Blueprint. However, Epic provides a few Classes to work with, including the Physics Thruster and Radial Force Actors.

Physics Thruster Actors

You can find a Physics Thruster Class in the Place tab in the Modes panel. Simply type **physics** in the Modes panel search box and then find the Physics Thruster Actor in the list. To use it, place it under the Physics Actor you want to affect in your level and rotate it in the direction you would like the force to be applied. Then, in the World Outliner panel, attach it to the Static Mesh Actor simulating physics. Set the amount of force you would like to apply under Thrust Strength in the level Details panel. Toggle on **Auto Activate** in the Activation section of the Level Details panel. The amount of force needed to move a physics body depends on the body's mass. So you may need a high value for thrust strength to have an effect, depending on the physics body.

TIP

Controlling Mass

Remember that scaling a physics body up or down changes its mass. You can also override the Mass setting of the Static Mesh in the Level Details panel and apply your own values. Select the Actor, go to the Level Details panel, and in the Physics section, look for the Mass In Kg property. Turn on Override and set the amount.

TRY IT YOURSELF ▼

Create a Cone Rocket

Follow these steps to create a simple cone rocket and use a linked Physics Thruster Actor to propel it into the air:

1. Drag out a Cone Static Mesh Actor from the Place tab in the Modes panel. Place it approximately 50 to 150 units above the floor.

2. Select **Simulate Physics** for the Cone Static Mesh Actor.

3. Drag out a Physics Thruster Actor from the Place tab in the Modes panel.

4. With the Physics Thruster selected, set its location under Transforms in the Details panel so that it has the same X and Y locations as the Cone Static Mesh Actor.

5. Rotate the Physics Thruster Actor so its yellow direction arrow is pointing straight down.

6. Attach the Physics Thruster to the cone in the World Outliner panel.

7. In the Details panel for the Physics Thruster Actor, set Thrust Strength to about **65,000** and select **Auto Activate**.

8. Preview the level; the cone should fly up in the air.

9. If the physics body is not moving, make sure the Physics Thruster direction is facing the correct direction. You can also reduce the mass of the Static Mesh Actor or increase the thrust strength of the Physics Thruster Actor. If the cone is flying erratically, make adjustments to the position of the Thruster Actor or set the constraints on the Static Mesh Cone to be locked on the X- and Y-axes under the Actor's Physics properties (refer to Figure 13.5).

NOTE
Copying and Pasting Actor Transforms

You can copy and paste the transforms of an Actor by right-clicking its Location, Rotation, or Scale property under Transforms in the Level Details panel and selecting Copy. Then apply it to another Actor by right-clicking on the second Actor's transforms and select Paste.

Radial Force Actors

A Radial Force Actor applies force in all directions from a single point of influence, so its orientation does not matter. A Radial Force Actor only affects Physics Actors that fall within its area of influence, and you can adjust the area of influence by scaling the Actor. The influence has a falloff value, so the applied force on a physics body is greater the closer it is to the center of the Radial Force Actor. To place a Radial Force Actor, locate it by using the search bar in the Modes panel. Drag it into your level; with the Actor selected, set the Force Strength properties.

▼ TRY IT YOURSELF

Use Radial Force Push

Follow these steps to set up a Radial Force Actor so that it pushes an Actor set to simulate physics:

1. Drag out a Cube Static Mesh Actor from the Place tab in the Modes panel. Place it 500 units above the floor.

2. With the placed Static Mesh selected, in the Level Details panel select **Simulate Physics** for the Static Mesh Actor and override its Mass in Kg property; set Mass to **10**.

3. Set the Linear Damping property of the cube to **1**.

4. Drag out a Radial Force Actor and place it on the floor, directly under the cube.

5. In the Details panel for the Radial Force Actor, set Force Strength to about **10,000**.

6. Preview the level. The cube should fall slowly toward the floor and get pushed to the side when it hits the floor.

Summary

This past hour you were introduced to working with physics in UE4. Having only the basic knowledge you now have, you can implement a large number of design possibilities in a project. There is, of course, always more to learn. Now that you are comfortable working with simple Physics Actors and properties, the next step you should be looking into is working with destructible Actors and the Physics Asset Tool (PhAT) Editor, which allows you to assign physical properties to skeletal meshes on the individual bones. You can use it for setting up anything from ropes to rag dolls to characters that respond differently each time they get hit. Remember to check out the Content Examples project from Epic. You can download the project from the Learn section of the Launcher. Just launch the project and open the physics and destructible level and preview them to see examples.

Q&A

Q. I don't see the crosshairs on the HUD when I preview my level. Why?

A. Make sure to set the current level's GameMode Override property to **SimplePhysicsGameMode** in the World Settings panel. You can also apply this setting to the entire project in the Project Settings panel of Maps & Modes.

Q. Why is the Simulate Physics property grayed out for my Static Mesh in the level?

A. Make sure the Static Mesh asset used has a collision hull. If it doesn't, open it in the Static Mesh Editor and assign one.

Q. I placed a Force Thruster Actor in a level, but it does not affect any of the physics bodies I have created. Why?

A. The Force Thruster Actor must be attached to the Static Mesh that you want to affect. Also, the Auto Activate property in the Details panel for the Force Thruster Actor needs to be selected.

Q. How do I change the force direction of a Force Thruster Actor?

A. Simply rotate the attached Force Thruster Actor using its transform gizmo so that the arrow points in the direction you want the force to be applied.

Q. When I use a Radial Force Actor and place a Static Mesh physics body on it, nothing happens. Why?

A. Make sure you are setting the Force value and not Impulse on the Radial Force Actor; be sure to apply a high Force value or reduce the mass of the physics bodies you are trying to affect.

Workshop

Now that you have finished the hour, see if you can answer the following questions.

Quiz

1. True or false: In the World Outliner panel, if you attach a Static Mesh Actor simulating physics to a Static Mesh Actor that has Mobility set to Static, the Physics Actor will not move.

2. True or false: Rigid bodies deform when they collide with other Actors.

3. True or false: Setting Linear Damping to a high value for a physics body will reduce its velocity over time.

4. True or false: A Physics material may not be a material, but they can be assigned to a material.

5. True or false: A Physics Thruster can move a physics body without the two Actors being attached.

Answers

1. False. Because the Static Mesh Actor is simulating physics attaching it to another Actor will not have an effect. If you want to attach an Actor simulating physic to another Actor you will need to use a Physics Constraint Actor.

2. False. Soft bodies deform when they collide with other Actors.

3. True. Linear Damping reduces the velocity of a physics body over time.

4. True. Physic Materials can be assign to either a Static Mesh Actors or a regular Materials.

5. False. For the Physic thruster to work it must be attached as the child to the Static Mesh simulating physic.

Exercise

Multiple Constraint Actors can affect a single Static Mesh Actor at the same time. Using Physics Constraint and Static Mesh Actors, create a platform that is suspended by four separate constraint chains in each corner.

1. Create a new level and set the GameMode Override setting to **SimplePhysicsGameMode** in the World Settings panel.

2. Create a constraint chain similar to the swinging lamp chain you made in a Try It Yourself exercise this hour but don't include the light. Add one more Physics Constraint Actor to the bottom of the chain and assign the last mesh to the Constraint Actor 1 property.

3. Once the chain has been made, select all the Actors that make up the chain at once and duplicate it three times. Position each copy so you have four separate constraint chains forming a square. You can do this duplication by using the **Move** transform gizmo and holding the **Alt** key as you move the selection.

4. Add a Static Mesh box and scale it so it makes a platform the player can stand on. Select **Simulate Physics** for this Actor and place it underneath the four constraint chains.

5. Assign the platform to the Constraint Actor 2 property to the last Physics Constraint Actor in each of the chains.

6. Preview the level and interact with the platform either with the physics gun or by jumping on the platform (see Figure 13.14).

FIGURE 13.14
Platform suspended by four separate constraint chains.

HOUR 14
Introducing Blueprint Visual Scripting System

What You'll Learn in This Hour:

▶ Learning the Blueprint Editor interface
▶ How to use events, functions, and variables
▶ Adding an event
▶ Declaring a variable

Just about every game engine has a scripting language that allows developers to add or modify functionality in their games. Some engines make use of existing scripting environments, such as LUA, and some have proprietary scripting environments. UE4 provides two methods for creating content: C++ and Blueprint. The Blueprint visual scripting system is a powerful and fully functional scripting environment that is used throughout the Editor. It gives artists and designers the ability to create entire games, prototype ideas, and modify existing gameplay elements. This hour introduces the Blueprint Editor and basic scripting concepts.

NOTE

Hour 14 Setup

For this hour, create a new Blank project without Starter Content.

Visual Scripting Basics

Developing in C++ requires an Integrated Development Environment (IDE), such as Microsoft Visual Studio, and can be used to script anything from new classes and gameplay to modifications of the Core Engine Components. Blueprint, on the other hand is a visual scripting environment. Although you can't use Blueprint to write a Rendering Engine, you can use it to create your own classes and gameplay functionality. A visual scripting environment, such as Blueprint, does not use a traditional text-based environment but instead offers nodes and wires. *Nodes* are visual representations of functions (pieces of code that perform specific operations), variables (which are used to store data), operators (which perform mathematical operations), and conditionals (which allow you to check and compare variables). In Blueprint you use wires to establish relationships between nodes to create and set the flow of your Blueprint; that is, you use wires to establish the order of operations. The Blueprint Editor is the interface that allows you to make and compile these sequences of nodes and wires.

NOTE

When to Use C++

You only need to work in C++ if your game demands 100% efficiency or requires some modification to the Core Rendering, Physics, Audio, or Networking Engine Components. Epic has even provided full access to all the source code used to create all the Core Engine Components. Some people simply prefer using a text-based scripting and programming environment, such as C++. If you are new to scripting, working in a visual scripting environment like Blueprint is a great way to learn fundamental programming concepts without having to worry about syntax.

Visual scripting allows artists and designers to script gameplay functionality, leaving programmers to work on more complicated tasks. A large percentage of most games can be created entirely in Blueprint, and because it compiles to the bytecode level, Blueprint scripts are very efficient. You can use Blueprint to make complete games for all the platforms that UE4 supports.

NOTE

Compiling Blueprint Scripts

Even though Blueprint is a visual environment, Blueprint scripts still need to be compiled. Blueprint scripts compile to the bytecode level. It's important to understand the following terms:

▶ **Compiler:** Software used to compile instructions (source code) written in a programming language.

▶ **Compiling:** The process of turning instructions into machine language (code) that can be executed by the CPU. Compiling requirements differ depending on the hardware and operating system.

▶ **Bytecode:** Compiled source code that is processed by a virtual machine instead of hardware. This means the source code can be compiled once and run on any hardware that has a virtual machine to process the bytecode.

▶ **Virtual machine:** Software that translates bytecode into instructions the hardware can understand and process.

Understanding the Blueprint Editor

The Blueprint visual scripting system is a key Component of the UE4 Editor and even in C++-based projects, you will most likely be utilizing Blueprints to some degree. There are five types of Blueprints to work with in UE4.

▶ **Level Blueprint:** This is used to manage global events for a level. There is only one Level Blueprint for each level, and it is automatically saved when the level is saved.

▶ **Blueprint class:** This is a class derived from an existing class that has been made in C++ or from another Blueprint class. It is used to code functionality for Actors placed in a level.

▶ **Data-Only Blueprint:** This only stores the modified properties of an inherited Blueprint.

▶ **Blueprint Interface:** Blueprint Interfaces (BPI) are used to store a collection of user-defined functions that can be assigned to other Blueprints. BPIs allow other Blueprints to share and pass data among each other.

▶ **Blueprint Macros:** These are self-contained node graphs of a commonly used sequence of nodes that can be reused throughout other Blueprints. Blueprint Macros are stored in a Blueprint Macro Library.

Level Blueprint and Blueprint classes are the two most common types of Blueprints you will use. In this hour, you focus on becoming familiar with the Blueprint Editor. Later hours show you more about how to work with Blueprint classes.

NOTE

Working with Blueprints

The following are some basic terms that are good to know when talking about Blueprint and programming in general:

▶ **Blueprint:** A Blueprint Class asset stored in the Content Browser.

▶ **Blueprint Actor:** An instance of a Blueprint Class asset placed in a level.

▶ **Object:** A variable or a collection of variables such as a data structures and functions that are stored in memory.

▶ **Class:** A code template for creating objects, which stores initial values assigned to variables along with functions and operations that fundamentally define the class.

▶ **Syntax:** In traditional programming and scripting environments, syntax refers to the spelling and grammatical structure that is expected by the language compiler in order to be able to compile code into machine language.

Blueprint Editor Interface

To open a level Blueprint and see the Blueprint Editor interface, from the Level Editor toolbar select **Blueprints > Open Level Blueprint** (see Figure 14.1). The Blueprint Editor's interface and workflow are easy to learn, but scripting is difficult to master. Even though you don't have to worry about syntax in a visual scripting environment, you still need to deal with logic and order of operations. This takes practice in any coding environment.

FIGURE 14.1
Opening the Level Blueprint in the Blueprint Editor for the current level.

The Blueprint Editor interface has a menu bar, a toolbar for quick access to common tools and operations, the Event Graph for building scripts, a Details panel for showing properties of whatever is currently selected in the Blueprint Editor, and a My Blueprint panel that is used to manage and keep track of node graphs, functions, macros, and variables used in the selected Blueprint. The features of the Blueprint Editor interface are indicated in Figure 14.2 and described in the following list:

- ▶ 1) **Toolbar:** The toolbar provides a number of buttons, described shortly, for controlling the Blueprint Editor.

- ▶ 2) **My Blueprint panel:** Is used to manage graphs, functions, macros, and variables that are in your Blueprint.

- ▶ 3) **Details panel:** Once a component, variable, or function is added to a Blueprint, you can edit its properties in the Details panel.

- ▶ 4) **Event Graph:** You use the Event Graph to script the core functionality of the Blueprint.

FIGURE 14.2
The Blueprint Editor interface.

NOTE

Blueprint Toolbar

When working with Level Blueprints, the Blueprint Editor toolbar does not have a save or find in Content Browser function because the Level Blueprint is tied to the level. To save the Level Blueprint, just save the Level.

Blueprint Editor Toolbar

The Blueprint Editor toolbar has only five tools on it. The two tools to focus on now are the Compile button and the Play button. You click the Compile button to compile script and see any issues in the compiler result window at the bottom of the Event Graph. The Play button here is the same as the Level Editor Play button for previewing a level. Notice that there is no Save button; this is because the Level Blueprint is tied to the level, so if you need to save a Level Blueprint, just save the level.

The Blueprint Editor's toolbar has a number of buttons for managing a Blueprints:

▶ **Compile:** Compiles a Blueprint

▶ **Search:** Opens a Find Results panel with a search box for locating nodes in a Blueprint

▶ **Class Settings:** Shows the options for the Blueprint in the Details panel

▶ **Class Defaults:** Displays the properties for the Blueprint in the Details panel

▶ **Play:** Previews the level

My Blueprint Panel

The My Blueprint panel keeps track of all the node graphs, functions, macros, and variables that your Blueprint uses. Each category is separated by title, and to the right of each title is a + symbol you can click to add to each section, as needed. You can use the My Blueprint panel to add, rename, and delete all these elements.

Event Graph

The Event Graph is the default node graph used to code your Blueprints. It is where you do most of your work when using the Blueprint Editor. You can add more node graphs to an existing Blueprint as needed. A node graph is like a sheet of graph paper. You can add as many graphs as you need to a Blueprint to help keep it organized. Table 14.1 lists the shortcuts used when working with nodes in the Event Graph.

TABLE 14.1   Blueprint Editor Shortcuts

Shortcut	Command or Action
Right-click an empty space	Opens the Blueprint Context Menu.
Right-drag an empty space	Moves the Event Graph to the clicked location.
Right-click a node	Brings up the node and pin actions.
Click a node	Selects the node.
Drag a node	Moves the node.
Drag an empty space	Selects the area.
Ctrl+click	Adds and removes the currently selected node to a selection of nodes.
Roll mouse wheel	Zooms the Event Graph in and out.
Home	Centers the Event Graph.
Delete	Deletes the selected nodes.
Ctrl+X	Cuts the selected nodes.
Ctrl+C	Copies the selected nodes.
Ctrl+V	Pastes the selected nodes.
Ctrl+W	Copies and pastes the selected nodes.

Blueprint Context Menu

The Blueprint Context Menu is one of the menus you use most often when working in the Blueprint Editor. You add events, functions, variables, and conditionals to a graph by right-clicking an empty area or dragging a pin. Either way allows you to open the Blueprint Context Menu (see Figure 14.3). This menu is *context sensitive* by default, which means it shows only actions that are relevant to what you currently have selected and/or the pin you are dragging from.

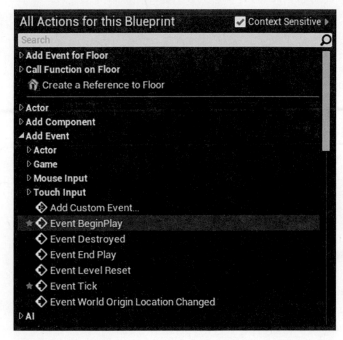

FIGURE 14.3
Blueprint Context Menu.

Nodes, Wires, Execs, and Pins

It can help to think of the flow of a visual script as electricity. A red event node sends out a signal that travels along wires and executes whatever node it passes through. When a node receives the signal, it retrieves any data it needs through data pins on the left side. It then performs its operation, passes the event signal along, and returns any results through data pins on the right side. Here's what you need to know about this process:

▶ Nodes are visual representations of events, functions, and variables and are color-coded to represent their use. A red node is an event node used to initiate the execution of a sequence of nodes. Blue nodes are functions to perform specific operations. Multicolored oval nodes, each with a single data pin, represent variables.

▶ "In" and "out" execution pins (execs) are the white right-facing triangles at the top of a node that denote sequence flow. A red event node has only an "out" exec pin because it is used to initiate a sequence, while blue nodes have both "in" and "out" exec pins (most of the time) to pass the signal along.

▶ Data pins are color-coded based on the type of data they need. Data pins on the left side of a node retrieve data, while data pins on the right side of a node return data.

▶ Wires connect nodes; white wires connect "in" and "out" exec pins, and colored wires connect data pins. The color of each wire represents the type of data it is passing.

To establish a connection between an exec pin or a data pin and with a wire, click the pin and drag to another pin of the same type. To break a wire going in or out of a pin, **Alt+click** on the pin. **Ctrl+click+drag** a pin or wire to move it to a new pin.

Fundamental Concepts in Scripting

All coding environments make use of events, functions, variables, and conditional operators. The following pages briefly introduce you to these core concepts.

Events

Blueprints in UE4 are based on events. An *event* is something that happens during gameplay and can be anything from the player pressing a key on the keyboard or a pawn entering a specific room in a level to an Actor colliding with another Actor or the game starting. Most events fall into common categories, which are described in Table 14.2. Events are used to initiate a sequence in Blueprint. When an event is fired, a signal is sent out from the event's execute out pin that travels along a wire and processes any functions it encounters along the way. When the signal comes to the end of a sequence of nodes, its signal is lost.

TABLE 14.2 Common Events

Event Name	Event Description
BeginOverlap	Fires when the collision hulls of two Actors overlap. (Assigned to an Actor or a Component.)
EndOverlap	Fires when the collision hulls of two Actors stop overlapping. (Assigned to an Actor or a Component.)
Hit	Fires when the collision hulls of two Actors touch but don't overlap. (Assigned to an Actor or a Component.)
BeginPlay	Fires every time a level is loaded into memory and played.
EndPlay	Fires when the level is over.

Event Name	Event Description
Destroyed	Fires when an Actor has been removed from memory.
Tick	Fires with every tick of the CPU.
Custom	Acts as the user has defined it to work, based on specific needs.

Some events need specific Actors or Components assigned to them, such as Collision Events—it is likely that more than one Collision Event is being broadcasted at a time. For example, if you have a Box Trigger Actor and a Sphere Trigger Actor in your level and you need each of them to respond when other Actors overlap with either of them, you need to assign each to their own OnActorBeginOverlap Collision Event. Being able to have events assigned to specific Actors allows you to script each Actor's individual responses. To assign an Actor in a level to a Collision Event, you select the Actor in the level and then right-click in an empty location in the Event Graph of the Level Blueprint. Then, in the Blueprint Context Menu search box, type **on Actor begin** and select **OnActorBeginOverlap** from the list to place the event node. Once the Collision Event node is placed, you can see the Actor's name assigned to the event node, so you know that the Actor has been assigned. Now when the Actor's collision hull is overlapped, this Collision Event node executes.

NOTE

Components

Components in UE4 are subobject elements found in Blueprint classes and are covered in Hour 16, "Working with Blueprint Classes."

While the Blueprint Editor provides predefined event nodes, you can also create your own custom events that can be called at any point in a Blueprint sequence. Creating a custom event allows you to define the name of the event and any data that is passed when the event is called. Figure 14.4 shows two preexisting events (EventBeginPlay and OnActorBeginOverlap) that call a custom event and pass a string variable. The custom event receives the signal and uses a Print String function to display the received string data to the screen. Custom events can help you manage and organize your Blueprints.

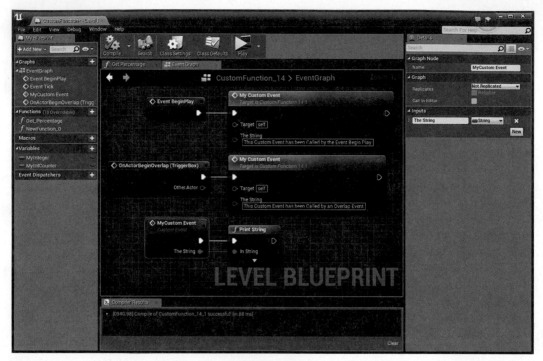

FIGURE 14.4
Blueprint custom events.

To make a custom event, right-click in the Event Graph, and in the Blueprint Context Menu search box, type **custom**. Then select **Custom Event** from the list to place a custom event node. Rename the event by clicking the default name. To assign a variable to the event, select the node and in the Details panel, add a variable. After you have made a custom event, you can call the event from another sequence by opening the Context Menu and typing in the search box the name you assigned to the event. You select the custom event from the list to place the node, and then you can wire it in a sequence.

Functions

A *function* is a piece of code that performs specific operations. It takes in data stored in variables, processes the information, and in most cases returns a result. The Blueprint Editor has a full suite of predefined functions that are similar to those in any other programming environment. When a function is placed in the Event Graph, you typically see a target data pin on the left side of the function's node. In a Blueprint, a target is typically a variable that stores a reference to an Actor or a Component of an Actor in the level on which the function operations will be performed. In the function example shown in Figure 14.5, you can see a SetActorLocation function that is used to change the location of an Actor in the level.

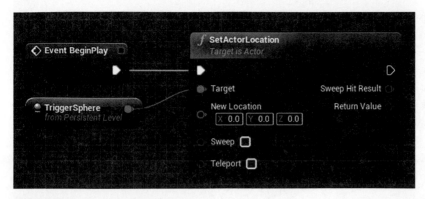

FIGURE 14.5
Blueprint function.

While Blueprint already has an extensive list of functions to work with, you can also make your own custom functions in the Blueprint Editor for individual Blueprints, or you can make your own Blueprint Functions Library, which allows you to make a collection of functions that can be reused in any Blueprint throughout a project. Figure 14.6 shows an example of a custom function created in the Blueprint Editor. This custom function, called Get Percentage, takes in two float variables (A and B), where A is a total value and B is the current value. The function divides the current value (B) by the total value (A) and then multiplies the result by 100 and returns the percentage as a float.

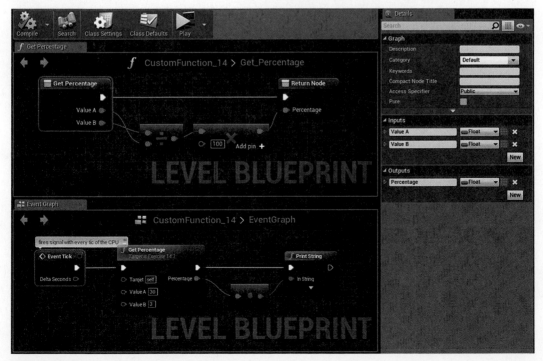

FIGURE 14.6
Blueprint custom function.

After you create a custom function, you can reuse it as many times as needed simply by dragging out the function from the My Blueprint panel to a node graph. To create a custom function in a Blueprint, simply click the + symbol next to Functions in the My Blueprint panel. You then have a node graph specific to the function. In the node graph you can see two purple nodes to assign input variables and output variables. You can define the input/output variable for a function by selecting the input or output nodes in the custom function graph and in the Details panel, you can create variables of different data types as needed. After you create input and output variables for the function, you can script the sequence as you would in any other node graph, but you need to wire the sequence up to the input and output nodes when you're finished.

NOTE

Custom Functions

You can also create a custom function by selecting a sequence of already-placed nodes and right-clicking on one of the nodes and selecting **Collapse to Function** from the menu. You get a new function that you can rename. If you often repeat a sequence of three or more predefined functions in a Blueprint, there is a good chance you would benefit from collapsing the sequence to a custom function.

▼ TRY IT YOURSELF

Add an Event

Follow these steps to add an event, BeginPlay, and use a Print String function to display text on the screen:

1. On the Level Editor menu, select **File > New** to create a new default level.

2. On the Level Editor toolbar, select **Blueprints > Open Level Blueprint**.

3. Select the **BeginPlay** and **Event Tick** events that have already been added and press **Delete**.

4. Right-click in the Event Graph and select BeginPlay. (Use the search box if you have trouble finding it.)

5. Click the exec on the BeginPlay event, drag to the right, and release.

6. Right-click in the Event Graph and in the Context Menu's search box type **print string**.

7. Select the **Print String** function to place a node for it.

8. To the right of the **String** data pin, where it says hello, type **Hello level**.

9. Click the **Compile** button on the Blueprint Editor toolbar and preview the level.

10. Every time you preview the level, you see **Hello level** in the upper-left corner of the Level Viewport for a few seconds, and then it disappears.

NOTE

The Print String Function

Using the Print String function is not the proper way to communicate with players. This function is typically used in development as a debugging tool to communicate what is happening in a Blueprint. If you want to send messages to the player, you need to use a Blueprint HUD class or learn to use the Unreal Motion Graphics Editor. See Hour 22, "Working with UMG."

Variables

Variables store different types of data. When a variable is declared (created), the computer sets aside a certain amount of memory, depending on the data type. That memory is then used to store or retrieve the information at that memory location. Different variable types use different amounts of memory. Some variables store as little information as a bit, and some store as much as an entire Actor. In the Blueprint Editor, variables are color coded so that you can quickly identify what variable type you need when working with functions.

Table 14.3 lists the most common variable types, their color assignment, and the type of data they store.

TABLE 14.3   Common Scripting Variable Types

Variable Type	Color	Description
Boolean (bool)	Red	Stores a value of **0** (off or false) or **1** (on or true).
Integer (int)	Cyan	Stores any whole round number, such as **1, 0, −100**, or **376**.
Float	Green	Stores any value with a decimal, such as **1.0, −64.12**, or **3.14159**.
String	Magenta	Stores text.
Vector	Gold	Stores three floats, X, Y, and Z, such as **100.5, 32.90, 100.0**.
Rotator	Purple	Is a vector that stores three floats, where X is roll, Y is pitch, and Z is yaw.
Transform	Orange	Is a struct that stores a vector for location, a rotator for orientation, and a vector for scale.
Object	Blue	Refers to an Actor in the level and stores all its properties in memory.

NOTE

What Is a Struct?

Short for *structure*, a struct is a collection of variables of any type represented as a single variable. The Vector and Rotator variables are technically structs because they store three separate Float variables. You can create your own structs in the UE4, but it is an advanced topic you should look into after you are more comfortable using the Blueprint Editor.

To declare a variable, click the + symbol next to Variables in the My Blueprint panel and give the new variable a name. Then, in the Details panel, you can set what type of variable it is and set its default values. To set the default values, you need to compile the Blueprint once, just after declaring the variable. After you have declared a variable, named it, and assigned a value, the most common operations performed on it are setting and getting the data for the variable. Getting retrieves the value stored in the variable, and setting stores a values. Figure 14.7 shows Get and Set nodes for common variable types.

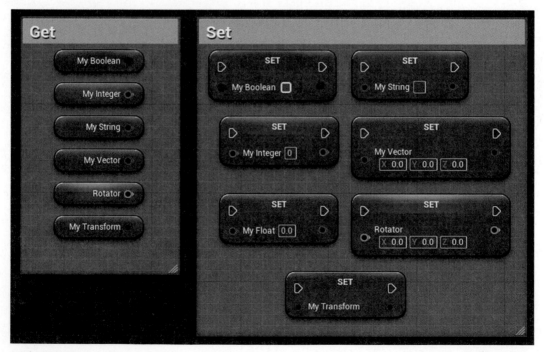

FIGURE 14.7
Get and set variable nodes.

NOTE
_____

Variable Lists

Every variable type in Blueprint can store a single value or an array. A variable converted to an array stores a list of its data type. You can use a group of functions to manage variable arrays—to set, get, remove, or add to spots in the array.

_____

TRY IT YOURSELF ▼

Declare Variables

Using the same Level Blueprint from the previous Try It Yourself, follow these steps to declare an integer variable, give it a name, and give it an initial value:

1. In the My Blueprint panel, click the + symbol next to Variables to add a new variable. Name this variable **MyInteger**. In the Details panel, set the variable type to **integer**.

2. To set the default value of the new MyInteger variable, click the **Compile** button on the Blueprint Editor toolbar. Then in the Details panel, under Default Value, set the variable's initial value to **100**.

3. To add an event called **Event Tick**, right-click in the Event Graph and, in the Blueprint Context Menu, select **Event Tick** to add the event node.

4. Press **Ctrl+W** to copy and paste the **Print String** function from the previous Try It Yourself, and wire it up to the Event Tick exec out pin.

5. In the My Blueprint panel, under Variables, click+drag the MyInteger variable into the Event Graph. Release the mouse, and you are asked if you want to set or get the variable. Choose **get** to place the variable on the graph.

6. Click the integer variable's data pin and drag it to the in string data pin on the Print String function. The Editor automatically adds a conversion node to convert the integer variable to a string variable. When finished, your Level Blueprint should look as shown in Figure 14.8.

7. Compile the script and preview the level. You see the default integer value repeatedly displayed on the left-hand side of the Level Viewport.

FIGURE 14.8
Event BeginPlay and Event Tick added to level Blueprint Event Graph.

NOTE

Event Tick

By default, Event Tick executes after every frame render (**Tick Interval 0**). The Delta Seconds data pin on the Event Tick node returns the amount of time it has taken to render each frame during that tick. If you are coming from a coding environment that uses game loops, you might recognize Event Tick as the Unreal equivalent to those loops. You can change Event Tick update intervals by clicking the **Class Settings** icon on the Blueprint toolbar. You can then change the settings in the Details panel, under **Actors Tick/Tick Interval (Sec)**.

Operators and Conditionals

Operators and conditionals are found in the Blueprint Context Menu under **Flow Control**. *Operators* are mathematical operation such as addition, subtraction, multiplication, and division. Operators allow you to modify the value of numerical variables such as floats, integers, and vectors. *Conditional expressions* allow you to check or compare the state of a variable and then respond accordingly. For example, you can check whether one variable is equal to another, or you can check whether one is greater than another.

Use Conditionals and Operators and Set a Variable

Using the same level Blueprint from the previous Try It Yourself, follow these steps to use math operators and set a variable to increase the MyInteger variable:

1. Disconnect MyInteger from the conversion node by pressing **Alt+click** on the **MyInteger** data pin.

2. Click the **MyInteger** data pin, drag to the right, and release. In the Blueprint Context Menu's search box, type +. Under Math/Integer, select **Integer + Integer** to add an integer addition operation node. The + operation node is placed with a wired connection. Set the lower integer pin to 1.

3. From My Blueprint panel, drag the **MyInteger** variable onto the graph and choose **Set** to place a set variable function.

4. Wire the exec out pin from **Event Tick** to the exec in pin on the **Set MyInteger** node.

5. Wire the exec out pin from the **Set MyInteger** node to the exec in on the **Print String** function.

6. From the **Set** function node, wire the integer data pin out to the **Convert to String** node that is already connected to the Print String function. When finished, your level Blueprint should look similar to Figure 14.9.

7. Compile and preview the level. You see the MyInteger value on the left-hand side of the Viewport incrementally increasing by 1.

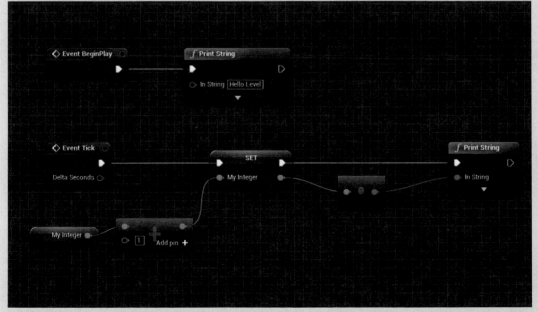

FIGURE 14.9
Level Blueprint example of getting an integer variable, adding a value of 1, and storing the result in the variable.

Script Organization and Commenting

In any scripting environment, organization and commenting are important, both when you are revisiting a script you wrote a month earlier and when other people on the development team need to make adjustments to something you scripted. Well-organized and commented scripts speed up development time. As described in the following sections, the Blueprint Editor has a few tools to help you keep things organized.

Node Comments

Node comments allow you to make notes on any node. Simply right-click the name of a placed node and look for the node comment box to pop up (see Figure 14.10) or hover the cursor over the node until the node comment box appears.

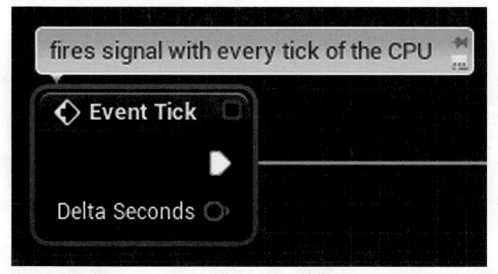

FIGURE 14.10
Example of a node comment.

Comment Box

Comment boxes (see Figure 14.11) allow you to wrap a selection of nodes inside a box and add a text comment. Another advantage to a comment box is that when you move a comment box, all the nodes inside the comment box move with it. To add a comment box to a selection of nodes, press the C key.

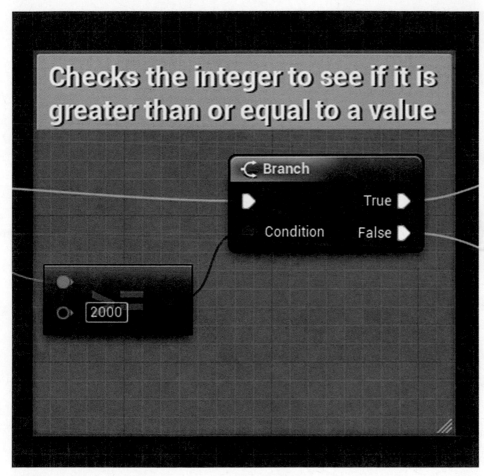

FIGURE 14.11
Example of a comment box.

Reroute Nodes

As your scripts get more complicated, you get more and more wires cluttering things up.
A reroute node can help you control the placement of a wire, as shown in Figure 14.12. To add
a reroute node, **right-click** an empty location on the Event Graph and in the Context Menu's
search box, type **reroute** and select **reroute** from the list to place the node.

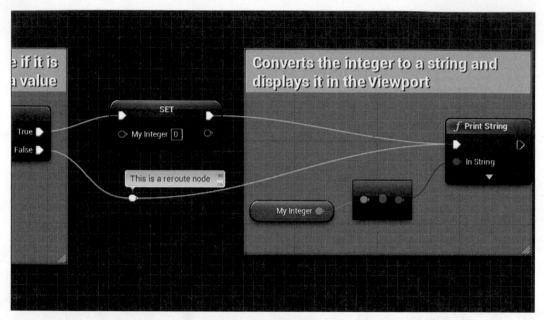

FIGURE 14.12
Reroute node used to control a wire.

Summary

This hour introduced you to the two methods used for coding in UE4, the fundamental concepts of scripting, and the Blueprint Editor interface. You learned to add events and functions, and you learned how to declare, get, and set variables. These core skills are needed to work in any Blueprint in UE4.

Q&A

Q. When I try to add a second event node, BeginPlay, the Editor shows me the first one already placed in the Event Graph. Why does this happen?

A. Some events, such as Event Tick and the BeginPlay event, can have only one instance per Blueprint. This might seem like it would be a problem when you start using multiple Event Graphs in a single Blueprint, but it's not. If you want to pass an event from one graph to another, you can create a custom event that Event Tick or BeginPlay calls every time it sends a signal.

Q. How do you determine a name for a variable?

A. You can give a variable any name you like. Try to choose a short, descriptive name that makes it easily identifiable. It is also best to establish a naming convention that can be applied across all the Blueprints in a project for consistency.

Q. Can I change the name of a variable after it has already been given one?

A. Yes, you can change the name of a variable in the My Blueprint window, or you can do it in the Blueprint Details panel with the variable selected. Changing the name updates all instances of the variable throughout the Blueprint.

Q. Can a variable type be changed after it has been created and used in the Event Graph?

A. Yes, you can change the variable type of an already-declared and used variable, but doing so affects the Blueprint. Remember that the data pins on functions are looking for specific data types, and if you change a variable type, you break any of the wires connecting the variable to data pins. You have to go back and adjust to the script manually.

Q. Can I reuse level Blueprint scripts from one level in another level?

A. No. Although, you can copy and paste event sequences from one Blueprint to another, the variables all need to be re-created in the new Blueprint's script. Also, many event sequences and actions in a Level Blueprint are tied to specific Actors in that level that do not exist in the new level. This is the advantage to using Blueprint Class Actors, which you learn about in later hours.

Workshop

Now that you have finished the hour, see if you can answer the following questions.

Quiz

1. True or false: Blueprint can be used to rewrite the Core Rendering Engine used in UE4.

2. True or false: Using the Print String function is not a good way to communicate with players.

3. True or false: Blueprint scripts compile to the bytecode level.

4. True or false: You can have more than one BeginPlay event in a single Blueprint script.

5. What is an array?

6. True or false: Commenting your scripts is a waste of time.

Answers

1. False. If you need to modify the Core Engine Components for your game, you need to work in C++.

2. True. The Print String function should only be used for debugging purposes.

3. True. Blueprints are compiled to the bytecode level.

4. False. You can only have a BeginPlay event in a Blueprint, but you can use a custom event to pass the signal or a Sequence node to split the signal.

5. An array is a variable that stores a list of values based on its type.

6. False. You should always comment your scripts.

Exercise

Building from the last Try It Yourself exercise in this hour, add a second integer variable that changes how much you increment the MyInteger integer variable for every tick. Then use a condition in the Event Tick sequence that checks the value of the MyInteger integer variable and resets MyInteger to 0 when it reaches a value of 2000 or above. Then finish the sequence with a custom event that when called, plays the print string. Figure 14.13 shows an example.

1. Open the Level Blueprint you have been working on this hour.

2. Declare a new variable, name it **MyIntCounter**, change its type to **integer**, and give it a default value of **5**.

3. Add **MyIntCounter** to the Event Graph and wire it up to the addition + node.

4. After the SET My Integer node, check whether it is greater than or equal to (>=) 2000. In the Blueprint Context Menu search box, type **integer >=**, and select **integer >= integer** to place the node. This node returns a value of **0** (false) or **1** (true).

5. Set the B integer data pin on the >= node to **2000**.

6. Check whether the condition is true or false by using a Branch node. Click and drag from the red Boolean data pin on the >= node to bring up the Blueprint Context Menu. In the Context Menu search box, type **Branch** and select it from the list to place the node.

7. Wire the exec out on the SET MyInteger node to the exec in on the Branch node.

8. Click and drag from the Branch True exec out pin to bring up the Blueprint Context Menu. In the search box, type **set myinteger** and select **Set MyInteger** to place the node.

9. On the SET my Integer, type **0** in the text box next to the My Integer Data pin.

10. Now create a custom event. Below the sequence in the Event Graph, right-click in the empty area to bring up the Blueprint Context Menu. In the Search box, type **custom** and select **Add Custom Event** from the list to place the event node. Rename the event **MyCustomEvent**.

11. Click-drag from the MyCustomEvent event node exec out pin, and in the Blueprint Context Menu search box type **print**. Select **Print String** from the list to place the node.

12. From the My Blueprint Panel, drag out the **MyInteger** variable onto the **In String** variable data pin on the Print String node. Blueprint automatically places the variable and adds a conversion node.

13. From the False exec, pin on the Branch node at the end of the first sequence. Click-drag to bring up the Context Menu. In the search box, type **mycustomevent** and select **MyCustomEvent** from the list to place the function.

14. Drag a wire from the exec out pin on the SET My Integer node wired to the branch and link it to the blue **MyCustomEvent** function. When finished, your Level Blueprint should look similar to Figure 14.13.

15. Save and preview the level.

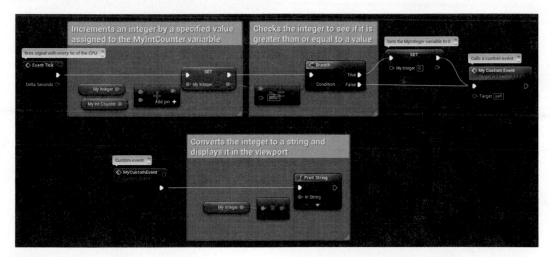

FIGURE 14.13
Exercise script example.

HOUR 15
Working with Level Blueprints

What You'll Learn in This Hour:

▶ Assigning Actors to events in a Level Blueprint
▶ Assigning an Actor as a Reference variable in a Level Blueprint
▶ Getting and setting the properties of an Actor in a Level Blueprint
▶ Using the Activate function
▶ Using the Play Sound at Location function

Every level has a Level Blueprint associated with it, although it may not be used. Although a level already stores a reference for every Actor placed in the level, the Level's Blueprint does not know about the Actors in the level unless you tell it. This hour teaches you how to assign placed Actors to Collision Events and how to add them as reference variables in a Level Blueprint. Then you learn to change an Actor's properties through the Level Blueprint Editor when an event is fired.

NOTE

Hour 15 Project Setup

Before you begin this hour, create a new project with the First Person template with Starter Content and create a default level.

In order to practice assigning Actors to events and reference variables this hour, you learn to create a simple event sequence. When the player moves into a defined area in the level, an Overlap Event executes and changes the Material assigned to a Static Mesh Actor, activates a particle system, and plays a sound.

To assign an Actor to an event, you need an Actor placed in the level. For this discussion, you can use a Trigger Actor.

There a few ways to define an area in a level where the player can interact. Epic has provided three common shape trigger classes (Box Trigger, Capsule Trigger, and Sphere Trigger) and a

Trigger Volume class that works with Collision Events (see Figure 15.1). This hour focuses on working with the Box Trigger, Capsule Trigger, and Sphere Trigger classes.

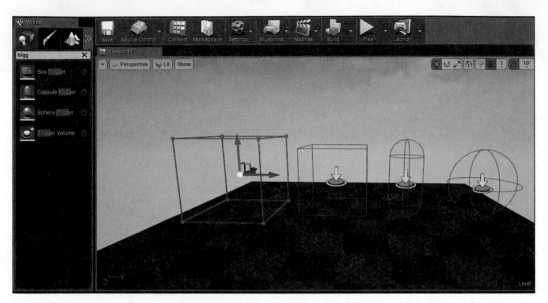

FIGURE 15.1
Placed Trigger Volumes.

All these classes can be found on the Place tab in the Modes panel. Search for a Trigger class by using the search box in the Place tab or select the Volumes category and drag out a Box Trigger and place it in your level. Before assigning the placed Box Trigger to an event, you need to modify some of its properties. With the Box Trigger placed and selected, change its name to **MyTriggerBox** in the Details panel, and in the Shape section, adjust the size by setting the Box Extent setting to **100** units on the X-, Y-, and Z-axes. You can adjust the shape settings at any time, but for now, you just need to make sure it is easy to enter the area defined by the Box Trigger Actor. Next, it is a good idea to change the rendering setting of the Box Trigger, so in the Rendering section of the Details panel, uncheck **Actor Hidden in Game**. This displays the Box Trigger's defined area when previewing and playtesting the level.

TIP

Rendering and Actor Visibility

Just about every placed Actor has rendering properties that can turn the visibility of the Actor on and off both in the Editor and in the level during gameplay. Typically, you do not want players to see the Trigger Actor because it might break immersion, depending on the visual style of the game. However, turning on visibility by unchecking **Actor Hidden in Game** temporarily helps you set up, playtest, and debug your Blueprint. Just remember to turn visibility off when you have everything working. Visibility settings for an Actor are found in the Rendering section of the Level Details panel when the Actor is selected.

Actor Collision Settings

With a default level created, the Game Mode set, and a Box Trigger Actor placed in your level, you can now create a Collision Event in the Level Blueprint. Collison-based events are directly related to the assigned Actor's collision properties—in this case, the Box Trigger Actor's collision properties. With the Box Trigger Actor selected, in the Level Blueprint Editor's Details panel, you can see several relevant properties (see Figure 15.2): Simulation Generate Hit Events, Generate Overlap Events, and Collision Responses.

GO TO ▶ HOUR 4, WORKING WITH STATIC MESH ACTORS, discusses collision responses types.

When Simulation Generates Hit Events and Generate Overlap Events are selected, they allow the Actor to broadcast Collision Events to the Level Blueprint. Hit Events happen when Actor collision hulls are touching but not intersecting. *Overlap Events* happen the moment two Actor collision hulls overlap or stop overlapping. Hit and Overlap Events are directly related to each Actor's collision presets. If two Actors are set to block each other, they will never overlap.

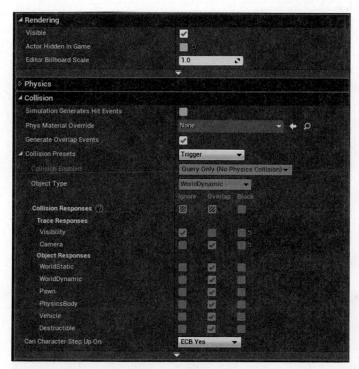

FIGURE 15.2
Trigger Actor Collision properties.

In Blueprint, the Event nodes responsible for receiving hit and overlap signals from Actors are as follows:

▶ **OnActorBeginOverlap event:** Fires once every time the assigned Actor's collision hull overlaps with another Actor's collision hull that meets the required collision response type. If the Actor leaves the collision area of the Event Actor and then reenters, the event fires again.

▶ **OnActorEndOverlap event:** Works the same way as the OnActorBeginOverlap event, but only when the other Actor leaves the area.

▶ **OnActorHit event:** Does not require the Actor's collision hulls to overlap but to touch. This event type is especially useful when you're working with Actors simulating physics. If a Physics Actor has a Hit Event assigned to it and is resting on the ground, this event continues to fire.

Assigning Actors to Events

Assigning an Actor to an event in the Level Blueprint is a straightforward process. It requires the Actor to be selected in the level and the event to be assigned in the Level Blueprint with the Blueprint Context Menu. Select the Actor in the level and right-click in the Level Blueprint Editor Event Graph to bring up the Context Menu. In the Context Menu, ensure that **Context Sensitive** is selected, expand the category **Add Event for MyTriggerBox**, and in the Collision subcategory, pick the Collision Event node type you need (see Figure 15.3).

FIGURE 15.3
Blueprint Context Menu with **Context Sensitive** turned on.

NOTE

Context Sensitive

In the upper-right corner of the Blueprint Context Menu is the Context Sensitive setting. Selecting this option organizes the content in the Context Menu based on your current selection, showing only events and functions that work with the selected Actor, component, or variable type.

TRY IT YOURSELF ▼

Assign an Actor to an OnActorBeginOverlap Event

Follow these steps to assign the Box Trigger Actor to the OnActorBeginOverlap event:

1. Open the Level Blueprint Editor.

2. Select the placed Box Trigger Actor in the level.

3. In the Level Blueprint Event Graph, right-click to bring up the Blueprint Context Menu. Make sure Context Sensitive is selected in the upper-right corner.

4. At the top of the list of actions in the Context Menu, expand **the MyTriggerBox** list by clicking the triangle to the left of the category.

5. Expand Collision and select **Add OnActorBeginOverlap** to add the Event node with the selected Actor assigned to it, designated by the Actor's name in parentheses after the event type name.

6. Click and drag off the exec out pin for the OnActorBeginOverlap Event. Releasing the mouse brings up the Context Menu again. Add a Print String (which you find under Utilities > String). Your event sequence should now look as shown in Figure 15.4.

7. In the Print String function, type **Hello Level**.

8. Preview the level by walking to and entering the Box Trigger area.

FIGURE 15.4
OnActorBeginOverlap event node with Actor assignment.

The OnActorBeginOverlap event node has an exec pin that passes the event signal, and it has a data out pin that returns a reference to the Actor that initiated the Overlap Event. If you drag the data out pin to the In String data pin on the Print String function, the Level Blueprint Editor automatically adds a Get Display Name function that returns the name of the Actor that instigated the event and passes it to the Print String function, as shown in Figure 15.5. Make these changes, preview the level, and walk into the area again. This time, the Print String function returns the name of the Pawn.

FIGURE 15.5
OnActorBeginOverlap event sequence that displays the name of the Other Actor—the Actor that initiates the event.

Assigning Actors to Reference Variables

In Blueprint, you can modify just about any properties you see in the Level Details panel for an Actor. An Actor Reference variable points to an assigned Actor in the level and gives the Level Blueprint access to the Actor's properties.

Assigning an Actor to an Actor Reference variable is a similar process to assigning an Actor to an event. With the Level Blueprint Editor open, select the desired Actor in the level (see Figure 15.6). In the Event Graph, right-click to open the Blueprint Context Menu and choose **Add Actor as Reference Variable** to place a variable with the selected Actor assigned to it into the Blueprint.

FIGURE 15.6
Actor Reference variable.

Actor Components

All Actors placed in a level have common settings found on every Actor, such as transform and rendering settings. These properties are on the Actor level, while other properties affect the Actor on the component level. A *component* is a subobject element of an Actor, and most (if not all) Actors have at least one component (see Figure 15.7). For example, Static Mesh Actors have a Static Mesh component, while Emitter Actors have a Particle System component, and Trigger Actors have a Collision component.

FIGURE 15.7
Component list of Static Mesh Actors in the Details panel.

NOTE

Components

There are many types of components. Some Actors have only one component, while others may have many components.

GO TO ▶ **HOUR 16, WORKING WITH BLUEPRINT CLASSES**, to learn more about working with components in Blueprint.

Getting and Setting Actor Properties

Much as when you work with any other variable types, you can get or set the properties of an Actor. Getting the property of an Actor creates a variable node that returns the data type of that property. For example, getting the location of an Actor returns a vector, as shown in Figure 15.8.

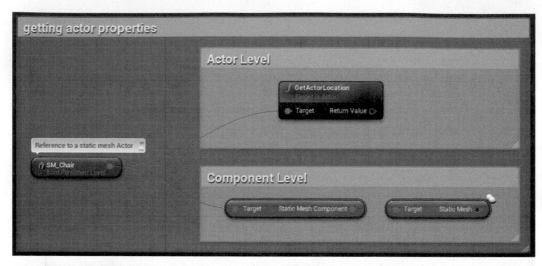

FIGURE 15.8
Getting an Actor's properties on the Actor level and the Component level.

Setting the properties of an Actor or its components requires a function that targets the Actor or the Actor's components, as shown in Figure 15.9.

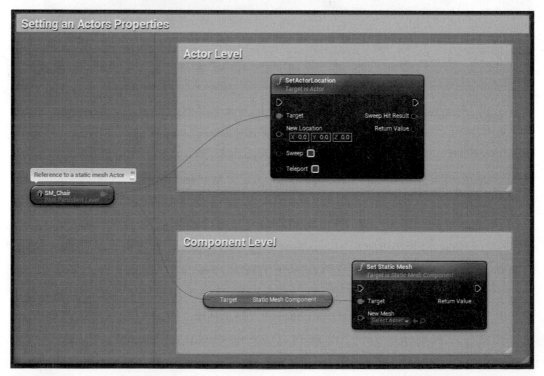

FIGURE 15.9
Setting an Actor's properties on the Actor level and Component level.

Function Targets

In many cases, for a function to execute properly, it needs to know what to affect. This is determined by a target data in pin. The blue Target pin tells a function which Actor or which component of the Actor the function should affect. Some functions work on the Actor level, while others work on the Component level. If you need to change a property of an Actor on the Actor level, you need a function that targets an Actor, but if you need to change a property of a component on the Actor, you need a function that targets a component. For example, if you want to change the location of an Actor, you work on the Actor level, but if you want to change the Static Mesh asset assigned to a Static Mesh Actor, you work on the Static Mesh Component level.

If you are changing a property on the Actor level, you need a function that works on the Actor level, and if you are changing a property on the Component level, you need a function that works on the Component level. Under the name of a function is a description that tells you if the function targets an Actor or a Component.

TRY IT YOURSELF ▼

Change the Material Properties of an Actor

Follow these steps to use a Box Trigger with an OnActorBeginOverlap event to change the material assigned to a Static Mesh Actor:

1. Add a Box Trigger Actor to the level. In the Level Detail panel, under Shapes, set Box Extents to **100** unit for the X-, Y-, and Z-axes.

2. In the Level Blueprint Editor Event Graph, add an OnActorBeginOverlap event with the Box Trigger Actor assigned to it.

3. Place a cone Static Mesh Actor in the center of the Box Trigger Actor and change its name to **MyCone**.

4. Find a material in the Content Browser under Starter Content in the Materials folder and drag it onto the placed cone Static Mesh Actor.

5. In the Level Blueprint Editor, with the Cone Static Mesh Actor selected, right-click in the Event Graph. In the Blueprint Context Menu, select **Create a Reference to** for the MyCone Static Mesh Actor.

6. With the Actor Reference variable placed, click the blue data out pin. Drag and release it to bring up the Context Menu. In the search box, type **set Material**.

7. Select **Set Material** from the list to add the Set Material function and Component Reference variable.

8. Link the OnActorBeginOverlap event exec out pin to Set Material's exec in pin.

9. Under the Set Material function, assign a new material from the material properties in the Content Browser. When you're finished, your event sequence should look similar to the one shown in Figure 15.10.

10. Preview the Level and move the pawn over to the cone.

FIGURE 15.10
The OnActorBeginOverlap event sequence changes the material assigned to a Static Mesh Actor.

As you walk over to the cone in the level you worked with in the preceding Try It Yourself and the Pawn Actor's collision hull overlaps with the Box Trigger Actor, the event fires and changes the material. But when the pawn moves away, the new material stays. In the next Try It Yourself, you will reset the material back to the originally assigned material when the Pawn leaves the Trigger Actor's area.

▼ TRY IT YOURSELF

Reset the Material Properties of an Actor

Follow these steps to use an OnActorBeginOverlap event to change the material back to the originally assigned material:

1. In the Level Blueprint Editor Event Graph, add an OnActorBeginOverlap event with the Box Trigger Actor assigned to it.

2. In the Level Blueprint Editor, with the cone Static Mesh Actor selected, right-click in the Event Graph. In the Blueprint Context Menu, select **Create a Reference to MyCone** to add a second reference variable for the MyCone Actor to the Level Blueprint.

3. With the new Actor Reference variable placed, click the blue data out pin. Drag and release to bring up the BP Context Menu. In the Search Box, type **set Material**.

4. Select **Set Material** from the list to add another Set Material function.

5. Link the OnActorBeginOverlap event and exec out pin to the **Set** Material's exec in pin.

6. Under the new Set Material function, assign to the material property the original material you placed on the MyCone Static Mesh Actor in step 4 of the previous Try It Yourself. When you're finished, your event sequence should look similar to the one shown in Figure 15.11.

7. Preview the Level and move the pawn in and out of the Box Trigger to see the material change.

FIGURE 15.11
Overlap Collision events.

Activate Property

For a few Actors, such as the Emitter Actor and the Ambient Sound Actor, an activate property tells the Actor to start playing the Particle Emitter or sound the moment the level is loaded. This property is on by default. Deactivating this property in the Levels Details panel for the Actor stops the Actor from playing until the property is changed. This property can be set, changed, or retrieved in Blueprint with several functions: Activate, Deactivate, IsActive, SetActivate, and

ToggleActive. In the next Try It Yourself exercise, you will place a Particle Emitter Actor into the level. You will also have the OnActorBeginOverlap sequence activate the Emitter Actor and an OnActorEndOverlap sequence deactivate the Actor.

▼ TRY IT YOURSELF

Activating and Deactivating a Particle Emitter Actor

Follow these steps to extend the previous Try It Yourself exercises and build off the OnActorBeginOverlap sequence:

1. Get a P_Explosion Particle System asset from the Starter Content Particles folder in the Content Browser and place it the in the center or near the Box Trigger Actor so you can see it when you interact with the trigger.

2. With the placed Emitter Actor selected in the level, right-click in the Level Blueprint Event Graph to open the Context Menu and select **Create a Reference to P_Explosion**.

3. With the P_Explosion Actor reference created, click and drag off of the blue data out pin of the variable node and release. In the Context Menu search box, type **activate** and select **Activate (ParticleSystemComponent)** this adds two nodes: an Activate function and a Component Reference variable that points to the Particle System assigned to the Emitter Actor.

4. Link the Set Material exec out pin to the Activate exec in pin.

5. Press **Ctrl+W** to copy and paste the P_Explosion reference variable. Drag out a Deactivate function and wire it to the end of the OnActorEndOverlap event sequence by linking it to the exec out pin of the Set Material function. When you're finished, your event sequence should look similar to the one shown in Figure 15.12.

6. Preview the level and walk in and out of the volume. Each time the Pawn Actor overlaps the sphere triggers, the event fires and activates the Particle Emitter.

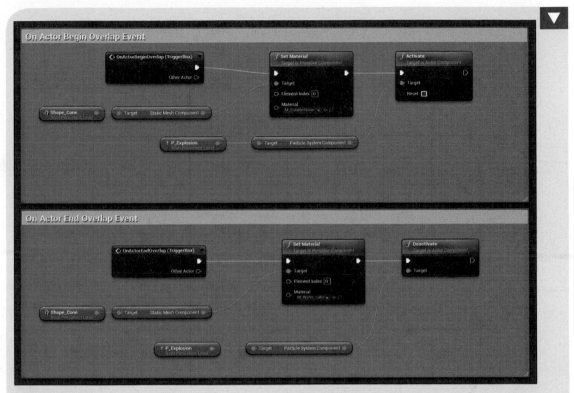

FIGURE 15.12
Toggle Particle Emitter Blueprint.

Play Sound at Location Function

In the previous examples, you have been using the Level Blueprint Editor to modify or control placed Actors. For the next example, you will use the Play Sound at Location function to play a Sound Cue asset on the fly. This function needs to know what Sound asset you want to play and the location in the level where it should play. The Sound asset to play can be assigned from the Content Browser or the function's drop-down list. You need to get the location from one of the already-placed Actors.

In the following Try It Yourself, you learn to add a Play Sound at Location function and get the location of a placed Actor.

▼ TRY IT YOURSELF

Add a Play Sound at Location Function

Continuing from the previous Try It Yourself, follow these steps to use a Play Sound at Location function to play a Sound Cue or Sound Wave asset when the OnActorBeginOverlap function fires:

1. Open the Level Blueprint for your level from the previous Try It Yourself.
2. In the Event Graph locate the OnActorBeginOverlap event sequence from the previous Try It Yourself.
3. Click the Activate function's exec out pin at the end of the sequence. Drag off and release so the Blueprint Context Menu opens. Type **Play Sound at Location** in the Search Box and select the **Play Sound at Location** function from the list.
4. Locate the Explosion_Cue Sound Cue asset in the Audio folder of the Starter Content in the Content Browser or use the drop-down menu on the function's node. **Click+drag** the Explosion_Cue Sound Cue asset to the Sound property on the Play Sound at Location function.
5. Select the Trigger Actor and add it as a reference variable to the Level Blueprint.
6. Click the blue data pin of the reference variable node and drag and release. In the Context Menu's search box, type **get Actor location** and select **Get Actor Location Function** from the list.
7. Click the yellow vector data out pin on the Get Actor function and drag a wire to the yellow vector data in pin on the Play Sound at Location function. When you're finished, your event sequence should look similar to the one shown in Figure 15.13.
8. Preview the level and walk the Pawn in and out of the Trigger Actor's defined area to hear the sound play.

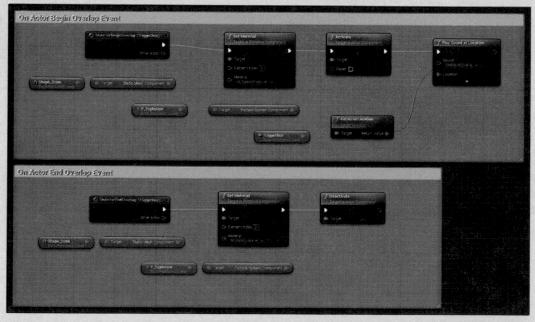

FIGURE 15.13
Placed Trigger Volumes.

NOTE

Ambient Sound Actor

If you prefer, you can use an Ambient Sound Actor and a ToggleActivate function to play a sound when the event fires. Just place a non-looping Sound Wave or Sound Cue in the level and follow the steps of the previous Try It Yourself. Replace the Particle Emitter Actor with an Ambient Sound Actor.

Using Physics Actors to Activate Events

So far, you have only been using the pawn to initiate Collision Events. Next you will set an event to fire when either a Static Mesh Actor that is set to Simulate Physics or a projectile overlaps with the Trigger Actor. You don't have to do any more scripting; you can just make some minor changes to the Collision properties in the Details panels of the Actors involved.

TRY IT YOURSELF ▼

Use a Physics Actor to Trigger Events

Continuing from the previous Try It Yourself, follow these steps to make the OnActorBeginOverlap event fire when a Static Mesh Actor that is set to simulate physics overlaps the volume:

1. From the Props folder in the Starter Content folder in the Content Browser, select a Static Mesh asset and place it above the Box Trigger from the previous exercises.

2. Under the placed Static Mesh Actor's Physics properties in the Details panel, select **Simulate Physics**.

3. Under the placed Static Mesh Actor's Collision properties in the Details panel, set **Generate Overlap Events**.

4. Preview the Level. As the Static Mesh Actor falls into the area defined by the Trigger Actor, the overlapped event is fired, and the material is changed.

NOTE

Using Projectile Actors to Activate Events

If you are using version 4.8 or earlier, the Trigger Actor's default Collision Presets setting is **Overlap with Everything but Projectiles**. To modify this, change Collision Presets to **Custom**. This unlocks the Object Response types, and you can set the Projectile category to Overlap. Preview the level again and shoot the Box Trigger. The Projectile category has been removed in later versions.

Summary

This hour, you learned to assign Actors to events and add them to a Level Blueprint as a reference variable. You were introduced to working with Trigger Actors and to modifying the properties of an Actor in the Level Blueprint Editor. You learned to activate and deactivate a Particle Emitter to play a Sound asset at a specified location when an event sequence fires. All these things are common event sequences found in many games. Remember to select the **Actor Hidden in Game** property for the placed Trigger Actors when you're done with everything else.

Q&A

Q. When I assign an Actor to a Collision Event in Level Blueprint, the event does not execute, Why?

A. When this happens, there are a few areas to check. First, look at the collision properties for the Actor assigned to the event and make sure Generate Overlap Events is selected. Then check the Collision Presets and Object Response types settings to make sure the Actor class type you need to instigate the event with is set to Overlap. Then check the Collision Presets and Object Response types settings for any of instigator Actors. If the instigators are Static Mesh Actors, check the Static Mesh assets to verify that they have collision hulls assigned to them.

Q. I assigned the wrong Actor to an event. Can I change it, or do I need to delete the event and start over?

A. Although you can easily delete the Event node and start over, you can also change which Actor is assigned to an already-created Event node. Select the new Actor in the level and then in the Level Blueprint Editor, right-click the title of the already-placed event node and select **Assign Selected Actor**. This will change which Actor the Event node is assigned to in the level.

Q. Why do the Particle Emitter and Sound Actors activate immediately when the level is played?

A. This has to do with the Auto Activate property on each of the Actors. By default, this property is set. To correct this for an Actor, select the Actor and in the Level Details panel, go to the Activate section and turn off the **Auto Activate** property.

Q. When I overlap the Trigger Actor in the level rapidly in succession, the Emitter does not always activate. Why?

A. The event is executing every time there is an overlap, but the Particle Emitter has a predetermined lifetime that must finish before it can be activated again.

Q. **What is the difference between the Box Trigger, Sphere Trigger, and Capsule Trigger classes and the Trigger Volume class?**

A. While all these classes can be used to trigger Collision Events, the primary difference is that the Trigger Volume class is based on BSPs and can be used to define more complex volume beyond simple primitive shapes. Since Trigger Volume Actors are based on BSPs, they are static, meaning they cannot move during gameplay.

Workshop

Now that you have finished the hour, see if you can answer the following questions.

Quiz

1. True or false: Trigger classes are found in the Place tab in the Modes panel.

2. True or false: If a Trigger Actor is not broadcasting an Overlap Event to its assigned OnActorBeginOverlap event node in the Level Blueprint, it's because Simulate Generate Hit Events has not been turned on for the Actor in the level.

3. A _____ is a subobject element of an Actor.

4. In order for a function to change the property of an Actor or a component, you need to assign an Actor or a component to the function's _____ data in pin.

5. True or false: If an Emitter Actor starts emitting particles immediately after the level is previewed, it is because the Auto Activate property is turned on for the Actor.

Answers

1. True. All the Trigger classes are located in the Place tab in the Modes panel.

2. False. Generate Overlap Events must be turned on for Overlap Events to work, and Simulate Generate Hit Events must be turned on for Hit events to work.

3. Components are subobject elements of Actors, and all Actors should have at least one component.

4. Target. The Target property on a function tells the function which Actor or component the function will affect when executed.

5. True. The Auto Activate property tells the Actor to play when turned on.

Exercise

For this hour's exercise, practice assigning Actors to events, adding Actors as reference variables, and modifying their properties. In a new default level, create three more OnActorBeginOverlap events, using different Trigger Actor types, and change the material property for each of three different Static Mesh Actors.

1. In the same project you've been working on this hour, create a new default level.

2. Place three Trigger Actors into the level: a Box Trigger, a Sphere Trigger, and a Capsule Trigger.

3. Resize each of the Trigger Actors and turn off **Actor Hidden in Game** in the Level Details panel for each of the Trigger Actors.

4. Place three Static Mesh Actors inside each Trigger Volume in the level and assign a unique material to each of them.

5. Open the Level Blueprint Editor and assign each Actor an OnActorBeginOverlap event.

6. Add each of the placed Static Mesh Actors as a reference variable to the Level Blueprint.

7. Use a Set Material function in each of the OnActorBeginOverlap event sequences for each of the Static Mesh Actors to change their material when the player shoots the Trigger Volume.

8. Use a Delay function to wait 1 second and another Set Material function in each of the OnActorBeginOverlap event sequences to change each Static Mesh back to its original material.

HOUR 16
Working with Blueprint Classes

What You'll Learn in This Hour:

- ▶ Creating a simple pickup class
- ▶ Adding and modifying components
- ▶ Working with Timelines
- ▶ Deriving a Blueprint class from an existing class

This hour introduces you to working with Blueprint classes. You start by learning to derive a Blueprint class from an Actor class and make a simple pickup class that bobs up and down and disappears when the character walks over it. Then you move on to learning how to derive a Blueprint class from the Point Light class and extend its functionality.

NOTE

Hour 16 Project Setup

Before you begin this hour, create a new project with the Third Person template and Starter Content. Then create two new folders in the Content Browser and name one **MyBlueprints** and the other **Maps**. Finally, create a new Default level and save it to the Maps folder.

Using Blueprint Classes

While Level Blueprints are great for creating event sequences, they are tied to the level that you are currently working on. Blueprint classes, on the other hand, allow you to script new Actors that can be reused in any level. This reuse speeds up production time because you only need to script the functionality of a Blueprint class once, but you can use it as many times and in as many levels as you like. When working with Blueprint classes, the Blueprint Editor has a few features specifically for working with Blueprint classes. You are introduced to some of these differences over the next hour.

Adding a Blueprint Class

In the Content Browser, navigate to the MyBlueprints folder you created earlier. With the folder selected, right-click in the Asset Management Area, and in the Context Menu that appears, select **Blueprint Class**. This opens the Pick Parent Class window, which allows you to create a Blueprint class asset. At the top is a Common Classes section that has quick links for commonly used class types (see Figure 16.1). Under this is the All Classes section, which lists all the existing classes from which you can derive a new Blueprint. For now, focus on creating a basic Actor class to learn how to add and position components. But later in this hour, you learn to create a new Blueprint from the Point Light class.

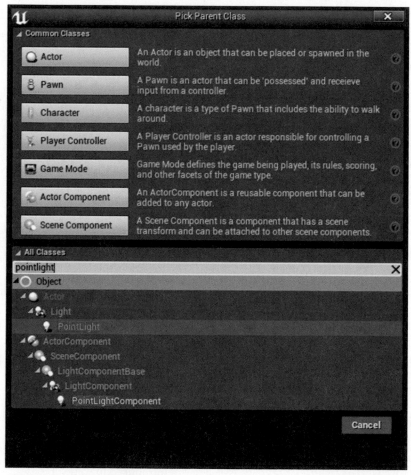

FIGURE 16.1
Pick Parent Class window.

All Blueprint classes are derived from existing classes, either classes originally created in C++ or other Blueprint classes. As you create new Blueprint classes, you will see them show up in the All Classes list. The Actor class is commonly used for deriving new Blueprints because it contains the base functionality needed for an Actor to be placed and rendered in a level.

In the next few Try It Yourself exercises, you create a simple pickup class that bobs up and down continually and, when a Pawn passes over the placed Actor of the class, it plays a sound, spawns a particle effect, and disappears. Then after a few seconds, the Actor plays another sound, another particle effect spawns, and the Pickup Mesh reappears, ready to be picked up again. To begin, you need to derive a Blueprint class from the Actor class.

TRY IT YOURSELF ▼

Create a Blueprint Class

Follow these steps to create a new Blueprint class:

1. In the Content Browser, in the MyBlueprints folder you created earlier, right-click an empty location in the Asset Management Area and select **Blueprint Class** from the Context Menu. The Pick Parent Class window appears.

2. In the Common Classes section of the Pick Parent Class window, click **Actor** and then click **Select** at the bottom of the window to create a Blueprint class. You now have a new Blueprint class asset in the Content Browser.

3. Rename the new asset **MyFirstPickup**.

4. Double-click **MyFirstPickup** to open the Blueprint Editor.

The Blueprint Editor Interface

Now that you have a Blueprint class created, look at the Blueprint Editor. The Blueprint Editor has a few windows and tools that are not found when working with Level Blueprints. These windows are identified in Figure 16.2 and described in the following list:

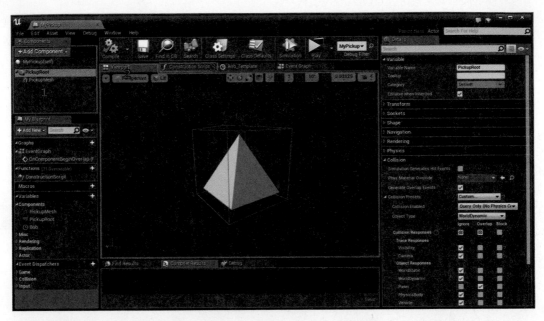

FIGURE 16.2
Blueprint Editor interface when working with a Blueprint class.

When working with a Blueprint class, the Blueprint Editor has a few features not found when working with Level Blueprints:

▶ **1) Components panel:** The Components panel lists all the components in the Blueprint and is used to manage them.

▶ **2) Viewport panel:** The Viewport panel displays the components in the Blueprint and is used to set up the spatial relationships of the component in the Actor.

▶ **3) Construction Script:** The Construction Script is a unique function that runs when an instance of the Blueprint (an Actor) is placed in a level. It is a node graph that, when executed, modifies each instance independently of the original Blueprint.

GO TO ▶ CHAPTER 17, USING EDITABLE VARIABLES AND THE CONSTRUCTION SCRIPT, to learn more about working with the Construction Script function in the Blueprint Editor.

When working with Blueprint classes, the Blueprint Editor's toolbar also has a few more buttons for managing a Blueprint class:

▶ **Save:** Saves changes made to a Blueprint as you work

▶ **Find in CB:** Locates the Blueprint in the Content Browser

▶ **Simulation:** Executes the Blueprint and displays the results in the Viewport of the Blueprint Editor

GO TO ▶ CHAPTER 14, INTRODUCING BLUEPRINT VISUAL SCRIPT SYSTEM, for a refresher on the core features found in the Blueprint Editor interface.

Working with the Components

One of the key concepts when working with Blueprint classes is components. A *component* is a subobject element of a Blueprint. Many different types of components can be added to a Blueprint, and a Blueprint can have many components at one time. You use the Components panel of the Blueprint Editor to manage all the components in a Blueprint. You can add, delete, rename, and organize components into hierarchical relationships by dragging one component onto another.

When a basic Blueprint class is first created, it already has a DefaultScene component assigned as the root component. While a Blueprint can have many components, there can be only one root component. The root component of the Blueprint is the only component that has transform limitations. It is the parent of all the other components in the Blueprint. It is the only component that cannot be moved or rotated, but it can be scaled. The root component's position and rotation are determined once the Actor is place in the level. All other components' transforms are relative to the root component by default. Just about any component type can be assigned as the root component.

Adding Components

The Components panel allows you to add components to an Actor in two different ways. If you click the green +**Add Components** button, you see an extensive list of components, organized in categories, that you can add to a Blueprint. To add a component from the Content Browser, **click+drag** the asset from the Content Browser into the Components panel in the Blueprint Editor. If there is a component type for that asset, it is automatically added to the Blueprint. You can easily do this for Static Meshes, Particle Systems, and Audio assets.

When a component is first added to a Blueprint, its parent is the DefaultScene root component. By dragging one component onto another, you can attach components, making one the parent and the other the child. They are both still subobject elements of the Actor, but the child component's transforms are relative to its parent component, and the parent component's transforms are relative to the root component, whose transforms are ultimately defined by the Actor's position in the world (the level).

Once a component is added to a Blueprint, you can edit its properties in the **Details** panel of the Blueprint Editor.

Many of the component types have properties that look familiar because they are similar to those of many of the Actors you have already been working with. For example, in a level you can place a Static Mesh Actor, but when working on the Blueprint class, you use a Static Mesh component. Both have the same properties used to modify a Static Mesh, but the component is a subobject element in Blueprint.

NOTE

Special Components

Some components, such as movement components, behave differently than a standard component. Movement components affect the entire Actor as a whole. They also do not have a physical representation in the Blueprint Viewport.

Viewport Panel

The Viewport panel allows you to see the spatial relationships of all the components added to an Actor. Much as in the Level Viewport, you can use transform gizmos to adjust the location, rotation, and scale of each of the components in the Blueprint. Select a component either in the Components panel or in the Viewport, and use the spacebar to cycle through the transform gizmos. There are also snap settings for all the transforms that you can turn on and off and adjust to help with the placement of each component.

TIP

Location Types: Relative and World

By default, added components' transforms are relative to their parent component and ultimately the root component of the Actor. You can change this separately for location, rotation, or scale. Select the component in the Blueprint Editor's Details panel, and in the Transforms category, click the triangle to the right of Location, Rotation, or Scale to change to relative or world based.

▼ TRY IT YOURSELF

Add Components

Now that you have created a Blueprint class, you need to add components. Follow these steps to add a Box Collision component and a Static Mesh component and to make the Static Mesh component a child of the Box Collision component:

1. Click the green **+Add Component** button at the top of the Components panel and click **Box Collision** in the drop-down to add this component to the Blueprint.

2. Right-click the newly added **Box Collision** component and rename it **PickupRoot**.

3. Click+drag the **PickupRoot** component onto **DefaultSceneRoot** to replace the DefaultSceneRoot component with the PickupRoot component.

4. In the Starter Content folder in the Content Browser, locate the **Shap_Quad** pyramid Static Mesh asset and drag it into the Components panel in the Blueprint Editor. You have now added a Static Mesh component to the Blueprint that references the pyramid Static Mesh asset.

5. Right-click the **Shap_Quad** in the Components panel and rename it **PickupMesh**.

6. Click the Viewport panel in the Blueprint Editor to see the components.

7. Select the Box Collision component either in the Components panel or in the Viewport panel. Then, in the Details panel, under Shape, set the Box Extent property to **60** for the X, Y, and Z categories.

8. Select the Static Mesh component in the Viewport panel and use the Move transform gizmo to reposition the Static Mesh component so it is inside the box collision.

9. Compile and save the Blueprint by clicking Compile and then Save on the Blueprint Editor toolbar. When you're finished, your Blueprint should look similar to the one in Figure 16.3.

10. On the Blueprint Editor toolbar, click **Find in CB** and locate your MyFirstPickup Blueprint class in the Content Browser.

11. From the Content Browser, click+drag an instance of the **MyFirstPickup** Blueprint class into your level.

FIGURE 16.3
Components panel and Viewport in the Blueprint Editor.

Blueprint Scripting with Components

When you're scripting a Blueprint class, you have functions that target the Actor and functions that target individual components in the Actor, but because you are working inside the Actor, you see/use the term *self* when referring to the Actor. So if you need to use a function that modifies the entire Actor, the target of the function is **self**. This also affects any events you might use. For example, you might have an event that is assigned to the Actor or an event that is assigned to individual component in the Actor. For example, there is an ActorBeginOverlap collision event that is assigned to Actors, and there is an OnComponentBeginOverlap collision event that is assigned to components in an Actor.

You can add any component in the Components panel to the Blueprint class Event Graph as a component reference variable by clicking and dragging the component into the Event Graph. In addition, every component you add to a Blueprint shows up in the Variables section of the My Blueprint panel. Once a component has been added as a component reference variable, you can use it as a target for functions that can modify the component's properties or behaviors.

In the following Try It Yourself, you script the main functionality of the pickup class so the player can walk over the Actor and make it disappear.

▼ TRY IT YOURSELF

Script the Functionality of a Simple Pickup

Now that you have components added to the Actor, the next step is to create a component overlap event, as described here:

1. In the Components panel select **PickupRoot(Box Collision)**. Then, in the Event Graph, right-click to bring up the Blueprint Context Menu. In the Context Menu's search box, type **on component begin overlap** and select the **OnBeginComponentOverlap** event to add it to the Event Graph.

2. Click+drag from the exec out pin on the **OnBeginComponentOverlap** node and release to bring up the Context Menu. Search for a **DoOnce** flow node and add it to the graph.

3. Click+drag from the completed exec out pin on the **DoOnce** node and release to bring up the Context Menu. Search for a **Set Hidden** mesh function and add it. This places the **Set Hidden in Game** node and a component reference variable that refers to the pickup mesh component. Click the **New Hidden Data Pin** check box to set it to true.

4. Click+drag off of the **Set Hidden in Game** function node's exec out pin and release to add a Play Sound at Location function. Assign a Sound Wave or Sound Cue asset (one that does not loop) to the Sound Data pin in by clicking the drop-down next to it.

5. Click+drag from the Play Sound at Location function node's exec out pin and add a Spawn Emitter at Location function node. Assign a Particle System to the Emitter Template data in pin by clicking on the drop-down next to the pin.

6. To set a location for Play Sound at Location and Spawn Emitter at Location, from the Components panel, drag **PickupRoot(Box Collision)** to the Event Graph to add a component reference variable for the component.

7. Click+drag from the blue data out pin on the placed component reference variable and add **GetWorldLocation (PickupRoot)**. Connect the Return Value Vector data out pin to the Location Vector data in pins on the Play Sound at Location and Spawn Emitter at Location function nodes.

8. To add a delay before the pickup reappears, click+drag and release and add a Delay function node. Set Duration to **3** (seconds).

9. Copy and paste all the nodes from the Set Hidden in Game function node to the Spawn Emitter at Location function node. Click+drag in an empty area in the Event Graph for a drag selection. Then press **Ctrl+C** to copy and **Ctrl+V** to paste duplicates of the selected nodes in to the Event Graph.

10. Move the pasted nodes so they are after the Delay function and link the Delay exec out pin to the pasted New Hidden in Game function.

11. Link the Pasted Spawn Emitter at Location exec out pin to the DoOnce Function Reset exec in pin all the way back at the beginning of the sequence.

12. When you are finished, your Blueprint sequence should look similar to the one shown in Figure 16.4. On the Blueprint toolbar, click **Compile** and then **Save**.

13. From the Content Browser, place a few copies of the **MyFirstPickup** Blueprint into the level.

14. Preview the level and walk over the pickup.

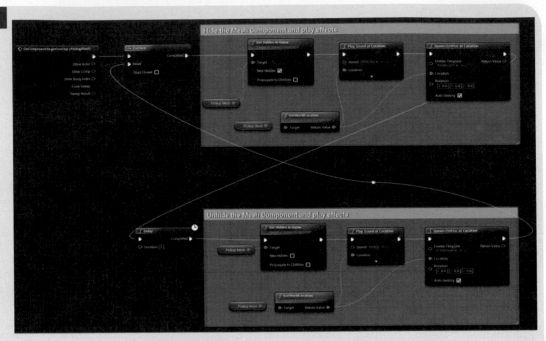

FIGURE 16.4
Pickup event sequence.

TIP

Blueprint Communication

Actors are self-contained, meaning they know information about themselves and their components. However, they do not know about other Actors in a level until an event fires—such as **OnActorBeginOverlap or OnComponentBeginOverlap**, which returns the Actor that initiated the event. There are a few ways around this, such as using event dispatchers, Blueprint interfaces, and casting. You can look further into these concepts when you are more comfortable with scripting basic Blueprint classes: https://docs.unrealengine.com/latest/INT/Engine/Blueprints/UserGuide/BlueprintCommsUsage/index.html

Working with the Timeline

A Timeline node allows you to create spline curve data that can be used in a Blueprint to change values over time. It can be used to animate the position of an Actor and/or its components or to change the intensity of the light component. To add a Timeline node to your Event Graph, right-click in the Event Graph to bring up the Blueprint Context Menu and in the search box type **Timeline**. Select **Add Timeline** from the list to place a Timeline node on the graph. You can have as many Timeline nodes as you need in a Blueprint, so it is good practice to rename each one you add with a descriptive name. To rename a Timeline, right-click it, choose **Rename**, and type in a new name. Once a Timeline has been add to an Event Graph, it also shows up in the My Blueprint panel, under Variables (or Components), and you can add a variable reference to the Timeline in other sequences in your Blueprint. Once you have a variable reference to a Timeline, you can change its properties through Blueprint.

A Timeline node has many exec in pins for playing, pausing, and rewinding the Timeline. It has an update exec out pin for running a sequence while the Timeline is playing and a finished exec out pin that executes when the Timeline is done (see Figure 16.5). If the Timeline is set to loop, the Finished exec out pin will not fire.

FIGURE 16.5
Timeline node.

Timelines have their own editor window that automatically opens when you double-click the node. With the Timeline Editor open, you see a toolbar for setting the properties of the Timeline and changing how it functions. You can set the length of the Timeline in seconds. You can set it to automatically play when the game begins, and you can set it to loop (see Figure 16.6).

FIGURE 16.6
Timeline Editor toolbar.

Timeline Tracks and Curves

On the Timeline Editor, you see buttons for adding different types of tracks. There are four types of tracks to work with in a Timeline: Float Track, Vector Track, Color Track, and an Event Track. Each of the track types is used to edit curve data with set keys and will create a data out pin on the Timeline node that returns the value of the specified variable type over the length of time the Timeline plays the track. The Event Track, however, adds an exec out pin to the Particle System node that fires at set times based on key placement.

A Timeline can have many tracks assigned to it. To add a track, simply click the track type you want, and Timeline adds it. You can rename a track by clicking the track title and typing in a new name. When you rename a track, the corresponding data pin on the Timeline node updates to reflect the new name. As you add tracks to a Timeline, new exec out and data pins are created, depending on the type of track added (see Figure 16.7).

Once a track has been added and renamed, you can start adding and editing keys along the curves in the track simply by **Shift+clicking** the curve. You can move an already-placed key manually by **click+dragging** the key. When a place key is selected, you can enter the precise time and value at the top of the track.

In the following Try It Yourself, you use a Timeline to animate the mesh component of the pickup Actor to bob up and down continually while the level is being played.

▼ TRY IT YOURSELF

Set Up the Timeline

Follow these steps to add a Timeline node to your Event Graph and edit a Float Track that will be used to animate your pickup Static Mesh component:

1. Add a Particle System node to your Blueprint if you have not already.

2. Rename the Particle System **PickupAnim**.

3. Double-click the Particle System node to open the Timeline Editor.

4. Set the Timeline length to **1** (second).

5. Select **Auto Play**.

6. Select **Loop**.

7. Add a Float Track to the Particle System by clicking the f+ button in the Timeline Editor.

8. Right-click **NewTrack_1** in the upper-left corner of the track and rename the track **bounce**.

9. Edit the curve in the track. To add a key, **Shift+click** the curve in the track. Add a key at Time **0** seconds with Value set to **0**.

10. Add a second key to the curve at Time **0.5** seconds with a Value setting of **1**. If the curve is off the track, use the left and right arrow buttons and the up and down buttons next to the Time input at the top of the track to fit the view of the track.

11. Add a final key at Time **1** second with Value set to **0**.

12. To change the interpolation of each key to Auto, right-click each key and choose **Auto** from the list. When you're finished, your curve should look like the one shown in Figure 16.7.

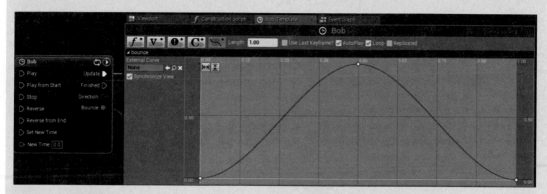

FIGURE 16.7
Timeline node with float data pin (left) and float curve track (right).

Once you have a Timeline set up, the next set is to use the float curve data to move the pickup Static Mesh component. You do this back in the Event Graph of the Blueprint. As the Particle System plays, it returns values ranging from 0 to 1 over 1 second. so you need to multiply the float values by the distance you want the pickup to move. Then you can apply the result to the Z-axis of the component to move it up and down.

Animate the Pickup with the Timeline

Follow these steps to animate the mesh component of your Blueprint with Timeline by making the mesh component bounce up and down rapidly:

1. From the Components panel, click+drag the **PickupMesh** component to the Event Graph to add it as a Reference variable.

2. **Click+drag** from the blue data pin on the PickupMesh Reference variable to open the Context Menu. In the search box, type **set relative location** and select **SetRelativeLocation** to add the function to the Event Graph.

3. Wire the Particle System update exec pin to the exec in on the SetRelativeLocation node.

4. Click+drag the green float data pin on the Particle System to open the Context Menu. In the search box, type **multiply** and select **Float * Float** to add it as a node.

5. In the text box next to the second float data pin on the Multiply node, type **10** to indicate the distance the component will move.

6. On the SetRelativeLocation node added in step 2, right-click the yellow vector data pin and choose **Split Struct Pin** from the list to split the vector to three green float data pins for X, Y, and Z locations.

7. Wire the green data pin out from the Multiply node to the green New Location Z float pin in on the SetRelativeLocation node.

8. Compile and save the Blueprint by clicking **Compile** and then **Save** on the Blueprint Editor toolbar. When you're finished, your Blueprint sequence should look similar to the one shown in Figure 16.8.

9. Preview the level. Your pickup Actors should now be moving up and down continuously.

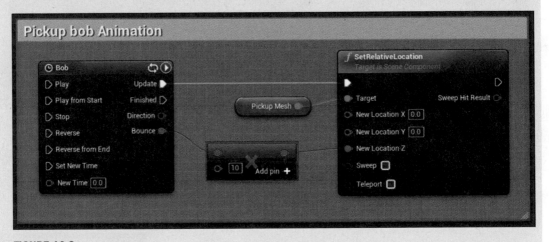

FIGURE 16.8
Animation sequence with a Particle System.

Scripting a Pulsating Light

Now that you have some experience creating a Blueprint class and working with components, for the second half of this hour, you're ready to learn to create a Blueprint class that extends the functionality of an existing class.

Over the next few Try It Yourself exercises, you create a pulsating light Blueprint derived from an existing class that randomly generates a light intensity within a specified range and then changes the Point Light intensity over time to meet that new value. Every time the light intensity equals the new intensity, the Blueprint randomly generates a new intensity. The Blueprint continues this process as long as the level is being played, so it needs an Event Tick event to constantly run the sequence.

Deriving a Blueprint from an Existing Class

In this section, you first create a new Blueprint class derived from a Point Light class (see Figure 16.9). This new class inherits the properties and components of the parent class. Then you can use the Blueprint Editor to create new functionality.

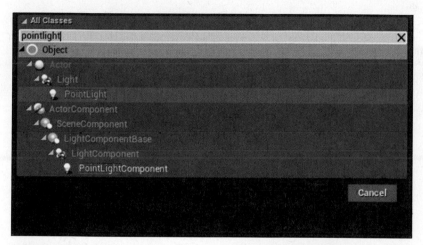

FIGURE 16.9
The All Classes section of the Pick Parent Class window.

Derive a Blueprint Class from the Point Light Class

Follow these steps to create a new Blueprint Actor from the Point Light class:

1. In the Content Browser, in the MyBlueprints folder you created earlier, right-click in an empty space in the Asset Management Area and select **Blueprint Class** from the dialog. The Pick Parent Class window appears.

2. In the All Classes section, type **pointlight** and select **Point Light**. Click **Select** at the bottom of the Pick Parent Class window.

3. In the Content Browser, rename the new asset **MyPulseLight_BP**.

4. Double-click **MyPulseLight_BP** to open it in the Blueprint Editor.

5. Drag **MyPulseLight_BP** from the Content Browser into your level and look at its properties in the level's Details panel. You see that it has the same Actor properties as the regular Point Light Actor.

Now you have a new Blueprint class derived. The next step is to create the variable types you need.

▼ TRY IT YOURSELF

Set Up a Variable

Follow these steps to create the variable you need for the Blueprint:

1. Open the MyPulseLight_BP asset from the previous Try It Yourself exercise by double-clicking it in the Content Browser.

2. In the My Blueprint panel, under **Variables**, click the + symbol to add a new variable.

3. With the new variable selected in the Details panel, name the variable **Target_Intensity** and set the Variable Type drop-down to **Float**.

4. Repeat steps 2 and 3 three more times to add the float variables Max_Intensity, Min_Intensity, and Pulse_Rate to your script. When you're finished with this, click the **Compile** button on the Blueprint Editor toolbar.

5. To set default values for some of the newly created variables, in the Details panel, set the Max_Intensity float variable's default to **10,000** and the Pulse_Rate float variable's default value to **100,000**.

NOTE

Point Light Component

You do not need to add a Point Light component to the Actor; one already exists because this Blueprint was derived from the original Point Light class.

The Max_Intensity float variable stores the maximum intensity that the light will ever be, and the Min_Intensity float variable stores the lowest intensity value, in this case **0**, which is no intensity at all. The Pulse_Rate float variable is used to set the speed at which the intensity changes from one to another. Now that you have the variables you need set up, you can start to script. The next step is to randomly generate a new intensity value and store it in the Target_Intensity float variable so you can use it to change the Point Light component's light intensity.

Generate a Random-Intensity Value and Set the Light Intensity

Follow these steps to create a script that randomly generates a float value between the minimum and maximum intensity values, store it in the target value, and use it to set the intensity of the light component:

1. Drag out the Target _Intensity float variable from the My Blueprint panel's Variables section to the Event Graph and select **Set**.

2. For now, link the exec out pin from the Event Tick event to the exec in on the Set node for Target_Intensity.

3. Click+drag from the green data in pin on Set and in the Context Menu that appears, search for **random float in range** and add **Random Float in Range** it to the Event Graph.

4. Drag the Min_Intensity float variable from the My Blueprint panel's Variables section to the Event Graph and select **Get**. Link its data out pin to the min data in pin on the Random Float in Range function.

5. Drag the Max_Intensity float variable from the My Blueprint panel's Variables section to the Event Graph and select **Get**. Link its data out pin to the max data in pin on the Random Float in Range function.

6. From the Components panel, click+drag **PointLightComponent(Inherited)** to the Event Graph to add a component reference variable that references the Point Light component.

7. Click+drag from the PointLightComponent(Inherited) variable's data pin, and in the search box of the Context Menu, type **set intensity**. Select the **Set Intensity** from the list to add this function.

8. Link the exec out pin from the set Target_Intensity node to the exec in on the Set Intensity node.

9. Drag the Target_Intensity float variable from the My Blueprint panel's Variables section to the Event Graph. Select **Get** to place a float variable reference for target intensity and link it to the new intensity on the Set Intensity function. When you're finished, your Blueprint sequence should look similar to the one shown in Figure 16.10.

10. Compile the script and make sure an instance of the Blueprint Actor is placed in your level. Preview the level. The New Point Light Actor should flicker rapidly.

FIGURE 16.10
Event Tick event sequence that randomly sets light component intensity.

CAUTION

Event Tick

The Event Tick event, by default, executes with every frame render during gameplay, which means it runs often. Therefore, it has the potential to affect performance.

At the moment, the light is generating a target intensity value within a range determined by the Min_Intensity and Max_Intensity float variables and setting the intensity to a new target value. The next step is to make the light blend smoothly between its current value and the target value. You do this by using the FInterp to Constant function. You also need to check whether the light's current intensity is equal to the target value and whether it generates a new target value, and then you need to repeat the interpolation function again.

▼ TRY IT YOURSELF

Make the Light Pulse Smoothly

Building on the previous Try It Yourself, follow these steps to make the light blend between its current intensity and the target intensity:

1. From the Components panel, click+drag **PointLightComponent(Inherited)** to the Event Graph to add a component reference variable that references the Point Light component.

2. Click+drag from the PointLightComponent(Inherited) reference variable's data out pin, and in the Context Menu search box type **get intensity**. Select **Get Intensity** from the list to add the node to the Event Graph.

3. Click+drag from the green float data out pin of the Intensity variable node, and in the Context Menu search box type **finterp to constant** and select **FInterp to Constant** from the list to add the node to the Event Graph.

4. Populate the data pin in on the FInterp to Constant function. Press **Alt+ click** to break the link from the already-placed Target_Intensity float variable connected to the Set Intensity function, added in the previous Try It Yourself, and connect it to the target data pin in on FInterp to Constant.

5. From the Event Tick event, drag the Delta Seconds data pin out to the Delta Time data pin in on FInterp to Constant node.

6. From the Variables section of the My Blueprint panel, drag out the **Pulse_Rate** floatvv variable and add it to the Event Graph. Link it up to the Interp Speed data pin on the FInterp to Constant function.

7. Take the return value data pin out from FInterp to Constant and link it to the Set Intensity function's new intensity data pin in.

8. On the Blueprint Editor toolbar, click **Compile** and then **Save**. When you're finished, your Blueprint sequence should look similar to the one shown in Figure 16.11.

9. Preview the level. You will see the light already pulsing and flickering.

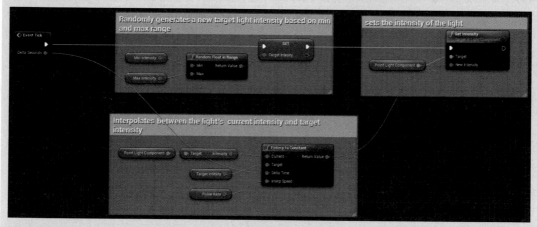

FIGURE 16.11
Pulsating light event sequence.

The light is pulsating, but the script is not yet finished. Although the light is flashing, the Event Tick event is continually generating a new target value every tick, so the light never reaches the target intensity value. You can fix this in the next Try It Yourself.

▼ TRY IT YOURSELF

Compare the Point Light Component's Current Intensity

The script needs to generate a new target intensity when the light component's current intensity is equal to the target intensity. For the final part of this script, you need to compare the light's current intensity to the new target value when they are equal and then repeat the process. Follow these steps:

1. From the Components panel, click+drag **PointLightComponent(Inherited)** to the Event Graph to add another component reference variable that references the Point Light component.

2. Click+drag from the **PointLightComponent(Inherited)** reference variable's data out pin, and in the Context Menu search box type **get intensity**. Select **Get Intensity** from the list to add the node.

3. Click+drag from the green float data pin out from the PointLightComponent(Inherited) node, and in the Context Menu search box type **equals**. Select **Equals (float)** from the list to add it. This node compares two float values and returns **1** (true) if they are equal and **0** (false) if they are not equal.

4. From the Variables section of the My Blueprint panel, drag out and add the **Target_Intensity** variable. Link it to the second float data in pin on the Equals node.

5. Click+drag from the **Equal** node's red data pin out, and in the Context Menu search box type **branch** to add the **Branch** node, which changes the flow of the sequence, depending on the state of a Boolean variable. If the Boolean is true, it passes the signal to the true exec out. If it's false, it passes the signal to the false exec out pin.

6. Link the exec out pin from **Event Tick** to the exec in on **Branch**.

7. Link the true exec out pin from the **Branch** node to the **Set Target Intensity** function node exec in pin.

8. Link the false exec out pin from the **Branch** node to the Set Intensity function's exec in pin.

9. Set the Pulse_Rate float variable's default value to **5,000**.

10. On the Blueprint Editor toolbar, click **Compile** and then **Save**. When you are finished, your Blueprint sequence should look similar to the one shown in Figure 16.12.

11. Preview the level. The light is still flickering, but it is a little less chaotic.

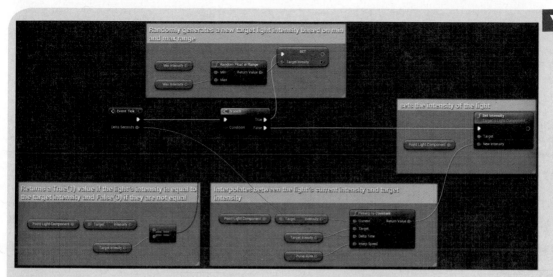

FIGURE 16.12
Comparing Point Light intensity.

Now when the Blueprint runs, the first thing it does is compare the Point Light component's current intensity to the target intensity, and if they are not equal, it continues to set the intensity based on the result of the FInterp to Constant function. As soon as the two values are equal, it randomly generates a new value for the target intensity within the min and max range, which makes the equals node return false again, causing the Set Intensity function to run again.

Summary

This hour, you learned to create Blueprint classes and to use the Blueprint Editor. You created two Blueprint classes: one derived from the Actor class and the other derived from the Point Light class. You scripted a simple pickup and pulsating Point Light Actor. You learned to use Timeline to animate a Static Mesh component. Blueprint classes are used to create just about any gameplay element you need. Although scripting gameplay functionality in a Level Blueprint is good, Blueprint classes are more powerful because they can be reused throughout a project. The more comfortable you become working with Blueprint classes, the more complexity you will be able to add to your own games.

Q&A

Q. The pickup Blueprint is animating, but the animation looks mechanical. Why?

A. As with keys on spline curves in Matinee, you can set the curve type. Right-click a key and set it to **Auto** to create a smooth transition out of the key.

Q. When I shoot the pickup Actor with a projectile, the projectile bounces off. Why?

A. By default, the box collision component of your pickup class has its collision set to block projectiles. In the Blueprint Editor, select the box trigger in the Components panel and in the Details panel, set Collision Presets to **Custom**. Then set Collision Response to **Ignore** so it ignores everything and set Pawn to **Overlap** so the box trigger only responds to the Pawn.

Q. When I walk the Pawn though the pickup, the Pawn gets hung up on the Static Mesh's collision. How can I fix it?

A. In the Blueprint Editor for the pickup Blueprint, select the Static Mesh component in the Components panel. Then set Collision Presets to **Custom**. Set Collision Response to **Ignore** to turn off collision for the Static Mesh component and allow the Pawn to run straight through the pickup.

Q. Animation plays once and then stops. How can I correct this?

A. Make sure **Loop** is selected in the Timeline Editor.

Workshop

Now that you have finished the hour, see if you can answer the following questions.

Quiz

1. True or false: Some functions target Actors, and some functions target components.
2. True or false: Timeline must be set to **Auto Play** all the time.
3. True or false: Timeline can only animate values between 0 and 1.
4. True or false: Blueprint classes can have multiple root components.
5. True or false: The root component position and rotation can be edited in a Blueprint class.

Answers

1. True. Depending on what you are trying to affect in your Blueprint, you need to use the correct function type. On a function node, underneath the name it says "Target is Scene Component" or "Target is Actor."

2. False. Auto Play only needs to be set if you want Timeline to start playing when the level is run; otherwise, you can use an Event to play the Timeline when needed.

3. False. Timeline can be used to animate any range of values.

4. False. Although a Blueprint class can have many components, it can only have one root component.

5. False. You can only modify the root component's scale.

Exercise

Go back to the pickup Actor from this hour's first set of Try It Yourself exercises and add continued rotation and make the respawn delay time a variable that can be edited when the Actor has been placed.

1. Add a new Float Track to the Timeline and rename the Float Track **Rotator**.

2. Add two keys to the new **Rotator** Float Track—one at time 0 seconds with a value of **0** and a second key at time 1 second with a value of **1**.

3. Use a setRelativeRotation function node that targets the Static Mesh component.

4. Right-click on the New Rotation Data pin on the SetRelativeRotation and select Split Struct Pin.

5. Multiply the **Rotator** float data pin out on the Timeline by **360**.

6. Connect the result of the multiplication to the New Rotation Z (Yaw) pin in on the SetRelativeRotation node. When finished, it should look similar to Figure 16.13.

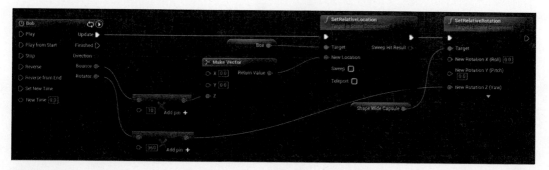

FIGURE 16.13
Rotating Pickup with Timeline.

7. Place a bunch of copies of your Blueprint pickup class into a level and preview the level. They should be bobbing up and down and rotating continuously.

Using Editable Variables and the Construction Script

What You'll Learn in This Hour:

▶ Making variables editable outside Blueprint
▶ Using the Construction Script
▶ Setting a variable value range

This hour teaches you how to make editable variables and to use the Construction Script in Blueprint. When you use editable variables and the Construction Script, each placed instance of a Blueprint can be modified independently of the original Blueprint class. The core functionality of the class is the same during gameplay, but the initial setup of the Actor can be unique for each instance. This hour walks you through the process of setting up editable variables and using the Construction Script.

NOTE

Hour 17 Setup

Create a new project with the First Person template and Starter Content and then create a new folder in the Content Browser called **Hour17Blueprints**.

Setting Up

Suppose you write a pickup Blueprint class like the one from Hour 16, "Working with Blueprint Classes." It would be nice to be able to change the Static Mesh or the rotation speed or the bob height of the pickup every time the pickup is placed in a level. In this hour, you will make a Blueprint class that creates a user defined number of Static Mesh components that can be positioned and rotated as needed. First, you set up the editable variable, and then you create a Blueprint sequence in the Construction Script.

Making Editable Variables

With the Blueprint Actor you created in Hour 16, you can place a few Light Actors throughout a level and have them pulse independently of each other. However, you may want some of the lights to be brighter than others, or maybe you want to be able to change the range from which the script generates the target intensity value. At the moment, these values are the same for every instance of the Blueprint placed in your level. You could duplicate the Blueprint asset and change the default variable's values, but doing so would increase the number of assets you have to work with—and in a large project that could become disorganized.

The Blueprint Editor allows you to make variables in a Blueprint editable, meaning that they can be modified outside the Blueprint Editor. Making variables editable causes them to show up in the level's Details panel when the Actor is placed in a level and selected. When making a variable editable, you should give it tooltip and define a category to store it. A tooltip pops up when the cursor rolls over the variable property, so if someone else uses your Blueprint, he or she will know what it's used for. Categories are used to organize variables, and this is important if you have to make many variables editable.

▼ TRY IT YOURSELF

MAKE BLUEPRINT VARIABLES EDITABLE

Follow these steps to create a Blueprint from an Actor class and make variables editable so that every placed instance of a Blueprint Actor can be modified independently:

1. In the Hour17Blueprints folder in the Content Browser, right-click and select **Blueprint Class**.

2. In the Pick Parent Class window that appears, select **Actor**. In the Content Browser, rename Blueprint to whatever you want and open it the Blueprint Editor by double-clicking it.

3. In the My Blueprint panel, under Variables, Click the + symbol to declare a new variable.

4. In the Variable Name property text box, type **NumComp** and set Variable Type to **Integer**.

5. Select the Editable Variable check box.

6. In the Tooltip text box type **Set the number of Components to Add**.

7. In the Category text box, type **Actor_Setup**.

8. Click **Compile** on the Blueprint Editor toolbar.

9. In the Details panel, under Default Value, set Default Value to **10**.

10. Create six more variables based on the information shown in Table 17.1. When you're finished, your My Blueprint panel's Variables category should look as shown in Figure 17.1.

11. Click **Compile** and then **Save** on the Blueprint Editor toolbar.

TABLE 17.1 Editable Variables to Add in the Try It Yourself

Variable Name	Variable Type	Tooltip	Category	Default Value
PivCompLocation	Vector	Sets the arrow component's location.	Actor_Setup	0,0,20
PivCompRotation	Rotator	Sets the arrow component's rotation.	Actor_Setup	0,0,15
MeshCompLocation	Vector	Sets the Static Mesh component's location.	Mesh_Setup	100,0,0
MeshCompRotation	Rotator	Sets the Static Mesh component's rotation.	Mesh_Setup	0,0,0
MeshCompScale	Vector	Sets the Static Mesh component's scale.	Mesh_Setup	1,1,1
SM_MeshAsset	Static Mesh (Reference)	Assigns a mesh asset to the mesh component.	Mesh_Setup	SM_CornerFrame

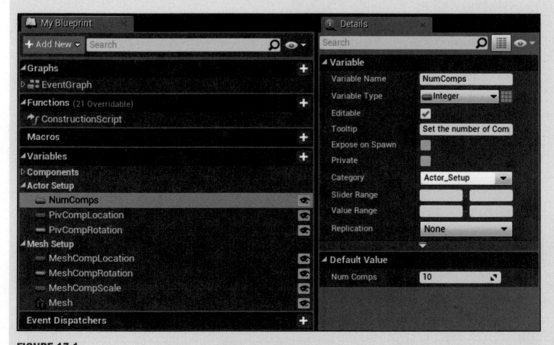

FIGURE 17.1
My Blueprint and Blueprint Details panels, showing declared editable variables.

Now that you have created all the variables you need, from the Content Browser drag your Blueprint into the level. With it selected, go the level's Details panel and look for the **Actor_Setup** and the **Mesh_Setup** categories you created. Under each category you should see all the variables you made, and if you hover the mouse cursor over each of the variables, the tooltips should show up. You can adjust the values for the variables, but your adjustments won't have an effect because you have not set up the Construction Script to utilize them yet.

Using the Construction Script

The Construction Script is available for every Blueprint class. It updates every time an Actor's properties or transforms change in the Blueprint Editor or when you compile the Blueprint. While editable variables allow you to modify each placed instance of an Actor, you don't see the changes until the game is run. The Construction Script, however, processes changes to an Actor while you are working in the Editor.

NOTE

Construction Script Execution

By default, the Construction Script is run every time a variable is changed in the level's Details panel for an Actor, every time an Actor transform is updated, when an Actor is spawned, and when the Blueprint is compiled.

Inside the Blueprint Editor you can see the Construction Script tab next to Event Graph. If it is not present, you can find Construction Script under the Functions tab in the My Blueprint panel, as shown in Figure 17.2. Double-clicking it opens the Construction Script. In the Construction Script, you can see an event node called Construction Script. This node executes a signal and processes the nodes that are wired to it.

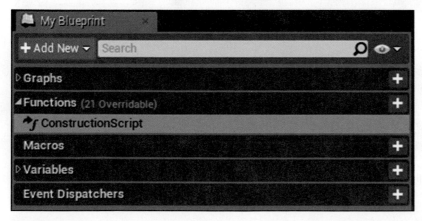

FIGURE 17.2
My Blueprint Construction Script.

If you click **Class Settings** on the Blueprint Editor toolbar, as shown in Figure 17.3, you see the Blueprint Options section in the in Details panel of the Blueprint Editor (see Figure 17.4). The first option here is Run Construction Script on Drag. With this set, when the Actor position, rotation, or scale is changed, the Construction Script of the Blueprint is called.

FIGURE 17.3
Blueprint Editor toolbar.

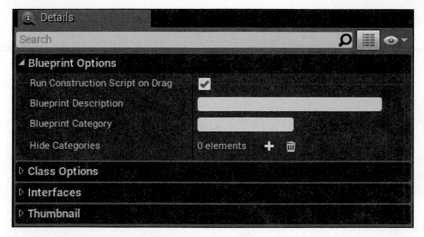

FIGURE 17.4
Blueprint Options section of the Details panel.

Because the Construction Script runs in the Editor and updates often, there are some limitations; some functions are not accessible in the Construction Script. For example, you can add components to the Blueprint on the fly, but you cannot spawn new Actors. Using the Construction Script is a great way to see the results of modified, editable variables on an Actor; the artist and level designer can use it to get feedback about your Blueprints.

Adding Static Mesh Components

Now that you have an understanding of how the Construction Script works, in the next Try It Yourself you will use the Construction Script and create a sequence that uses a ForLoop node and add arrow components to your Blueprint.

▼ TRY IT YOURSELF

ADD ARROW COMPONENTS TO A BLUEPRINT

Follow these steps to use the Construction Script and a For loop to add multiple arrow components to a Blueprint:

1. Open the Blueprint you created in the previous Try it Yourself (if it's not already open).

2. Select the **Construction Script** under the toolbar.

3. Click+drag the already-placed **Construction Script** node exec out pin and release it. In the Context Menu search box, type **forloop** and select **ForLoop** from the list to add the node.

4. In the ForLoop node's **First Index** text box type **0**.

5. Click+drag the **NumComp** integer variable from the My Blueprint panel to the last index on the ForLoop node to automatically select **Get** for the variable and add it to the Event Graph.

6. Click+drag from the **ForLoop** node's exec out pin and in the Context Menu search box type **add arrow**. Select the **Add Arrow** component to add it to the graph.

7. Right-click the orange Relative Transform data pin and select **Split Struct Pin**.

8. Click+drag from the integer data pin on the ForLoop node and in the Context Menu search box type **vector**. Select **Vector * Int** to place the node.

9. Click+drag the **PivCompLocation** Integer variable from the My Blueprint panel onto the Multiplies Vector Data pin in to select **Get** for the variable. Wire the Multiplies vector data pin out to the Relative Transform Location data pin in on the Add Arrow Component node.

10. Repeat steps 8–9, but this time use a **Rotate * Int** and **PivCompRotation** and wire it to the **Relative Transform Rotation**.

11. Right-click the **Return Value** data pin on the Add Arrow Component node and select **Promote to Local Variable**. In the My Blueprint panel, under Local Variables, rename the variable **TempArrowComp**. When you're finished, your Blueprint's Construction Script should look similar to the one shown in Figure 17.5.

12. Click **Compile** and **Save** on the Blueprint Editor toolbar.

FIGURE 17.5
Your Construction Script should look similar to this.

So what did you just do? You set a ForLoop event to execute a set number of times based on its first and last index values. For example, if the first value is **0** and last value is **10**, the ForLoop event executes 11 times. The add arrow component simply adds an arrow component to the Blueprint at a specified relative transform. In this case, it adds 11 arrow components, and each time, it offsets the position and rotation by multiplying the PivCompLocation and the PivCompRotation variables by the index count of the ForLoop event. The local variable temporarily holds the arrow component added to the Blueprint during that execution. (You will use it later in the hour.)

NOTE

Local Variables

Local variables are temporary variables created in a function. They are accessible only to that function. Once a function is finished executing, the variable is no longer used.

So far, you have used only three of the variables you created earlier, but now that you have the first half of your Construction Script set up, you can test it in the Blueprint Editor. Select the Viewport panel so you can see the components and then click **Class Defaults** on the Blueprint

Editor toolbar. In the Blueprint Details panel, you see your categories and all the variables you created. If you adjust the NumComp property, you see arrow components added and removed from the Viewport.

CAUTION
Class Defaults

Changing variable properties in the Blueprint Details panel changes their default values. When you are finished, make sure you set all the variables back to their original settings, as shown in Table 17.1.

Adding Static Mesh Components

Now that you have arrow components added to the Blueprint, you need to add Static Mesh components. After you add a Static Mesh component, you can assign a Static Mesh asset to the component so you can see it. Finally, you attach it to the arrow component. The arrow components will serve as a pivot point for the Static Mesh components.

▼ TRY IT YOURSELF

ADD STATIC MESH COMPONENTS

Follow these steps to add Static Mesh components and assign a Static Mesh asset to each component and attach them to the already-made arrow components:

1. In the Construction Script, click+drag from the TempArrowComp exec out and in the Context Menu search box type **add static**. Select **Add Static Mesh Component** from the list.

2. On the **Add Static Mesh Component** node, right-click the Orange Relative Transform data pin and select **Split Struct Pin**.

3. From the My Blueprint panel's Variables section, drag the vector **MeshCompLocation** variable onto the Relative Transform Location data pin on the Add Static Mesh Component node to select **Get** for the variable.

4. Repeat step 3 for MeshCompRotation but assign it to the Relative Transform Rotation data pin. Also repeat step 3 for MeshCompScale but assign it to the Relative Transform Scale data pin.

5. Right-click the Return Value data pin on the Add Static Mesh Component node and select **Promote to Local** Variable. In the My Blueprint panel, under Local Variables, rename the variable **TempMeshComp** to select **Set** for the node.

6. Click+drag from the exec out pin on the Set node and in the Context Menu search box, type **set static**. Select **Set Static Mesh** from the list to add the node.

7. Wire the blue data out pin from the Set node to the blue target in pin on the Set Static Mesh node.

8. From the My Blueprint panel's Variables section, drag the Static Mesh reference variable SM_MeshAsset onto the blue New Mesh data in pin on the Set Static Mesh node to select **Get** for the variable.

9. Click+drag from the exec out pin on the Set Static Mesh node and in the Context Menu search box, type **attach**. Select **AttachTo** from the list to place the node.

10. From the My Blueprint panel's Local Variables section, drag the **TempMeshComp** variable created in step 5 onto the blue target in pin on the AttachTo node to **Get** the variable.

11. From the My Blueprint panel's Local Variables section, drag the TempArrowComp variable onto the In Parent blue data in pin on the AttachTo node to select **Get** for the variable. When you're finished, your Blueprint should look similar to the one shown in Figure 17.6.

12. Click **Compile** and **Save** on the Blueprint Editor toolbar.

FIGURE 17.6
The second half of the final Construction Script.

Now that you have finished the Construction Script, from the Content Browser drag your Blueprint into the level. With the Blueprint selected, go the level's Details panel and look for the Actor_Setup and Mesh_Setup categories you created. Play around with the variables' values until you get something you like. Then drag out a second Actor onto your Blueprint and give it different settings and assign a different mesh to it. Both of your Actors are instances of the same Blueprint class but can modified independently of each other.

Limiting Editable Variables

You will notice that as you increase the NumComp variable, there may be a delay as the Blueprint Editor updates the Construction Script. When using editable variables, it is a good ideas to set limitations so anyone using your script can't choose extreme values. Back in the Blueprint Editor, select your NumComp variable and in the Blueprint Details panel, look for the Slider Range and Value Range properties. Slider Range lets you control the values other developers can choose when using your Blueprint, but users can still type in any value they want. The Value Range property locks the value down so users can only pick values within your defined range. In the first text box for both properties, type **1** and in the second text box type **100** (see Figure 17.7). After you set these properties, compile and save your Blueprint. Then select the Actor in the level and in the level's Details panel, adjust the NumComp property to see the changes.

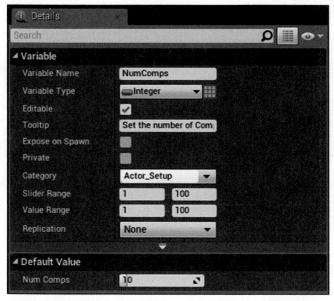

FIGURE 17.7
Slider Range and Value Range variable properties.

Show 3D Widget

Some editable variables can be displayed in the Level Viewport so you can interact with them directly by using the transform gizmo. Back in the Blueprint Editor, select the vector PivCompLocation variable and in the Blueprint Details panel, select **Show 3D Widget**. Compile and save your Blueprint. Then, in the Level Viewport, look for a wireframe diamond widget at the base of your Actor. The name of the variable should also be visible. Click the diamond widget and move it up and down, and you see each component's position update in real time;

also, the PivCompLocation values in the level's Details panel also change accordingly (see Figure 17.8). When you get a chance, do the same thing for the MeshCompLocation variable in your Blueprints as well.

FIGURE 17.8
Selecting Show 3D Widget.

Summary

This hour you learned how to use the Construction Script to update changes made to Actors with editable variables in the Blueprint Editor. As you can see, using editable variables and the Construction Script can be extremely powerful. Other people on your project will be able to use your Blueprint without ever having to open up the Blueprint Editor to make changes. The more comfortable you become with using the Construction Script, the more effective you can make Blueprint Actors for other people on a development team to use.

Q&A

Q. What are the green and yellow eyes next to the variable in the My Blueprint panel?

A. You can use the green and yellow eyes to quickly make a variable editable. A closed eye means the variable is not editable, and a yellow eye means it's editable but does not have a tooltip. A green eye means it is editable and has a tooltip.

Q. I can't edit the names of my local variables in the Blueprint Details panel. How can I rename them?

A. You have to rename local variables in the My Blueprint panel. Locate a variable in the Local Variables section in the My Blueprint panel, right-click it, select **Rename**, and type a new name.

Q. Why can't I see the Static Mesh components?

A. There are two likely reasons for this. The first is that you may not have assigned a Static Mesh asset to the SM_MeshAsset variable you created in the first Try It Yourself. The second is that the MeshCompScale variable has values of 0,0,0. Change it to **1,1,1**.

Workshop

Now that you have finished the hour, see if you can answer the following questions.

Quiz

1. True or false: While it is possible to add different components to a Blueprint in the Construction Script, you cannot spawn new Actors from the Construction Script.

2. True or false: A local variable is accessible outside the function in which it is created.

3. True or false: The Add Arrow component adds a Static Mesh component.

4. True or false: If you want to be able to interact with a vector variable in the Level Viewport, you need to set the Show 3D widget variable property.

5. True or false: The Construction Script updates every time an Actor's properties or transforms change.

Answers

1. True. While you can spawn new Actors into a level during runtime from the Event Graph in a Blueprint, You cannot spawn Actors into the level from the Construction Script.

2. False. Local variables are only accessible to the function they are declared in.

3. False. The Add Arrow adds an arrow.

4. True. Some variable types, such as vector variables, have a Show property that displays a visual representation of the variable in the level when an instance of the Blueprint has been placed in the level.

5. True. Under Class settings in the Blueprint Editor, the **Run Construction Script on Drag** property is set to True.

Exercise

For this exercise, use a Set Material node and editable material interface reference variable to change the materials of all the added Static Mesh components.

1. Open your Blueprint and go to the Construction Script.

2. Click+drag the local **TempMeshComp** variable from the My Blueprint panel to the end of the sequences in the Construction Script and select **Get** for the variable and add it to the Event Graph.

3. Click+drag from the **TempMeshComp** variable and in the Context Menu search box, type **set material**. Select **Set Material** from the list to add the node to the Event Graph.

4. Wire the Set Material exec pin to the end of the AttachTo node.

5. Create a variable in the **My Blueprint** panel.

6. Set Variable Type to **Material Instance**, rename the variable, make it editable, give it a tooltip, and assign it to the Mesh_Setup category.

7. Click **Compile** and **Save** on Blueprint Editor toolbar.

Making Key Input Events and Spawning Actors

What You'll Learn in This Hour:

▶ Setting variables to be exposed on spawn
▶ Spawning an Actor from a Blueprint class
▶ Scripting a keyboard input event

In the previous hour, you learned to make variables editable and use the Construction Script. This hour teaches you how to set up key input events in a Blueprint and how to spawn one Actor from another at runtime.

NOTE

Hour 18 Setup

Create a new project with the First Person template and Starter Content, and then create a new folder in the Content Browser called **MyBlueprints**.

Why Spawning Is Important

Most games require more than just Collision Events to respond to player actions. In this hour, you create a Blueprint class that will spawn a new Actor every time the player walks up to it and presses a key. Being able to spawn new Actors on the fly opens the door to creating more dynamic and interactive experiences, whether it's pickups being randomly spawned throughout a level or waves of enemies increasing in number based on player skill. Without spawning, level designers would have to manually place every single Actor for every single scenario that might unfold during gameplay, and that, of course, is not feasible. To spawn an Actor during gameplay through Blueprint, you use the Spawn Actor function, and you need to create two new Blueprint classes: a spawner class and a spawned class. The spawner spawns an Actor of another class by adding it to the level during gameplay. The spawned is the Actor that is created.

Creating a Blueprint Class to Spawn

Before you can make one Actor spawn another from a class, you need to make the Blueprint class to spawn. In the first part of the hour you make a Blueprint class that has a Static Mesh component set to simulate physics. You will use the Construction Script to change properties of each spawned instance of the Physics Actor. Then you create the UseKeySpawner Blueprint class to spawn an instance of the physics Blueprint class.

▼ TRY IT YOURSELF

Set Up the Physics Blueprint Class

Follow these steps to create the physics Blueprint class that you will spawn at runtime:

1. To create a new Blueprint class, right-click the **MyBlueprints** folder in the Content Browser and select **Blueprint Class** from the Context Menu. Then select **Actor** from the Common Classes tab.

2. Name your new Blueprint class **PhysicsActor_BP** and then open this Actor in the Blueprint Editor by double-clicking it in the Content Browser.

3. In the Component tab, click the green **+Add Component** button and select **Cube** to add a cube Static Mesh component.

4. Rename the new component **PhysicsMeshComp** and assign it to the root component of the Blueprint by dragging it onto the default scene component and selecting **Make Root**.

5. With **PhysicsMeshComp** selected in the Blueprint Details panel, under Physics, select **Simulate Physics**.

6. Click **Compile** and **Save** on the Blueprint Editor toolbar and place your Blueprint in a Default level.

7. Preview the level and shoot the box; it should move.

Using the Construction Script

You have created a Blueprint class that will be spawned, and you need to now use the Construction Script so the mesh and materials assigned to the Static Mesh component can be changed. Later on, this will allow you to change the appearance of the Actors being spawned and take advantage of the Expose on Spawn variable property. First, you set up the Construction Script and create a Static Mesh and material reference variables. Then you can set each variable to be exposed on spawn.

TIP

The Sequence Node

The Sequence node splits the event signal into as many signals as you need. Because the results of the branch comparison are unknown, you should make sure other signals are processed. You can add more exec out nodes to the Sequence node by clicking **Add Pin**, and you can remove them by right-clicking an exec out pin you want to remove and selecting **Remove**.

TRY IT YOURSELF

Swap Out the Static Mesh Assigned to the Mesh Component

Follow these steps to use the Construction Script to change the Static Mesh and Material assets that are assigned to the Static Mesh component of the PhysicsActor_BP Blueprint:

1. Open the PhysicsActor_BP Blueprint.

2. Open the Construction Script by selecting its tab or clicking **Construction Script** in the Functions tab in My Blueprint panel.

3. Click+drag the already-placed Construction Script node exec out pin and release. In the Context Menu search box, type **sequence** and select **Sequence** from the list to add the node.

4. Click+drag the Sequence node's then 0 exec out pin and release. In the Context Menu search box, type **set Static Mesh**. Select **Set Static Mesh (PhysicsMeshComp)** to place a Set Static Mesh function node that targets the Static Mesh component.

5. On the Set Static Mesh function node, right-click the blue data in pin to the left of the NewMesh property and choose **Promote to Variable**.

6. Rename the new variable **NewMesh** and then compile the Blueprint. Because the Set Static Mesh variable you created does not have a mesh assigned to it, the component's mesh disappears from the Blueprint Viewport when the Construction Script runs.

7. To check whether a mesh has been assigned to the variable before the Set Static Mesh function is executed, click+drag from the NewMesh variable data out pin. In the Context Menu search box, type **isvalid** and select **?IsValid** from the list to place the node.

8. Click+drag from the ?IsValid exec out pin and wire it to the Set Static Mesh node exec in pin.

9. Link the then 0 exec out pin to the **?IsValid** node's exec in pin.

10. Repeat steps 4–9 but this time use the then 1 exec out on the Sequence node to change the material of the PhysicsMeshComp using a Set Material function node and a material reference variable named NewMaterial. When you're finished, your Blueprint should look similar to the one shown in Figure 18.1.

11. Compile and save the Blueprint.

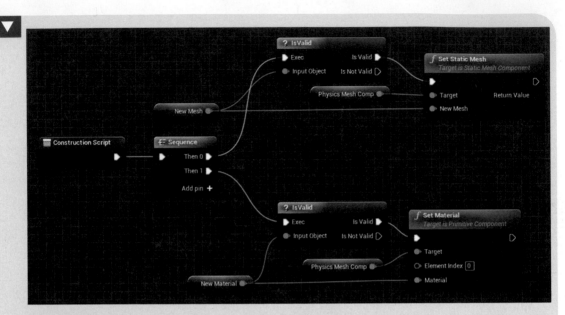

FIGURE 18.1
Your Construction Script should look similar to this.

Using the Expose on Spawn Variable Property

Just as the Editable Variable property makes a variable accessible in a level's Details panel for an Actor, the Expose on Spawn property exposes the variable to whichever Blueprint is spawning the new Actor. When a class is assigned to the Spawn Actor from Class function, any variable in the class that has Expose on Spawn turned on shows up as a data pin in on the spawn function. Every variable created in a Blueprint can be set to Exposed on Spawn.

Before you move on to creating the spawner Blueprint that will spawn the Physics Actor, you need to prepare the two variables created in the previous Try It Yourself.

▼ TRY IT YOURSELF

Prepare Variables to Be Exposed on Spawn

Follow these steps to edit the properties of the variables you have created so far this hour:

1. Open the PhysicsActor_BP Blueprint.

2. Locate and select the **NewMesh** variable in the Variables section of the My Blueprint tab.

3. In the Blueprint Details panel, turn on the **Editable** property, as shown in Figure 18.2.

4. In the Tooltip text box, give an informative description, such as **This will change the mesh of the physics Actor**.

5. Turn on **Expose on Spawn**, as shown in Figure 18.2.

6. In the Category text box, type **Mesh Setup** to create a new property category called Mesh Setup.

7. Repeat steps 3–5 for the NewMaterial variable and under Category pick the already-made **Mesh Setup** category from the list.

8. Compile and save the Blueprint.

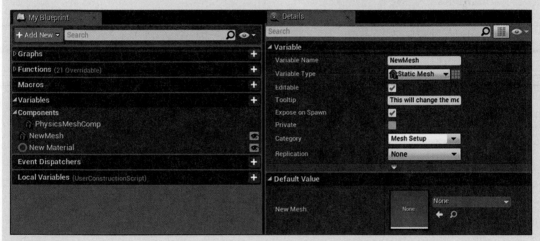

FIGURE 18.2
The My Blueprint and Details panels in the Blueprint Editor.

Setting Up the Spawner Blueprint

Scripting an input event that requires the player to press a key to initiate a Blueprint sequence is a fairly easy process. You need an input event that is assigned to a specific key, such as the **E** key. You also need to tell the Actor to temporarily enable input for a specific player controller. If you simply enable input for an Actor and place multiple instances of the Actor in your level, they will all execute at the same time when the input key is pressed. So you need to enable inputs only on the Actor the player is trying to interact with directly. This can be done with an overlap event that enables input for the Actor when the pawn overlaps with a collision component and disables the input when the player moves away and ends the overlap.

This method is fine for a single-key input that has a very specific function, such as spawning an Actor or opening a door. For Actors that require more robust input systems such as pawns, characters, and vehicles, it is best to set up key mapping.

GO TO ▶ CHAPTER 20, CREATING AN ARCADE SHOOTER: INPUT SYSTEM AND PAWNS, to learn more on input mappings.

For the setup of this Blueprint, you need a box collision component for the Overlap event, a Static Mesh for a visual representation of the Actor location in the level, and an arrow component to define the spawn location of the Physics Actor when the user presses the key.

▼ TRY IT YOURSELF

Set Up and Use a Key Spawner Blueprint Class

Now that the Physics Actor is ready, it's time to set up the UseKeySpawner Actor, so follow these steps:

1. Create a new Blueprint class, Select the **MyBlueprints** folder in the Content Browser, right-click in the Asset Management Area, and select **Blueprint Class** from the Context Menu. Then select *Actor* from the Common Classes tab.

2. Name your new Blueprint class **UseKeySpawner_BP** and open it in the Blueprint Editor (see Figure 18.3).

3. Add a box **collision** component and set the relative Z location to **100**. Then set the box extents to **100** for X, **100** for Y, and **100** for Z.

4. Add a cylinder Static Mesh component under Basic Shapes and set its relative Z location to **50**.

5. Compile and save the Blueprint.

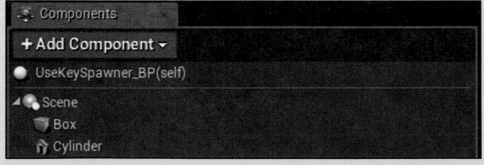

FIGURE 18.3
Component setup.

With the necessary components in place, you now need to script an overlap event sequence for the box collision component that enables the Actor to receive input from the player controller and disable input when the overlap has ended.

TRY IT YOURSELF ▼

Script Overlap Events to Enable and Disable Player Inputs

Follow these steps to use the Construction Script to modify the properties of the Actor:

1. Open the UseKeySpawner_BP Blueprint.

2. Select the box collision component from the Components tab. In the Event Graph, add an OnComponentBeginOverlap event node.

3. Add an Enable Input Function node and wire the OnComponentBeginOverlap(Box) exec out pin to the enable input exec in pin.

4. Add a player controller with **Get** selected and wire its blue data pin out to the blue player controller pin in on the Enable Input node.

5. Select the box collision component from the Components tab, and in the **Event Graph** add an OnComponentEndOverlap event node.

6. Add a Disable Input function node and wire the OnComponentEndOverlap(Box) exec out pin to the Disable Input exec in pin.

7. Wire the blue data out pin from the player controller you added in step 4 to the blue **player** controller pin in on the Disable Input node. When you're finished, your Blueprint should look similar to the one shown in Figure 18.4.

8. Compile and save the Blueprint.

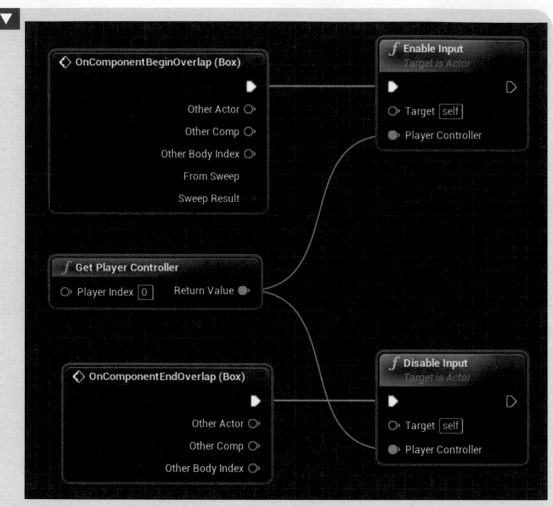

FIGURE 18.4
The Event Graph in Blueprint for showing overlap event sequences.

Spawning an Actor from a Class

Actors are added during gameplay via spawning. If you couldn't spawn Actors, you would have to pre-place every Actor you would ever need, which would limit the type of gameplay events and encounters you could create. Spawning allows you to script dynamic experiences. There are spawn functions for adding specific common types of Actors. For example, there is a spawn emitter for spawning Particle Effects, and there is a spawn sound for adding Sound Actors to a level when needed. Actors can be spawned with specific transforms, or they can be attached to other Actors. When spawning an Actor, you need to consider the location because you don't typically want the Actor to spawn inside the collision hull of another Actor or component.

For this demonstration, you use a Spawn Actor from Class function that can spawn any Blueprint class you create.

TRY IT YOURSELF ▼

Add the Keyboard Input Event and Spawn an Actor from a Class

Now that you have the enable and disable input events set up, you need to add a keyboard input event that executes when the player presses the **E** key. Follow these steps:

1. Open the UseKeySpawner_BP Blueprint.

2. In the Event Graph, right-click in an empty location to bring up the Context Menu. In the search box type **e** and select **E** from the list to add it to the graph.

3. Add a Spawn Actor from Class function, and wire its exec in to the E key event's released exec out pin.

4. To the right of the purple data in pin, click to select a class and use the search box to search for the PhysicsActor_BP Blueprint you scripted earlier.

5. Add a **world** transform to define the location in the world to add the spawned Actor. Select the arrow component from the Components panel and drag it to the Event Graph.

6. Click+drag from the blue data out pin of the component reference. In the Context Menu search box, type **get world transform** and select **GetWorldTransform** to add it to the Event Graph.

7. Wire the GetWorldTransform orange data out pin to the orange spawn transform data in pin on the Spawn Actor From Class function node. When you're finished, your Blueprint should look similar to the one shown in Figure 18.5.

8. Compile and save the Blueprint. Then place an instance of it into your level.

9. Preview the level, move the pawn over to the placed instance of the UseKeySpawner_BP Actor, and press the **E** key. The Physics Actor should be added to the level.

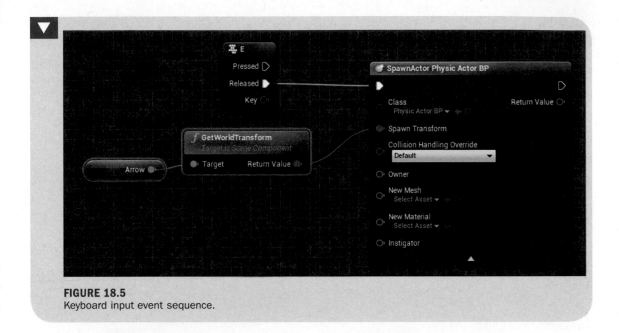

FIGURE 18.5
Keyboard input event sequence.

NOTE

Keyboard Inputs

You could also use the keyboard input event setup done here to play or stop a timeline that animates a mesh component, such as a door opening or closing.

The last thing you need to do is make use of the variables you exposed on spawn in the PhysicsActor_BP. When you added PhysicsActor_BP to the class property of the Spawn Actor from Class function, the exposed variables were added to the function as well because of the Expose on Spawn property. Now you need to add those as variables to the UseKeySpawner_BP Actor and make them editable so that when you place an instance in the level, you will be able to pick a new mesh and material for the spawned Physics Actor.

Promoting Variables and Making Them Editable

In order to change the exposed on spawn variables that are displayed on the Spawn Actor from Class function node, you need to create two new variables in the Blueprint and make them editable. Follow these steps:

1. Open the UseKeySpawner_BP in the Blueprint Editor.

2. On the Spawn Actor from Class function node, right-click the blue data in pin to the left of the NewMesh property and choose **Promote to Variable**.

3. Now select the variable and in the Blueprint Details panel make the variable **Editable**.

4. Repeat steps 2–3 for the NewMaterial property as well.

5. Compile and save the Blueprint.

6. In the level, select the placed instance of the UseKeySpawner_BP Actor, and in the Details panel, assign a new mesh and material.

7. Preview the level and interact with the UseKeySpawner_BP.

8. Place multiple instances of the UseKeySpawner_BP Actor and assign different meshes and materials. When you're finished, your Blueprint should look similar to the one shown in Figure 18.6.

9. Preview the level again and interact with each of the placed Actors.

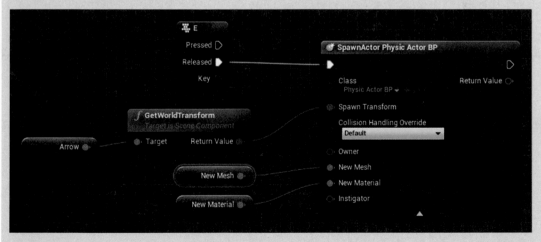

FIGURE 18.6
Promoted editable variables added to the sequence.

Summary

This hour, you learned how to make one Actor spawn another with modified properties. You also learned how to use the Expose Variable on Spawn property and how to enable and disable player controller input on an Actor. Now you can start to build on these skills to make more dynamic Actors that your player can interact with.

Q&A

Q. **Will the keyboard input method described this hour work in a multiplayer game?**

A. No, because the input is enabled only for Player Controller 0, which is the default controller for a single-player game.

Q. **How do I change the scale of a spawned Actor?**

A. You can do this in the spawn transform. Disconnect the orange wire from the arrow component's GetWorldTransform and right-click the orange transform node and select **Split Struct Pin** to separate the transform struct into its individual location, rotation, and scale properties.

Q. **Every time my Physics Actor spawns into the level it flies off. Why?**

A. The spawned Physics Actor may be colliding with another Actor or component in the level. Because the spawn location is determined by the arrow component in the UseKeySpawner_ BP Blueprint class, adjusting the arrow components location in the Blueprint will fix the issue.

Q. **After the second spawned Actor, the input event stops working. Why does this happen?**

A. The box collision component's OnComponentEndOverlap event is being triggered by one of the spawned Actors. In the UseKeySpawner_BP, edit the box collision component's collision properties so that it responds only to the pawn.

Workshop

Now that you have finished the hour, see if you can answer the following questions.

Quiz

1. True or false: The Key input event works only with the E key.

2. True or false: Turning on the Expose on Spawn property for a variable in a Blueprint makes the variable show up in the Spawn Actor from Class function node.

3. If you want to spawn an Actor through Blueprint, which function do you need?

    A. GetWorldTransform

    B. Spawn Actor from Class

    C. OnComponentBeginOverlap

    D. Enable Input

4. True or false: If you Enable input for a Blueprint Class and place multiple instances of the Actor in a level, they will all execute at the same time when the input key is pressed.

Answers

1. False. There are input events for every key on your keyboard.

2. True. The Expose on Spawn property for variables makes them accessible through the Spawn Actor from Class function.

3. B. While there are several spawn functions, the Spawn Actor from Class function allows you to spawn your own Blueprint classes.

4. True. You need to use events to enable and disable input in the Blueprint class when needed.

Exercise

Spawning the Physics Actor when the player press the E key functions is not very exciting. It also does not provide any feedback for the player when he or she interacts with it other than showing the spawned Actor. In this exercise you create a lever in your UseKeySpawner Blueprint that animates and spawns a Particle Effect and plays a sound when the Physics Actor spawns in.

1. In the UseKeySpawner_BP Blueprint add the **Shape_Cylinder** Static Mesh asset from the Starter Content Folder as a component and rename it **LeverMesh**.

2. Scale the LeverMesh Static Mesh component so it looks like a lever. Set **0.1** for X and Y and **2.0** for Z.

3. Position the LeverMesh component at 0,70,0 to the right of the cylinder mesh component that you added in the Set Up and Use a Key Spawner Blueprint Class Try It Yourself exercise.

4. In the UseKeySpawner_BP Event Graph, add a timeline with **Auto Play** and **Loop** unselected and Time set to **1** (second).

5. Add a float curve and name it **LeverRotation**.

6. Add three keyframes to the float curve: Keyframe 1 (with Time set to **0** and Value set to **0**), Keyframe 2 (with Time set to **0** and Value set to **1**), and Keyframe 3 (with Time set to **1** and Value set to **0**).

7. From the E Input event node wire the Released exec out pin to the Play from Start exec in pin on the timeline.

8. Click+drag LeverMesh and select **Get** for it to add it as reference variable to the Event Graph.

9. Click+drag from the LeverMesh blue data pin and in the Context Menu search box, type **Set relative rotation**. Select **SetRelativeRotation** from the list to place the node.

10. Wire the Timeline Update exec out pin to the exec in pin on the SetRelativeRotation node.

11. Click+drag from the green LeverRotation pin created in step 5 and in the Context Menu search box, type **multiply**. Select **Float ∗ Float** to add the node. In the text box type **60** as the number of degrees the lever will rotate when animating.

12. On the SetRelativeRotation function node, right-click the rotation data pin and select Split Pin and wire the float data pin out from the multiplication node to the New Rotation Y (Pitch) on the SetRelativeRotation node.

13. Click+drag from the timeline node's Finished exec out pin and in the Context Menu search box, type **spawn emitter**. Select **Spawn Emitter at Location** to add the node. Under Emitter Template, assign **P_Explosion**.

14. Click+drag from the Spawn Emitter at Location exec out pin and in the Context Menu search box, type **play sound**. Select **Play Sound at Location** to add the node. Next to the Sound property, assign the **Explosion01** Sound asset.

15. Wire the Timeline Finished exec out pin to the exec in pin on the Spawn node.

16. Use the arrow component's transform to set the **Location** and **Rotation** properties of the Spawn Emitters at Location and Play Sound at Location nodes.

17. Wire the Play Sound at Location exec out pin to the Spawn Actor node you placed in the Add the Keyboard Input Event and Spawn an Actor from a Class Try It Yourself earlier in the hour.

18. When you're finished, your Blueprint should look similar to the one shown in Figure 18.7. Compile and save the Blueprint.

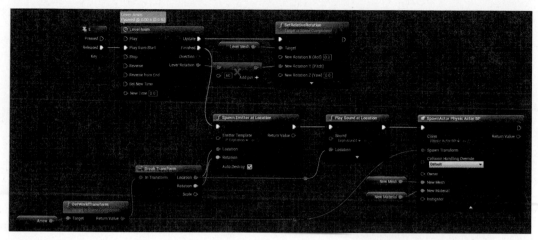

FIGURE 18.7
Blueprint Sequence that animates a lever and spawns an Actor when the player presses the E key.

19. Preview the level and interact with the spawned Actor. When you press the E key, the lever animates, the explosion particle plays, you hear the explosion sound, and you see Physics Actor spawn.

HOUR 19
Making an Action Encounter

What You'll Learn in This Hour:

▶ Working with an existing Blueprint class to make an obstacle course
▶ Modifying character movement properties
▶ Assigning a Game Mode to a level
▶ Assigning an Actor tag

In earlier hours, you were introduced to Blueprint. In this hour, you use existing Blueprints classes to build your own action-based encounter. Using one of the provided Game Modes, you will place and modify existing Blueprint classes to create a time-based obstacle course.

NOTE

Hour 19 Setup

For this hour, you need to open the Hour_19 project, available on the book's companion website at www.sty-ue4.com. Here, you will find everything you need to complete the hour and create a simple encounter for First person shooter and/or Third Person Game Mode. In the Content Browser of the Hour_19 project, you will see a folder called BasicFPSGame, and in it is a Game Mode called BasicFPSGameMode. In the Content Browser of the project, you will also see another folder called Basic3rdPGame. In this folder is a Game Mode called Basic3rdPGameMode. You will also find a collection of Blueprint classes organized in folders based on functionality.

Project Game Modes

For this hour, we have provide two Game Modes to work with: a first-person shooter (FPS) Game Mode called BasicFPSGameMode and a third-person Game Mode called Basic3rdPGameMode. The FPS Game Mode uses a character Blueprint called BasicFPSCharacter, and the third-person Game Mode uses a character Blueprint called Basic3rdPCharacter.

Heads-Up Displays (HUDs)

Both of the Game Modes for this hour have simple Unreal Motion Graphics (UMG) HUDs. The HUDs for both Game Modes display the health of the character, the number of pickup items collected, and the time since the level was started. In both Game Modes, the characters can be killed by falling off a ledge or by taking damage.

GO TO ▶ HOUR 22, WORKING WITH UMG, to learn more about creating interfaces and working with Unreal Motion Graphics (UMG) UI Designer.

Game Timer and Respawn System

Both Game Modes for this hour already have respawn and timer systems scripted into their Game Mode Blueprints. The timer starts counting when a level is started and is displayed on the HUD. The respawn system works in conjunction with the CheckPoint_BP and KillVolume_BP Blueprint Actors, which you can find in the BP_Respawn folder in the Content Browser.

Knowing Characters' Abilities

When creating a level encounter, it is a good idea to know everything about the characters' abilities. How fast do they move? How high and far can they jump? What weapons do they have? The more you know about the characters' abilities, the better you can design encounters in your levels.

The FPS Game Mode character you are using this hour has common weapons scripted in the character Blueprint class. There is a trace weapon, a projectile weapon, and a physics gun. Pressing the **1**, **2**, or **3** number keys switches between weapons. You can fire the trace weapon and the projectile weapon by pressing the left mouse button. When the physics gun is active, you can click to pick up Physics Actors and right-click to throw a picked-up Actor or poke a physics item if it is on the ground.

In the Content Browser, go to Hour_19/Basic3rdPGame/Blueprints/Basic3rdPCharacter and open up the Blueprint in the Blueprint Editor. On the Components panel, select the CharacterMovement Component and look through the properties on the Blueprint Details panel for this component. Here you will find most of the information you need. Most of the character movement is based on acceleration and velocity. With a little bit of testing, you can get a better idea of how this equates to world units.

In the following Try It Yourself, you will become familiar with the CharacterMovement Component's settings.

Establish Third-Person Player Abilities

Follow these steps to use the JumpTest level to establish the player jump height and distance:

1. In the Content Browser, go to Hour_19/Maps and open the **JumpTest** level. In this level you see several BSP Actors set to different sizes. You will use these to get an idea of how fast, high, and far the character can run and jump.

2. Preview the level and practice jumping from one end to the other. Try jumping from a standstill and then try jumping from a run. You should see some slight variation in distance based on player speed and acceleration. From these tests, you can get an estimate of the third-person player jump height and distance. With the default values, the player can jump roughly a distance of 600 units and a height of 200 units.

3. In the Content Browser, search for the **Basic3rdPCharacter** Blueprint and open it.

4. In the Blueprint Editor, in the Components panel, select the **CharacterMovement** Component.

5. In the Details panel, locate the Max Walk Speed property in the Character Movement: Walking section (see Figure 19.1). Change its value to **300**.

6. Compile the Blueprint and then preview the level and interact with the BSP Actors again.

7. In the Details panel, locate the Jump Z Velocity property under Character Movement: Jumping/Falling (see Figure 19.1). Set it to **1000**.

8. Compile the Blueprint and then preview the level and interact with the BSP Actors again.

9. Play around with some of the other character properties. You can always reset a property back to its default value simply by clicking the yellow arrow to the right of a property value.

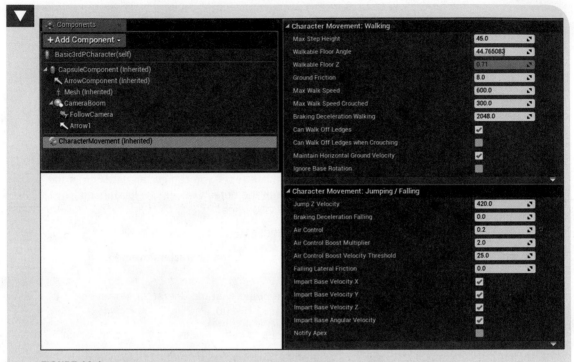

FIGURE 19.1
CharacterMovement Component properties.

NOTE

Basic First-Person Game Mode

The steps you took in the preceding Try It Yourself also work for the basic first-person Game Mode (BasicFPSCharacter), but you need to change the Game Mode Override setting for the JumpTest level to **BasicFPSGameMode** in order to test it.

Using Blueprint Classes

All the Blueprint classes you can use to build your obstacle course encounter level are organized into folders based on functionality. There is a folder for moving platforms and obstacles that cause damage to the player. Another folder contains turret and projectile Actor Blueprints. Another folder contains levers and switches, and yet others have pickups and spawn checkpoints and kill volumes.

Each of the Actors makes use of Construction Script and editable variables so that each placed Actor can be modified as needed. All the Actors have properties relative to their core functionality that can be modified using the level's Details panel. Some have mesh, material, and particle properties that can be swapped out with your own assets.

TIP

Grids and Snaps

When placing many of the Blueprints used in this hour, it can help to turn on grid snaps and set the units to **100**, as shown in Figure 19.2.

FIGURE 19.2
Grids and snaps.

The following sections describe the folders provided with this hour and their contents.

BP_Common Folder

The BP_Common folder contains Blueprint classes that can be used with either of the provided Game Modes. This folder contains a sample map called ActorGallery that demonstrates the basic functionality of all the Blueprint classes. In the Content Browser, go to Hour_19/BP_Common, open the ActorGallery map, and preview the level.

There are six Actors in this folder that you can use to create an obstacle course:

▶ **Launcher_BP:** This Actor launches the player's character in the air, using a specified distance and height. To change the direction, simply rotate the placed Actor.

▶ **Mover_BP:** This Blueprint animates a Mesh Component between two locations. You can set the Move Speed and the Delay time before it changes direction. You can also set whether it starts at the ending location or the beginning location. You set the destination by selecting the Destination transform and moving and rotating it to any desired transform.

▶ **Pendulum_BP:** This Actor swings back and forth and causes a specified damage amount to the player character if it hits them. You can set the swing speed and the start direction. This Actor can be rotated and uniformly scaled.

▶ **Smasher_BP:** This Actor animates two spiked pistons back and forth and causes damage to the player if caught in the middle. You can change the end location, return and attack speed, hit and attack delay, and damage amount. This Actor can be rotated and scaled.

▶ **Stomper_BP:** This Actor animates a Mesh Component between two locations based on the distance from where it is placed. It causes a specified damage to the player character. This Actor can be rotated and uniformly scaled.

▶ **SpikeTrap_BP:** This Actor releases spikes out of the floor when the character walks over it. You can change the speed, damage amount, and sound effects for this Actor.

In the next Try It Yourself, you practice creating a level, setting the Game Mode for the level, and working with one of the provided Blueprint Actors. To bring up the World Settings panel for the current level, on the Level Editor toolbar select **Settings > World Settings** (see Figure 19.3).

FIGURE 19.3
Opening the World Settings panel.

The World Settings panel opens next to the Details panel in the Level Editor interface. The World Settings panel allows you to set properties such as Lightmass, Physics, and Game Mode for the level you are currently working on. If you assign the Game Mode class, all the Blueprint classes assigned to the Game Mode are added automatically. The next Try It Yourself walks you through this process.

▼ TRY IT YOURSELF

Work with the Provided Blueprints Classes

Follow these steps to create a default level and practice using the Mover_BP class:

1. Create a new default map and save it to the Hour_19/Maps folder.

2. On the World Settings panel, set Game Mode Override to **Basic 3rdPGameMode** (see Figure 19.4).

3. Select the Mover_BP Actor from the Content Browser and place it in the level.

4. Select the placed Mover_BP and then select the blue diamond (called a Destination transform) and move it to a new location.

5. Preview the level and notice how it moves. Then move the character onto the platform to ride it.

6. Stop the preview and, with the Actor selected, go the Details panel and change the Move Speed. Larger values add more time and slow down the movement; smaller values reduce the time and speed up the movement of the platform.

7. When you have a movement speed you like, change the Return and Destination Delay times to make the platform pause before each movement.

8. Make a copy of the Mover_BP Actor. With the Actor selected, hold the **Alt** key and move the Actor or press **Ctrl+W** to duplicate the Actor.

9. Move the duplicated Actor to a new location and then drag its Destination transform so that it lines up with the Destination transform of the first Actor.

10. Preview the level and have the character ride the first mover to the second mover.

11. Make adjustments to both Actors' Start and Destination transforms, Move Speed, and Delay times to refine movement.

FIGURE 19.4
Setting the Game Mode.

BP_Turrets Folder

The BP_Turrets folder contains three types of turret Blueprints and their projectile Blueprints. There are two tracking turrets that track the character when it is in a specified distance from their position. There is also a pattern-based turret that spawns projectiles in a set direction in a specific pattern. All the turrets work with both of the provided Game Modes.

In the Content Browser, go to Hour_19/BP_Turrets/, open the TurretGallery map, and preview the level.

These are the Blueprints in this folder:

▶ **Pattern_Projectile_BP:** This is a projectile Blueprint that is spawned by the PatternTurret_BP Blueprint. It causes damage to the player when hit.

▶ **PatternTurret_BP:** This Blueprint spawns the **Pattern_Projectile_BP** Blueprint in a pattern based on specified properties. It can be placed, rotated, and uniformly scaled as needed.

▶ **ProjectileTurret_BP:** This turret tracks the player character and fires a projectile (TurretProjectile_BP) at the character when he or she moves within a specified range. The Turret Range, Track Speed, and Fire Rate can be adjusted as needed. This Blueprint can be placed, rotated, and uniformly scaled as needed.

▶ **TraceTurret_BP:** This turret tracks the player character and fires a trace weapon at the character when he or she moves within a specified range. The Turret Range, Track Speed, and Fire Rate can be adjusted as needed. This Blueprint can be placed, rotated, and uniformly scaled as needed.

▶ **TurretProjectile_BP:** This Blueprint is spawned by the ProjectileTurret_BP Blueprint. It causes damage to the player when hit.

BP_Respawn Folder

In the BP_Respawn folder are two Blueprint classes that can be used to respawn at checkpoints or to destroy the player when he or she falls off a ledge.

In the Content Browser, go to Hour_19/BP_Respawn, open the Respawn_Gallery map, and preview the level.

These are the Blueprints in this folder:

▶ **Checkpoint_BP:** This Blueprint class works with the respawn system in the provided Game Modes. When the character walks over this Actor, it sends its location to the Game Mode. Then when the player dies, he or she respawns to the Actor's location. If there are multiple Actors of this class in a level, the last one to be interacted with is the character's respawn location.

▶ **KillVolume_BP:** This Blueprint class destroys the player character when touched, forcing the destroy event in the provided Game Modes to fire and respawn the player at the last touched checkpoint Actor.

BP_Pickup Folder

In the BP_Pickup folder are three pickup Blueprint classes. One is a health pickup that gives the player health. Another is a collection pickup that the player can collect while playing the level. The third is a physics-based pickup that can be picked up with a physics gun, so the player can pick up the Actor and move it from one location to another. This Blueprint works only with the provided basic first-person Game Mode when the player uses the physics gun.

In the Content Browser, go to Hour_19/BP_Pickup, open the Pickup_Gallery map, and preview the level.

These are the Blueprints in this folder:

▶ **CollectionPickup_BP:** For this Blueprint, you can change the mesh, material, and point assignment. It works with both the provided first- and third-person Game Modes. This Blueprint can be scaled and placed anywhere.

▶ **HealthPickup_BP:** For this Blueprint, you can change the mesh, material, and health amount. This Blueprint works with both the provided first- and third-person Game Modes. It can be scaled and placed anywhere.

▶ **PhysicsPickup_BP:** For this Blueprint, you can change the mesh material. It works only with the physics gun in the first-person Game Mode. It has an Actor tag already assigned to it so that it works with the physics gun.

BP_Levers Folder

The BP_Levers folder contains a collection of Blueprint classes used to activate or turn on and off other Blueprints. There is a Blueprint that requires the player to press the **E** key to use the lever, and there is a touch-based Blueprint that requires the character or a tagged Physics Actor to be placed on it to activate another Actor.

Lever and switch plate Blueprints can be used to open and close the Door_BP Blueprint and the Stomper_BP Blueprint class found in the BP_Common folder.

In the Content Browser, go to Hour_19/BP_Levers, open the Lever_Gallery map, and preview the level.

This folder contains the following Actors:

▶ **UseKeyLever_BP:** This Actor works when the player character walks up to it and presses the **E** key. It animates the lever and sends a signal to any Actor in the level that has been assigned to its list of Actors to activate.

▶ **Door_BP:** This touch trigger door opens when the player walks up to it. It can be set to a locked state that requires another Actor, such as the UseKeyLever_BP or the TouchActivation_BP Actor, to unlock the door before it can be used by the player.

▶ **PhysicSpawner_BP:** When placed in the level, the player can walk up to this Actor and press the **E** key to spawn a physics pickup (found in the BP_Pickup folder). There is a property that lets you assign the tags that are spawned to the Physics Actor.

▶ **TouchActivation_BP:** This Blueprint class works when either the character or a physics Pickup_BP Actor with Actor tag set to **Key** interacts with it. It can unlock Door_BP or turn on ActivateStomper_BP. You can manually assign other Actors in the level you want to be activated by using TouchActivation_BP when it is interacted with.

▶ **ActivateStomper_BP:** This stomper Actor can be turned on when it receives a signal from UseKeyLever_BP or TouchActor_BP.

All these Actors use Blueprint Interface (BPI) to communicate. When placing these Actors, you need to assign which placed Actor they should affect.

Actor and Component Tags

For the physics gun to work with a Physics Actor, the Physics Actor must have an Actor tag. A *tag* is name that can be assigned to either an Actor or a Component of an Actor, and it can be used to differentiate between two or more of the same Actor or Component types in Blueprint. In this case, the physics gun sequence in the FPS character Blueprint only looks for Physics Actors with the assigned Actor tag of Pickup. For example, you may have two Static Mesh Actors simulating physics but want only one of them to be usable with the physics gun. In this case, you would need to assign the Pickup tag to the Physics Actor you want the player to be able to pick up.

In the Content Browser, go to Hour_19/BP_Pickups, open the ActorTagExample map, and preview the level. Press the **3** key to switch to the physics gun.

There are two Static Mesh Actors here, both simulating physics. Both Actors can be pushed around when you walk into them, but the Static Mesh Actor on the right has been assigned an Actor tag called Pickup and can therefore be picked up, dropped, poked, and thrown. With the physics gun selected, try to pick up both Actors.

Figure 19.5 shows the level's Details panel properties for the tagged Static Mesh Actor.

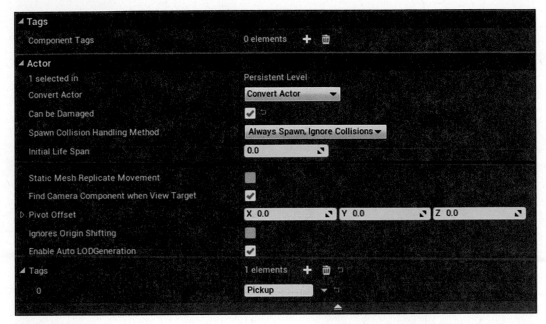

FIGURE 19.5
Actor and Component tags.

Because the PhysicsPickup_BP Actor already has the Pickup tag assigned, it already works with the physics gun when placed or spawned into the level.

Summary

This hour you learned about a collection of Blueprint classes you can place and modify to create obstacle-based level encounters for first- or third-person Game Modes. You learned how to change the players' default movement abilities and were introduced to the concepts of Actor and Component tags.

Q&A

Q. When I play the level I made in this hour, I don't have a first- or third-person character to control. Why?

A. Remember to set Game Mode Override to **BasicFPSGameMode** or **Basic3rdPGame** for the level on the World Settings panel.

Q. When I assign Actors to the Actor Activate List property of TouchActivation_BP, they don't turn on. Why?

A. While the TouchActivation_BP Actor broadcasts a signal to any Actor in the list through a Blueprint Interface (BPI), not all the Actors in the list know how to receive the signal. Only the Door_BP and ActivateStomper_BP Blueprint classes are set up to respond to the signal.

Workshop

Now that you have finished the hour, see if you can answer the following questions.

Quiz

1. To change the player's default movement properties, which component do you need to edit in the character Blueprint class assigned to the Game Mode?

2. If you want to be able to pick up a Static Mesh Actor simulating physics with the physics gun, what do you need to assign for it?

3. If you need more control or accuracy when placing Actors in the level, it helps to turn on _____ for grid, rotation, and scale transforms.

Answers

1. Character Movement Component contains the character's default movement properties.

2. Actor tag. The Physics gun in the First Person Game Mode only interacts with Static Mesh Actors simulating physics that have been given an Actor tag of Pickup.

3. Snapping. Turning on snapping allows you to control the number of grid Units, rotation Degrees, and scale percentage.

Exercise

For this exercise, you create an obstacle course level in the Hour_19 project, using the provided Blueprint classes and one of the Game Modes. When you are finished creating the obstacle course, you can download one of the free Infinity Blade environment asset packs and the free Infinity Blade FX pack from the marketplace and add them to the project so you can set dress your level.

1. In the Hour_19 project, create a new default level, give it a name, and save it to the Maps folder.

2. Open the World Settings panel for the level and set the Game Mode Override property of the level to the first-person (BasicFPSGameMode) or third-person (Basic3rdPGameMode) Game Mode.

3. Block out the level using primitive Static Mesh Actors and/or BSP Actors.

4. Using the Blueprint classes in the BP_Common, BP_Pickups, and BP_Respawn folders, design an obstacle course for the player.

5. Make adjustments to Actor properties and preview and refine the level as needed.

6. When you are happy with the level, download one of the free Infinity Blade asset packs from the marketplace in the Unreal Launcher and add the content to the project.

7. Download the free Infinity Blade FX pack from the marketplace in the Unreal Launcher and add it to the project.

8. Using the Infinity Blade assets, set dress the level, and place lights and the Ambient Sound Actor throughout as needed.

9. Build lighting and play the level.

Creating an Arcade Shooter: Input Systems and Pawns

What You'll Learn in This Hour:

▶ Identifying requirements with a design summary

▶ Creating a new project

▶ Making a custom Game Mode

▶ Creating a custom Pawn and Player Controller

▶ Controlling a Pawn's movement

▶ Setting up a fixed camera

When making a new video game, you almost always have the player take control of something in the game world. This can mean a full character or a simple object. What is important is that the player does something, like press a key or pull a trigger, and something in the game responds. In UE4, you use *Player Controllers* to interpret those physical actions and *Pawns* to act them out. This hour explores these concepts and helps you create your first game—a simple arcade shooter. You will learn how to determine requirements from a design brief, how to create and set up a new project, how to spawn and use a Pawn, and how to set up a game camera.

NOTE

Hour 20 Setup

In this hour, you begin to create a game from scratch. You will create a Blank project with Starter Content. In the Hour_20 folder (available on the book's companion website at www.sty-ue4.com), you will find the assets that you need to work with along with a version of the game called H20_AcradeShooter that you can use to compare your results.

Identifying Requirements with a Design Summary

No two games are exactly alike. It is important to focus on the fundamental elements you want to include in a game. In this hour, you will make a simple arcade shooter, similar to *Space Invaders* or *Asteroids*. Before you can create the game, you need to determine the requirements and features.

Your design in this case is simple: The player controls a spaceship that can move left or right and has to either dodge or destroy asteroids that are in the way.

Identifying Requirements

It is crucially important to take some time when starting a project to determine what types of interactions are necessary to make the design a reality. Understanding the requirements for a game helps you focus production. For the game you create in this hour, you can break down the design summary into the following component parts:

▶ The player controls a spaceship.

▶ The spaceship can move left or right.

▶ Asteroids are in the player's way, moving downward.

▶ The spaceship can shoot the asteroids to destroy them.

Breaking down the summary brings up some things you need to keep in mind. The design tells you that you will need an Actor in the game that the player can control; in UE4, these are called *Pawns*. The design also tells you that the movement of the spaceship is limited to one axis. This requirement means you need to set up input bindings for that one axis. Because you know the player is constrained, you can also assume that the camera is fixed and that the player does not control it. You also see what obstacles the player will face and that another type of input is needed to fire a projectile.

Creating a Game Project

The first thing you always need to do when creating a new game is create a new project in UE4. UE4 provides a lot of great starting content and templates for new projects. You can also create fantastic experiences from scratch by using the Blank Project template during project creation.

TIP

Setting Your Startup Level

You can change the default start level that the game and the Editor use by selecting **Project Settings >
Maps & Modes**. Changing **Editor Default Map** to the map you are currently working on can speed up
your process, and changing **Game Default Map** changes the map the game uses to start (when playing in Standalone).

In the following Try It Yourself, you create a new blank project and an empty map to use as a
blank canvas to build your game-creation experience.

TRY IT YOURSELF ▼

Create a New Project and Default Level

Follow these steps to create a new blank project and replace the default level with a new empty
level as the foundation for your arcade shooter:

1. Launch the UE4 Project Browser and go to the **New Project** tab, as shown in Figure 20.1.

2. Select the **Blank Project** template.

3. Target the project to **Desktop/Console**.

4. Set the Quality setting to **Maximum Quality**.

5. Set the folder location for your project to be stored.

6. Name the new project **ArcadeShooter**.

7. Click the **Create Project** button to create your new project.

8. When your new project loads, select **File > New Level** (or press **Ctrl+N**).

9. Choose the **Default** template from the New Level dialog.

10. Select **File > Save As** (or press **Ctrl+Shift+S**).

11. In the Save Level As dialog, right-click the **Content** directory and select **New Folder**. Rename
the new folder **Maps**.

12. Make sure the **Maps** directory is selected and in the **Name** field, name the map **Level_0**.

13. Click **Save**.

14. In the Project Settings panel, click **Maps & Modes**.

15. Set both Game Default Map and Editor Startup Map to **Level_0**.

FIGURE 20.1
The New Project tab in the UE4 Project Browser.

TIP

The Maps Folder

While you can store level UAssets in any directory inside the Content directory, it is highly recommended that you store all levels in a directory named Maps. As long as your level is within a folder named Maps, it will show up in drop-down lists like the ones for the game default map. It will also make using the UE4 Front End executable for distribution and cooking slightly simpler by finding your levels automatically.

Now that you have created a basically empty level, you can move on to setting up the game's logic and systems.

Creating a Custom Game Mode

You need a place to store your game's logic and behaviors. In UE4, each level has its own Blueprint, which is one place to store game logic, but putting too much scripting in the Level Blueprint means a lot of copying and pasting down the road to transfer that logic to new levels and maps. Instead, UE4 has the concept of a Game Mode. Like Level Blueprints, Game Modes can store complex behaviors related to a game, but unlike with Level Blueprints, that behavior can be shared between multiple levels.

The Game Mode is responsible for defining the behavior of the game being played and enforcing rules. The Game Mode holds information about items a player begins the game with, what happens when the player dies or the game ends, game time limits, and scores.

Game modes are the glue between many of the different systems in a game. Game mode Blueprints hold the characters or Pawns you are using and also reference which HUD class to use, which spectator class to used, and the game state and player state classes that control the information necessary for multiplayer experiences.

At the most basic level, the Game Mode sets the rules of the current game—for example, how many players can join, how level transitions are handled, information about when the game is paused or active, and game-specific behaviors like win and loss conditions.

Creating a new Game Mode is easy. In the Content Browser, right-click and select **Blueprint Class** to open the **Pick Parent Class** window, which is where you can select **Game Mode**, as shown in Figure 20.2.

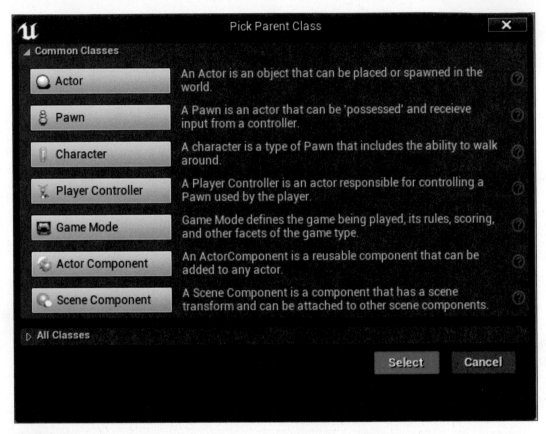

FIGURE 20.2
The Pick Parent Class window. This commonly used window offers several class options, including the Game Mode option you need now.

▼ TRY IT YOURSELF

Create a New Game Mode Blueprint Class

Follow these steps to create a new Game Mode Blueprint class to store the game's logic:

1. In the Content Browser, right-click and select **Folder**.

2. Name this folder **Blueprints**.

3. Double-click the **Blueprints** folder to open into it.

4. In the Content Browser, right-click and select **Blueprint Class**.

5. In the Pick Parent Class window that appears, select **Game Mode**.

6. Name your new Game Mode **ArcadeShooter_GameMode**.

7. Select **File > Save All** (or press **Ctrl+S**).

Now that you have a new Game Mode, you need to tell UE4 to load it instead of the default Game Mode. You do this in the Project Settings panel.

TIP

Level Overrides

Sometimes it is necessary to use different Game Modes during different parts of a game. Each level can also override the Game Mode and class settings. To change these settings on a per-level basis, select **Window > World Settings** and find the Game Mode Override property. This property works exactly as it does in the Project Settings panel. Also, when you add a Game Mode Override setting, you can override other properties, such as those for Pawns or HUD classes, which can be especially useful when you're prototyping new features.

There is only ever one Game Mode present per level—either the default Game Mode set in the Project Settings panel or the Game Mode set on a per-level basis. In a multiplayer game, the Game Mode only ever runs on the server, and the results of the rules and state are sent (replicated) to each client.

TRY IT YOURSELF ▼

Set the New Default Game Mode

Follow these steps to use the Maps & Modes section of the Project Settings panel to set the default Game Mode for your game:

1. Select **Edit > Project Settings**.

2. In the Project Settings panel, click the **Maps & Modes** section.

3. In the Default Modes section, click the **Default GameMode** field to open the search box for all Game Modes.

4. Select your newly created **ArcadeShooter_GameMode** Game Mode.

Creating a Custom Pawn and Player Controller

In UE4, Actors that are controlled directly by players or artificial intelligence (AI) are called Pawns. These Pawns can be practically anything: dinosaurs, humans, monsters, vehicles, bouncy balls, spaceships, even animate food. Any player- or AI-controlled entity in a game is a Pawn. Some games may not have physical or visible representations of players, but Pawns are still used to represent the physical locations of players in the game world.

Pawns define the visible appearance of the controlled objects and also can control movement, physics, and abilities. It is often useful to think of them as the physical bodies of the player in the game world.

The non-physical representation of a player is a Controller. Controllers are the interface between a Pawn and the player or AI controlling it.

Controllers are Actors that can possess and control Pawns. Again, Controllers are non-physical and usually do not directly determine physical properties (e.g., appearance, movement, physics) of the possessed Pawn. Instead, they are more the representation of the *will* or *intent* of the player.

There is a one-to-one relationship between Controllers and Pawns—in other words, one Controller per Pawn and one Pawn per Controller. With this in mind, Pawns can be possessed (i.e., controlled) by AI through an AI Controller or by a player through a Player Controller.

The default Player Controller handles most behavior you need for your game, but you should create your own Pawn.

Inheriting from the Default Pawn

To create a Pawn, you can create a new Blueprint class. This time, however, you start with a class from the All Classes section of the Pick Parent Class window that has a few more features already premade for you. When you create a Blueprint class, you expand the **All Classes** to get access to all the classes in the project. As shown in Figure 20.3, you can look through this list for specific classes. In this case, you want to use the DefaultPawn class because it automatically sets up some of the behaviors that you are going to need in your game.

FIGURE 20.3
In the Pick Parent Class window, expand the All Classes subsection and search for the Pawn you want, such as DefaultPawn.

TIP

Class Inheritance

Inheriting from an existing class allows generalized behaviors to be shared with extreme ease. By inheriting from the DefaultPawn class, for example, you create a class that is a clone of several generalized behaviors but that has the ability to make specific changes. If improvements are made to the DefaultPawn class (or any of its parents), your Pawn will automatically receive those improvements as well.

Using inheritance throughout a project helps you avoid repetition and inconsistent work.

Create Custom Pawn and Player Controller Classes

Follow these steps to create a new Blueprint class that inherits from the DefaultPawn class and create a new Blueprint class that inherits from the Player-Controller class:

1. In the Content Browser, navigate to the **Blueprints** folder.

2. Right-click in the Content Browser and select **Blueprint Class**.

3. In the Pick Parent Class window that appears, expand the All Classes category.

4. In the Search field, type **defaultPawn** and select the **DefaultPawn** class from the results. Click **Select** at the bottom of the window.

5. Rename the new Pawn Blueprint class **Hero_Spaceship**.

6. Right-click in the Content Browser and select **Blueprint Class**.

7. In the Pick Parent Class window that appears, expand the Common Classes category and select **Player Controller**.

8. Rename the new Player Controller Blueprint class **Hero_PC**.

You now have a new Pawn class, and you need to understand the different parts that make up the class. Double-click your new **Hero_Spaceship** class in the Content Browser to open it in the Blueprint Class Editor.

Look at the component hierarchy. By default, there are three components in a DefaultPawn class: CollisionComponent, MeshComponent, and MovementComponent (see Figure 20.4). These three components handle the major types of behaviors a Pawn is responsible for.

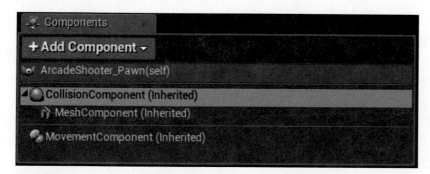

FIGURE 20.4
The component hierarchy in the Blueprint Class Editor for a DefaultPawn class.

`CollisionComponent` handles both physics collisions of the Pawn and trigger overlaps of the Pawn with volumes or Actors in the level. It represents the physical volume of the Pawn and can be shaped to fit the Pawn's simplified form. `CollisionComponent` does not show up in a game and is not part of the Pawn's visual representation.

`MeshComponent` controls the visuals in a game. Right now for your game, this `MeshComponent` class is a sphere, meaning that the visual representation of your Pawn is a sphere. You can replace or modify `MeshComponent` to make your Pawn look like anything you desire. You can add other types of components here to change the visuals, including Particle Emitters, Skeletal Meshes, 2d Sprites, and complex hierarchies of Static Meshes.

`MovementComponent` controls your Pawn's movement. Using `MovementComponent` is a convenient way of handling player movement. Complex tasks (such as checking for collision and handling velocity) are simplified through the convenient interface of `MovementComponent`.

Because you haven't changed it yet, your Pawn is currently just a simple sphere. You can change this by replacing MeshComponent completely or by changing its Static Mesh reference. In the next Try It Yourself, you will import the UFO mesh used by many of the UE4 content examples and then replace the current Pawn's mesh with it.

▼ TRY IT YOURSELF

Make the Spaceship Look Good

Your new Pawn is pretty drab as a sphere. Follow these steps to improve its looks:

1. In the root folder in the Content Browser, right-click and select **New Folder** to create a new folder.

2. Rename this new folder **Vehicles**.

3. Open the **Vehicles** folder and click the **Import** button.

4. In the Import dialog, navigate to the **Hour_20/RawAssets/Models** folder that comes with the book.

5. Select the **UFO.FBX** file and click **Open**.

6. In the FBX Import Options dialog that appears, leave all the settings at their defaults and click **Import All**.

7. In the Content Browser click **Save All** (or press **Ctrl+S**).

8. In the Content Browser, navigate to the **Blueprints** folder and double-click the **Hero_Spaceship** Blueprint class UAsset to open it in the Blueprint Class Editor.

9. If the Editor shows only the Class Defaults panel, then in the note beneath the panel title, click the **Open Full Blueprint Editor** link.

10. In the Components panel, select **MeshComponent**; in the Details panel, select the Static Mesh drop-down, type **UFO** in the search box, and select the **UFO UAsset** from the search results.

11. In the Details panel, set the transform's Scale property to **0.75, 0.75, 0.75** to fit the UFO's bulk inside the CollisionComponent's radius.

12. In the toolbar, click **Compile** and then click **Save**.

Controlling a Pawn's Movement

UE4 makes controlling a Pawn's movement very easy. Because you inherited your Pawn from the DefaultPawn class, all the heavy lifting has already been done. To see just how simple it is to control your Pawn's movement, you can test your work.

First, you need to tell the Game Mode to spawn the player using your new **Hero_Spaceship** Pawn by default. You set this in the class Defaults panel in the Game Mode's Blueprint Class Editor or in the Maps & Modes section of the Project Settings panel.

In the next Try It Yourself, you set the Hero_Spaceship Pawn class as the default Pawn class in **ArcadeShooter_GameMode**. You also set the Player Controller class to **Hero_PC**.

TRY IT YOURSELF ▼

Set the DefaultPawn and PlayerController Classes

The Game Mode needs to know which Pawn and Player Controller you want to be spawned when the game starts. Follow these steps to set these things now:

1. In the Content Browser, navigate to the **Blueprints** folder and double-click the **ArcadeShooter_GameMode** Blueprint class UAsset.

2. In the class Defaults panel, in the Classes category, find the Default Pawn Class property and click its down arrow.

3. Select the **Hero_Spaceship** Blueprint class.

4. Also in the class Defaults panel, click the down arrow next to the Player Controller property and select the **Hero_PC** Blueprint class.

5. In the toolbar, click **Compile** and then click **Save**.

With Hero_Spaceship set up to be the Game Mode's default Pawn, you are ready to test your Pawn's movement. In the Level Editor toolbar, click **Play**, as shown in Figure 20.5. When the game starts, use the **arrow keys** or **WSAD** to move around. You can also use the mouse to look around. When you are done, press the **Esc** key to stop.

CAUTION

Using a Player Start

If things don't seem to be working, it may be because there is no Player Start Actor in the scene. If you don't see Player Start in your World Outliner panel, you can easily add a new one by going to **Modes > Basic > Player Start** and dragging it into the world. Remember to rotate the Player Start Actor to the direction in which you want your Pawn to come out looking!

FIGURE 20.5
Click the Play button on the toolbar to instantly test your game while staying in the Editor.

Although your Pawn can move freely, a couple things don't seem to match your design brief. First, the camera is first person instead of top-down and fixed. Second, your Pawn is moving forward and backward as well as side to side. In this case, you want to pull back from all the features that UE4 has provided you and put in some logic to lock things down.

Disabling the Default Movement

The DefaultPawn class does a lot automatically, but in this case, you want to more manual control. Luckily, it's pretty simple to get that control. The DefaultPawn class's Defaults panel contains a property called Add Default Movement Bindings, which is selected by default. By unselecting this property, you can disable the DefaultPawn class's basic movement and overwrite its behavior and bindings with your own (see Figure 20.6).

FIGURE 20.6
In the Class Defaults of the Pawn, disable the Add Default Movement Bindings check box.

Disable Default Movement

In the game you are creating, the default Pawn is doing more than you need. Follow these steps to disable this behavior through the Hero_Spaceship Pawn's Blueprint class defaults:

1. In the Content Browser, navigate to the **Blueprints** folder and double-click the **Hero_Spaceship** Blueprint class.

2. In the Class Defaults panel, in the Pawn category, ensure that the **Add Default Movement Bindings** property's check box is unchecked to disable this feature.

3. In the toolbar, click **Compile** and then click **Save**.

4. Play again and notice that you can no longer move around. The camera is still in first person, but your spaceship is now locked where it was spawned.

Setting Up Input Action and Axis Mappings

A locked spaceship isn't exactly what you want. It looks like you quickly swung from too much freedom to none at all, and you need to add back some user control. One part of this is binding different keypresses to different actions. Taking an input—like a joystick movement, a keypress, or a trigger pull—and registering a specific action with that input is called *input binding*, and you do this at the Project level.

To set input binding, select **Settings > Project Settings** and then open the **Input** section of the Project Settings panel. At the top of this section are two lists in the Bindings section: Action Mappings and Axis Mappings. The difference between these two sections is subtle but important. *Action mappings* are for single keypress and release inputs. These are usually used for jumping, shooting, and other discrete events. *Axis mappings* are for continuous input, such as movement, turning, and camera control. Both types of mappings can be used simultaneously and picking the right type of binding for your actions will make creating complex and rich player interactions easier.

Axis mappings work slightly differently depending on the hardware generating an input. Some hardware (such as mice, joysticks, or gamepads) return input values to UE4 in a range from -1 to 1. UE4 can scale that value, depending on how much the user wants to let the input influence the game. Keyboards, however, separate up and down and left and right to different keys and don't provide a continuous range of input. A key is either pressed or it isn't, so when you're binding a key as an axis mapping, UE4 needs to be able to interpret that pressed key as a value on that same -1 to 1 scale.

For movement, you use axis mappings, and in your arcade shooter, you are limiting the player's movement to a single axis, so the player can move either left or right. In the next Try It Yourself, you set up the input bindings to support left and right movement for your Pawn.

▼ TRY IT YOURSELF

Create the MoveRight Set of Mappings

In the following steps, you set up the game to be prepared for user input. Bind all the appropriate keys and the left gamepad thumbstick to left and right movement. Any bindings that will cause the user to move left instead of right should have a value of −1.0 set for their scale.

1. Select **Edit > Project Settings**.

2. In the Project Settings panel, select the **Input** category.

3. Under the Bindings category, find the Axis Mappings property, click the + icon beside it.

4. Expand the Axis Mappings field by clicking the arrow to the left of it, and rename the mapping **MoveRight**.

5. Click the arrow to the left of the MoveRight binding to expand the key binding list.

6. Click the + icon beside the MoveRight field four times to create five None mappings.

7. Click the down arrow next to each None field and replace each field to match Figure 20.7.

8. Ensure that each Scale property is set to match Figure 20.7.

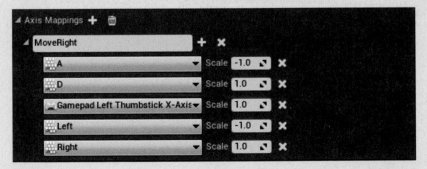

FIGURE 20.7
The Axis Mappings settings for MoveRight, which have three parts each: the name of the mapping, the key or axis that is being bound, and the amount positive or negative of the input that should be accumulated each second.

At the top of the Axis Mappings properties in the Project Settings panel is a field where you input the name for the action that is to be performed. You click the + symbol beside the action name to add a new binding. Each binding has two parts: the input that is being bound and a scale next to it that modulates the result.

You want the game to treat keypresses, like **A** and **D**, as a continuous axis. To do this, you need to have some of those keys be negative; in other words, when you press left, you want the axis to go down, and when you press right, you want the axis to go up.

For thumbstick axes (e.g., **Gamepad Left Thumbstick X-Axis**), the negative values are already calculated, so the scale should usually just be **1.0**.

In this example, the keys **A** and **D**, the **left arrow** and **right arrow** keys, and the **Gamepad Left Thumbstick** are all being bound to the **MoveRight** action. This brings up an important distinction: By using Action Mappings and Axis Mappings, you can bind multiple different input methods to the same event. This means less testing and duplication of Blueprint scripts in your project, and it means everything becomes more readable. Instead of having Blueprint scripts checking whether the **A** key is pressed, the Blueprint can just update movement when the MoveRight event is triggered.

But just creating an input binding doesn't make things move. Now you need to actually use the MoveRight action.

Using Input Events to Move a Pawn

You are now ready to set up movement again. You have a fancy input axis called MoveRight and a Pawn that is just itching to move again. First, you need to open the Blueprint Class Editor of your Pawn and go to the Event Graph. Here, you can begin to lay down behaviors that will fire when your MoveRight action is triggered.

In the Event Graph, right-clicking and searching for your action by name, **MoveRight**, brings up the InputAxis MoveRight event into the graph, as shown in Figure 20.8.

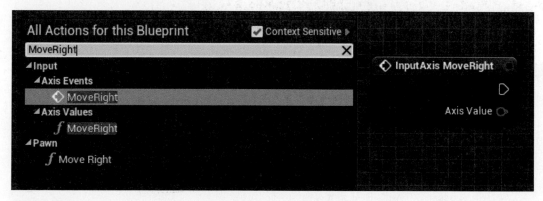

FIGURE 20.8
Axis mappings show up by name under Axis Events. There are also Axis Values functions and Pawn functions, but these functions are not what you are looking for in this case.

Once you have an axis event, you can query the axis value and convert it into movement. To do this you need a few more Blueprint nodes, starting with Add Movement Input. This function works with MovementComponent to interpret a value and a world space direction to move the Pawn in.

By hooking up the **InputAxis MoveRight** event's execution pin and the value that is returned in **Axis Value** to **Add Movement Input**, MovementComponent can take the player's inputs and move the Pawn in a world direction.

Since you want the spaceship to move left or right on input, you need to take the vector coming from the Pawn's right axis. You can get this vector by using the Get Actor Right Vector node and plugging its Return Value into the Add Movement Input's World Direction (see Figure 20.9).

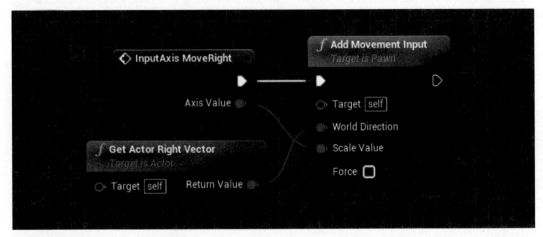

FIGURE 20.9
The finished graph of the Add Movement Input.

▼ TRY IT YOURSELF

Hook Up the MoveRight Axis Mapping to the Pawn's Movement

With the MoveRight axis mapping, the Pawn needs to know how to interpret the values that come from the mapping. Follow these steps to hook up the simple graph required to tell the Pawn how to move on player input:

1. In the Content Browser, navigate to the **Blueprints** folder and double-click the **Hero_Spaceship** Pawn's Blueprint class to open the Blueprint Class Editor.

2. Right-click in an open space in the **Event Graph** and enter **moveright** in the search box.

3. Select **Axis Events > MoveRight** from the search results.

4. Click+drag from the InputAxis MoveRight event node's exec out pin and place an **Add Movement** input node.

5. Hook the InputAxis MoveRight event node's Axis Value output pin to the Add Movement Input node's Scale Value input pin.

6. Click+drag from the Add Movement Input node's World Direction input pin and place a **Get Actor Right Vector** node.

7. On the toolbar, click **Compile** and then click **Save**.

8. When this graph is all hooked up, test the game again. Pressing any of the input keys (A, D, left arrow, right arrow) or using a compatible gamepad's left thumbstick should move the camera either right or left.

TIP

Default Pawn Goodness

In your game, you use Add Movement Input, which takes a world direction. This powerful function can move the Pawn in any direction. The DefaultPawn class, however, gives you some convenience functions for this exact use case. Try replacing the Add Movement Input and Get Actor Right Vector with the DefaultPawn class's MoveRight function. This will have exactly the same result, but it keeps the graph a little bit cleaner, as shown in Figure 20.10.

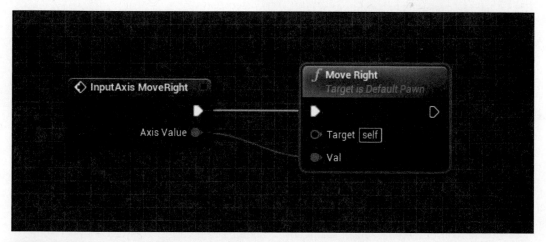

FIGURE 20.10
Alternative setup, showing the DefaultPawn class's MoveRight function instead of the Add Movement Input node.

Setting Up a Fixed Camera

Right now, your game has a camera that follows your Pawn around. This is the default, but for the game you want to make, it isn't quite right. Instead, you want a camera to stay fixed, looking down at the spaceship from above. You also don't want it to move when the Pawn does.

To solve this quandary, you can use Camera Actors and view targets and the built-in PlayerController class to set the view that a player sees. This setup could be done in the Level Blueprint, but it would then be more difficult to port your game logic to a new level. Instead, you are going to bundle this camera logic into a Game Mode. When the game begins, the Game Mode will spawn a camera for your game and then tell the PlayerController class to use that new camera.

In the next Try It Yourself, you use the BeginPlay event and the SPawn Actor from Class node to create a new camera and position it with a Make Transform node before setting it as the PlayerController class's view target.

▼ TRY IT YOURSELF

Create and Set a Fixed-Position Camera

Follow these steps to use the ArcadeShooter_GameMode to spawn a new camera and set it as the PlayerController class's view target:

1. In the Content Browser, navigate to the **Blueprints** folder and double-click the **ArcadeShooter_GameMode** Blueprint class to open the Blueprint Class Editor.

2. If the Editor shows only the Class Defaults panel, then in the note beneath the panel title, click the **Open Full Blueprint Editor** link.

3. In the EventGraph, locate the Event BeginPlay node, and if it doesn't exist, create it by right-clicking and searching for **begin play**.

4. Click+drag from the Event BeginPlay node's exec out pin and place a **SPawn Actor from Class** node.

5. On the SPawn Actor from Class node, click the down arrow in the Select Class field, and select **CameraActor**.

6. Click+drag from the SPawnActor CameraActor node's SPawn Transform property and place a **Make Transform** node.

7. Set the Make Transform node's Location property to **0.0, 0.0, 1000.0**.

8. Set the Make Transform node's Rotation property to **0.0, −90.0, 0.0**.

9. To the right of the SPawnActor CameraActor node place a new **Get Player Controller** node.

10. Click+drag from the Get Player Controller node's Return Value output pin and place a **Set View Target with Blend** node.

11. Hook the SPawnActor CameraActor node's Return Value output pin into the Set View Target with Blend node's New View Target input pin.

12. Hook the SPawnActor CameraActor node's Exec Out pin to the Set View Target with Blend node's exec in pin. Figure 20.11 shows the completed GameMode Event Graph.

13. On the toolbar, click **Compile** and then click **Save**.

14. Give the game another test run. At this point the camera should be looking straight down at your Pawn, which moves left or right when its input keys are pressed.

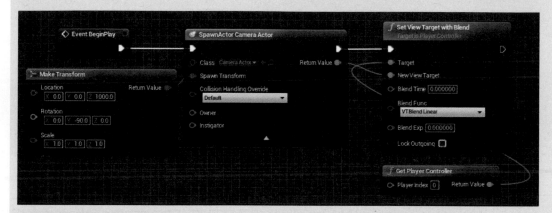

FIGURE 20.11
The finished Event Graph to set up a fixed camera in the Game Mode.

Summary

In this hour, you learned how to make a new UE4 project from scratch and how to get it set up with a custom level and a new Game Mode. You learned what Pawns and Player Controllers are and how to use them. You also learned how to disable the default movement of the DefaultPawn class and how to hook up your own movement and inputs through the Project Settings panel. Finally, you explored one way of setting up a fixed camera in a game.

Q&A

Q. Why should I put all the game logic in a Game Mode instead of in a Level Blueprint?

A. There is no requirement that game logic be put in one place or the other. Instead, it helps to think of the separation as a way to reduce repeated work later. All the logic that is shared between multiple levels should probably be put in a Game Mode or individual Actors, while level-specific logic (like triggers that cause doors to open or lights to turn on) should usually be put in Level Blueprints. You can choose to put everything in Level Blueprints, but if you decide to make a new level, you will have a harder time making sure everything works there and stays up to date than if you primarily use a Game Mode.

374   HOUR 20: Creating an Arcade Shooter: Input Systems and Pawns

Q. Does a Pawn need to inherit from the default Pawn?

A. Not at all! DefaultPawn is just a convenience class, but all its features can be replicated with a bit of work. UE4 also comes with some other convenient Pawn classes, such as the Character class, which contains a Skeletal Mesh component and some logic dedicated to locomotion.

Q. Positioning a camera by inserting raw numbers is difficult. Do I have to spawn a camera this way?

A. No. Another option is to place a camera in a level and then reference it in level script when calling Set View Target with Blend. This brings the logic out of the Game Mode and makes it level specific, allowing easier artistic control of the camera.

Q. I don't like the speed at which my Pawn moves. Can I change it?

A. Absolutely. To change the Pawn's movement speed, open up the Pawn's Blueprint Class Editor and select MovementComponent. In the Details panel, set the three float values that control the Pawn's max speed, acceleration, and deceleration.

Q. Do I have to use only the single MeshComponent in the Hero_Spaceship Pawn Blueprint class?

A. No, you can use any number of components to define the visuals of a Pawn. If you are adding several components (or even if you are sticking with the single one), you might want to disable the physics simulation of your Static Mesh components. You can change the collision presets by clicking on the individual component and finding the **Collision Presets** property in the Details panel. Setting Collision Presets to **No Collision** ensures that it incurs the lowest physics cost possible. Make sure CollisionComponent has **Pawn Preset** and **Generate Overlap Events** enabled; if you don't do this, in the next hour nothing will work. Also, if you disable collision of any individual Static Mesh or visual components, make sure the CollisionComponent's sphere encapsulates your visuals.

Workshop

Now that you have finished the hour, see if you can answer the following questions.

Quiz

1. True or false: Pawns are Actors that players or AI control directly.

2. True or false: UE4 automatically knows which Game Mode to use by detecting it in the Content Browser.

3. True or false: Action bindings and axis bindings only work with fixed names such as MoveRight.

4. True or false: Axis bindings are for continuously pressed inputs like holding down a key or moving a joystick.

Answers

1. True. Any Actors in the scene that AI or players directly control are called Pawns.

2. False. The Game Mode must be set either in the Project Settings panel or the level's World Settings panel.

3. False. Any string can be put into the input binding's Name field and work. For example, you could replace MoveRight with Strafe.

4. True. Any time you need more input information than a simple on or off switch, an axis binding is what you should map your actions to.

Exercise

In this hour's exercise, practice setting up new input bindings to control your Pawn, modifying your Pawn, and customizing your level. Hook the left and right movement of your Pawn to your mouse input, and add walls or other affectations to your level. Then make the floors and walls invisible. The following steps should be done in the same Project and Level made for this hour.

1. Select **Project Settings > Input** and in the Move Right binding found, add a new axis.

2. Set the new axis to **Mouse X** and the Scale property to **1.0**.

3. Preview your game to see the mouse affect your Pawn's location.

4. Select the MovementComponent of your Pawn in the Pawn's Blueprint Class Editor.

5. Modify the **Max Speed** and **Acceleration** settings of MovementComponent to change how fast the Pawn moves.

6. Select the floor of your level and duplicate it several times by pressing **Ctrl+W**.

7. Position the duplicated floors to box out the left and right sides of your level and stop your Pawn from being able to leave the camera's view.

8. Select all the duplicate floors and enable the **Actor Hidden In Game property** in the Rendering category to make all the floors invisible while the game is running.

HOUR 21
Creating an Arcade Shooter: Obstacles and Pickups

What You'll Learn in This Hour:

- ▶ Creating an obstacle base class
- ▶ Making an obstacle move
- ▶ Damaging the Pawn
- ▶ Restarting the game on player death
- ▶ Creating a health pickup
- ▶ Creating a Blueprint that spawns other Actors
- ▶ Cleaning up old obstacles

In the previous hour, you made a new Game Mode and created a spaceship that can move back and forth. Currently, however, your game isn't really much of a game. To change this, in this hour, you add some challenges to the game by introducing obstacles that can hurt and destroy your spaceship. You also create new ways for the player to heal from damage. In this hour, you learn how to create an Obstacle Blueprint class that your obstacles will inherit from, how to set up your Pawn to receive damage, how to create a pickup Blueprint class to heal that damage, and how to create a spawner Blueprint class that can automate the creation of your various Actors.

NOTE

Hour 21 Setup

This hour you will continue working on the ArcadeShooter project you started in Hour 20, "Creating an Arcade Shooter: Input System and Pawns." If you prefer, as a starting point you can also use the provided H20_ArcadeShooter project found in the Hour_20 folder that comes with the book (available on the book's companion website at www.sty-ue4.com).

After you finish this lesson, compare your results to the H21_ArcadeShooter Project found in the Hour_21 folder that comes with the book.

Creating an Obstacle Base Class

Your game needs something to challenge the player. Obstacles come in many shapes and forms; some are Actors that simply act as blockers for player progression, and others can cause damage or a change of behavioral states in the player. You are making a spaceship game, so an asteroid would be a good first obstacle. You need to create a new Actor in the world that has a Static Mesh component to show what it is, a collision component to interact with the player's Pawn, and the ability to move down toward and past the player.

Since you may want to create several variations on this theme, you should take advantage of Blueprint class inheritance to avoid rewriting the same logic over and over again. Because directional movement is one of the primary features of the obstacles and pickups that you need, you should create a base class that consolidates that movement ability. In the following Try It Yourself, you set up a new Blueprint class that has all the requisite components that you will inherit when you make your Obstacle classes.

▼ TRY IT YOURSELF

Set Up Your Obstacle Base Class

An obstacle can be as simple as a single Static Mesh or as complicated as a homing missile launcher. There are a variety of options that all require similar base features, so you can create the basic features necessary for movement and collision and later add custom logic. Follow these steps to set up your Obstacle base class:

1. In the Content Browser, navigate to the **Blueprints** folder.

2. Right-click in the Content Browser and select **Blueprint Class**.

3. In the Pick Parent Class window that appears, select **Actor** from the Common Classes category.

4. Rename the new Actor Blueprint class **Obstacle**. Save it and open it in the Blueprint Class Editor.

5. In the Components panel, add a new sphere collision component.

6. Make the sphere collision component the Actor's root by dragging and dropping it on **DefaultSceneRoot**.

7. In the Details panel for the sphere collision component, set the Sphere Radius property to **50.0** and set the Collision Presets property to **Overlap All Dynamic**.

8. In the Components panel, add a new sphere Static Mesh component.

9. Select the new Static Mesh component, which is currently named Sphere1, and rename it **StaticMesh**.

10. In the Details panel for the **StaticMesh**, set the Collision Presets property to **No Collision**.

11. In the Components panel, and a new rotating movement component.

Let's take a moment to go over everything you did in this Try It Yourself. First, you made several components (shown in Figure 21.1), but not all of them have obvious purposes.

The Static Mesh component is pretty self-explanatory; you need to be able to see obstacles, so you need a mesh to represent it. You use UE4's default Sphere Mesh for now, but you can import and use any Static Mesh to fill this role.

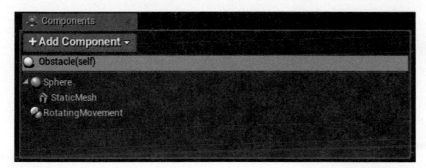

FIGURE 21.1
The Obstacle Blueprint class's components.

The sphere collision component is what you are going to use to handle all the game collision and overlap information you need. When you added it, you changed the Collision Presets property to **Overlap All Dynamic**. You want the Actor to know when it has overlapped your Pawn, and later you'll want it to know when it has overlapped other obstacles. Because you want to test against the sphere instead of the Static Mesh, you also set the Static Mesh component's Collision Presets property to **No Collision**.

GO TO ▶ HOUR 4, WORKING WITH STATIC MESH ACTORS, to learn more about the Collision Presets property.

Finally, you added a rotating movement component, which is similar to the floating Pawn movement component you added to your Pawn in the previous hour. It is a component that contains the behaviors necessary to cause an Actor to rotate in an arbitrary direction. You use it and the Construction Script to cause an obstacle to rotate in a random direction each time it is created.

▼ TRY IT YOURSELF

Make Each Obstacle Unique

If you place your obstacle In the level right now, nothing happens. If you place many copies of it in the level, they all look and act exactly the same. Follow these steps to use the rotating movement component and the power of Construction Script to change that:

1. In the Content Browser, navigate to the **Blueprints** folder.

2. Double-click the **Obstacle** Blueprint class to open it in the Blueprint Editor.

3. Drag the rotating movement component from the Components panel and drop it into the Construction Script to create a reference to the component.

4. Click+drag from the Rotating Movement reference node's output pin and place a **Set Rotation Rate** node.

5. Hook the Construction Script node's exec out pin to the Set Rotation Rate node's exec in pin.

6. Place a **Random Rotator** node underneath the Set Rotation Rate node.

7. Hook the Random Rotator node's Return Value output pin into the Set Rotation Rate node's Rotation Rate input pin.

8. In the My Blueprint panel, create a new float variable and name it **Random Scale Min**.

9. In the My Blueprint panel, create a new float variable and name it **Random Scale Max**.

10. On the toolbar, click **Compile**.

11. In the Class Defaults panel, set Random Scale Min to **0.7**.

12. In the Class Defaults panel, set Random Scale Max to **1.5**.

13. Click+drag from the Set Rotation Rate node's exec out pin and place a **Set Actor Scale 3D** node.

14. Place a **Random Float in Range** node underneath the Set Actor Scale 3D node.

15. From the My Blueprint panel, drag and drop the Random Scale Min variable onto the Random Float in Range node's Min input pin.

16. Drag and drop the Random Scale Max variable onto the Random Float in Range node's Max input pin.

17. Hook the Random Float in Range node's output pin into the Set Actor Scale 3D node's New Scale 3D input pin. A Float to Vector conversion node is automatically placed in between the two nodes.

You've now modified your rotating movement component to pick a random rotation at the creation of each Obstacle Actor, and you have made the Obstacle Actor range from 70% to 150% of the default size (see Figure 21.2).

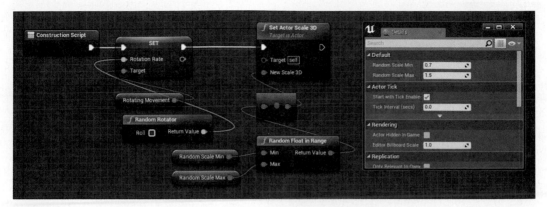

FIGURE 21.2
The Obstacle Blueprint class's Construction Script, setting the random rotation rate and random scale of each Obstacle class Instance.

Making Your Obstacle Move

You can't really make a difficult game from a set of spinning but stationary asteroids. You need to make these obstacles move. Since your game is locked to a single axis, the requirements are rather simple, but you still need to put in a small bit of effort to get everything moving smoothly.

NOTE

Moving the World

This hour, you are constraining the player to a set axis and moving the world (or elements in the world) past the player. In a fully fleshed-out version of the game, you would create the illusion of the player's Pawn moving through panning background elements and particle effects. It would also be possible to make this game by having the character move forward instead of moving the world.

There is no right or wrong answer, although sometimes "faking it" and moving the world makes behaviors and interactions easier to handle. Other times, actually moving the Pawn can make level building easier and, depending on how complex the world is, potentially more efficient.

For your Pawn, you used a Flying Pawn Movement component to handle its motion. Your obstacles and pickups aren't Pawns, and you only want really simple movement. Instead of adding a component, you use your Event Tick event to move the obstacle down past the player each frame. Also, because you don't want all the obstacles to move at exactly the same speed, you give each asteroid a different velocity through the Construction Script.

In the following Try It Yourself, you use an Event Tick event, a Random Float in Range node, and the AddActorWorldOffset node to get the obstacle moving along.

▼ TRY IT YOURSELF

Move Your Obstacle

Your Obstacle Actors are stationary, so follow these steps to use the Blueprint Event Graph and Construction Script to make them move:

1. In the Content Browser, navigate to the **Blueprints** folder.

2. Double-click the **Obstacle** Blueprint class to open it in the Blueprint Class Editor.

3. Click on the **Event Graph**.

4. In the My Blueprint panel, create a new Float variable and name it **Speed Min**.

5. In the My Blueprint panel, create a new Float variable and name it **Speed Max**.

6. In the My Blueprint panel, create a new Float variable and name it **Current Speed**.

7. In the My Blueprint panel, create a new Vector variable and name it **Movement Direction**.

8. On the toolbar, click **Compile**.

9. In the Class Defaults panel, set Speed Min to **200**.

10. In the Class Defaults panel, set Speed Max to **500**.

11. In the Class Defaults panel. set Movement Direction to **–1.0, 0.0, 0.0**.

12. Click+drag from the Event Tick node's Delta Seconds output pin and place a **Float * Float** node.

13. Drag the Current Speed variable and drop it onto the Float * Float node's second input pin.

14. Click+drag from the Float * Float node's output pin and place a **Vector * Float** node.

15. Drag the Movement Direction variable and drop it onto the Vector * Float node's vector input pin.

16. Click+drag from the Event Tick node's exec out pin and place an **AddActorWorldOffset** node.

17. Hook the Vector * Float node's output pin into the AddActorWorldOffset node's Delta Location pin.

18. Click on the Construction Script.

19. Click+drag from the Set Actor Scale 3D node and place a **Set Current Speed** node.

20. Place a **Random Float in Range** node underneath the Set Current Speed node.

21. Drag the Speed Min variable and drop it onto the Random Float in Range node's Min input pin.

22. Drag the Speed Max variable and drop it onto the Random Float in Range node's Max input pin.

23. Hook the Random Float in Range node's Return Value output pin into the Set Current Speed node's Current Speed input pin.

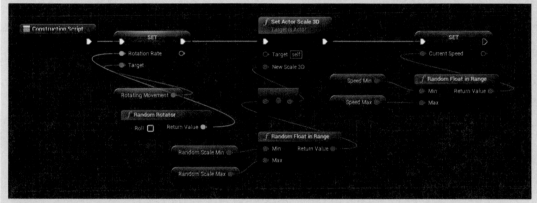

FIGURE 21.3
Here the Event Graph and Construction Script together cause your Obstacle Actor to move at a random speed in the negative X direction every frame. This random speed is calculated only once, during each Actor's construction. This means each Actor will have a unique speed but that individual Actors' speeds will remain consistent.

So now, each obstacle will have a different speed, but the obstacles will all move in the same direction, down the X-axis. Place several Obstacle Actors into the level and try the game in Play in Viewport, and all the obstacles should move down the screen.

You may notice that you can fly your spaceship right into the obstacles, and nothing happens. This is because even though the ship and the obstacles have collision, you haven't hooked up any overlap behaviors.

Now that you have implemented the majority of the sharable behaviors in your Obstacle class, you can now create an asteroid class. In the following Try It Yourself, you create a new Blueprint class that inherits from your Obstacle Blueprint class.

▼ TRY IT YOURSELF

Create the Asteroid Child Class

With the majority of behaviors defined in the base Obstacle class, you can create variations through inheritance. Follow these steps to create an Asteroid version of the Obstacle class and change the Static Mesh to match:

1. In the Content Browser, navigate to the **Blueprints** folder.

2. Right-click in the Content Browser and select **Blueprint Class**.

3. In the Pick Parent Class window that appears, expand the All Classes Category and in the search field, type **obstacle**.

4. Select **Obstacle** from the list and click **Select** at the bottom of the window.

5. Rename the new Obstacle Blueprint class **Asteroid**.

6. Double-click the **Asteroid** Blueprint class to open it in the Blueprint Class Editor.

7. In the Components panel, select the Static Mesh component.

8. In the Details panel, click the Static Mesh property field's down arrow and then search for **sm_rock** and select **SM_Rock**.

9. Reset the Element 0 Material property to the defaults assigned on the Static Mesh by clicking the yellow **Reset to Base Material** arrow next to the property.

10. Set the Static Mesh component's Location property to **0.0, 0.0, −30.0**.

11. Set the Static Mesh component's Scale property to **0.5, 0.5, 0.3**.

Now you have created a new Blueprint based on your original Obstacle Blueprint class. You've given it a rocky Static Mesh and a simple sphere for collision. Because you want to use the sphere component for all collision testing, in the preceding Try It Yourself, you needed to make sure it encompassed your rock entirely. Instead of resizing the collision sphere to fit the rock mesh, you scaled the rock down to fit inside its collision bounds. By doing this, you have made sure that the asteroid's collision and Static Mesh aren't vastly different.

Damaging the Pawn

Taking damage or reducing health is a common concept in video games. Some games have complex systems for regenerating health that show the character's health through a moving scale of effects and visuals and user interfaces. Other games are "one hit kill" games, often with the player getting multiple lives, or chances to try again. Some games are a mix of these concepts, with state-based damage.

For this game, you want to allow the player to be damaged once, but if he or she is damaged again, the player dies. You will later introduce a healing option that allows the player to regenerate health. Because you will use your Obstacle class as the base for both your health pickups and the asteroids, you need to have a way to differentiate between the two. To set up the damage state, you need a property on your Pawn to monitor whether the player is damaged, and you need something to show that to the player. In the following two Try It Yourself sections, you'll set up the Pawn to have a damage state, and you'll teach the Asteroid class to know when it has hit the Pawn.

Prep a Damage State and a Take Damage Function

Space is a dangerous place. Your Pawn needs to know when it is hurt and needs to be able to communicate that damage to the player. Follow these steps to prepare the Event Graph so it looks like the one shown in Figure 21.4:

1. In the Content Browser, navigate to the **Blueprints** folder.

2. Double-click the **Hero_Spaceship** Blueprint class.

3. In the My Blueprint panel, create a new Boolean variable and name it **Is Damaged**.

4. On the toolbar, click **Compile**.

5. Ensure that Is Damaged defaults to **False**.

6. In the Components panel, add a new Particle System component and name it **Damage Particle System** to create the Particle System you use to show when your spaceship is damaged.

7. Set Damage Particle System's Template property to **P_Fire**.

8. Set Damage Particle System's Auto Activate property to **False**.

9. In the My Blueprint panel, create a new function by clicking the **Add New** button and name the new function **Take Damage**.

10. In the My Blueprint panel, double-click the **Take Damage** function to open the function's Event Graph.

11. Click+drag from the Take Damage node's exec out pin and place a **Branch** node.

12. Drag the **Is Damaged** variable onto the Condition input pin of the Branch node.

13. Click+drag from the Branch node's False pin and place a **Set Is Damaged** node.

14. Set the Set Is Damaged node's input pin to **True**.

15. Drag the **Damage** Particle System and place it to the right of the Set Is Damaged node.

16. Click+drag from the Damage Particle System reference node's output pin and place an **Activate** node.

17. Hook the Set Is Damaged node's exec out pin into the Activate node's exec in pin.

18. On the toolbar, click **Compile** and then click **Save**.

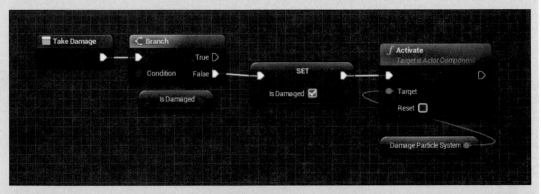

FIGURE 21.4
The Take Damage function. Whenever the Pawn receives damage and this function is called, the Pawn tests to see if it is already damaged, and if it's not, sets the Is Damage variable to **True** before activating the damage Particle System.

You have finished the prep work for your damage state. Right now, if you click Play, nothing new happens. So you need to begin hooking up the asteroid Actors to cause the Pawn to receive damage. To do this, you can use two nodes: Event ActorBeginOverlap and Cast To. These events will let the asteroid determine when it touches the hero. Event ActorBeginOverlap works like an Event Begin Play or Event Tick, only it fires whenever an Actor overlaps another Actor. It provides a reference to the Actor it overlaps, but you need a good way to make sure it is one of your asteroids. That is where the Cast To node comes in.

Using the Cast To Node

The Cast To set of nodes turns a targeted object into the specific class you are attempting to access. When placing a Cast To node, you must pick a specific class, such as Cast To Pawn or Cast To Game Mode. The Cast To node then attempts to convert the target object to that particular type. It is successful if the object is (or inherits from) the specified class.

If the target object can be interpreted as the specified class (that is, the condition is True), the Cast To node continues execution through the Success exec pin and returns the object as the requested class. At this point, variables and functions that are exclusive to the requested class can be used.

If the target object cannot be interpreted by the specified class, the Cast To node continues execution through the Failed exec pin instead, and the returned object is a null reference pointer.

It is important to note that no extra data is converted with a Cast To node. It may be helpful to think of the Cast To node as providing you the same object but interpreted differently. The targeted object is still exactly the same as it was before it was cast into a different class, only the reference that was returned may know more or less about that object.

For example, the Hero_Spaceship class inherits from the Actor class, but the Actor class doesn't have a function called Take Damage. Because Event ActorBeginOverlap returns the overlapping Actor as an Actor reference, you need to use the Cast To Hero_Spaceship node to interpret it as the Hero_Spaceship that it really is. Once you have a reference to the Pawn as a Hero_Spaceship, you can call the Take Damage function on it. Any Actors that are being overlapped that aren't your spaceship are then safely ignored.

In the following Try It Yourself, you use the Event ActorBeginOverlap and Cast To Hero_ Spaceship nodes to trigger the Take Damage function on Hero_Spaceship.

TRY IT YOURSELF ▼

Handle Overlaps

The Asteroid Actors need to call the Take Damage function whenever they overlap with the Pawn, and they also need to be able to destroy themselves. Follow these steps to prepare your Event Graph so it looks like the one shown in Figure 21.5:

1. In the Content Browser, navigate to the **Blueprints** folder.

2. Double-click the **Asteroid** Blueprint class.

3. Click the **Event Graph**.

4. Click+drag from the Event Actor Begin Overlap node's Other Actor output pin and place a **Cast To Hero_Spaceship** node.

5. Ensure that the Event ActorBeginOverlap node's exec out pin is hooked into the Cast To Hero_Spaceship node's exec in pin.

6. Click+drag from the Cast To Hero_Spaceship node's As Hero Spaceship output pin and place a **Take Damage** node.

7. Ensure that the Cast To Hero_Spaceship node's exec out pin is hooked into the Take Damage node's exec in pin.

8. Click+drag from the Take Damage node's exec out pin and place a **Spawn Emitter at Location** node.

9. Set the Spawn Emitter at Location node's Emitter Template input pin to P_Explosion.

10. Place a **GetActorLocation** node underneath the Spawn Emitter at Location node.

11. Hook the GetActorLocation node's Return Value output pin into the Spawn Emitter at Location node's Location pin.

12. Click+drag from the Spawn Emitter at Location node's exec out pin and place a DestroyActor node.

13. On the toolbar, click **Compile** and then click **Save**.

14. Place several Asteroid Actors into the level in front of the player start.

15. In the level toolbar click the **Play in Viewport** button to test your work. When the asteroids collide with the Hero_Spaceship Pawn, they should explode and disappear, and the spaceship should catch on fire.

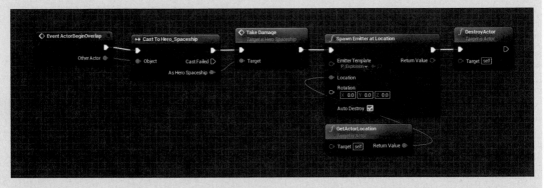

FIGUE 21.5
The Asteroid Blueprint class's Event ActorBeginOverlap node. Whenever another Actor overlaps the asteroid, it is first cast into the Hero_Spaceship Blueprint class. If it turns out to be the Hero_Spaceship class, Hero_Spaceship takes damage through the Take Damage function, and the asteroid spawns a explosion particle emitter before destroying itself.

CAUTION

Obstacle Placement Height

If asteroids aren't colliding with the ship, it could be because they aren't at the same vertical level as the Pawn. The easiest way to fix this is to just raise your Asteroid Actor up in the Z-axis so it is at the same level as your Pawn.

Restarting the Game on Death

Currently in your game, damage is only cosmetic. No matter how many obstacles the player blindly collides with, the spaceship will never be destroyed. To rectify this design flaw, you need to modify the Take Damage function to create a death state. You can then restart the level using a timer and the Game Mode's Restart Game function.

NOTE
_____

Timers

Sometimes it is necessary to have a function or an event fire after a specifiable interval. Using a timer is a convenient way to trigger actions at specified times. For example, after blowing up the spaceship, you will want to wait a short time before restarting the game. By using a timer, you can ensure that the player has time to watch your particle effect and realize what has happened before triggering the Restart Game function.

In Blueprints, you can set timers a couple ways. You can, for example, trigger specific functions by name with the Set Timer by Function node. Or you can connect a custom event to the Set Timer by Event node. A timer takes a set float time that controls how long the timer waits before triggering its action.

Timers can also be set to loop through a Boolean on either function.

_____

In the following Try It Yourself, you create a new On Death function to call whenever the spaceship has taken too much damage, and you use a timer to wait a few seconds before restarting the game through the Game Mode.

TRY IT YOURSELF ▼

Create a Death State

After the spaceship has hit two asteroids, you want the spaceship to explode and the game to restart. Follow these steps to prepare your Event Graph to look like the one shown in Figure 21.6:

1. In the Content Browser, navigate to the **Blueprints** folder.

2. Double-click the **Hero_Spaceship** Blueprint class.

3. In the My Blueprint panel, create a new function by clicking the **Add New** button and name the new function **On Death**.

4. In the My Blueprint panel, double-click the **On Death** function to open the function's Event Graph.

5. Click+drag from the On Death node's exec out pin and place a **Spawn Emitter at Location** node.

6. Place a **GetActorLocation** node underneath the Spawn Emitter at Location node.

7. Hook the GetActorLocation node's Return Value output pin into the Spawn Emitter at Location node's Location input pin.

8. Click+drag from the Spawn Emitter at Location node's exec out pin and place a **Set Actor Hidden In Game** node.

9. Set the Set Actor Hidden In Game node's New Hidden input pin to **True**.

10. Click+drag from the Set Actor Hidden In Game node's exec out pin and place a **Set Actor Enable Collision** node.

11. Click+drag from the Set Actor Enable Collision node's exec out pin and place a Set Timer by Function Name node.

12. Place a **Get Game Mode** node underneath the Set Timer by Function Name node.

13. Hook the Get Game Mode node's Return Value pin into the Set Timer by Function Name node's Object input pin.

14. Set the Set Timer by Function Name node's Function Name input to **RestartGame**.

15. Set the Set Timer by Function Name node's Time input to **3.0**.

16. In the My Blueprint panel, double-click the **Take Damage** function to open the function's Event Graph.

17. Click+drag from the Branch node's True exec pin and place an **On Death** node.

18. In the Level toolbar, click the **Play In Viewport** button to test your work. When the Asteroid Actors collide with Hero_Spaceship, they should explode and disappear, and the spaceship should catch on fire. After the second collision, the ship should explode and disappear, and three seconds later, the game should restart.

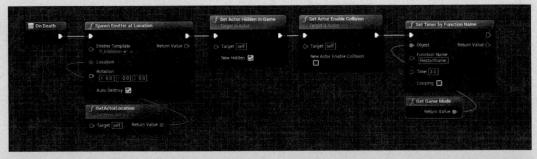

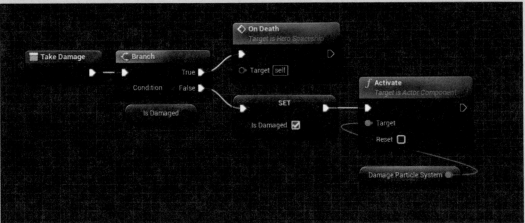

FIGURE 21.6
The Hero_Spaceship Blueprint class's On Death and Take Damage functions. The On Death function uses a timer to call the Game Mode's built-in RestartGame function. In the Take Damage function, the On Death node is placed after the Branch node's True pin. This means Take Damage first checks whether the Pawn is already damaged, and if it is, calls the On Death function.

Creating a Health Pickup

You've created a way for your player to take damage, but you haven't done anything to heal the player after damage. In this section, you'll duplicate your Asteroid class and quickly make some subtle modifications to it to make it a healing pickup instead.

The primary difference between the Asteroid class you've made before and a health pickup is how it reacts to touching a Pawn. The motion, rotation, and collision can all stay the same. Therefore, instead of remaking everything from scratch, you can start by inheriting from the Obstacle class you created earlier in this hour.

In the next few Try It Yourself sections, you create a new Health_Pickup class that inherits from the Obstacle class and then you make changes to the visuals and the Construction Script variables.

Add a Health Pickup

Your Pawn is having a hard time staying alive. Make a repair pack pickup to extinguish flames. Follow these steps to start by creating a new Blueprint class and creating a cross shape inside of a sphere:

1. In the Content Browser, navigate to the **Blueprints** folder.

2. Right-click in the Content Browser and select **Blueprint Class**.

3. In the Pick Parent Class window that appears, expand the All Classes Category, and in the search field type **obstacle**. Select **Obstacle** from the list of classes and click **Select** at the bottom of the window.

4. Rename the new Obstacle Blueprint class **Health_Pickup**.

5. In the Class Defaults panel, set Random Scale Min default to **1.0**.

6. In the Class Defaults panel, set Random Scale Max default to **1.0**.

7. If the editor shows only the Class Defaults panel, then in the note beneath the panel title, click the **Open Full Blueprint Editor** link.

8. In the Components panel, add two cube Static Meshes through the **Add Component** drop-down.

9. Select the first cube Static Mesh component and set its Transform Scale property to **0.2, 0.2, 0.6**.

10. Select the second cube Static Mesh component and set its Transform Scale property to **0.6, 0.2, 0.2**.

The Health_Pickup class now exists, but it won't be recognizable to the user because it looks like a plain sphere. You need to create some special materials to better communicate the pickup's purpose.

▼ TRY IT YOURSELF

Create Materials for the Pickup

It isn't yet visually obvious to the user what the Health_Pickup pickup does. You can create two new materials to change that—one for the sphere boundaries and one for the Cross Mesh inside. Follow these steps to prepare your material Event Graph so they look like the ones shown in Figure 21.7:

1. In the Content Browser, create a new folder at the root level and name it **Pickups**.

2. Right-click in the Content Browser and select **Material**.

3. Rename the new material **M_Pickup_Orb**.

4. Double-click **M_Pickup_Orb** to open it in the Material Editor.

5. In the Details panel, set the Blend Mode property to **Translucent**.

6. In the Details panel, set the Shading Model property to **Unlit**.

7. In the material Event Graph, right-click and place a **Constant3Vector** node.

8. Hook the Constant3Vector node's output pin into the M_Pickup_Orb output node's Emissive Color pin.

9. In the Details panel, set the Constant3Vector node's Constant property to **0.0, 10.0, 0.0**.

10. In the material Event Graph, right-click and place a **Fresnel** node.

11. Hook the Fresnel node's output pin into the M_Pickup_Orb output node's Opacity pin.

12. On the toolbar, click **Save**.

13. Right-click in the Content Browser and select **Material**.

14. Rename the new material **M_Pickup_Cross**.

15. Double-click **M_Pickup_Cross** to open it in the Material Editor.

16. In the material Event Graph, right-click and place a **Constant3Vector** node.

17. Hook the Constant3Vector node's output pin into the M_Pickup_Cross output node's Base Color pin.

18. In the Details panel, set the Constant3Vector node's Constant property to **0.0, 1.0, 0.0**.

19. On the toolbar, click **Save**.

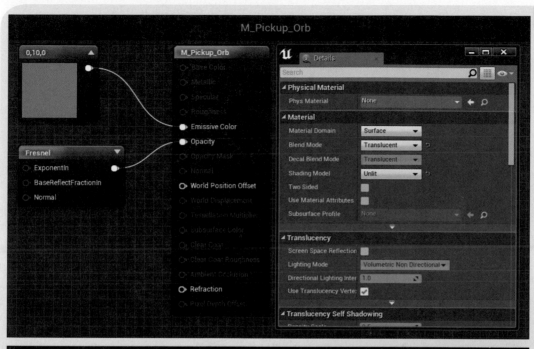

FIGURE 21.7
The M_Pickup_Orb and M_Pickup_Cross material Event Graphs and properties.

You have created the new materials created but still need to assign them to the Health_Pickup Blueprint class's Static Mesh components.

▼ TRY IT YOURSELF

Apply the Pickup Materials

The materials have been created, but they need to be applied to the different Static Mesh components in the Health_Pickup Blueprint class to create the visuals shown in Figure 21.8. Follow these steps:

1. In the Content Browser, navigate to the **Blueprints** folder.

2. Double-click the **Health_Pickup** Blueprint class.

3. In the Components panel, select the **StaticMesh** component.

4. Set Element 0 Material to **M_Pickup_Orb**.

5. In the Components panel, select the first **Cube** component.

6. Set Element 0 Material to **M_Pickup_Cross**.

7. In the Components panel, select the **Cube1** component.

8. Set Element 0 Material to **M_Pickup_Cross**.

9. On the toolbar, click **Compile** and then click **Save**.

FIGURE 21.8
The health pickup with the appropriate materials assigned to each Static Mesh component.

Now that the visuals are handled, the next step is to add the game logic that allows the Health_ Pickup to change the Is Damaged state of the Pawn. You can follow the same pattern you used with the asteroid for dealing with damage, only this time you will create a Heal Damage function that sets the Is Damaged variable to False and deactivates the Damage Particle System component.

In the following two Try It Yourself sections, you create the Heal Damage function the Pawn needs to heal itself and deactivate the fire particles, then you use the Event ActorBeginOverlap even of the Health_Pickup Blueprint class to call that Heal Damage function.

TRY IT YOURSELF ▼

Create the Heal Damage Function

With your new Health_Pickup created and moving appropriately, you need to set up the function to fix the spaceship. Follow these steps to prepare your Event Graph so it looks like the one shown in Figure 21.9:

1. In the Content Browser, navigate to the **Blueprints** folder.

2. Double-click the **Hero_Spaceship** Blueprint class.

3. In the My Blueprint panel, create a new function by clicking **Add New** and name the new function **Heal Damage**.

4. In the My Blueprint panel, double-click the **Heal Damage** function to open the function's graph.

5. Click+drag from the Heal Damage node's exec out pin and place a **Set Is Damaged** node.

6. Ensure that the Set Is Damaged node's Is Damaged input pin is set to **False**.

7. Drag the Damage Particle System component and drop it to the right of the Set Is Damaged node.

8. Click+drag from the Damage Particle System reference node's output pin and place a **Deactivate** node.

9. Hook the Set Is Damaged node's exec out pin into the Deactivate node's exec in pin.

10. On the toolbar, click **Compile** and then click **Save**.

FIGURE 21.9
The Heal Damage function Event Graph of the Hero_Spaceship Blueprint class.

With the Heal Damage function in place, the pickup now needs to know when to call the Heal Damage function on the Pawn.

▼ TRY IT YOURSELF

Call the Health Damage Function on Overlap

The Pawn is now capable of healing itself, and the Health_Pickup Blueprint class needs to be able to tell the Pawn when it should be healed. Follow these steps to prepare your Event Graph so it looks like the one shown in Figure 21.10:

1. In the **Content Browser**, navigate to the **Blueprints** folder.

2. Double-click the **Health_Pickup** Blueprint class.

3. Click the **Event Graph**.

4. Click+drag from the Event Actor Begin Overlap node's Other Actor pin and place a **Cast To Hero_Spaceship** node.

5. Ensure that the Event ActorBeginOverlap node's exec out pin is hooked into the Cast To Hero_Spaceship node's exec in pin.

6. Click+drag from the Cast To Hero_Spaceship node's As Hero Spaceship output pin and place a **Heal Damage** node.

7. Ensure that the Cast To Hero_Spaceship node's exec out pin is hooked into the Heal Damage node's exec in pin.

8. Click+drag from the Heal Damage node's exec out pin and place a **DestroyActor** node.

9. On the toolbar, click **Compile** and then click **Save**.

10. Place an **Asteroid** Actor in the level in front of the player start and then place a **Health_ Pickup** Actor further away.

11. In the Level toolbar, click the **Play In Viewport** button to test your work. When the Asteroid Actor overlaps Hero_Spaceship, the spaceship catches fire, and then when Health_Pickup collides with Hero_Spaceship, that fire goes out.

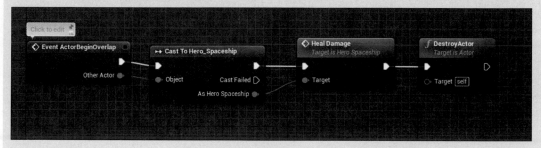

FIGURE 21.10
The Health_Pickup class's Event ActorBeginOverlap Event Graph, triggering the Heal Damage function when the Actor overlaps the Hero_Spaceship Pawn.

Creating an Actor Spawner

At this point, you could create a game just by placing a set of asteroids and pickups in a fixed level. This is a valid way to build levels, and a lot of great games use hand-placed elements to create a heavily crafted player experience. In this case, though, you want a less labor-intensive way to build out a level.

One simple way to do this is to create a Blueprint class that is dedicated to spawning other Actors. This "spawner" Blueprint handles how often new Actors are introduced as well as when to randomly select different types of elements. In your game, you need to randomly spawn asteroids or health pickups.

Creating a system that waits a random (but controlled) amount of time between spawning new Actors and does so continually can be a bit of a difficult concept to deal with. There are multiple solutions, such as using timers and events or functions or using functions with recursion. One simple but discouraged method is to build your own countdown timer and use the Event Tick event to check whether you need to spawn a new object. The concept is that a float variable stores a randomly created countdown time, and every tick, the frame's time is subtracted from it. Once the variable hits zero, it spawns an Actor and sets the countdown back to a new random time. This continues indefinitely. The problem with this system is that it is performance intensive and when used frequently can cause real performance issues in a game. It can also be difficult to maintain. One tick-based countdown can be simple to deal with, but as the rules of the game get more complex, it can be hard to manage the game flow if everything is done in a single Event Tick.

Instead of building a tick-based pattern, you can use the Set Timer by Function Name node and a custom function to create an endless stream of Actors. In the following two Try It Yourself sections, you create a Blueprint class that spawns other Actors and randomly decides which Actor to spawn. You create a new function that uses Set Timer by Function Name to continually spawn new Actors.

▼ TRY IT YOURSELF

Prepare the Spawn Function

Your game has Actors to avoid and Actors to aim for, but hand-placing them can be a pain. You can have UE4 do the heavy lifting for you. Follow these steps to prepare your Event Graph so it looks like the one shown in Figure 21.11:

1. In the Content Browser, navigate to the **Blueprints** folder.

2. Right-click and create a new Blueprint class whose parent class is Actor. Name your new class **Obstacle_Spawner**.

3. Double-click the **Obstacle_Spawner** Blueprint class.

4. In the My Blueprint panel, create a new float variable and name it **Spawn Time Min**.

5. In the My Blueprint panel, create a new float variable and name it **Spawn Time Max**.

6. In the My Blueprint panel, create a new float variable and name it **Health Pickup Probability**.

7. On the toolbar, click **Compile**.

8. In the Class Defaults panel, set Spawn Time Min to **5.0**.

9. In the Class Defaults panel, set Spawn Time Max to **10.0**.

10. In the Class Defaults panel, set Health Pickup Probability to **0.1**.

11. In the My Blueprint panel, create a new function by clicking **Add New** and name the new function **Spawn**.

12. In the Event Graph, click+drag from the Event BeginPlay node's exec out pin and place a **Set Timer by Function Name** node.

13. Set the Set Timer by Function Name node's Function Name input pin to **Spawn**.

14. Place a **Random Float in Range** node beneath the Set Time by Function Name node.

15. Drag the Spawn Time Min float variable onto the Random Float in Range node's Min input pin.

16. Drag the Spawn Time Max float variable onto the Random Float in Range node's Max input pin.

17. Hook the Random Float in Range node's Return Value output pin into the Set Timer by Function Name node's Time input pin.

18. On the toolbar, click **Compile** and then click **Save**.

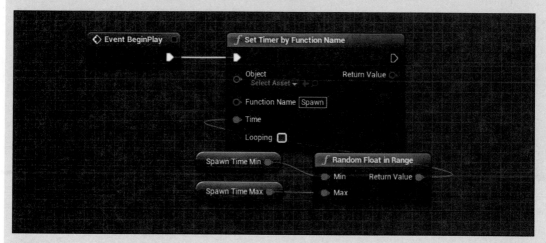

FIGURE 21.11
The Obstacle_Spawner Blueprint class's Event BeginPlay event, calling the Spawn function with a random time between specified minimum and maximum values.

At this point the Spawn function doesn't contain any logic, so nothing happens if you test the game. You need to fill out the Spawn function to create new Actors and continue indefinitely.

Pick Which Class to Spawn

The Spawn function doesn't do anything yet, but you can use a Branch node to determine which Blueprint class to spawn, and then you can set a timer to create a recursive pattern. Follow these steps to prepare your Event Graph so it looks like the one shown in Figure 21.12:

1. In the Content Browser, navigate to the **Blueprints** folder.

2. Double-click the **Obstacle_Spawner** Blueprint class.

3. In the My Blueprint panel, double-click the **Spawn** function to open the function's Event Graph.

4. Click+drag from the Spawn node's exec out pin and place a **Branch** node.

5. Place a **Random Float** node underneath the Branch node.

6. Click+drag from the Random Float node's Return Value output pin and place a **Float < Float** node.

7. Drag the Health Pickup Probability variable onto the second input of the Float < Float node.

8. Hook the Float < Float node's Boolean output pin into the Branch node's Condition input pin.

9. Click+drag from the Branch node's True exec pin and place a **Spawn Actor by Class** node.

10. Set the Spawn Actor by Class node's Class input to **Health_Pickup**.

11. Place a **GetActorTransform** node underneath the SpawnActor Health Pickup node.

12. Hook the GetActorTransform node's Return Value output pin into the SpawnActor Health Pickup node's Spawn Transform input.

13. Click+drag from the Branch node's False exec pin and place a **Spawn Actor by Class** node.

14. Set the Spawn Actor by Class node's Class input pin to **Asteroid**.

15. Place a **GetActorTransform** node underneath the SpawnActor Asteroid node.

16. Hook the GetActorTransform node's Return Value output pin into the SpawnActor Asteroid node's Spawn Transform input.

17. Click+drag from the SpawnActor Health Pickup node's exec out pin and place a **Set Timer by Function Name** node.

18. Hook the SpawnActor Asteroid node's exec out pin into the Set Timer by Function Name's exec in pin.

19. Set the Set Timer by Function Name node's Function Name input pin to **Spawn**.

20. Place a **Random Float in Range** node beneath the Set Time by Function Name node.

21. Drag the Spawn Time Min float variable onto the Random Float in Range node's Min input pin.

22. Drag the Spawn Time Max float variable onto the Random Float in Range node's Max input pin.

23. Hook the Random Float in Range node's Return Value output pin into the Set Timer by Function Name node's Time input pin.

24. On the toolbar, click **Compile** and then click **Save**.

25. Remove any Asteroid Actors or Health_Pickup Actors from the level.

26. Place a few Obstacle_Spawner Actors into the scene.

27. In the level toolbar, click the **Play In Viewport** button to test your work. After approximately five seconds, the Obstacle_Spawner Actors should begin spawning Asteroid or Health_Pickup Actors.

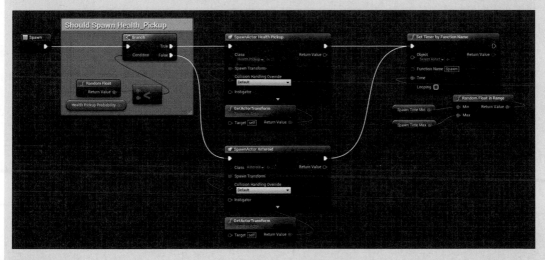

FIGURE 21.12
The Obstacle_Spawner Blueprint class's Spawn function, which determines which Blueprint class to spawn by comparing a random float value to a set threshold. When the random float is less than the probability threshold, the Health_Pickup Blueprint class is spawned; otherwise, the Asteroid Blueprint class is spawned. Regardless of which Blueprint class is created, the function then sets a timer to call itself with a randomly generated time.

With your Obstacle_Spawner complete, you no longer have to hand place your asteroids and health pickups. Instead, off camera, you can place multiple Obstacle_Spawner Actors to create a variety of places for either of your obstacles to spawn. Figure 21.13 and Figure 21.14 show examples of potential spawner placement and what the results in game look like.

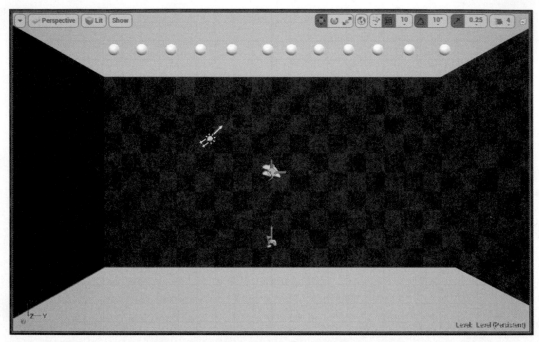

FIGURE 21.13
An example of placement of Obstacle_Spawner Actors where they are spread out across the play space.

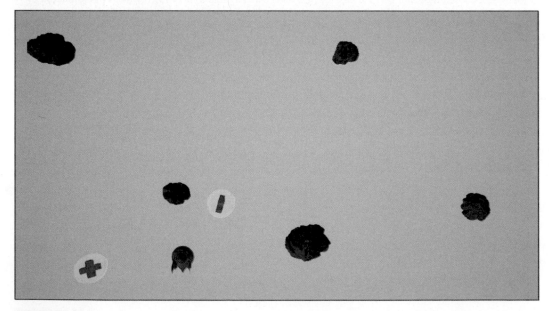

FIGURE 21.14
An in-game screenshot from the placement of Obstacle_Spawner Actors shown in Figure 21.13.

Give it a try by placing some Obstacle_Spawner Actors of your own and giving the game a run.

Cleaning Up Old Obstacles

Now that you are spawning a potentially infinite number of asteroids and pickups, you may start running out of memory or having performance problems due to having too many asteroids and pickups in your scene. Luckily, Unreal Engine makes such a situation easy to fix.

From the Modes panel, place a new Kill ZVolume at the bottom edge of the screen so it spans the entire play area. Whenever an Actor enters a Kill ZVolume, that Actor is destroyed and cleaned up (see Figure 21.15).

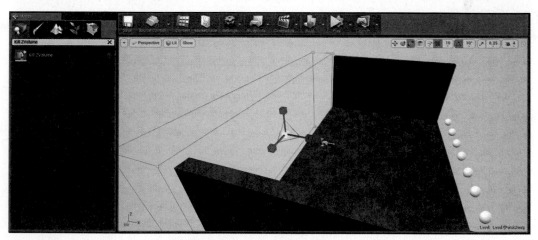

FIGURE 21.15
An example of level placement for a Kill ZVolume used to clean up asteroids as they exit the screen.

After you place a Kill ZVolume, click **Simulate** to make sure your asteroids get cleaned up properly as they enter this Kill ZVolume.

Summary

In this hour, you learned how to make a set of Blueprint classes that interact with your Pawn. You created a damage state and a healing mechanism for your game. You learned how to spawn Actors in a controlled random fashion and destroy Actors when interacting with them. At this point, you have a mostly functioning game and a decent framework to build on.

Q&A

Q. My asteroids and pickups aren't interacting with my Pawn. Why?

A. There could be a couple of issues. First, make sure that each of your obstacles and pickups has a sphere collision and that its Collision Presets property is set to **OverlapAll**. Then also make sure that your Pawn has collision. Finally, check to make sure that the Pawns and the obstacles are at the same height and that they are actually touching. It can be hard to tell from a top-down point of view.

Q. I want to add some more specific behavior to the Construction Script of the Health_Pickup Actor, but I don't want the Asteroid Actor to be affected. How do I do this?

A. There are two primary ways to achieve this sort of separation between multiple children of the same parent class. The first way is similar to the way you disabled the scale randomization of the Health_Pickup. The scaling behavior was implemented in the parent class's Construction Script, but variables were set up to allow the different child classes to scale themselves separately.

Alternatively, in the Health_Pickup class's Construction Script graph, right-click on the Construction Script node and select **Add Call to Parent Function**. This will create a special **Parent: Construction Script** node. This node will run all of the parent class's (for example, the Obstacle class) construction behavior before running any child-specific behavior that you add afterward.

Q. Why do you test for overlaps inside the obstacles instead of inside the Hero_Spaceship Blueprint?

A. Although all the overlap interactions could be done in the Hero_Spaceship Blueprint class, that approach is discouraged. The problem is that when you follow the pattern of the Pawn testing to see what affects it, the logic can become very difficult to maintain. To handle the same two interactions from the Pawn's point of view would require creating a much longer and slightly more complicated single graph with several branch nodes to handle the different behaviors.

As the game becomes even more complete and complicated, such a monolithic graph would become much harder to maintain. Instead, it helps to keep the applicable behaviors close to their logical units. For example, an asteroid doesn't know what it means to damage Hero_Spaceship; all it knows is that when it touches Hero_Spaceship, it should call the Take Damage function. Meanwhile, Hero_Spaceship doesn't know what might cause it to call Take Damage, but it is aware of what to do when that function is called on it.

Q. Why do you use another timer in the Spawn function instead of using the looping Boolean on the timer itself in the Event Graph on Begin Play?

A. You can use the looping Boolean input on the Set Timer by Function Name node instead of calling the timer again in the function itself. This does, however, result in slightly different behavior, where each *instance* of the spawner has a different interval between spawning new obstacles but those *intervals* are consistent. By setting a new random time with every Spawn function call, you ensure that the Obstacle_Spawner Actors are always creating new obstacles at random intervals, creating a more chaotic game.

Workshop

Take a few moments to review and see if you can answer the following questions.

Quiz

1. True or false: The rotating movement component rotates the Actor it is attached to around an axis at a set velocity.

2. True or false: The DefaultPawn class contains logic to handle damage and health information about itself.

3. True or false: The Cast To node only works for casting Actors to other Actors.

4. True or false: The Set Timer by Function Name node needs the exact name of the function you are trying to call.

Answers

1. True. However, the component is able to do even more than that. It is definitely worth playing around with the component to unlock all its abilities.

2. False. The DefaultPawn class does a lot, but it leaves health and damage behaviors up to you.

3. False. The Cast To node works with all types. Any type (such as textures, materials, particle effects) can be cast to other types as long as they share a common class hierarchy.

4. True. The Set Timer by Function Name node can't guess what function you mean if it isn't spelled properly; even whitespace in the function name matters here.

Exercise

On your own, consider other types of pickups and simple collision-based behavior Actors you could introduce into the game. Then use what you have learned in Hour 20 and this hour to create an obstacle that can destroy asteroids, which the player shoots with a keypress. If you are feeling especially adventurous, on your own, consider changing the lighting and the environment to better fit the theme of the game.

1. Create a new Blueprint class that inherits from the Obstacle class, and name it **Plasma_ Bolt**.

2. Give the StaticMesh component a custom material. Since this is supposed to be a weapon blast, consider going with a highly emissive red or electric blue material.

3. In the Class Defaults panel for your new Plasma_Bolt class, change the Movement Direction Vector from −1.0, 0.0, 0.0 to **1.0, 0.0, 0.0**.

4. Set both Random Scale Min and Random Scale Max to **0.2**.

5. Set both Speed Min and Speed Max to **1000**.

6. Add a new Event ActorBeginOverlap node in the obstacle's Event Graph and use a Cast To Asteroid node to detect when it overlaps with an asteroid.

7. When Plasma_Bolt overlaps with an asteroid, spawn an explosion particle emitter and use DestroyActor to destroy both the asteroid and the Plasma_Bolt Actor.

8. Create a new input action binding for a shoot action and bind the spacebar and another key or gamepad button to it.

9. In your pawn's Event Graph, create a new event for your action binding.

10. From the Pressed exec pin, use SpawnActor to spawn the Plasma_Bolt Actor at your pawn's location.

11. Test your game and use the bound key or gamepad button from step 8 to shoot those pesky asteroids!

Working with UMG

What You'll Learn in This Hour:

▶ Using the Unreal Motion Graphics (UMG) UI designer
▶ Creating a Widget Blueprint
▶ Making a Start menu Game Mode
▶ Making a menu interface

Unreal Motion Graphics UI Designer (UMG) is an Editor in UE4 that is used to design, animate, and script user interfaces and HUD functionality. This hour introduces you to UMG and how to create a Start menu.

NOTE
___

Hour 22 Setup

For this hour, create a new project with the Flying template and include Starter Content. Then, after the project is made, in the Content Browser create a folder called **StartMenuGame**.

___

Creating a Widget Blueprint

There are two common methods to create interfaces and HUDs in Blueprint. One is to code in the Blueprint HUD class assigned to a Game mode. The second, and more artist-friendly, way is to use the UMG UI designer. UMG allows you to interactively place interface assets called *widgets* and code functionality with Blueprint. When you understand the basics of UMG, creating an interface is fairly easy.

Before you can start to use UMG, you need to create a Widget Blueprint, as described in the following Try It Yourself.

Create a Widget Blueprint Asset

To see the UMG interface, follow these steps to create a Widget Blueprint asset:

1. Right-click in the StartMenuGame folder you created for this chapter and select **Widget Blueprint** to add a new Widget Blueprint to the Content folder.

2. Name the new Widget Blueprint **StartMenuWidget_BP**.

3. Double-click **StartMenuWidget_BP** to open it in UMG.

Navigating the UMG Interface

The UMG interface has two modes, as shown in Figure 22.1: Designer mode for placing widgets such as images and text and Graph mode for adding functionality in Blueprint. UMG defaults to Designer mode when it's first opened.

FIGURE 22.1
UMG modes.

Designer Mode

The Designer mode has a Palette panel that lists all the widgets you can use, organized by functionality (see Figure 22.2). The Hierarchy panel shows all the placed widgets in your interface. You can attach widgets to one another and detach them from each other in the Hierarchy panel as needed. The root of the Widget Blueprint is the Canvas panel, and all placed widgets are attached to it. There is also a Details panel that shows the properties of any selected placed widgets in the interface. This mode also has an Animations panel and a Timeline for creating, managing, and editing the animations of your widgets. In the center is the Designer panel, which is where you create your interface layout by dragging elements from the Palette panel and placing them in the Designer panel.

The following areas are identified in Figure 22.2 with numbers: 1) Toolbar; 2) Palette panel; 3) Hierarchy panel; 4) Designer panel; 5) Details panel; 6) Animation panels.

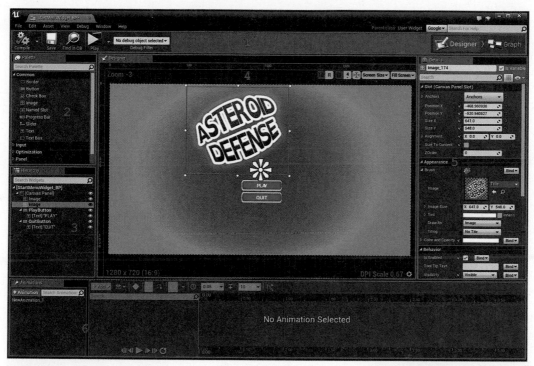

FIGURE 22.2
UMG Designer mode interface.

NOTE

Default Root Widget

On a new Widget Blueprint, the Canvas panel is the default root widget to which widgets can be attached. You can, however, delete the Canvas panel and place any other widget to make it the root. Typically you do this when that Widget Blueprint is going to be used as part of another Widget Blueprint.

Graph Mode

The Graph mode is the Blueprint Editor for Widget Blueprints (see Figure 22.3). This is where you code functionality for placed widgets, either as functions or event sequences. The Graph mode Blueprint Editor has a My Blueprint panel for managing graphs, functions, macros, variables, and event dispatchers; a Details panel that shows properties of selected nodes; and an Event Graph for scripting. Typically widgets placed in the Designer mode show up here as variables.

NOTE

Widget Reference Variables

If a placed widget in the Designer mode does not show up as a variable in Graph mode but you need it to do so, you can go back to the Designer mode, select the widget, and then in the Designer mode's Details panel, select the **IsVariable** property.

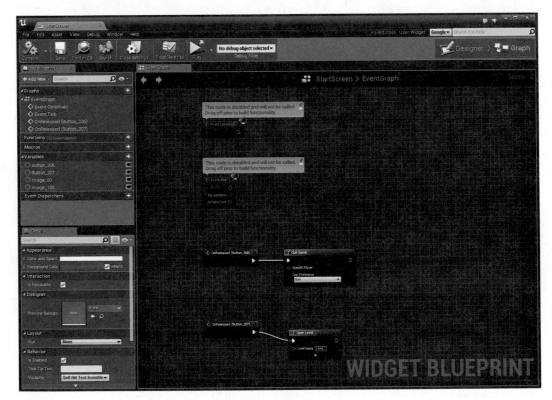

FIGURE 22.3
UMG Graph mode interface.

Setting the Resolution

The Designer mode allows you to set the resolution for which you are creating an interface or a HUD. Although UE4 scales your game to whatever resolution the target platform can support, interfaces should be designed around common resolutions and aspect ratio settings.

To pick a resolution setting for your interface in Designer mode, select the Screen Size drop-down in the upper-right corner and pick a resolution from the common resolution presets list (see Figure 22.4).

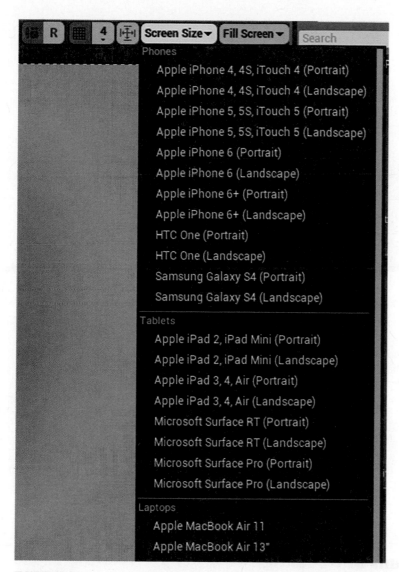

FIGURE 22.4
Screen Size presets.

When developing a game for a target platform such as a PC or a game console, you can never be certain about the monitor the end user will have, so you should build your interface to be adaptable to different screen resolutions and aspect ratios. Table 22.1 shows common preview resolutions—not actual settings for the Widget Blueprint or the project—because the resolution will ultimately be determined by the end user's hardware. Preview settings give you a "working scale" to author your UIs.

NOTE

Resolution Setting

Regardless of platform resolution and aspect ratio, the upper-left corner on any screen is the 0,0 coordinate, where X is horizontal and Y is vertical. HD and UHD refer to the pixel density, which is total pixels across multiplied by the total number of pixels down. For example, $1280 \times 720 = 921,600$ pixels.

TABLE 22.1   Common Aspect Ratios and Screen Resolutions

Aspect Ratio	Common Resolutions
4:3 (1.33)	320×240, 640×480, 1024×768, 2048×1536 (HD)
16:10 (1.6)	1280×800, 1440×900, 2560×1600 (UHD)
16:9 (1.77)	1280×720 (HD), 1920×1080 (HD), 3840×2160 (4K UHD)

NOTE

Aspect Ratios

The aspect ratio determines whether you are working in wide screen (16:9) or 4:3 (NTSC/PAL). The aspect ratio refers to the number of pixels across to the number of pixels down on the monitor. For example, 16:9 means that for every 16 pixels across, you have 9 pixels down.

You could build an interface for each resolution you want your game to support, but doing so requires more art assets and Widget Blueprints, which increase the memory size of the project and adds complexity.

A good rule of thumb is to design one interface at the highest target resolution and the most common aspect ratio you want your game to support. Then scale down the interface to lower resolutions and different aspect ratios. Epic has provided tools to do this: anchor points and DPI scaling.

Anchor Points and DPI Scaling

You use anchors when working with Widget Blueprints with a Canvas panel as the root. Every widget placed has an anchor point, which establishes a normalized reference point for widget placement onscreen. An anchor point's position onscreen is percentage based, not pixel based. This means that anchor points are resolution and aspect ratio independent. For example, an anchor point with an X,Y position of .5,.5 will always be in the center of the screen, regardless of resolution and aspect ratio, and an anchor point with a position of 1,1 will always be in the lower-right corner, regardless of screen resolution and aspect ratio. However, a widget's relationship to its anchor point is pixel based, meaning it will always be a set distance away from the anchor point, no matter what the resolution or aspect ratio of the interface is.

This is where DPI scaling comes in. DPI scaling scales the interface resolution up or down, depending on the target platform resolution and aspect ratio so that all the anchor points adjust accordingly and, in turn, adjust the positions of their widgets onscreen. To adjust the DPI Scaling settings, you select **Edit > Project Settings > Engine > User Interface**.

While you can micromanage DPI Curve as shown in Figure 22.5, the defaults are already good; the only thing you may need to change is the DPI Scale Rule property, which sets what axis will be used to determine how the interface should be scaled. Horizontal is always the X, and vertical is always the Y. The shortest and longest sides change depending on whether the game is in portrait or landscape mode.

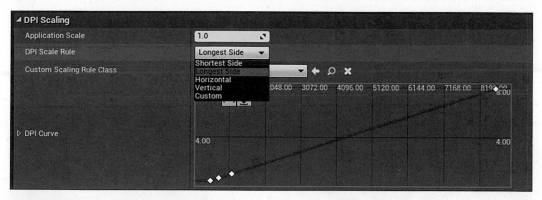

FIGURE 22.5
DPI Scaling settings.

Creating a Start Menu

For the rest of this hour, you create a Start menu. To do this, you will create a new Game Mode and Player Controller Blueprint, as well as an empty level. The Player Controller will be set to display the mouse cursor, and the Game Mode will be assigned to the level so every time the level is loaded, it will automatically display the Start menu. Finally, you will set level to be the game default map so that the level will be the first level to load every time the game executable is run.

Importing Assets

Before you can create an interface, you need images and audio files to work with.

In the Hour_22 folder that comes with this book, find the folder called **InterfaceAssets**, which contains all the assets you need to make a basic Start menu interface. The images will import as textures, and the audio files will import as sound waves.

When importing images for interfaces, the three main things you have to worry about are mipmap generation, texture streaming, and assigning the texture to a texture group.

When you create and import images that will be used in an interface, the powers of 2 rule does not apply. While using images that follow the powers of 2 guideline is important for textures that are being used in materials that may need to be tiled or assigned to Static Meshes, textures used in interfaces do not have these constraints.

GO TO ▶ CHAPTER 6, USING MATERIALS, to learn more about working with textures, materials, and powers of 2.

When you import images, UE4 wants them to be assigned to texture groups so that the Editor knows how to process them. To open a Texture asset in the Texture Editor, locate it in the Content Browser and double-click the Texture asset. With textures that are going to be used for an interface, you should set the Texture Group property in the Texture Editor to **UI** (see Figure 22.6).

FIGURE 22.6
Texture Editor showing texture Mip Gen Settings and Texture group assignment.

The *mip* in mipmap stands for *multum in parvo* ("a great deal in a small space"), and *mipmapping* is the process of generating a sequence of lower-resolution images from a larger one. In UE4, mipmaps are generated automatically when an image that adheres to the powers of 2 guideline is imported. This is an efficiency technique in 3D graphics. As an object moves farther and farther away from the camera, its resolution becomes smaller and smaller, and therefore the object can use lower resolution textures. Images used in an interface, however, do not typically need mips because they are displayed in the foreground, usually in front of everything else.

Texture streaming refers to the process of loading textures into memory at runtime. This is noticeable when game levels load on the fly. The lower-resolution images created with mipmapping load into memory and are displayed on the surfaces of models first. The low-resolution textures are eventually replaced as the higher-resolution textures are loaded. The transition from a low to high resolution can cause texture popping. This is one reason many games make you watch a load screen first, before displaying the level. Texture popping is something you don't want players to see on interfaces. Each texture can be set to **Never Stream**.

CAUTION

Texture Streaming

It is good practice to turn on **Never Stream** only for textures you are using in interfaces. The Never Stream setting for a texture is found in the Texture Editor Details panel, under the Texture category. You need to expand the category to locate this setting.

When a texture that is not a power of 2 is imported, it is automatically set to **Never Stream**, and its Mip Gen setting is automatically set to **NoMipmaps**. You should still to set Texture Group to **UI** in the Texture Editor.

The provided InterfaceAsset folder contains a background texture, a title texture, a button texture, and two audio files—Mouse Hover and Mouse Pressed. Import all the provided assets. When the images are added to the Content Browser, open each texture in the Texture Editor, switch their Texture Group setting to **UI**, and turn on **Never Stream**.

TIP

Texture Resolution

If you need to know the resolution of an image after it's imported, in the Content Browser, hover the mouse over the imported asset to see relevant information, or open it in the Texture Editor.

In the StartMenuGame folder in the Content Browser of the project you created earlier, you should now create a new folder and import all the imported project assets into it.

Placing Widgets on the Canvas

With the assets imported, it's time to start setting up the interface in the Widget Blueprint. First you need to place a background image and the game title image using Image widgets in UMG.

Place an Image Widget

Follow these steps to add an image widget and assign a texture.

1. Double-click **StartMenuWidget_BP** to open it in UMG.

2. In Designer mode, set Screen Size to **1080p(HDTV,Blu-ray)**.

3. Drag an Image widget from the Palette panel to the [Canvas Panel] of the Hierarchy panel in the Designer mode window.

4. With the placed Image widget selected, in the Slot section of the Details panel, set the anchor point to the center of the screen either by using the presets or manually setting Minimum X,Y to **.5,.5** and Maximum X,Y to **.5,.5** (see Figure 22.7).

5. Drag the Background Image Texture asset from the Content Browser to the Image property of the Appearance section of the Details panel.

6. In the Slot section of the Details panel, set the Size X property to **1920** and the Size Y property to **1080**.

7. In the Designer Viewport, position the image so it fills the entire Canvas panel.

8. Drag out another image widget and repeat steps 3–6 to place the Title Image Texture asset. The anchor point for this widget should also be in the center, but the Size X and Size Y properties should match the new image size **641 × 548**.

9. Save the Widget Blueprint. At this point, your Start menu should look like the one shown in Figure 22.7.

FIGURE 22.7
UMG Designer panel displaying background image and title image.

Next, you need to use a button and a text widget to create a Play button and a Quit button. A button widget is already set up with basic button functionality for dealing with mouse interactions, such as MouseOver and MouseDown events. All you need to do is place it on the Canvas panel and assign the correct assets. The following Try It Yourself describes this process, and Table 22.2 shows button states for mouse interaction with a button widget.

TABLE 22.2   Button Widget Style Properties

Button State	Description
Normal	The image that will be displayed when there is no mouse interaction
Hovered	The image that will be displayed when the mouse cursor rolls over the button
Pressed	The image that will be displayed when the mouse cursor is over the image when the mouse button has been pressed
Disabled	The image that will be displayed if the button is deactivated in Blueprint

▼ TRY IT YOURSELF

Place a Button and Text Widget

Now you are going to create Play and Quit buttons for your Start menu. A button widget will hold the images that represent the button, and a text widget will display the text for the button. The text widget should be attached to the button widget so that if you decide to reposition the button, the text widget will follow. Here are the steps:

1. Open UMG (if it's not already open) by double-clicking **StartMenuWidget_BP**.

2. Drag a button widget from the Palette panel and place it in the Canvas Panel section of the Hierarchy panel.

3. With the placed button widget selected at the top of the Details panel, rename the widget **PlayButton**.

4. With the placed button widget selected in the Details panel, in the Slot section, set the anchor point to the center of the screen either by using the presets or manually setting Minimum X,Y to .5,.5 and Maximum X,Y to .5,.5.

5. Set the size of the widget to match the button texture in the Slot section of the Details pane, set the Size X property to **256** and the Size Y property to **64**.

6. In the Details panel, go to the Appearance section and assign the **NormalButton** texture to the Normal Image property.

7. In the Details panel, go to the Appearance section and assign the **HoverButton** texture to the Hovered Image property.

8. In the Details panel, go to the Appearance section and assign the **PressedButton** texture to the Pressed Image property.

9. To set up sound for the button, in the Details panel go to the Appearance section and assign the **MPressed_sw** sound wave to the Pressed Sound Property.

10. In the Details panel in the Appearance section, assign the **MHover_sw** sound wave to the Hovered Sound property.

11. Add text to the button; drag a text widget from the Palette panel onto the PlayButton widget in the Designer Viewport.

12. With the text widget selected, in the Details panel, go to the Content section and set Default Text to **PLAY**.

13. To create the Quit button, repeat steps 2–11 but this time set the name of the button widget to **QuitButton** and set Default Text to **QUIT**.

When you're finished, the Start menu should look like the one shown in Figure 22.8.

FIGURE 22.8
UMG Designer panel displaying button widget Appearance properties in the Details panel.

Scripting Functionality

Now you need to script some basic Blueprint functionality for each of the buttons you have created. There are three common event types you can assign to a button: OnClicked, OnPressed, and OnReleased.

Script Events for Your Button

With the PlayButton widget selected in Designer mode, in the Events section of the Details panel you can see three event types that you can add to your button. Follow these steps to script a simple OnReleased event for the Play and Quit buttons:

1. In Designer mode in the Designer Viewport, select the **PlayButton** widget.

2. In the Details panel, navigate to the Events section and click the + symbol next to **OnReleased**, as shown in Figure 22.9. This switches UMG to Graph mode and places an OnReleased event in the Event Graph.

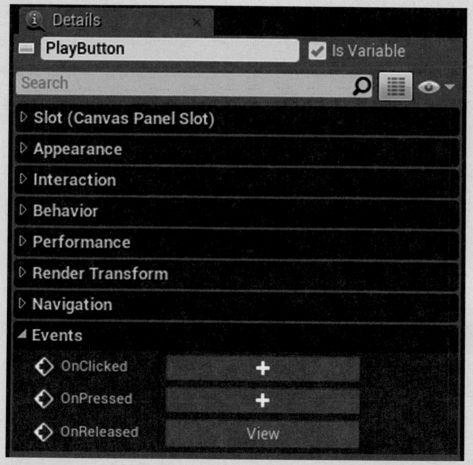

FIGURE 22.9
Button widget Events properties in the Details panel.

3. Click+drag from the exec out of the OnReleased event node and in the context menu search box, type **open** and select **Open Level** to place the node.

4. With the Open Level function node placed, set Level Name to **FlyingExampleMap**.

5. In Designer mode in the Designer Viewport, select the **QuitButton** widget, and in the Details panel navigate to the Events section and click the + symbol next to **OnReleased** to add an OnReleased event node for QuitButton in the Event Graph.

6. Click+drag from the exec out of the OnReleased event node and then, in the Context Menu search box, type **quit** and select **Quit** to place this function. When you're finished, the Widget Blueprint should look like the one shown in Figure 22.10.

7. Compile and save the Widget Blueprint.

FIGURE 22.10
UMG Event Graph showing button widget assigned to OnReleased events.

The ability to toggle the display of the mouse cursor is handled by the Player Controller Blueprints. Now that your Start Menu widget is finished, you need to add the Widget Blueprint to the Viewport when the game begins. To do this, you need to create a new Game Mode and controller class that will be assigned to the level that will be the first level to load when the game is started.

With the Start Menu Widget Blueprint set up and ready to go, you need to create a simple Game Mode that uses a Player Controller to display the mouse cursor.

TRY IT YOURSELF ▼

Create a Simple Game Mode and Display the Mouse Cursor

Follow these steps to create a Game Mode and Controller Blueprint that shows the mouse cursor.

1. To create a new Game Mode Blueprint, in the Content Browser navigate to the **StartMenuGame** folder.

2. Right-click in the Content Browser Asset Management area and select **Blueprint Class** from the Dialog menu.

3. In the Pick Parent Class window that appears, select **Game Mode** from the Common Classes category.

4. Name the Game mode **StartMenuGameMode**.

5. To create a new Player Controller, in the Content Browser navigate to the **StartMenuGame** folder.

6. Right-click in the Content Browser and select **Blueprint Class**.

7. In the Pick Parent Class window that appears, select **Player Controller** from the Common Classes category.

8. Name the Player Controller **StartMenuController**.

9. Assign the Player Controller to the Game Mode, open the StartMenuGameMode Blueprint, and select Class Defaults on the Blueprint Editor toolbar. In the Details panel under the Classes section, assign the **StartMenuController** Blueprint to the Player Controller Class property (see Figure 22.11).

FIGURE 22.11
StartMenuGameMode Class Default properties in the Blueprint Details panel.

10. Compile, save, and close the StartMenuGameMode Blueprint.

11. Next, you need to tell the Player Controller Blueprint to show the mouse cursor. Open the StartMenuController Blueprint. With Class Defaults selected in the Blueprint Editor toolbar, in the Details panel, under Mouse Interface turn on **Show Mouse Cursor, Enable Click Events,** and **Enable Mouse Over Events.** See Figure 22.12.

FIGURE 22.12
StartMenuController Class Default properties in the Blueprint Details panel.

12. Compile and save the StartMenuController Blueprint.

NOTE

Resolution Setting

While the ability to toggle the display of the mouse cursor is handled by the Player Controller, you can set it from any Blueprint—not just inside the Player Controller. Click+drag from the GetPlayerController node in any Blueprint class, and use the SetShowMouseCursor node to toggle the cursor's visibility.

With the Game Mode set up, you need to create a Blueprint sequence that adds the Widget Blueprint to the player's Viewport during gameplay.

▼ TRY IT YOURSELF

Add a Widget Blueprint to the Player's Viewport

Follow these steps to add a Widget Blueprint to the Viewport.

1. Open the StartMenuController Blueprint in the Blueprint Editor and navigate to the Event Graph.

2. In the Event Graph, locate the Event BeginPlay event node.

3. Left-click and drag from the Event BeginPlay event node exec out pin; in the context menu search box, type **create widget** and select **Create Widget** from the list to place the node.

4. On the newly placed Create Widget function node next to the Class property, select the **StartMenuWidget_BP** you created at the start of the hour from the drop-down menu.

5. Left-click and drag from the Create Widget nodes exec out pin, and in the context menu search box type **add to Viewport** and select **Add to Viewport** from the list to place the node.

6. Link the **Return Value** from the Create Widget to the target of the Add to Viewport node. When you're finished, the Blueprint should look like the one shown in Figure 22.13.

7. Compile and save the StartMenuController Blueprint.

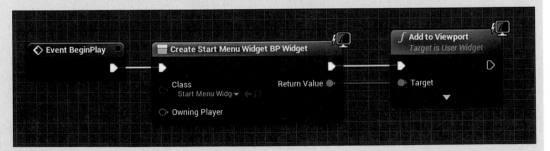

FIGURE 22.13
Start menu Player Controller Blueprint sequence that adds a Widget Blueprint to the player Viewport.

The last thing you need to do is create a new level that will be the first level to load when the game is played. You need to assign the level to the game default map in the Project Settings panel, under Maps & Modes. After you do this, when the game is first launched, this level and Game Mode are loaded and the Start menu is displayed.

TRY IT YOURSELF ▼

Add a Game Default Map

Follow these steps to assign a Game Mode to a level and then set the level as the Game Default Map.

1. In the Content Browser, create a new folder and name it **Maps**.

2. Create a new empty level and save it to the Maps folder. Name the map **StartLevel**.

3. Open the World Settings panel by going to the Setting button on the Level Editor's toolbar and selecting **World Settings**.

4. In the World Settings panel, under Game Mode assign the **StartMenuGameMode** Blueprint to the GameMode Override property.

5. Save the Level again to save the changes.

6. Open the Project Setting panel by going to Settings on the Level Editor's toolbar and selecting **Project Settings**.

7. In Project Setting panel, under Maps & Modes/Default Maps assign the **StartLevel** to the Game Default Map.

8. Preview the level. The Start menu should appear, and the cursor should stay. Roll over the buttons to see if they change and whether the audio plays.

9. Click and release the **Play** button. The FlyingExampleMap level should load.

Sample Menu System

The Hour_22 folder contains a sample project that has a complete menu system for you to look at and deconstruct. The system has been set up using the Flying template. This project has a Start menu that was created using the method shown earlier—along with two other Widget Blueprints used to create a pause menu and a simple HUD. The Pause menu Widget Blueprint has been added to the Viewport in the FlyingController Blueprint in the Flying Game Mode template, and a HUD Widget Blueprint has been added to the Viewport in the FlyingPawn Blueprint of the Flying Game Mode template.

If you open up the FlyingController Blueprint, you can see that the Pause menu Widget Blueprint is added to the Viewport when the player presses the **Q** or **Esc** key. This is because the Esc key in preview mode is controlled by the Editor. When the game is ready to be packaged and made into an executable, you can disconnect the Q key input event, and the Esc key will function properly.

The PawnHud Widget Blueprint gets variable data from the FlyingPawn Blueprint by casting to the flying pawn. This is done in two functions—one for the speed and one for the health of the pawn. Both of the text widget text properties have been bound to functions that cast to the flying pawn and retrieve the variables that store the pawn health and speed.

Summary

This hour, you learned how to create a Widget Blueprint, use UMG, and place image, button, and text widgets. You learned about prepping textures for use in an interface and how to set up a Game Mode for mouse interaction. As always, there is more to learn; for example, you can embed a Widget Blueprint in other Widget Blueprints to add complexity to your menus. For now, you know how to create a basic menu system that's found in every game.

Q&A

Q. Why is my interface texture pixelated when the level first loads?

A. You have not set Texture Group to **UI** in the Texture Editor, so your texture is still generating mipmaps.

Q. Why does UE4 warn me when I import a texture that is not powers of 2?

A. Depending on the version of the Editor you are using, you may get a warning. The majority of textures are typically used in materials assigned to Static Meshes and should be powers of 2. Interface textures are not bound by this constraint.

Q. What is Blueprint casting?

A. In a traditional programming or scripting environment, casting allows you to convert one variable type to another. But Blueprint casting also allows one Actor to reference another Actor in a game and call functions or get and set variables in the Cast Actor.

Q. When I bring in my own textures into UE4, I want to be able to see through an image. What do I need to do?

A. If you want a texture to be transparent or masked, you need to create an alpha for the image in your image editing application. Then save the image as a 32-bit image so that transparency or masked data will import with the image. File types .tga and .psd both store alpha channels and import into UE4.

Workshop

Now that you have finished the hour, see if you can answer the following questions.

Quiz

1. True or false: Interface textures must be powers of 2.

2. _____ is the process of generating multiple resolutions of an image when it is imported.

3. True or false: When importing a texture to be used in an interface, you want to assign the texture to the World Texture group.

4. What is *mip* short for?

5. What are the four style properties of a button widget?

Answers

1. False. Textures for interfaces do not need to be powers of 2.

2. Mipmapping is the process of generating multiple resolutions of an image when it is imported.

3. False. You should assign texture for interface to the UI Texture group.

4. Mip stands for *Multum in parvo.*

5. Normal, Hovered, Pressed, and Disabled are the four style properties of a button widget.

Exercise

For this exercise, use the provided images and audio assets to create a Start menu for the arcade shooter project you created in Hours 20, "Creating an Arcade Shooter: Input System and Pawns," and 21, "Creating an Arcade Shooter: Obstacles and Pickups." If you have not worked through those hours yet, use the arcade shooter project provided with this hour.

1. Open the arcade shooter project you created during Hours 20 and 21, or use the version provided with this hour, ArcadeShooter22.

2. Create a Start Menu Game Mode and Widget Blueprint and make the Start menu interface, using the provided assets. Follow the process outlined in all the "Try It Yourself" sections in this hour.

Making an Executable

What You'll Learn in This Hour:

▶ Contrasting cooked and uncooked content
▶ Packaging a project for Windows
▶ Resources for Android and iOS packaging
▶ Accessing advanced packaging settings

After having done the heavy lifting for making a unique mind-blowing user experience, the next step is to get your creation into the hands of users. With many game engines, this can be a long, convoluted process fraught with many pitfalls and traps. Thankfully, Unreal Engine 4 makes creating packaged builds a painless process. In this hour, you learn about cooked content and how to use UE4 to create an executable with the shipping configuration.

NOTE

Hour 23 Setup

The process used in this hour can be done with any Windows or OSX-compatible UE4 projects.

This hour you continue working on the ArcadeShooter project you started in Hour 20 and continued in Hours 21 and 22. If you prefer, as a starting point for this hour you can also use the provided H22_ArcadeShooter project found in the Hour_22 folder (available on the book's companion website at www.sty-ue4.com).

After you have finished this lesson, compare your results to the H23_ArcadeShooter Project found in the Hour_23 folder that comes with the book.

Cooking Content

Unreal Engine 4 stores content in formats for internal use inside UAsset files. These formats are guaranteed to work with the UE4 Editor, but they aren't necessarily available on all platforms or when the Editor is not installed. Instead of requiring a developer to prepare different versions of assets for different platforms, UE4 uses a cooking stage to ensure that content is usable on the target device.

The cooking step in a development process is functionally a conversion step. It involves performing the necessary data handling to convert editor-specific data assets into assets that are ready for use on a myriad of platforms. This stage also involves other tasks, like stripping away unnecessary or redundant information.

Cooking also ensures that a game project is ready and that it isn't missing information that may cause problems later. The cooking process involves a number of steps that help prevent bugs, such as compiling Blueprints and checking for errors, ensuring that all shaders are completely compiled, and checking for missing assets in levels that are being cooked.

The amount of time the cooking process takes depends on how much content you are cooking at one time. By default, UE4 cooks all the content required to make a game playable, starting from your default game level. Luckily, UE4 also knows what information has changed since the last time you cooked, and usually the process is faster after you cook the first time.

TIP

Cooking for Windows

Even if you are targeting the same platform that you develop on, you need to cook content. Unreal Engine does not support standalone projects working with uncooked content at this time. Because cooking can take a while, it can sometimes be a good idea to give it a head start. You can start cooking before going to packaging by selecting **File > Cook Content for Windows**.

Packaging a Project for Windows

Prepping your content is only one step in the process of getting your project out to users. The next step is taking all that cooked content and packaging it up in a nice bundle with an executable your users can run. How packaging happens depends on the platform you choose to target. If you use a Windows operating system and are targeting your game for play on Microsoft systems, Unreal Engine 4 makes creating distribution-ready packages of your content and code simple.

While the UE4 Editor requires a 64-bit process to run, UE4 supports packaging projects for both 32-bit and 64-bit processors. For many projects, the difference will be unnoticeable. In addition, 64-bit processors are capable of running 32-bit projects. Today 64-bit processors are adopted more heavily with modern hardware, and the need to support 32-bit computers continues to decrease. Developing for 64-bit allows you to utilize more of the features of modern-day hardware.

Generally, you should develop for 32-bit only if you are particularly targeting older hardware or have some other explicit reason to.

Packaging your project is exceptionally simple thanks to two menu options under the File menu: Shipping and Windows (64-bit) (see Figure 23.1).

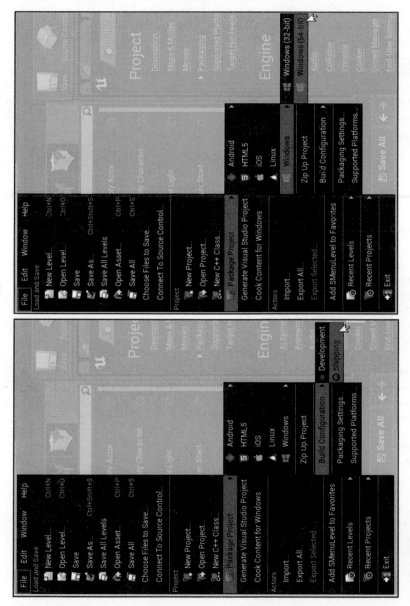

FIGURE 23.1
The two menu options needed to quickly package a project for Windows. The left image sets the build configuration to Shipping, and the right image shows the Windows (64-bit) option.

NOTE

Shipping Configuration

The first image in Figure 23.1 shows the project's build configuration being set to Shipping. With this option, many debug commands are disabled. Some of the debug features enabled with the Development setting can be used improperly and may create game-breaking bugs for you users. Therefore, any distributed packages should probably be created using the Shipping configuration.

When you're testing locally, however, Development is a good selection.

Selecting **File > Package Project > Windows > Windows (64-bit)** brings up the Browse For Folder dialog, shown in Figure 23.2, which you use to specify where you want the package to live. It is important to place the package on a hard drive that has enough space to potentially store your entire project a second time and to give the folder a project-specific name.

FIGURE 23.2
The Browse For Folder dialog box, where you specify where to place the new project.

After you click **OK**, a processing message appears in the bottom-right corner of the screen, noting the progress of the packaging step (see Figure 23.3).

FIGURE 23.3
The progress message that appears while the project is being packaged.

The packaging process can take a while, especially if content needs to be cooked. Detailed information about the process is presented in the Output Log panel, although this can sometimes be hard to visually read through because of the sheer volume of logs that are printed to the screen.

A simplified (and categorized) version of the output is also available through the message log, which you can open by selecting **Window > Developer Tools > Message Log**. Figure 23.4 shows the Message Log panel, set to the Packaging Results category when an error arises, and Figure 23.5 shows the same error in more detail in the Output Log panel.

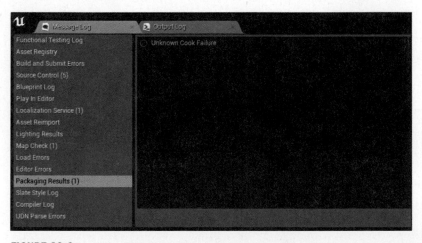

FIGURE 23.4
The Message Log panel, presenting an error in the packaging results due to an unknown cook failure.

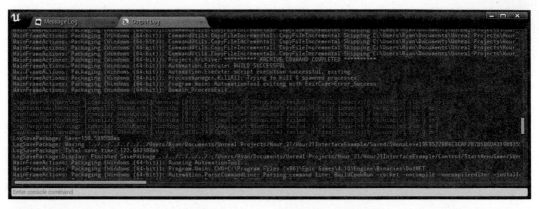

FIGURE 23.5
The cook failure mentioned in Figure 23.4, shown in the Output Log panel. This error is due to a broken Blueprint network that cannot compile properly.

Once the cooking and packaging are complete, the content is placed in the location you specified in the Browse For Folder dialog. If you navigate to that folder in File Explorer, you can now see the available packages. By default, the folder contains a new directory called WindowsNoEditor, which contains the entire packaged project necessary to run the project on Windows.

In the WindowsNoEditor folder, double-clicking *ProjectName*.exe starts the project. as shown in Figure 23.6.

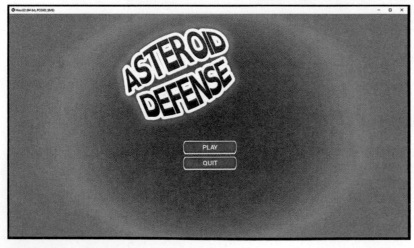

FIGURE 23.6
The Hour 23 project, running from a standalone version.

Package Your Project

Follow these steps on a Windows machine to practice packaging your project in Windows:

1. Open the Hour 23 project (or a project of your choosing).

2. Select **File > Package Project > Build Configuration > Shipping**.

3. Select **File > Package Project > Windows > Windows (32-bit)**.

4. In the Browse For Folder dialog that appears, create a new folder in a location of your choosing and rename it something relevant, such as Hour23_packaged.

5. Select this new folder and click **OK**.

6. Wait for the notification in the bottom-right corner to say Package Success and then disappear.

7. Open File Explorer and navigate to the folder created in step 4.

8. Open the WindowsNoEditor folder inside your package folder.

9. Double-click the **.exe** file in this folder, which should follow the pattern *ProjectName*.exe (for example, it should be Hour23.exe).

10. Enjoy your new standalone game!

Resources for Android and iOS Packaging

The two primary mobile platforms, iOS and Android, handle packaging and deployment slightly differently. The process for getting a project onto Android or iOS can be daunting and does require a certain amount of setup beforehand.

The process requires that you first set up your environment with either the Android Works SDK or iTunes. To ensure that you are getting the most up-to-date information, check out the excellent UE4 documentation at https://docs.unrealengine.com/latest/INT/Platforms/Android/GettingStarted/ and https://docs.unrealengine.com/latest/INT/Platforms/iOS/QuickStart/. Reading these living documents is the best way to be certain you are following the most accurate steps for working with mobile in Unreal Engine 4.

Keep in mind that to submit and develop for iOS's App Store or Android's Google Play Store, you first need to become a registered developer for each service. Both services require one-time registration fees to get a game onto their stores. At this writing, you do not need to pay the App Store or Google Play Store fees until you want to deploy your game to their services. However, to test your app on iOS without first registering, you can use Xcode 7 or later on an OSX machine to deploy the project directly. If you are developing from Windows, you need to first become a part of the developer program and pay a registration fee.

In addition, both services provide certification steps for your apps that you must follow before distributing a project. When you have supplied all the appropriate information detailed in the UE4 Quick Start documentation, you need to set your app to be in Distribution mode. To switch to Distribution mode, select **File > Package Project > Packaging Settings**, then select the **Packaging** category, and toggle the **For Distribution** option. By doing this, you tell UE4 to package all the necessary certificates and packaging signing that the respective stores require.

Accessing Advanced Packaging Settings

Although the steps mentioned in the previous sections are often sufficient to package most projects, occasionally you need more control over the process. UE4's packaging settings allow you to easily modify a number of advanced package configurations. Using these configuration options is the key to a smooth packaging process, especially when you're preparing a game for multiple platforms.

To access the packaging settings, select **File > Package Project > Packaging Settings** and then select the **Packaging** category (see Figure 23.7).

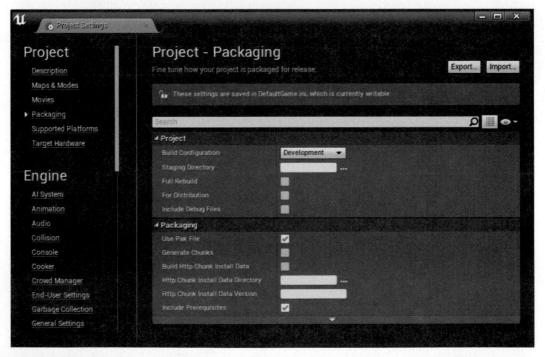

FIGURE 23.7
The Packaging tab's common properties.

The Packaging tab allows you to set properties such as the following:

▶ **Build Configuration:** You can specify the build configuration for which to compile your code-based project. If you are using Blueprint projects, there isn't much difference here between testing using the Development configuration and testing for the final release using the Shipping configuration.

▶ **Staging Directory:** You can specify the directory for storing the packaged build. Whenever you pick a new directory by using **File > Package Project** in the File Browser dialog, this field will update automatically to match.

▶ **Full Rebuild:** For code-based projects, this property determines whether to rebuild all code or only modified code. In Blueprint projects, it is safe to leave this unchecked.

▶ **For Distribution:** This option determines whether your game is in Distribution mode. Packaging with this option enabled is a requirement for submitting a game to the Apple App Store or the Google Play Store.

▶ **Use Pak File:** This option determines whether to package all assets in the project as individual files or a single package. When it is enabled, all the assets are bundled together in a single .pak file. If a project has a large number of files, enabling this option may make distribution much easier.

▶ **Include Prerequisites:** When this option is enabled, all the required prerequisites for a packaged game are included in the package itself. This is important for distributing to unknown systems, where you cannot guarantee that the target systems already have all the prerequisites installed.

Summary

In this hour, you learned how to free your UE4 projects from the Editor and get them into the wild. You learned what it means to cook content and how to preemptively cook your content for Windows, as well as how to package content into a standalone folder, ready for distribution.

Q&A

Q. When I run the standalone game, the wrong map loads. How do I fix this?

A. Select **Edit > Project Settings** and then select the **Maps & Modes** tab and change the **Default Game Level** property to whichever map you want your game to start up with.

Q. When I copy the packaged directory onto a new computer, I get an error, but it works fine on my machine. What is happening?

A. Although this could be a number of problems. depending on what the error is, one of the most common reasons this might happen is because the target computer is missing required prerequisites that Unreal Engine 4 projects need to run. You should bundle prerequisites with your packaged game; to do so, in the Packaging window, ensure that the Include Prerequisites property is selected.

Q. The cooking process is throwing an unknown error in the message log. What is going on?

A. A huge number of problems can occur when you're cooking a project. If you get an unknown error in the message log, take some time to look through the output log instead. The output log color codes errors using red, so scroll through the log looking for red text. Often the problem might be as simple as a deleted object or file, so checking the output log first for any obvious fixes is a great way to go.

Workshop

Now that you have finished the hour, see if you can answer the following questions.

Quiz

1. What is the name of the process that involves converting content in Editor-specific formats to work on target platforms:

2. True or false: 64-bit processors can run 32-bit executables made in Unreal Engine 4.

3. True or false: When you package a project from the Editor, the currently open level is the one that loads first.

Answers

1. Cooking. This is distinct from staging, which is the process that stores the cooked data in a local location before deploying to a target device.

2. True. 64-bit processors can run 32-bit programs, but 32-bit processors cannot run 64-bit programs.

3. False. The level that is loaded when a standalone package is created is the level designated in the Maps & Modes tab of the Project Settings dialog.

Exercise

Create and package a brand-new project to thoroughly practice packaging.

1. In the Launcher, create a new UE4 project with the template of your choice. For speediness, do not include the Starter Content.

2. Open the new project.

3. Select **File > Package Project > Build Configuration > Shipping**.

4. Select **File > Package Project > Windows > Windows (32-bit)** to package the project for Windows.

5. Choose a good location for the project to live.

6. When the project is done packaging, in the File Explorer, navigate to the folder and find the project's .exe file. Double-click the .exe file to complete this exercise.

HOUR 24
Working with Mobile

What You'll Learn in This Hour:

▶ Developing for mobile devices

▶ Using touch

▶ Using a device's motion data

The largest and fastest-growing market in video games isn't console or PC games; it is mobile games. The mobile phone market has exploded in recent years, and the number of games being made (and profiting) on the various mobile platforms is incredible. Mobile devices are less powerful than consoles and PCs, however, so you need to exercise a fair amount of care to make sure your games will run on mobile. In this hour, you will learn the limitations of most mobile platforms, how to have touch events interact in a game, how to use virtual joysticks to control a Pawn, and how to use the gyroscope to create a unique mobile-only control scheme.

NOTE

Hour 24 Setup

This hour you will continue working on the ArcadeShooter project you started in Hour 20 and continued in Hours 21, 22, and 23. If you prefer, as a starting point you can also use the provided H23_ArcadeShooter project found in the Hour_23 folder that comes with the book (available on the book's companion website at www.sty-ue4.com).

After you have finished this lesson, compare your results to the H24_ArcadeShooter Project found in the Hour_24 folder that comes with the book.

NOTE

Testing on Mobile

When you're creating mobile games, you need to do extra testing on actual hardware. This process can be convoluted and is constantly changing, and the various operating systems and devices handle the process slightly differently.

To ensure that you are able to set up an Android device properly, go to https://docs.unrealengine.com/latest/INT/Platforms/Android/GettingStarted/.

To ensure that an iOS device is ready for deployment, go to https://docs.unrealengine.com/latest/INT/Platforms/iOS/QuickStart/index.html.

Developing for Mobile Devices

In general, mobile devices are inferior to consoles and PCs in many respects. They are slower, and they have weaker graphics abilities, less memory, less storage space, and smaller screens. However, computer hardware devices are advancing more and more each year, so the limitations in one year will be greatly reduced in the next.

In some ways, the year-over-year advances in the mobile hardware space exceed the same yearly improvements in consoles and PCs. This makes the mobile arena harder to track, although device adoption is still important. The most recent iPhone or Samsung device may be able to handle high-end graphics and features, but the broad adoption of the newest hardware isn't immediate, and the vast majority of potential users may be working with two- or three-year-old technology. To make matters more confusing, the rise of tablet and touch-enabled laptops means some devices will rival full desktops but still fall in the category of mobile.

Because these devices are improving at such a rapid rate, it is important to figure out the minimum requirements for a project. Unreal Engine 4 allows for variable quality and features, so it is possible to take advantage of the latest graphical techniques on a Microsoft Surface or iPad but have those same features disabled for a mobile phone.

With the knowledge that the requirements of the mobile space are rapidly changing, this section covers some of the best practices when dealing with mobile devices (at this writing).

Previewing for Mobile

When developing for mobile devices, several best practices should be kept in mind. It can be difficult, however, to know how the constraints of your device will affect the visual appearance of a project while working in the Editor. Luckily, Unreal Engine 4 allows you to preview the material feature set and rendering levels of your mobile device.

To enable this visualization feature, in the Viewport toolbar, select **Settings > Preview Rendering Level > Mobile/HTML 5 > Default Mobile/HTML5 Preview** (see Figure 24.1).

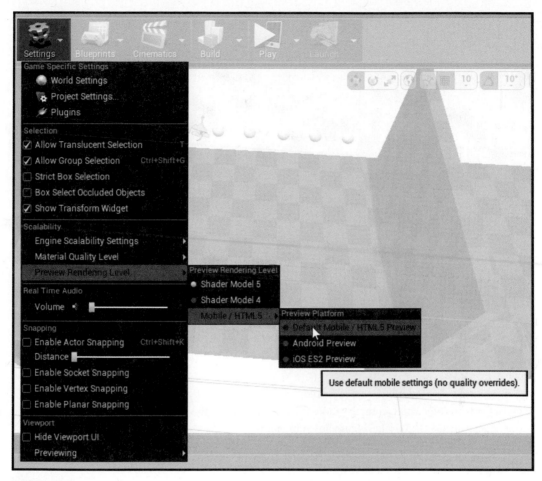

FIGURE 24.1
Setting the preview rendering level causes all materials and shaders to recompile with stricter display settings that are similar to those used on actual mobile devices.

When you choose the **HTML5 Preview** option, the visual preview of your level is likely to change to a more accurate representation of what your project will look like on a mobile device. However, the rendering level is not completely indicative of the final result on your device, and you should always strive to test on the actual hardware.

Since mobile hardware varies so wildly, sometimes the automatic material optimizations on each device are not enough. In these cases, for expensive materials you should use the Quality Switch node to remove the costlier operations from the material. Figure 24.2 shows an example of an expensive material feature being removed except from the highest-end configurations.

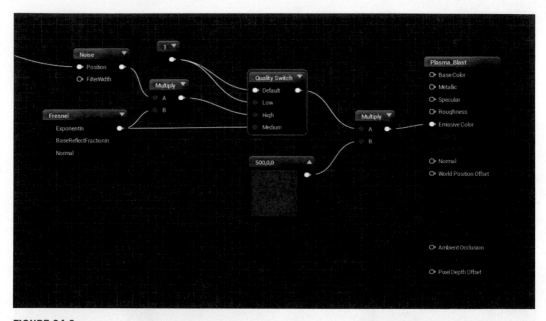

FIGURE 24.2
The Quality Switch node is used here to remove the expensive Noise node from the material when the material quality level is set to medium or low. The Fresnel node is then removed when the material quality level is set to low.

When you have Quality Switch nodes placed throughout the materials in a project to remove expensive operations, you can set the material quality level for the project by selecting **Settings > Material Quality Level**, as shown in Figure 24.3. The three options here—Low, Medium, and High—make a difference only when you have used Quality Switch nodes for the materials in the project.

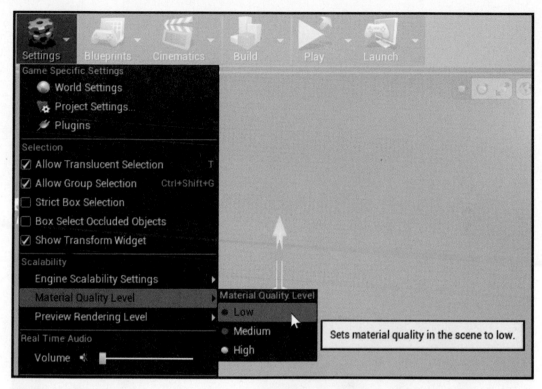

FIGURE 24.3
You can use the Settings menu to set the project's material quality level to one of three options: Low, Medium, or High.

Different devices have unique aspect ratios and resolutions. It is important to test your project at the same resolutions you expect to use when you ship a project.

Figure 24.4 shows how to set the mobile resolution in the Play section of the Editor Preferences panel, under **Play in Standalone Game**. Common device resolutions are available through the **Common Window Sizes** drop-down. You can then use the toolbar to select **Play > Mobile Preview**.

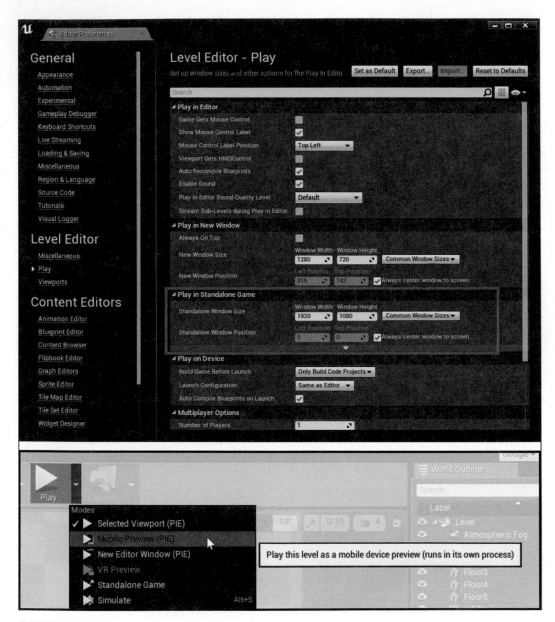

FIGURE 24.4
Using **Play > Mobile Preview** creates a standalone process version of your game running in a mobile-ready resolution.

Optimizing for Mobile

There are a number of best practices you should consider when developing for mobile. Sometimes the design of a project requires you to disregard one of these recommendations, but be extremely wary about doing so as ignoring these optimizations may significantly reduce your project's performance:

▶ **Always bake lighting.** Dynamic lighting can greatly affect the cost of rendering on any platform, and most mobile devices are especially slow when processing dynamic lights. Whenever possible, set your lights to static and at most use only one dynamic Directional Light set to Stationary. However, higher-end mobile devices can use more dynamic Point Lights, thanks to a feature called Max Dynamic Point Lights, which is available via the Rendering section of the Project Settings panel. Max Dynamic Point Lights can help make dynamic lights in a scene much cheaper by limiting the number of Point Lights that can affect a pixel at a single time.

▶ **Avoid using movable lights when working on mobile devices.** Even with the Max Dynamic Point Lights setting, movable lights are always more expensive than stationary or static lights.

▶ **Disable most post-processes.** You can leave Temporal AA, Vignettes, and Film post-process settings on, but even these cause performance loss. Make especially sure to disable Bloom, Depth of Field, and Ambient Occlusion.

▶ **Use masked and translucent materials sparingly.** Overdraw is the process that occurs when the hardware has to shade the same pixel more than once, and it is extremely expensive. When you use translucent or masked materials, make sure only small parts of the screen are covered by them. You can use the Shader Complexity view mode (see Figure 24.5) to identify when you have too much overdraw or materials that are too complex. Alternatively, you can use the console command **viewmode shadercomplexity** in the mobile preview.

The Shader Complexity view mode shows the per-pixel instruction cost of the view. The view is color coded from bright green (very cheap), through red (expensive), to white (extremely expensive). Because with translucent and masked materials, the same pixel has to be evaluated multiple times, overdraw can cause great expense and often shows up as hot white.

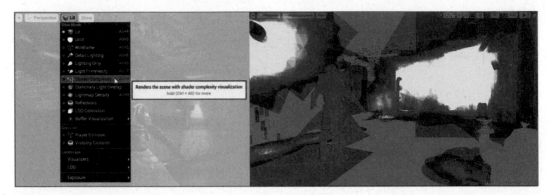

FIGURE 24.5
The Shader Complexity view mode is very helpful for finding expensive materials and overdraw in a project.

▶ **Keep your materials extremely simple, with low instruction counts and very few textures.** On most mobile devices you have only five texture samplers available, but on any platform, it is a good idea to use as few texture samplers as possible.

▶ **Make sure lit opaque materials use only two textures.** With UE4's physically based shading model, there is a simple way to achieve this optimization with some texture packing. In the first texture, the RGB channels should be the Base Color pin, and the Alpha should hold the Roughness pin. For this first texture, TC_Default compression should be used. The second texture should hold the Normal Map in RGB and use TC_NormalMap Compression, and Alpha should be empty. This means that there are no texture samplers for Specular and Metallic, so instead constants should be used in place of these pins. Figure 24.6 shows an example of a material that follows this format.

Because the rock in this example is not metallic and in a physically based shading model specularity is primarily controlled by roughness, the Metallic and Specular input pins can be replaced with constants. Meanwhile, the Roughness input can be packed into the same texture that holds the RGB base color. Finally, the Normal input needs its own RGB texture to describe the normal variation of the rock's surface.

This technique does not work as well for objects that have mixed metal and nonmetal parts. In those cases, another Texture Sampler may be needed to control the metalness of the material.

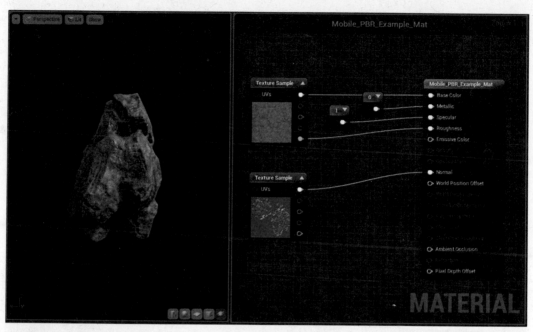

FIGURE 24.6
For most materials, this simple two-texture sample setup can create efficient yet high quality physically based materials.

▶ **Do not plug UV modifications (like scaling) into texture samplers in the material graph.** Instead, enable the **Num Customized UVs** option for a material to do UV scaling on the vertex (see Figure 24.7). You can enable customized vertex UVs through the Details panel when nothing is selected in the material graph. This makes UV calculations per vertex instead of per pixel, which is important for mobile graphics processors. When you plug scaled texture coordinates into a customized UV input, the vertex shader processes the graph and replaces the texture coordinates on each vertex with the scaled (or modified) result.

This process allows you to scale UVs without the expense of scaling them when each pixel is rendered and without the inconvenience of scaling them in the source 3D package (for example, Maya, Max, Houdini, Blender).

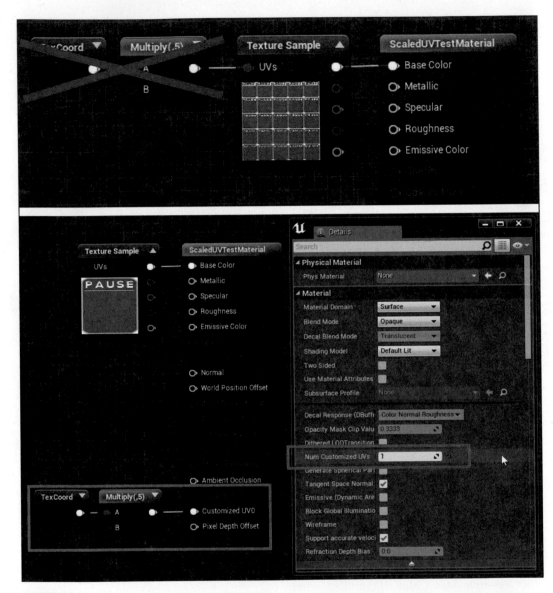

FIGURE 24.7
Both of the graphs in this figure produce the same visual result, but the second graph is much cheaper on many devices.

▶ **Keep the triangle count of any view as low as possible for a project.** Using simplified art styles is one way to lower the triangle count in a project. If this is not possible for a project and you need high poly count meshes, take care to reduce the number of Actors and Mesh components in each view. Using the **Stat RHI** console command in the mobile preview can help you determine the number of triangles in a scene. In the Counters section, the Triangle Drawn line shows the number of triangles in the current view (see Figure 24.8).

Draw calls (the number of objects that are being rendered to the screen in a single frame) should be kept as low as possible for any view. The number of DrawPrimitive calls can be seen by typing **Stat RHI** in the mobile preview console (see Figure 24.8).

The maximum number of draw calls in each project differs depending on the hardware you are targeting. No matter the device, however, keeping the number of draw calls as small as possible will always help ensure a stable framerate.

FIGURE 24.8
Using **Stat RHI** to view the current number of triangles and draw calls being processed in any frame. Bring up the console by pressing ~.

▶ **Always use square textures that are power of 2 dimensions (for example, 32×32, 64×64, 128×128, 256×256, 512×512, 1024×1024).** Doing this ensures that you have the lowest amount of memory waste possible. You can use the command **listtextures** in the mobile preview console to see where you are using your texture memory.

Setting Editor Targets

Unreal Engine 4 contains general presets for projects, depending on whether the project is targeted at the console/PC market or the mobile/tablet market. These presets touch several rendering and input features, and by informing Unreal Engine what platform you are developing for, you can save yourself some headache down the line.

When you first create a project, you may select Console/PC. If you later determine that you should make a mobile/tablet focused project, you can change your setting to Mobile/Target. To do this, go to the Project Settings panel, and in the Target Hardware category, set Optimize Project Settings For to **Mobile/Tablet** and **Scalable 3D or 2D**. Some changes then appear in the Pending Changes section of this window, and you need to restart the Editor to see all the modifications (see Figure 24.9).

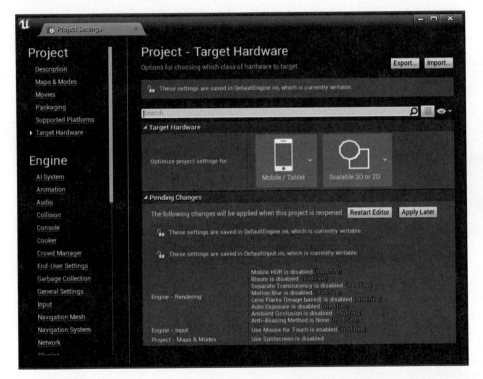

FIGURE 24.9
The Project Settings panel target hardware after you change the Optimize Project Settings For settings to Mobile/Tablet and Scalable 3D or 2D.

The Pending Changes section shows all the project settings that will automatically be set. Click the **Restart Editor** button to confirm these changes. Making these changes causes every lit material in your Content Browser to need to be recompiled, which can take a while but should happen only once.

The **Mobile/Tablet** preset disables a few rendering features and post-process effects:

▶ **Separate Transparency:** This is the ability to render some translucent materials after the post-process passes happen. It is commonly used for rendering glass in combination with depth of field, and is a very expensive feature that is not included on mobile devices.

▶ **Motion Blur:** This is a post-process that blurs the screen and Actors based on relative movement. This feature has a fair amount of overhead that is too expensive for mobile, and it is therefore not available on mobile devices.

▶ **Lens Flares (Image Based):** This is a post-process feature to render lens flare approximations based on the high dynamic range light values in the scene. This evaluative full-screen post-process is relatively expensive and is not included on mobile devices.

▶ **Auto Exposure:** This post-process feature evaluates the light values in the current scene and adjusts the exposure to help with visibility. Like the other post-process effects, this feature is not available on mobile devices. As a side note, the Auto Exposure Bias setting is supported.

▶ **Ambient Occlusion:** This is another expensive post-process feature. It disables the screen-space ambient occlusion process, which requires that the rendering sample the depth buffer multiple times to generate contact shadows. This type of effect is prohibitively expensive on most mobile devices and is therefore not available for mobile devices.

▶ **Anti-Aliasing Method:** This is a post-process that attempts to remove jagged edges and remove sub-pixel artifacts. Anti-aliasing is not included on mobile hardware. Temporal anti-aliasing is available for use on mobile but may result in small jittering artifacts on moving objects.

In addition to disabling various high-cost features, the Mobile/Tablet preset enables the input feature **Mouse for Touch**, which lets the mouse emulate a finger touch.

Setting the **Scalable 3D or 2D** preset disables two more high-cost features:

▶ **Mobile HDR:** This core feature lets a mobile device render high dynamic range buffers. This is the feature that allows for all lighting effects to function. These HDR render buffers are used in a variety of rendering features and effects, and removing this option substantially reduces the memory used by the renderer. As a side effect, all rendering features that rely on those HDR buffers no longer work the same way.

▶ **Bloom:** This post-process feature takes a blurred form of the highlights present in the scene and lays them on top of the render. This feature allows heavily emissive features or brightly lit objects to seem to glow, and it heavily relies on mobile HDR rendering being enabled, since in many cases only pixels with values greater than 1.0 are expected to bloom.

CAUTION

Scalable 3D or 2D and Lighting on Mobile

When you select the **Scalable 3D or 2D** preset, the Mobile HDR rendering feature is disabled. This results in all lighting features being disabled on mobile devices, including static baked lighting.

The mobile preview in the Editor does not show this change, so the visual result of your project may change considerably from the mobile preview to use on an actual device. To emulate the effect while working in the Editor, you should delete or disable all lights in the scene.

Again, if you require lighting effects in a mobile project, you should not switch to the Scalable 3D or 2D preset.

Using Touch

One of the major innovations of mobile devices has been the rise of touch input. The one-to-one relationship between a finger press and an onscreen action is definitely a huge drawing point for mobile devices.

The nature of touch allows you to create a myriad of interaction styles based on the same input. Some interaction styles mimic those of hardware inputs, virtual keyboards, and virtual joysticks, while other uses of touch are entirely new.

Virtual Joysticks

When you switch a project to a mobile project, UE4 handles one of the more complicated input styles for you by creating a set of virtual joysticks for you. These joysticks (shown in Figure 24.10) are two digital representations of axis input. The inner circle is the joystick's representation, while the outer circle shows how far the joystick can be moved.

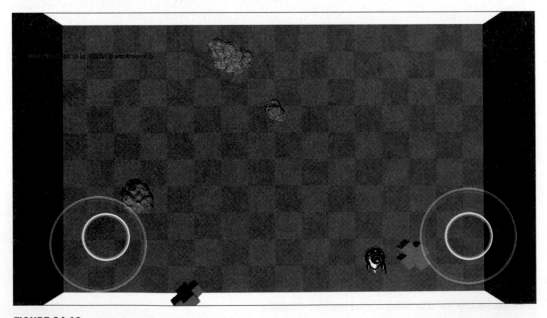

FIGURE 24.10
A mobile version of the Hour 23 project. The two sets of white circles are the left and right virtual joysticks created by UE4. The left joystick is currently bound to movement.

These virtual joysticks can be especially convenient when you're creating twin-stick control scheme games. You can disable the joysticks on the Project Settings panel by going to the Input category and selecting the Default Touch Interface dropdown and selecting Clear (see Figure 24.11).

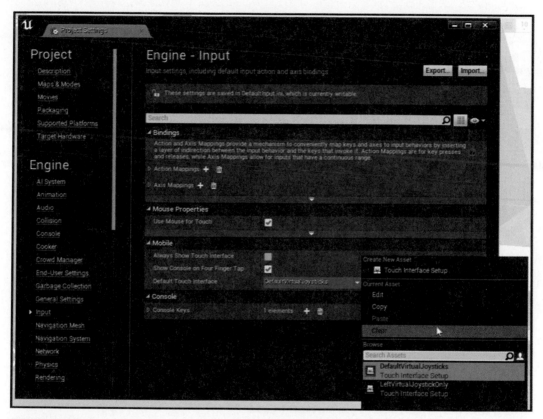

FIGURE 24.11
The Input category in the Project Settings panel, with the Clear option highlighted for the touch interface.

A touch interface is a UAsset that allows you to build and display a touch-enabled user interface. These interfaces allow you to create virtual joysticks and buttons.

In your arcade shooter game, for example, you use only one directional input to control movement, so you do not need the right joystick. You can easily remove the right joystick by setting Default Touch Interface to **LeftVirtualJoystickOnly** in the Input category of the Project Settings panel.

▼ TRY IT YOURSELF

Remove the Right Joystick

Your game needs only one virtual joystick. You can use the default available settings to replace the dual joystick with a single one:

1. In the Hour 23 project, open the **Project Settings** panel.

2. Navigate to the **Input** category.

3. Locate the Default Touch Interface field.

4. Click the down arrow in the property field.

5. In the bottom-right corner of the selection dropdown, click the **View Options** eye icon.

6. Ensure that **Show Engine Content** is selected. This enables you to find and select the default engine Touch Interfaces provided by UE4.

7. In the selection dropdown, find the **LeftVirtualJoystickOnly** Interface UAsset.

8. Use the toolbar to preview your changes and ensure that only one joystick appears.

Touch Events

While the touch interface is great for setting up virtual joysticks, some inputs are better handled directly through Blueprints. Throughout this book, when you have added new inputs, you have simply hooked up the input with Action Mappings in the Input category of the Project Settings panel. Touch events are a little different, in that they are handled directly in Blueprints.

TIP

Using a Touch Interface for a Button Press

You can use a touch interface to emulate controller buttons, but only for axis mappings. If you are making your own touch interface, all the inputs should be axis mappings *not* action mappings.

For the most fine-tuned control, set up touch events with the InputTouch node in the Event Graph. Figure 24.12 shows the InputTouch node and properties.

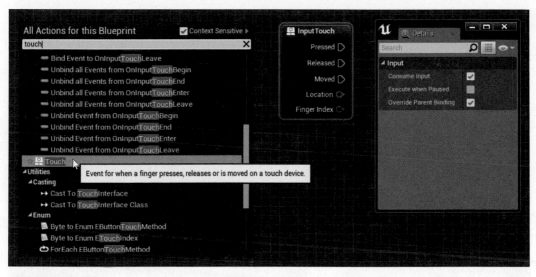

FIGURE 24.12
The InputTouch event node can be found by searching for **touch** in the Blueprint Context Menu; the inputs and the details work much like those for any other event node.

The InputTouch event node has three execution pins and two property pins:

▶ **Pressed:** Fires once for each finger each time that finger touches down.

▶ **Released:** Fires once whenever a finger is lifted from the sensor.

▶ **Moved:** Fires every tick while a finger is down and the current location is changing.

▶ **Location:** The current location of the finger in screen space, with [0,0] being the top-left corner and the units being pixels. This location can be converted to world space by using the Deproject Screen to World node.

▶ **Finger Index:** A unique index that identifies which finger's input is currently being handled. This is based on touch order, not on the user's actual physical fingers. You can use this in conjunction with branch and comparison nodes to handle multiple inputs.

There is one property on this node worth mentioning:

▶ **Consume Input:** Whenever more than one Actor is bound to the touch, the first Actor that has this flag checked is the *only* Actor to process the touch event. If you want multiple different Actors to be able to handle the touch event, all InputTouch nodes on each Actor should have the Consume Input flag disabled.

▼ TRY IT YOURSELF

Set Up Tap to Shoot

Because a mobile device doesn't have a mouse or trigger, in the arcade shooter, you need to set up your Pawn to shoot a projectile whenever the user taps the device. Here's how you make that happen:

1. In the Content Browser for the Hour 23 project, double-click **Hero_Spaceship** in the Blueprints folder.

2. Below the InputAction Shoot node, search for **touch** and place a new **InputTouch** event.

3. Click+drag the Released pin from the InputTouch event node and connect it to the same SpawnActor node used by InputAction Shoot. Both events should hook up to the same node. Figure 24.13 shows how the Event Graph should look. You can compare your results to those in the Hour 24 project.

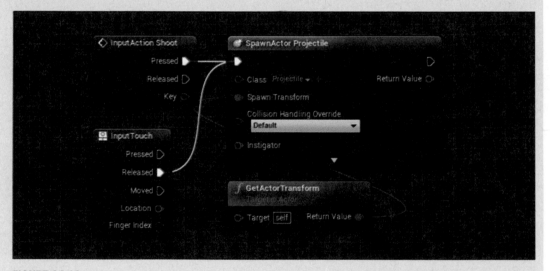

FIGURE 24.13
Both the InputAction Shoot and InputTouch Released events are hooked up to the same spawn behaviors.

NOTE

Touch Interactions with UMG

From the project from Hour 22, "Working with UMG," you have a UMG start screen. Luckily, UMG handles touch events as if they were mouse clicks, so you are still capable of using your main menu.

Using a Device's Motion Data

Most handheld devices ship with built-in gyroscopes and accelerometers. These small sensors allow the mobile device to detect changes in orientation. This experience differentiator is another strength of mobile devices.

Unreal Engine 4 makes using these sensors exceptionally simple through the Inputs section of the Project Settings panel. By adding the Tilt option to an existing axis mapping, you can offer another way to use the input controls you've already built.

Figure 24.14 shows the Tilt option added to the MoveRight axis mapping. In this case, you want to invert the value that comes out of Tilt and scale it down so the movement is easier to control.

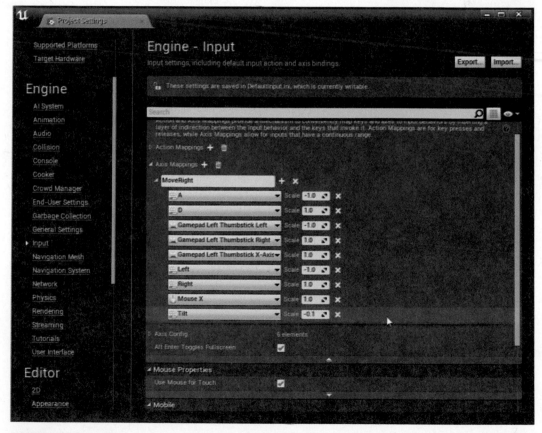

FIGURE 24.14
The Tilt axis mapping added to the existing MoveRight axis mapping.

Although axis inputs can be extremely convenient, sometimes you want to access the values of the gyroscope or accelerometer in another place. As with the InputTouch event node, you can access the values currently being processed by the gyroscope directly through the Event Graph.

Unlike with the InputTouch event, however, the device's motion data is accessed not as an event. Instead, the data can be accessed from a Player Controller, in the form of the Get Input Motion State function. These nodes are shown in Figure 24.15.

FIGURE 24.15
The Get Input Motion State node pulled off the default Player Controller.

The Get Input Motion State function node offers four motion states:

▶ **Tilt:** The rotation around the device's X- and Z-axes.

▶ **Rotation Rate:** The *speed*, or change in rotation per second, of each axis.

▶ **Gravity:** A non-normalized vector pointing toward the earth from the Player Controller's point of view.

▶ **Acceleration:** The change in speed of the device's rotation per second of each axis. For example, a consistently spinning device would have zero acceleration but a nonzero rotation rate.

Using the input mappings, while functional, may not give you all the control you need. The primary issue is that the input mappings versions do not have dead zones, which means if the mobile device isn't perfectly calibrated and you hook the tilt up to your character's movement, it will always be moving, even when the device is lying flat on a table. Instead, by using an Event Tick node and the Get Input Motion State, you can create your own gravity-based control scheme for the ship.

Use Your Device's Gravity

Here you use Get Input Motion State and Event Tick in your Pawn to create a control scheme that works when the player tilts the device left or right. You need a compatible mobile device to test this behavior. Follow these steps to hook up the gravity vector to your device's movement controls:

1. In the Content Browser for the Hour 23 project, open **Hero_Spaceship** in the Blueprints folder.

2. Add a new **Event Tick** node (or use the existing one, if there already is an Event Tick node).

3. Near the Event Tick node, place new **Get Actor Right Vector** and **Get Player Controller** nodes.

4. Click+drag from the Get Player Controller node's Return Value pin and place a new **Get Input Motion State** node.

5. Click+drag from the Gravity pin and place a new **Normalize** node.

6. Create a new **Vector * Vector** node and hook up the Return Values of the Get Actor Right Vector and Normalize nodes.

7. Create a new variable of type Vector and name it **Internal Gravity Vector**.

8. Set the Internal Gravity Vector to the result of the Vector * Vector node and hook it up to the exec out pin of the Event Tick node.

9. Create a new **Branch** node and hook it up to the exec out pin of the Internal Gravity Vector's Set node.

10. From the Internal Gravity Vector's Set node, pull off the yellow Vector pin and drop a new **VectorLength** node.

11. Click+drag from the Return Value of the VectorLength node and place a **Float > Float** node. Set the B float value to **0.1**.

12. Hook the Boolean output of the **Float > Float** node to the Branch node's Condition input.

13. From the Branch node's True exec out pin, create a new **Add Movement Input** node.

14. Place an **Internal Gravity Vector get** into the World Direction input of the Add Movement Input node.

15. To increase the acceleration speed of your Pawn when tilting the device, put the value **2.0** into the Add Movement Input node's Scale Value input. Figure 24.16 shows the resultant node network in Hero_Spaceship.

16. Deploy your application to your personal mobile device to test the new behavior. You can compare your results to those in the Hour 24 project.

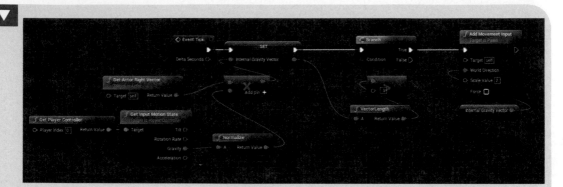

FIGURE 24.16
The required Event Graph to hook a mobile device's motion inputs up to a Pawn's left and right movements.

The math you are using in this Event Graph is simple. The Get Input Motion State Gravity pin returns a non-normalized vector in the world space direction of real-world gravity. You want your Pawn to slide toward the real-world earth, wherever that may be. However, because you don't want the Pawn to ever move forward, backward, upward, or downward, you multiply that gravity vector by the Pawn's right vector. This removes the impact from any gravity that is not aligned with the Pawn's right axis.

Checking the length of the resultant vector allows you to set a dead zone, but whenever the vector's length is greater than 0.1, you add a Movement Input node in that direction.

Summary

Mobile project development is a burgeoning field, and using Unreal Engine 4 is an excellent way to begin quick mobile development. This hour you've learned about the current hardware limitations of mobile devices and how to hook up touch, virtual joysticks, and gyroscopic inputs. These core input models are key to making a touch-enabled mobile-ready experience.

Q&A

Q. **I have converted a previous project to mobile, but several of my materials are now gray checkerboards when I test on a mobile device. What happened?**

A. Although this could be a number of potential problems, one of the most likely is that the reduction of texture samplers has caused your materials to fail to compile. Opening the broken materials in the Editor and clicking the **Mobile Stats** button in the toolbar will display any compilation errors your material has on mobile.

Q. I'm using the Gravity pin from the Get Input Motion State, but it is causing my Pawn to move really fast and become hard to control. What is the problem?

A. You most likely have not normalized the value that comes out of the Gravity pin. If the Gravity vector isn't normalized, its values can be way over 1 in length resulting in uncontrollable acceleration.

Q. I'm having trouble using the input bindings with the motion controls, like tilt. How do I get them to map properly to the behavior I want?

A. Whenever you encounter difficulties with the input bindings with motion states, it is best to switch to the method shown in Figure 24.14. By moving the input into an Event Graph, you can more carefully and accurately map the behavior in your own way. You can use the Print String node to print the outputs of the Get Input Motion State results to debug what is happening with your device.

Q. I'm trying to set up multi-touch input using the InputTouch event on my Windows device, but it isn't working. What is wrong?

A. Unfortunately, at this writing, UE4 does not support multi-touch on Windows devices, and there is not yet a good workaround.

Q. Several of my materials render fine in the Editor but are just checkerboards on my device. What is wrong?

A. If you are seeing default material checkerboard, then you may be using a node that is not supported at the target level. Find the material that is rendering incorrectly in the Content Browser and double-click on it to open its Editor. Next, click the **Mobile Stats** icon in the Material's toolbar. A Stats panel should appear, showing any compilation errors for mobile devices.

Workshop

Now that you have finished the hour, see if you can answer the following questions.

Quiz

1. True or false: Mobile devices are phones only.

2. True or false: Unreal Engine 4 can work only for iOS mobile devices.

3. True or false: You can handle touch inputs only directly in the Event Graph, not through the Input Binding category in the Project Settings panel.

4. True or false: The Finger Index property of the InputTouch event node is the user's finger, starting with 0 being the thumb and 4 being the little finger.

Answers

1. False. Tablets and many new laptops have touch inputs, broadening the definition of mobile devices to include more than just phones. In terms of graphics limitations, however, you usually are targeting smart phones or lower-end tablets.

2. False. Unreal Engine 4 supports Android, iOS, and Windows 10 devices.

3. True. Touch inputs (tapping or dragging) cannot be utilized through the Input Bindings category.

4. False. The Finger Index property doesn't identify which finger is being used; rather, it identifies different finger taps based on order. For example, the first finger to touch the screen is given the index 0, and if another finger touches the screen before the first one is removed, that new finger is given the index 1.

Exercise

Now use what you have learned about Action Bindings and mobile to modify your Hero_Spaceship Pawn's Event Graph to allow the user to fire a constant stream of projectiles without having to tap each time.

1. Open the Hero_Spaceship Blueprint class's Event Graph.

2. Find the InputAction Shoot event and move all of its outputs into a new function called **Shoot**.

3. Place the new Shoot function beside the InputAction Shoot event and hook up their exec pins.

4. Detach any outputs for the Event Touch node.

5. Click+drag from the Event Touch node's Pressed exec pin and place a **Set Timer by Function Name** node.

6. Set the Function Name input to **Shoot**.

7. Set the Time input to **0.1**.

8. Set the Looping input to **True**.

9. Click+drag from the Set Timer by Function Name node's Return Value output pin and select the **Promote to Variable** option.

10. Rename the new variable **ShootTimerHandle**.

11. Click+drag from the Event Touch node's Released exec pin and place a **Clear Timer by Handle** node.

12. Drag the ShootTimerHandle variable and drop it onto the Clear Timer by Handle node's **Handle** input pin.

Index